2ND EDITION

THE COPYRIGHT HANDBOOK

HOW TO PROTECT AND USE WRITTEN WORKS

BY ATTORNEY STEPHEN FISHMAN

NOLO PRESS, BERKELEY

Your Responsibility When Using a Self-Help Law Book

We've done our best to give you useful and accurate information in this book. But laws and procedures change frequently and are subject to differing interpretations. If you want legal advice backed by a guarantee, see a lawyer. If you use this book, it's your responsibility to make sure that the facts and general advice contained in it are applicable to your situation.

Keeping Up-To-Date

To keep its books up-to-date, Nolo Press issues new printings and new editions periodically. New printings reflect minor legal changes and technical corrections. New editions contain major legal changes, major text additions or major reorganizations. To find out if a later printing or edition of any Nolo book is available, call Nolo Press at (510) 549-1976 or check the catalog in the *Nolo News*, our quarterly newspaper.

To stay current, follow the "Update" service in the *Nolo News*. You can get a free two year subscription by sending us the registration card in the back of the book. In another effort to help you use Nolo's latest materials, we offer a 25% discount off the purchase of any new Nolo book if you turn in any earlier printing or edition. (See the "Recycle Offer" in the back of this book.)

This book was last revised in: **January 1995**.

Second Edition

Second Printing	JANUARY 1995
Editor	STEPHEN ELIAS
Illustrations	MARI STEIN
Book Design	TERRI HEARSH
Cover Design	SUSAN WIGHT & TONI IHARA
Index	SAYRE VAN YOUNG
Proofreading	ANNE HAYES
Printing	DELTA LITHOGRAPH

Fishman, Stephen.
    The copyright handbook / by Stephen Fishman. -- 2nd national ed.
        p.   cm.
    Includes index.
    ISBN 0-87337-241-7
    1. Copyright--United States--Popular works. 2. Copyright,
International--Popular works.   I. Title.
KF2995.F53 1994
346.7304'82—dc20
[347.306482]   94-975
                                       CIP

Printed on paper with recycled content.

PRINTED IN THE USA

Acknowledgments

Many thanks to:

Jake Warner for giving me the opportunity to write a book on such an interesting subject and for his editorial contributions.

Steve Elias, whose ideas and superb editing made this a much better book.

M. J. Salone for permission to borrow from the chapters on international copyright protection and copyright infringement in her book *How to Copyright Software* (Nolo Press).

Kent Dunlap, Assistant General Counsel, U.S. Copyright Office, and Lisa Goldoftas for reviewing the chapter on copyright registration.

Attorney Katherine Hardy for reviewing portions of the manuscript.

Susan Wight and Toni Ihara for their imaginative front cover design.

Dedication

This book is dedicated to my mother, Helen F. Poellot.

Table of Contents

1 How to Use This Book

2 Copyright Basics

3 Copyright Notice

4 Copyright Registration

5 Correcting or Changing Copyright Notice or Registration

PART I: DEALING WITH ERRORS OR
OMISSIONS IN COPYRIGHT NOTICE

PART II: DEALING WITH ERRORS OR CHANGES
AFFECTING COPYRIGHT REGISTRATION:
SUPPLEMENTAL REGISTRATION

6 What Copyright Protects

11 Using Other Authors' Words

12 Copyright Infringement: What It Is, What to Do About It, How to Avoid It

13 International Copyright Protection

14 Electronic Publishing

15 Help Beyond This Book

A Appendix

Sample Forms

Blank Forms

1

How to Use This Book

Here's a book about copyright for written works. It is for the entire universe of people who deal with the written word.

> ### WHO THIS BOOK IS FOR
>
> Novelists, short story writers, poets, playwrights, screenwriters, biographers, historians, authors of how-to books, writers of scientific and technical works and other works of nonfiction, published and unpublished authors, journalists, freelance writers, persons employed by others to create written works, persons who employ others to create written works, editors who work for magazines and book publishers, established publishers, self-publishers, librarians, teachers and literary agents.

A. How This Book Is Organized

This book has two parts:
- Part I (Chapters 2–4) consists of a short overview of copyright law (Chapter 2, *Copyright Basics*), and a "how-to" guide on copyright notice and registration with the Copyright Office.

- Part II (Chapters 5–15) serves as your copyright resource; it discusses the most important aspects of copyright law in detail. If you are unable to find the answers to your questions in Part II, the final chapter (Chapter 15, *Help Beyond This Book*) tells you how to do further research on your own and, if necessary, find a copyright attorney.

B. Which Parts of This Book You Should Read

Not everyone will want to read the whole book. Which parts you do want to read will of course depend on why you bought the book.

Most of you bought the book for one of these three reasons:
- You want to know how to satisfy the procedural requirements to obtain maximum copyright protection for a written work.
- You have a specific copyright question or problem.
- You want a general education about copyright law.

Assuming you fall into one of these three categories, here is how you can make best use of this book.

1. Readers Who Want to Know How to Satisfy the Procedural Requirements for Maximum Copyright Protection

If you just want to know how to place a valid copyright notice on your work (that's the © followed by a date and name you usually see on published works) read Chapter 3, *Copyright Notice*. Placing a valid copyright notice on your work will make it easier to enforce your copyright.

If you want to register your work with the Copyright Office, refer to Chapter 4, *Copyright Registration,* for a step-by-step explanation. You'll find all the registration forms you need in the tear-out appendix at the end of the book. You will obtain important benefits by registering your work after it is published.

2. Readers Who Have a Specific Copyright Question

If you have a specific question or problem, start with the table of contents at the front of the book. For example, suppose you want to know whether you need permission to use a quotation from Abraham Lincoln that you found in a recent civil war history. By scanning the table of contents you would discover Chapter 11, *Using Other Authors' Words*—probably the place to start. And by examining the section headings under Chapter 11, you would find that Section A is the place to start reading.

If you didn't find what you were looking for in the table of contents, you could use the index at the back of the book and search under such terms as "quotations" and "public domain."

3. People Who Want to Learn All About Copyright

If you simply want to learn more about copyright, read Chapter 2, *Copyright Basics,* and then read as much of Chapters 5 through 13 as you wish. You can skip Chapters 2, 3 and 4, since these chapters are intended for people who want to take specific steps

to obtain maximum copyright protection for a written work.

C. What This Book Is Not About

This book only covers copyright for written works. This means it is not about:

- copyright protection for music, artwork, photography or audio-visual works
- publishing contracts—although we discuss the copyright aspects of publishing contracts, this is not a book about how to negotiate or draft contracts
- protecting inventions—see *Patent It Yourself,* by David Pressman (Nolo Press), if you want to know about this
- protecting computer software—see *Copyright Your Software* and *Software Development: A Legal Guide,* both by Stephen Fishman (Nolo Press), if you want to know about this
- protecting titles, logos or slogans—these items may be protected under the federal and state trademark laws, which have nothing to do with copyright; see *Trademark: How to Name Your Business & Product*, by Kate McGrath and Stephen Elias (Nolo Press).
- protecting ideas—copyright only protects words, not ideas. Ideas can be protected as trade secrets, which involves committing anyone who learns of the ideas to secrecy, and maintaining security procedures to prevent the ideas from leaking out.

2

Copyright Basics

This chapter is an introduction to some basic copyright concepts and vocabulary. It is designed to pave the way for more detailed discussions in later chapters. We therefore urge you not to use this material to reach a final conclusion about any particular issue. Only after reading one or more of the later chapters will you be in a position to make a judgment about a particular question or course of action.

A. Why Have a Copyright Law?

The Founding Fathers recognized that everyone would benefit if creative people were encouraged to create new intellectual and artistic works. When the United States Constitution was written in 1787, the framers took care to include a copyright clause (Article I, Section 8) stating that "The Congress shall have Power... To promote the Progress of Science and useful Arts, by securing for limited times to Authors... the exclusive Right to their... writings."

The primary purpose of copyright, then, is not to enrich authors; rather, it is to promote the progress of science and the useful arts—that is, human knowledge. To pursue this goal, copyright encourages authors in their creative efforts by giving them a mini-monopoly over their works—termed a copyright. But this monopoly is limited when it appears to conflict with the overriding public interest in encouraging creation of new intellectual and artistic works generally. (See Section E, below.)

B. What Is Copyright?

Copyright is a legal device that provides the creator of a work of art or literature, or a work that conveys information or ideas, the right to control how the work is used. The Copyright Act of 1976—the federal law providing for copyright protection—grants authors a bundle of intangible, exclusive rights over their work. These rights include:

- reproduction right—the right to make copies of a protected work
- distribution right—the right to sell or otherwise distribute copies to the public
- right to create adaptions (or derivative works)— the right to prepare new works based on the protected work, and
- performance and display rights—the right to perform a protected work such as a stageplay, or display a work in public.

An author's copyright rights may be exercised only by the author—or by a person or entity to whom the author has transferred all or part of her rights. If someone wrongfully uses the material covered by the copyright, the copyright owner can sue and obtain compensation for any losses suffered.

In this sense, a copyright is a type of property—it belongs to its owner (usually the author) and the courts can be asked to intervene if anyone uses it without permission. And, like other forms of

property, a copyright may be sold by its owner, or otherwise exploited for her economic benefit.

C. How Is a Copyright Created and Protected?

A copyright automatically comes into existence the moment an author fixes her words in some tangible form—for instance, the moment a book or article is typed, handwritten or dictated. No further action need be taken. However, it is wise to place a valid copyright notice on all published works and to register these works in the U.S. Copyright Office shortly after publication.

WHAT CONSTITUTES PUBLICATION

Knowing whether a work has been published or not can be important because many important copyright rules differ for published and unpublished works. A work is published for copyright purposes when copies are sold, rented, lent, given away or otherwise distributed to the public by the copyright owner or by others acting with the owner's permission—for example, a publisher. It is not necessary to sell thousands of copies of a work for it to be considered published. So long as multiple copies of a work are made available to the public, the work is "published" for copyright purposes even if no copies are actually sold or otherwise distributed.

---

1. Notice

In the past, all published works had to contain a copyright notice (the © symbol followed by the publication date and copyright owner's name) to be protected by copyright. This is no longer true. Use of copyright notices is now optional. Even so, it is always a good idea to include a copyright notice on all published works so that potential copiers will be informed of the underlying claim to copyright ownership.

2. Registration

Prompt registration in the U.S. Copyright Office makes your copyright a matter of public record and provides a number of important advantages if it is ever necessary to go to court to enforce it. To register a work you must fill out a registration form and deposit copies of your work with the Copyright Office.

D. What Copyright Protects

Copyright protects an author's words if and to the extent they are original—that is, not copied from other authors' works. Since the main goal of copyright is to encourage creation of new intellectual and artistic works, it follows that copyright protection extends only to material authors write themselves.

There is also no reason to protect works whose creation is a purely mechanical or clerical act. Protecting works such as phone books or certain blank forms would not help develop the arts and sciences. An author must employ a minimal amount of creativity in creating the work. This does not mean that to be protectible a work has to be a great work of art, but a minimal amount of thought or judgment must have been involved in its creation.

A work need not be entirely new to be protectible. Copyright protects new material an author adds to a previously existing work. For example, copyright protects derivative works. A derivative work is a work that is created by adapting or transforming previously written material into a new work of authorship. Examples include a screenplay or stageplay based on a novel, an English translation of a work written in a foreign language and condensed versions of articles (such as those found in *Reader's Digest*). Copyright can also protect "compilations." These are works in which preexisting materials are selected, coordinated and arranged so that a new work of authorship is created—for example, anthologies or catalogs.

E. Limitations on Copyright Protection

We've seen that the purpose of copyright is to encourage intellectual and artistic creation. Paradoxically, giving authors too much copyright protection could inhibit rather than enhance creative growth. To avoid this, some important limitations on copyright protection have been developed.

1. Ideas and Facts Are Not Protected

Copyright only protects the words with which a writer expressed facts and ideas. Copyright does not protect the facts or ideas themselves; facts and ideas are free for anyone to use. To give an author a monopoly over the facts and ideas contained in his work would hinder intellectual and artistic progress, not encourage it. For example, imagine how scientific progress would have suffered if Charles Darwin could have prevented anyone else from writing about evolution after he published *The Origin of Species*.

Because copyright only extends its protection to words rather than the underlying facts and ideas, works in which the particular words used by the author are important and distinctive—such as poems, novels and plays—enjoy the most copyright protection. Works that readers buy primarily for the ideas and facts they contain, not their language,

receive less protection. This includes most types of factual works, such as histories, biographies, how-to books, news stories and so forth.

2. Fair Use

To foster the advancement of the arts and sciences, there must be a free flow of information and ideas. If no one could quote from a protected work without the author's permission (which could be withheld or given only upon payment of a permission fee), the free flow of ideas would be stopped dead. To avoid this, a special fair use exception to authors' copyright rights was created. An author is free to copy from a protected work for purposes such as criticism, news reporting, teaching or research so long as the value of the copyrighted work is not diminished.

3. Works in the Public Domain

Any work that is not protected by copyright is said to be in the public domain. This includes works in which the copyright was lost, works in which the copyright expired and works authored or owned by the federal government. Public domain means what it says—such works belong to the public as a whole. Anyone is free to use them any way she wishes without asking anyone's permission. And no one can ever obtain copyright protection for public domain material, no matter how she transforms it. Everything published more than 75 years ago is now in the public domain, freely available to us all.

F. Copyright Ownership and Transfer of Ownership

The copyright in a protectible work is initially owned by the work's author or authors. But a person need not actually create the work to be its "author" for copyright purposes. A protectible work written by an employee as part of her job is initially owned by the employer—that is, the employer is considered to be the work's author. Such works are called works made for hire. Works created by nonemployees who sign work for hire agreements may also be works made for hire.

Like any other property, a copyright can be bought and sold. This is the way authors other than self-publishers profit from their work. Typically, authors sell their work to publishers for a fee or royalty. However, transfers of copyright ownership are unique in one respect: Authors or their heirs have the right to terminate any transfer of copyright ownership 35 years after it is made.

G. How Long a Copyright Lasts

Few things in this world last as long as copyright protection. Indeed, an author's work is likely to be long forgotten before her copyright in it expires. The copyright in works created after 1977 by individuals usually lasts for the life of the author plus an additional 50 years. The copyright in works created by employees for their employers lasts for 75 years from the date of publication, or 100 years from the date of creation, whichever occurs first.

The copyright in works *created and published* before 1978 lasts for 75 years from the date of publication if they were (or are) timely renewed (see the sidebar as to what constitutes publication). As a result, it may be necessary to do some legwork to find out if certain pre-1978 published works are still under copyright. The copyright in works created *but not published* before 1978 lasts at least until December 31, 2002.

H. Copyright Infringement

Copyright infringement occurs when a person other than the copyright owner exploits one or more of the copyright owner's exclusive rights without the owner's permission. This type of theft is also commonly termed copyright piracy.

The Copyright Act doesn't prevent copyright infringement from occurring, just as the laws against auto theft do not prevent cars from being stolen. However, the Copyright Act does give authors a legal remedy to use after an infringement has occurred—they may sue the infringer in federal court.

An author who wins an infringement suit can stop any further infringement, get infringing copies destroyed, obtain damages from the infringer—often the amount of any profits obtained from the infringement—and recover other monetary losses. This means in effect that an author can make a copyright pirate restore the author to the same economic position she would have been in had the infringement never occurred. And, in some cases, the copyright owner may even be able to obtain monetary penalties that may far exceed her actual losses.

I. Other Protections for Intellectual Property

The copyright law is not the only means available to protect products of human intellect that have some economic value. The state and federal trademark laws protect distinctive words, phrases, logos and other symbols that are used to identify products and services in the marketplace. The federal patent law protects new inventions. State trade secret laws may protect novel and generally unknown ideas, processes or technical designs that provide a commercial advantage in the marketplace.

1. Trademarks

The copyright laws do not protect names, titles or short phrases. This is where trademark protection comes in. Under both federal and state laws a manufacturer, merchant or group associated with a product or service can obtain protection for a word, phrase, logo or other symbol used to distinguish that product or service from others. If a competitor uses a protected trademark, the trademark holder can obtain a court injunction and monetary damages.

EXAMPLE: The word "Kleenex" is a registered trademark of the Kimberly-Clark Corporation. None of Kimberly-Clark's competitors can use this word on a box of facial tissues without Kimberly-Clark's consent. If they do, Kimberly-Clark could get a court to order them to stop and could sue for damages.

The trademark laws are often used in conjunction with the copyright law to protect advertising copy. The trademark laws protect the product or service name and any slogans used in the advertising and the copyright laws protect any additional literal expression that the ad contains.

2. Patents

By filing for and obtaining a patent from the U.S. Patent and Trademark Office, an inventor is granted a monopoly on the use and commercial exploitation of her invention for a limited time. A patent may protect the functional features of a machine, process, manufactured item, composition of matter, ornamental design or asexually reproduced plants. A patent also protects new uses for any such items. However, to obtain a patent, the invention must be novel and non-obvious.

EXAMPLE: Mickey invents an entirely new and non-obvious type of mousetrap. He applies for a patent on his invention. If and when it's issued, no one can make, use or sell Mickey's invention without his permission for the term of the patent (17 years). If they do, Mickey can sue them for patent infringement.

The basic difference between a patent and a copyright is that a patent protects ideas as expressed in an invention, whether a machine or process of some type. Copyright protects only the words an author uses to express an idea, not the idea itself.

EXAMPLE: Mary has invented the widget, a device only dreamed about for decades. She obtains a patent for her invention. She manufactures and sells the widget herself. She also writes and publishes a technical manual, *The Widget Owner's Survival Guide*. The patent law prevents anyone from manufacturing and selling widgets without Mary's permission. The copyright law prevents anyone from copying the manual without Mary's permission.

Obtaining a patent can be a difficult and time-consuming process (it usually takes years). See *Patent It Yourself*, by David Pressman (Nolo Press) for a detailed discussion.

3. Trade Secrets

A trade secret is information or know-how that is not generally known in the community and that provides its owner with a competitive advantage in the marketplace. The information can be an idea, written words, formula, process or procedure, technical design, list, marketing plan or any other secret that gives the owner an economic advantage.

If a trade secret's owner takes reasonable steps to keep the confidential information or know-how secret, the courts of most states will protect the owner from disclosures of the secret by:

- the owner's employees
- other persons with a duty not to make such disclosures
- industrial spys, and
- competitors who wrongfully acquire the information.

That is, the trade secret's owner may be able to sue the infringer and obtain an injunction and/or damages. However, the more widely known a trade secret is, the less likely the courts are to protect it.

Since trade secret protection is available for the expression of an idea as well as the idea itself, certain expressions may be protected by both copyright and trade secret law. And, of course, an idea may also qualify for patent protection.

EXAMPLE: Recall that Mary, in the second patent law example above, wrote a training manual for her widget invention. This manual was automatically protected by copyright. If the manual is also kept confidential (Mary only allows her employees to read it and makes them sign agreements to keep it confidential), it may also be entitled to trade secret protection. However, once Mary publishes and distributes the manual widely to the public, any trade secret protection would cease.

Since most authors want their work to be published and as widely read as possible, trade secret laws usually have little application to written works. However, trade secret protection may be important to authors of written works containing competitively advantageous information that has been kept confidential. Trade secret protection is provided only under state law, and varies from state to state.

4. Contract Protection for Ideas

Consider this example: Manny, a TV producer, agrees to pay Sally $10,000 for telling him an idea she has for a new TV show. Sally tells Manny the idea, but he fails to pay. Does Sally have any recourse against Manny?

We know that copyright does not protect ideas, so Sally cannot sue Manny for copyright infringement. Her idea is not for a new invention, so she gets no help from the patent laws. And let's assume the idea is not a trade secret.

All is not lost for Sally because some courts have held that if a person agrees to pay another person for disclosing an idea she has, the agreement constitutes an enforceable contract. This means that if the person fails to pay what he promised, the person who disclosed her idea may be able to sue and collect the promised payment. This might mean that Sally can sue Manny for breach of contract and collect the $10,000. Some courts would permit Sally the $10,000 only if her idea was novel and concrete and Manny actually used it. Others would not require this. See *Copyright Principles, Law and Practice,* by Paul Goldstein (Little, Brown and Co.), Chapter 15.

However, there are very few Mannys or Sallys in the real world. Rarely, if ever, will a producer, publisher, editor or other person agree to pay an author for a mere idea. Thus, contract protection for ideas is usually more theoretical than real. The best way to protect your ideas is to disclose them only to people whose integrity can be trusted.

SOME COMMON COPYRIGHT MISCONCEPTIONS

Copyright is a fast-changing area of the law. The copyright laws were completely rewritten in 1978 and major changes were made again in 1989. Many people who are unaware of the impact of these changes have ideas about copyright that are no longer true. For example:

- A work must be registered with the U.S. Copyright Office to be protected by copyright.

  This hasn't been true since 1978. Copyright protection begins automatically the moment a work is set to paper or otherwise fixed in a tangible form.

- Only works that have a copyright notice on them are protected by copyright.

  Use of copyright notices has been optional since March 1, 1989.

- No one can use or photocopy a protected work without the owner's permission.

  This has never been true. You can photocopy or otherwise use protected works so long as the use comes within the bounds of fair use—that is, does not diminish the value of the protected work.

- You can copyright your great ideas.

  This also has never been true. Copyright only protects the expression of an idea, not the idea itself.

Copyright Notice

A. Introduction

This chapter is about copyright notice. That's the "c" in a circle, followed by a publication date and name, usually seen on published works. The purpose of such a notice is to inform the public that a work is copyrighted, when it was published and who owns the copyright. Before March 1, 1989, a notice was required on all published works as a condition of keeping the copyright. For works published after that date, a notice is not required. Nonetheless, it's a very good idea to provide a notice anyway on all your published works.

The use of a copyright notice is the responsibility of the copyright owner and does not require any advance permission from, or registration with, the Copyright Office.

The extent to which you need to be concerned with the material in this chapter depends upon your particular situation.

Authors of books published by established companies. As a practical matter, you don't have to worry much about the copyright notice if you're being published by an established publisher. The publisher, as a matter of course, will include copyright notices on all copies of the books they print and distribute. The author just needs to make sure that the information in the notice is correct.

Freelance writers. Freelance writers whose work appears in magazines and other periodicals are protected by the notice the publisher provides for the periodical as a whole. But some freelancers choose to include a separate notice on their work. (See Section F, below.)

Self-published authors. Persons who self-publish their work must compose and format their copyright notices themselves and should carefully read this chapter, as should those who work in the publishing field.

B. When Copyright Notice Is Required

Copyright notice is mandatory for some works and not for others, depending upon the date of publication.

1. Works published before 1978

Until 1978, all works published in the United States had to contain a valid copyright notice to be protected by copyright. Failure to provide the notice resulted in loss of the copyright in the work—that is, the work was injected into the public domain, meaning that anyone could copy or otherwise use it without the author's permission.

> **EXAMPLE:** Bernie self-published his poetry collection in 1977. He knew nothing about copyright law and failed to provide a copyright notice on the work. Shirley finds a copy of the collection in a used bookstore in 1990 and decides to include several of Bernie's poems in

HOW IMPORTANT ARE THE DATES OF PUBLICATION?

THEY'RE "OF THE ESSENCE"
(DARLING - "OF THE ESSENCE."

a compilation of modern American poetry. Since the book did not contain a copyright notice, it is considered to be in the public domain and Shirley may reproduce all or part of it without Bernie's permission.

2. Works published between January 1, 1978 and March 1, 1989

As the example above illustrates, the pre-1978 notice requirement often had draconian results—authors lost their copyright protection just because they failed to comply with a mere technical formality. The harshness of this rule was moderated somewhat by the Copyright Act of 1976, which provided that a work without a valid notice that was published after January 1, 1978, did not enter the public domain if— within five years after the publication—the work was registered with the Copyright Office and a reasonable effort was made to add a valid notice to all copies of the work distributed after the omission was discovered. (See Chapter 4, *Copyright Registration*, for detailed discussion.)

3. Works published after March 1, 1989

The copyright notice requirement for published works ended altogether when the United States signed the Berne Convention, an international copyright treaty. The Berne Convention is discussed in detail in Chapter 13, *International Copyright Protection*. All you need to know about it now is that it required the U.S. to get rid of its notice requirement, which happened on March 1, 1989. Any work printed after that date need not contain a copyright notice, even if it was originally published prior to that date.

EXAMPLE: George self-publishes a book in 1981. The work had to contain a valid copyright notice to be protected by copyright. He then reissues the book in 1991. The newly printed copies need not contain a copyright notice, but it is a good idea to provide one anyway (see below).

C. Why Provide a Copyright Notice on Published Works?

Even though a notice is not required for works printed after March 1, 1989, you should still make sure that a valid copyright notice appears on every copy of every work you publish. There are several excellent reasons for this.

1. Notice Makes Infringement Suits Economically Feasible

Authors and other copyright owners enforce their copyright rights by suing persons who copy their work or otherwise exercise their copyright rights without their permission. Unfortunately, copyright infringement litigation is usually very expensive (copyright attorneys usually charge at least $150 an hour). As a result, copyright infringement lawsuits may be economically feasible only if the author can obtain substantial damages (money) from the infringer.

The way to get substantial damages is to prove that the infringement was *willful*—that is, that the infringer knew that he was breaking the law but did so anyway. Courts usually award far more damages where the infringement was willful than where the infringer didn't realize what he was doing was wrong. (See Chapter 12, *Copyright Infringement*, for a detailed discussion of infringement suits.)

Proving willfulness can be difficult if a work lacks a valid copyright notice. The reason for this is what's known as the innocent infringement defense. If a person copies a published work that does not contain a copyright notice, the copier can claim in court that the infringement was innocent—that is, he or she didn't know the work was protected by copyright. If the judge or jury believes this, the copier may still be liable for infringement, but the damages (monetary compensation) may be drastically reduced from what they otherwise would have been. On the other hand, if there is a valid copyright notice on the work, the infringer cannot claim innocence and will be treated as a willful infringer.

EXAMPLE 1: Mary self-publishes a book without a copyright notice. Izzy copies a substantial amount of it in a book of his own. Mary sues Izzy for copyright infringement. Mary proves to the court that she suffered $25,000 in damages due to the infringement. However, Izzy, while admitting that he copied Mary's work, claims that he did not realize it was copyrighted because it lacked a copyright notice. The judge buys Izzy's story, and as a result rules that Izzy need only pay Mary $5,000 in damages rather than the $25,000 required to fully compensate her.

EXAMPLE 2: Assume instead that Mary included a valid copyright notice in her book. She sues Izzy for copyright infringement. Since her book contained a valid notice, Izzy cannot argue that he did not realize the book was protected by copyright. As a result, Mary is awarded the full amount of damages required to fully compensate her—$25,000.

2. Copyright Notice May Deter Potential Infringers

Another important reason to place a copyright notice on all copies of your published work is that it may help deter copyright infringement. The notice lets readers know that the work is protected by copyright and may not be copied without the owner's permission. Moreover, since copyright notices appear on the vast majority of published works, a reader of a work not containing a notice might mistakenly assume that the work is not copyrighted, and feel free to copy it.

3. Notice Protects Your Work in Countries Not Adhering to the Berne Convention

There are some 20 foreign countries that do not afford copyright protection to works not containing valid copyright notices. (See Chapter 13, *International Copyright Protection,* for detailed discussion.) Providing a copyright notice on your work will enable your work to be protected in these countries.

Copyright tip
Placing a copyright notice on your published work costs nothing and may end up saving you thousands of dollars by deterring others from copying your work and enabling you to recover your full measure of damages against those who do copy it. **Always, always, always place a valid copyright notice on your published work!**

D. When to Provide Notice

A copyright notice should be included on a work when it is first published and on every subsequent published edition. A work is published for copyright purposes when it is made generally available to the public by the copyright owner or others acting with the owner's permission—a publisher, for example. It is not necessary to sell or otherwise transfer any copies of the work—publication occurs if the work is made available to the public without restriction. For example, leaving copies of a work in a public place would constitute publication, as would distributing copies on a busy street. But distributing copies to a restricted group would not constitute publication. Sending five copies of a manuscript to five publishers would not be a publication, nor would circulating copies to colleagues (a restricted group) for comment.

A copyright notice has never been required for unpublished works, and will not bar an infringer from raising the innocent infringement defense. But, under certain circumstances, it might be desirable to provide a notice on an unpublished manuscript. (See discussion in Section I, below.)

E. Form of Notice

There are strict technical requirements as to what a copyright notice must contain. Follow these rules exactly or your notice may be found to be invalid and not accomplish its intended purpose. A valid copyright notice contains three elements:

- the copyright symbol
- the year in which the work was published
- the name of the copyright owner.

It is not required that these elements appear in any particular order in the notice, but most notices are written in the order set forth above. We'll discuss each element in turn.

1. Copyright Symbol

You should use the familiar © symbol—that is, the lowercase letter "c" completely surrounded by a circle. The word "Copyright" or the abbreviation "Copr." are also acceptable in the United States, but

not in many foreign countries. So if your work might be distributed outside the U.S., be sure to always use the © symbol.

ADDING THE WORD "COPYRIGHT" TO NOTICE

Often, you'll see the word "Copyright" or the abbreviation "Copr." followed by or preceeding the © symbol—for instance, "Copyright ©." Technically, this is not required—the © symbol alone is sufficient. However, it is a good idea to include the words anyway because they will further clarify that the work is protected by copyright.

---

2. Year of Publication

The copyright notice must also state the year the work was published. For first editions, this is easy. Put the year the work was actually published. (See Section D, above.)

a. New versions

The copyright notice for a new version of a work must contain the date that version was published. (See Chapter 7, *Adaptions and Compilations*, for when changes in a work make it a new version for copyright purposes.) The notice need not contain the date or dates of the prior version or versions. However, it is common practice to include such dates in the copyright notice. One reason is to let the reader know when the earlier versions were created. Another reason to do this is that it is not always easy to tell if a work qualifies as a new version under copyright office rules.

EXAMPLE: Sally Bowles published the first edition of her high school textbook on French in 1981. The copyright notice read "Copyright © 1981 by Sally Bowles." The book is revised and republished as a second edition in 1992. If the second edition qualifies as a new version, the notice need only state "Copyright © 1992 by Sally Bowles." However, Sally is not sure whether the changes she made were substantial enough to make the second edition a new version. She decides to err on the side of caution and writes the notice like this: "Copyright © 1981, 1992 by Sally Bowles."

b.   Form of date

The date is usually written in Arabic numerals—for instance, "1991." But you can also use abbreviations of Arabic numerals—for instance, "'91"; Roman numerals—for instance, "MCMXCI"; or spelled out words instead of numerals—for instance, "Nineteen Hundred Ninety-One."

Copyright tip

Copyright owners sometimes state the year of publication in Roman numerals in the hope readers won't be able to decipher it and will think the work more recent than it really is. However, dates not written in Arabic numerals may not be acceptable in some foreign countries.

3.   Copyright Owner's Name

The name of the copyright owner must also be included in the notice. Briefly, the owner is:
- the author or authors of the work
- the legal owner of a work made for hire, or
- the person or entity (partnership or corporation) to whom all the author's exclusive copyright rights have been transferred.

a.   Author or authors

Unless a work is made for hire (see below), the original author or authors own all the copyright rights. Where all these rights are retained, the author's name should appear in the copyright notice.

EXAMPLE: Eli Yale self-publishes a book on ivy gardening in 1992. Eli wrote the book himself and owns all the copyright rights. The copyright notice should state: "Copyright © 1992 by Eli Yale."

If there are multiple authors, they should all be listed in the copyright notice. The authors' names can appear in any order.

EXAMPLE: Joe Sixpack, Louis Loser and Benny Bigmouth write a book together about nuclear physics. All their names should appear in the copyright notice. For example: "Copyright © 1992 by Joe Sixpack, Louis Loser and Benny Bigmouth."

b.   Works made for hire

A work made for hire is a work made by an employee as part of her job, or a work specially ordered or commissioned under a written work for hire contract. (See Chapter 8, *Initial Copyright Ownership.*) The writer's employer or other person for whom the work was prepared is the copyright owner and that person's (or entity's) name should appear in the copyright notice. The writer-employee's name should not be included in the notice.

EXAMPLE: Archie and Marion are technical writers employed by Datavue Publications, Inc. As part of their job, they write a technical manual that Datavue publishes. Only Datavue's name should appear in the copyright notice: "Copyright © 1992 by Datavue Publications."

c. Transferees

If all of the copyright rights owned by the author—or by the owner of a work made for hire—are transferred to another person or entity, that name should appear in the copyright notice on all copies printed and distributed after the transfer. However, any copies printed before the transfer occurred may be distributed without updating the notice.

EXAMPLE: Eli Yale self-publishes his book on ivy gardening in 1993. His name alone appears on the copyright notice. He prints 1,000 copies and by January 1994, 500 have been sold. In February 1994, Eli transfers his entire copyright in the book to Joe Harvard, the owner of a small bookstore. Joe is now the copyright owner. However, Joe can distribute the 500 unsold copies without updating the copyright notice they contain, even though the notice states that Eli is the copyright owner. But if Joe prints and distributes any new copies, his name alone should appear in the copyright notice.

The most common form of transfer of rights is by a writer to her publisher. A writer can sell all or part of her copyright rights to a publisher. This is a matter for negotiation. Trade book publishing contracts typically provide the publisher with an exclusive license to exercise the rights the publisher needs (for example, the right to publish the book in all English-speaking countries). In this event, the author's name should appear in the copyright notice, not the publisher's name, because the author has retained some of her copyright rights. Another approach, commonly used in textbook publishing, is for the author to transfer all his copyright rights to his publisher. Where this occurs, the publisher's name should appear in the notice.

WHAT NAME GOES ON NOTICE WHERE RIGHTS ARE TRANSFERRED TO DIFFERENT PEOPLE?

We explain in Chapter 9, *Transferring Copyright Ownership*, that a copyright is completely divisible—that is, the owner may transfer all or part of her exclusive copyright rights to whomever and however she wishes. For example, a copyright owner can transfer less than all of her rights and retain the others, or transfer some rights to one person or entity and all the others to other transferees. In this event, it can be confusing to determine just who the owner of copyright is for purposes of the copyright notice. The general rule is that unless the author—or owner of a work made for hire—transfers all her copyright rights to a single person or entity, the author's name should appear in the notice.

EXAMPLE: Lucy has written a novel. She sells to Schultz Publishing Co. the right to publish the book in hardcover in North America. Lucy sells the paperback rights to Pequod Press. Finally, Lucy sells the right to publish her novel outside of North America to Linus Publications. Lucy's name alone should appear in the copyright notice on the hardcover, paperback and foreign editions of her book. In contrast, if Lucy sold all her rights to Schultz, its name should appear in the notice.

The one exception to this general rule is where a collective or derivative work is created from preexisting material. (See Section F, below.)

d.   Form of name

Usually, the owner's full legal name is used. However, it is permissible to use an abbreviation of the owner's name, a last name alone, a trade name, nickname, fictitious name, pseudonym, initials or some other designation as long as the copyright owner is *generally known* by the name or other words or letters used in the notice. For example, the novelist David Cornwell could use the pseudonym John le Carré (by which he is generally known), or the International Business Machines Corporation could use the abbreviation "IBM." However, if the author is generally known only by her full name, only that name should be used in the notice.

IF YOU WANT TO REMAIN ANONYMOUS

The word "anonymous" should not be used in a copyright notice because an author is obviously not generally known by that name. Likewise, it is not advisable to use a pseudonym by which you are not generally known. You can avoid revealing your name in a copyright notice, and still ensure the notice's validity, by transferring all of your copyright rights to your publisher. This way, the publisher's name may appear in the notice. Another approach would be to form a corporation, transfer your entire copyright to it, and then use the corporation's name in the notice.

If the copyright owner is a corporation, it is not necessary to include the word "Inc." in the name, even if this is part of the corporation's full legal name. Nor is it necessary for the word "by" to precede the copyright owner's name, although it is commonly used—for example, a notice can be written as "Copyright © 1993 by Joe Blow" or "Copyright © 1993 Joe Blow."

F.   Notice on Compilations and Adaptions

Compilations and adaptions are formed all or in part from preexisting material. Nevertheless, it is usually not necessary that the copyright notice for this type of work refer to the preexisting material.

1.   Compilations

A compilation may be a collective work—that is, a work that consists of separate and independent works assembled into a collective whole, such as encyclopedias, anthologies and serial works like magazines, periodicals, newspapers, newsletters and journals. A compilation may also be a work in which preexisting materials—usually data of various types—are selected, coordinated and arranged so that a new work is created—for example, a catalog. (See Chapter 7, *Adaptions and Compilations*, for detailed discussion.)

Unless a person who creates a compilation uses material in the public domain, he must either own the preexisting material used in the work or obtain the permission of those who do own it. If the creator of a compilation does not own the preexisting material, all he owns is the copyright in the compilation as a whole—that is, the copyright in the creative work involved in selecting, combining and assembling the material into a whole work. Nevertheless, a compilation need only contain one copyright notice in the name of that copyright owner.

EXAMPLE: James Henry compiles and publishes an anthology of the best American short stories of 1992. The anthology contains 12 stories. The authors of the stories gave Henry permission to publish them in the anthology, but still retain all their copyright rights. The anthology need contain only one copyright notice in Henry's name: "Copyright © 1992 by James Henry." Separate copyright notices need not be provided for the 12 contributions owned by persons other than Henry.

Although an individual contribution to a compilation does not have to have its own copyright notice, a notice is permissible where the copyright in the contribution is owned by someone other than the owner of the compilation as a whole. This may help deter a potential infringer and make clear that the owner of the copyright in the compilation does not own that particular contribution. (See Section H.3 below for where to place this notice.)

a.   Publication date for compilations

The copyright notice for a compilation need only list the year the compilation itself is published, not the date or dates the preexisting material was published.

EXAMPLE: Josephine self-publishes an anthology of her short stories in 1992. The stories were published in various literary journals between 1985 and 1992. The notice on the anthology need only state 1992 as the publication date.

b.   Advertisements

The rule that a single notice for a compilation as a whole covers all the material in the work does not apply to advertisements. Advertisements in serial publications such as periodicals, magazines and newspapers must carry their own copyright notice. However, an advertisement inserted in a compilation on behalf of the copyright owner of the compilation need not contain its own notice—for example, an ad inserted in *Time* magazine by its owners urging readers to subscribe would not need its own notice.

COMPILATIONS FIRST PUBLISHED BEFORE MARCH 1, 1989

Individual contributions to compilations first printed and distributed before March 1, 1989, are not required to bear their own copyright notices. However, it can be a good idea to provide a notice for such contributions if they have not been registered with the Copyright Office or if a transfer or license agreement was never recorded with the Copyright Office. This is because if the person named in the notice for a pre-March 1, 1989, compilation as a whole fraudulently transfers the right to copy an unnoticed contribution to a third person, the third person might not be held liable for infringement. (See discussion in Chapter 5, *Correcting or Changing Copyright Notice or Registration.*)

---

2.   Adaptions (Derivative Works)

An adaption—called a derivative work in copyright jargon—is a work that is created by recasting, transforming or adapting a previously published work into a new work of authorship. Examples include a screenplay or play based on a novel, an English translation of a work written in a foreign language, condensed versions of articles, such as those found in *Reader's Digest*, and annotations to literary works.

Unless the preexisting material used by a derivative work is in the public domain or owned by the creator of the derivative work, the creator must obtain the copyright owner's permission to use it. (See Chapter 7, *Adaptions and Compilations*.)

As with compilations, the copyright notice for a derivative work need only contain the name of the owner of the copyright to the derivative work itself, not the owner of the preexisting material upon which the derivative work is based.

> **EXAMPLE:** Sally obtains Sue's permission to write a screenplay based on a novel written by Sue. Only Sally's name need appear in the copyright notice to the screenplay.

a. Publication date

As with collective works, the publication date in the notice for a derivative work should be the year the derivative work was published, not the year or years the preexisting material was published.

> **EXAMPLE:** Joe writes a play based on his previously published novel. The novel was published in 1991, the play in 1993. The copyright notice on the published copies of the play need only state 1993 as the publication date.

3. Works Containing United States Government Materials

The rule that a single general notice is sufficient for a compilation or derivative work does not always apply to publications incorporating United States government works. United States government publications are in the public domain—that is, they are not copyrighted and anyone can use them without asking the federal government's permission. However, if a work consists preponderantly of one or more works by the U.S. government, the copyright notice must affirmatively or negatively identify those portions of the work in which copyright is claimed—that is, that part of the work not consisting of U.S. government materials. This enables readers of such works to know which portions of the work are government materials in the public domain.

It's up to you to decide if your work consists preponderantly of U.S. government materials. Certainly, if more than half of your book or other work consists of federal government materials, your notice should enable readers to determine which portions of the work are copyrighted and which in the public domain.

> **EXAMPLE:** Databest Incorporated publishes a book containing analyses of U.S. census data and including several appendices containing U.S. Census Bureau material. The book is a collective work in which independently created contributions have been combined to form a collective whole. The appendices amount to over half the book. The copyright notice for the work could state: "Copyright © 1992 by Databest Incorporated. No protection is claimed in works of the United States government as set forth in Appendices 1, 2, 3, 4, 6." Alternatively, the notice could affirmatively identify those portions of the work in which copyright is claimed—that is, those portions not containing government materials, say chapters 1–10. In this event, the notice might look like this: "Copyright © 1992 by Databest Incorporated. Copyright claimed in Chapters 1 through 10."

Failure to follow this rule will result in the copyright notice being found invalid. This means that an infringer of the material in which you claim a copyright would be allowed to raise the innocent infringement defense at trial. (See Section C above.)

G. Book Dust Jackets

The copyright notice contained in a book does not serve as notice for copyrightable material on the dust jacket, even if the notice says so. This is because the dust jacket is not permanently attached to the book. If the dust jacket contains valuable material that you do not wish copied, it should bear its own copyright notice. The notice can be placed anywhere on the dust jacket. Publishers often place it on the back cover or the back inside flap.

H. Multimedia Works

Multimedia works, or "electronic books," combine text with visual images (both still photos and video and film clips) and sound (including music, ordinary speech and dramatic performances). Some multimedia works consist of a printed text combined with a CD-ROM disk or other computer diskette (the book-disk *From Alice to Ocean* is one outstanding example); others are stored only on CD-ROMs or other magnetic media.

Where a work consists of a book and disk, both should contain their own copyright notice. The computer disk should have a label containing a notice. In addition, it's a good idea to include a notice on the title screen on the computer when the disk is activated, or in an "about" or credit box. Alternatively, the notice could be displayed on screen continuously when the disk is used.

I. Where to Place Copyright Notice

Where to place your copyright notice depends on the nature of the work. The main idea is to make it legible and readable without the aid of a magnifying glass. Remember, you want the notice to be seen by the readers so that they will know that the work is protected by copyright and who owns the copyright.

1. Books

If the work is a book (bound or unbound), booklet, pamphlet or multipage folder, place the copyright notice in one of the following locations:
- the title page
- the page immediately following the title page (this is the most commonly used location for books)
- either side of the front cover
- if there is no front cover, either side of the back leaf of the copies—that is, the hinged piece of paper at the end of a book or pamphlet consisting of at least two pages
- the first or last page of the main body of the work
- if there are no more than ten pages between the front page and the first page of the main body of the work, on any page between the front page and the first page of the main body of the work provided that the notice is reproduced prominently and is set apart from other matter on the page where it appears, or
- if there are no more than ten pages between the last page and the main body of the work, on any page between the last page of the main body of the work and the back page provided that the notice is reproduced prominently and is set apart from other matter on the page where it appears.

2. Magazines and Periodicals

The copyright notice for a magazine, periodical, newsletter, journal or other serial publication may be placed in any of the locations provided for books (above), or:
- as part of, or adjacent to, the masthead (the masthead typically contains such information as the periodical's title, information about the staff, frequency of issuance and subscription policies)
- on the same page as the masthead, but not as part of the masthead itself, provided that the

notice is reproduced prominently and set apart from the other matter appearing on the page, or

- adjacent to a prominent heading appearing at or near the front of the issue containing the periodical's title and any combination of the volume and issue number and date of the issue.

3. Individual Contributions to Compilations

As explained earlier, individual contributions to compilations normally do not need to contain their own copyright notices; however, it is permissible to provide one anyway.

a. Contributions of one page or less

If the contribution consists of a single page or less, the optional copyright notice may be placed:

- under the title of the contribution on that page
- adjacent to the contribution, or
- on the same page if, through format and/or wording, it is clear that the notice applies only to that particular contribution.

b. Contributions containing more than one page

If the contribution contains more than one page, the optional copyright notice may be placed:

- under a title appearing at or near the beginning of the contribution
- on the first page of the main body of the contribution
- immediately following the end of the contribution, or
- on any of the pages where the contribution appears if it is less than 20 pages and the notice is prominent and set apart from the other matter on that page.

c. On same page as copyright notice for compilation

Regardless of the individual contribution's length, the copyright notice may always be placed on the same page as the copyright notice for the compilation as a whole or in a table of contents or list of acknowledgments appearing near the front or back of the compilation. However, the contribution must be listed separately by title or, if it's untitled, by a description reasonably identifying it. These locations may be the most convenient if you need to include a large number of copyright notices.

> **EXAMPLE 1:** The *Nutne Reader*, a literary magazine, publishes an article called "Deconstructionism at a Crossroads" written by Joe Fogel, a freelance literary critic. Joe owns all the copyright rights in the article. Although the *Nutne Reader* contains its own copyright notice, at Joe's insistence it prints the following notice on the same page containing the copyright notice for the *Nutne Reader* as a whole: "'Deconstructionism at a Crossroads' Copyright © 1992 by Joe Fogel."

> **EXAMPLE 2:** Praetorian Publishing, Inc. publishes a new translation of Caesar's *Gallic Wars*. The book also contains many new illustrations. The translation was done by Gus Augustus and the illustrations by Rene Renior. Gus and Rene have sold Praetorian only the right to publish their work in the United States and have retained their other copyright rights. The copyright notice for this compilation, combining Gus's translation with Rene's illustrations to form a collective whole, could simply state "Copyright © 1992 by Praetorian Publishing." However, if they so wish and Praetorian agrees, separate notices can also be provided for Gus's and Rene's contributions. If these notices were placed on the same page as Praetorian's notice, the copyright notice would look like this:

Copyright © 1992 by Praetorian Publishing
Translation copyright © 1992 by Gus Augustus
Illustrations copyright © 1992 by Rene Renior

4. Single-Leaf Works

A single-leaf work is a work consisting of one page, whether printed on one or both sides. A book dust jacket is a good example. The copyright notice for a single leaf work may be placed anywhere on the front or back of the work.

K. Other Information Near Notice

Certain other information in addition to the copyright notice itself is commonly included on the same page as the notice.

FIRST THE WORD COPYRIGHT OR THE © SYMBOL OR COPR. THEN THE DATE, THEN YOUR NAME, THEN ALL RIGHTS RESERVED.

1. "All Rights Reserved"

Bolivia and Honduras require the words "All rights reserved" to appear in the copyright notice. (See Chapter 13, *International Copyright Protection*.) If you intend to distribute your work south of the border, include these words at the end of your copyright notice.

> **EXAMPLE:** Eli Yale thinks there might be a market for his gardening book in South America, so he writes his copyright notice like this:
>
> *Copyright © 1992 by Eli Yale. All rights reserved.*

2. Warning Statements

Since many people do not really understand what a copyright notice means, many publishers include various types of warning or explanatory statements on the same page as the copyright notice. The purpose is to make clear to readers that the work is copyrighted and may not be reproduced without the copyright owner's permission. It does not cost anything to place this type of statement near the copyright notice, and it may help deter copyright infringement. But remember, such statements do not take the place of a valid copyright notice as described earlier in this chapter.

a. Statements commonly used in books

Here are some examples of warning statements that are commonly used in books:

Except as permitted under the Copyright Act of 1976, no part of this book may be reproduced in any form or by any electronic or mechanical means, including the use of information storage and retrieval systems, without permission in writing from the copyright owner. (Some publishers add: *Requests for* permissions should be addressed in writing to [publisher's name and address].)

Or, more simply:

Except as permitted under the Copyright Act of 1976, this book may not be reproduced in whole or in part in any manner.

b.   Screenplays and stage plays

Here is an example of a warning statement that may be used on a published version of a stage play or screenplay:

Caution: Professionals and amateurs are hereby warned that this material is fully protected by copyright and is subject to royalty. This play may not be used for stage production (professional or amateur), motion pictures, radio, television, public reading, mechanical or electronic reproduction, or for any other purpose without written permission of the copyright owner. Contact [publisher's name] at [address] for information concerning licenses to dramatize this material.

3.   Granting Permission to Use Excerpts

If you don't mind if portions of your work are copied, and want to avoid having to formally grant a license each time others want to do so, you can include a statement after the copyright notice granting permission to copy the work. This permission can be as broad or narrow as you wish. For example:

Permission is hereby granted to reprint quotations from this work up to [number] words in length provided that such quotations are not altered or edited in any way and provided that an appropriate credit line and copyright notice are included.

4.   Other Material on Copyright Page

Particularly in books, certain other types of material are commonly placed on the same page as the copyright notice, even though it has nothing to do with copyright.

a.   ISBN or ISSN number

An International Standard Book Number (ISBN) is a ten-digit number preceded by the letters ISBN. An ISBN is assigned to each book by its publisher under a system administered by the R. R. Bowker Co. The number identifies the country of publication, the publisher and the title of the book itself. It is designed to facilitate handling orders and keeping track of inventory by computer. The number has nothing to do with copyright and has no official legal status. Although not legally required, the ISBN is important for cataloging and order fulfillment.

If you're a self-publisher, you'll need to obtain an ISBN yourself. Contact ISBN Agency, 121 Chanlon Road, New Providence, NJ 07974, 908-665-6770, and ask for a publisher identifier number. A fee must be paid for this. It is then the publisher's responsibility to assign numbers to each published title, enter them on computer sheets supplied by Bowker and return the sheets to Bowker. The ISBN should be printed in nine-point type or larger on the book's copyright page. The ISBN should also appear in the lower right-hand corner of the back of the book jacket.

An eight-digit International Standard Serial Number (ISSN) is utilized for serial publications such as magazines, periodicals, journals, newsletters, numbered monograph series, etc. The ISSN remains the same for each issue of a serial publication. The ISSN should be printed on the same page as the copyright notice, in the masthead area or on the page containing instructions for ordering the publication. The ISSN program is administered by the National Serials Data Program of the Library of Congress, Washington, DC 20540, 202-287-6452. To obtain an

ISSN, a serial publisher need only call or write the program, which will supply the necessary forms and assign an ISSN without charge.

b. Library of Congress Catalog Number

The Library of Congress will preassign a Library of Congress Catalog Number (LCCN) upon request. The LCCN is the stock control number for the Library of Congress's records. The number is used by librarians for classification and ordering purposes. According to the Library of Congress, the LCCN benefits publishers because books with LCCN are listed on a computer database that alerts librarians of forthcoming publications and enables them to select and promptly order new books.

Publishers normally obtain these on an author's behalf. However, self-publishers will have to get them themselves. To obtain an LCCN, call or write the Library of Congress, Cataloging In Publication Division, Washington, DC 20540, and ask for a form called "Request for Preassignment of Library of Congress Catalog Card Number." Complete the form and send it back to the Cataloging In Publication Division along with a copy of the title page of your book, if available; the publisher's name must appear on the title page.

The division will mail the LCCN back to you in about a month. The LCCN should be printed on the reverse of the title page, which is usually the page where the copyright notice is placed on books. There is no charge for an LCCN, but a complimentary copy of the book must be sent to the CIP Division after it is published. This is in addition to the copies furnished to the Copyright Office as part of the registration process. (See Chapter 4, *Copyright Registration.*)

Note, however, that an LCCN may not be obtained for books paid for or subsidized by individual authors or for serial publications.

J. Copyright Notice on Unpublished Manuscripts

It has never been necessary to place a copyright notice on an unpublished manuscript, and doing so will not prevent an infringer from raising the innocent infringement defense. However, it does not seem likely that a copier could convince a judge or jury that his infringement of an unpublished manuscript was innocent if the manuscript contained a copyright notice. In addition, as with published works, placing a copyright notice on an unpublished manuscript may help to deter potential infringers.

a. Manuscripts sent to book and magazine publishers

Literary agents and editors advise against placing a copyright notice on a manuscript you submit to a book or magazine publisher. Publishers and editors are aware of the copyright laws and know that unpublished manuscripts are copyrighted whether or not they have a notice. Typing a notice on your manuscript makes you look like an amateur who doesn't understand the rules of the publishing game.

The one exception to this rule is where all or part of the material in the manuscript has been previously published or will be published. In this event, you should state at the bottom of the title page where the publication took place and include a notice for that publication.

> **EXAMPLE:** Nora Zorbas has written a book on Greek cooking. A portion of chapter three was previously published as an article in *Culinary Magazine.* Nora should state at the bottom of the title page of her manuscript: "Portions of Chapter Three originally published in *Culinary Magazine,* December 1992. Copyright © 1992 by Culinary Publications."

b.   Other distributions of unpublished manuscripts

It is sensible to place a copyright notice on your unpublished manuscript before sending it to persons other than publishers or editors. For example, you might want to include a notice on a manuscript that you intend to send to a colleague (or colleagues) to read. It is impossible to know just who will get their hands on your manuscript once it leaves your possession. The notice might deter a potential infringer.

c.   Form of notice

A copyright notice for an unpublished manuscript should be in one of the following forms:
Copyright © by John Smith (This work is unpublished.)
or
Copyright © by John Smith (Work in Progress.)

You should not include a date in such a notice because the date on a copyright notice denotes the date of publication.

Copyright Registration

This chapter is about how to register your work with the Copyright Office. It covers the reasons why you should register, what types of works can be registered and who can accomplish the registration. The chapter also explains step-by-step how to complete the application forms, deposit the correct material with the Copyright Office and take the other necessary steps to complete the registration process.

A. What Is Copyright Registration?

Copyright registration is a legal formality by which a copyright owner makes a public record in the U.S. Copyright Office in Washington, DC of some basic information about a copyrighted work, such as the title of the work, who wrote it and when, and who owns the copyright. When people speak of copyrighting a book or other work, they usually mean registering it with the Copyright Office.

To register, you must fill out the appropriate preprinted application form, pay an application fee, and mail the application and fee to the Copyright Office along with one or two copies of the copyrighted work.

Contrary to what many people think, it is not necessary to register to create or establish a copyright. This is because an author's copyright comes into existence *automatically* the moment an original work of authorship is written down or otherwise fixed in a tangible form. (See Chapter 2, *Copyright Basics.*)

B. Why Register?

If registration is not required, why bother? There are several excellent reasons.

1. Registration Is a Prerequisite to Infringement Suits

If you're an American citizen or legal resident and your work is first published in the United States (or simultaneously in the U.S. and another country) you may not file a copyright infringement suit in this country until your work has been registered with the Copyright Office. You may be thinking, "Big deal, I'll register if and when someone infringes on my work and I need to file a lawsuit." If you adopt this strategy, you may end up having to register in a hurry so you can file suit quickly. You'll have to pay an extra $200 for such expedited registration. (See discussion in Section O, below.)

COMPARE—WORKS FIRST PUBLISHED ABROAD

Copyright owners who are not U.S. citizens or residents and whose work is first published in foreign countries that are members of the Berne International Copyright Convention need not register to sue for infringement in the U.S. (See Chapter 13, *International Copyright Protection,* for a list of Berne countries). But, if they do timely register their copyrights, they will receive the important benefits discussed in the next section.

---

2. Benefits of Timely Registration

You won't need to pay the extra $200 if you register right away. Far more important, however, if you register within the time limits discussed in Section 3, below, you will receive a huge bonus: the right to receive special statutory damages and possibly your attorney fees if you successfully sue someone for infringing upon your work.

Normally, a copyright owner who registers her work and successfully sues an infringer is entitled to receive the amount of her losses caused by the infringement (for example, lost sales) plus any profits the infringer (and his publisher, if there is one) earned; these are called actual damages. See Chapter 12, *Copyright Infringement,* for detailed discussion. Unfortunately, this remedy is not as good as it sounds. Because an infringer's profits are often small, and the copyright owner's losses equally modest, actual damages are often quite small in comparison with the costs of copyright litigation (copyright lawyers typically charge between $150 and $300 per hour).

EXAMPLE: Kay writes and publishes a mystery novel. Six months later, she discovers that C.C. Copycat has copied a substantial number of her words in a novel published under his own name. Copycat and his publisher earned a $10,000 profit from publishing the novel. Kay sees a knowledgeable copyright attorney. He informs her that if the case goes to trial, his attorney fees would be at least $20,000. If the only damages Kay could recover are the profits earned by Copycat and his publisher, she would lose $10,000 on the suit (assuming it goes to trial).

To give copyright owners a strong incentive to register their works and to help make copyright infringement suits economically feasible, the Copyright Act permits copyright owners who *timely* register their work and later successfully sue an infringer to be awarded statutory damages up to $100,000, plus attorney fees and court costs.

Statutory damages are special damages a copyright owner may elect to receive instead of actual damages. The amount of statutory damages awarded depends on the nature of the infringement—the more deliberate and harmful the infringement the better the chance of obtaining a large award. (See detailed discussion in Chapter 12, *Copyright Infringement.*)

EXAMPLE: Kay sues Copycat and his publisher and elects to receive statutory damages. The case goes to trial and Kay wins. In addition to ordering Copycat's publisher to stop selling his book, the court orders Copycat and his publisher to pay Kay $15,000 in statutory damages and to pay Kay's attorney fees and court costs—about $35,000 in all.

IMPORTANCE OF TIMELY REGISTRATION TO VALUE OF COPYRIGHT

If you fail to qualify for an award of statutory damages and attorney fees—by not timely registering your copyright—you probably can't afford a copyright infringement suit. And even if you can, the amount you will be able to collect from the infringer may not serve as a disincentive to infringement, since actual damages are hard to prove. As a practical matter, a lack of timely registration therefore makes it difficult if not impossible to enforce a copyright, and accordingly reduces its value.

EXAMPLE: Assume that Kay does not timely register her novel, and therefore cannot afford to sue Copycat and his publisher. This means she cannot prevent his copycat novel from being sold. As a result, the sales of her own novel are substantially reduced. In addition, Copycat sold a screenplay based on his novel to Repulsive Pictures. Since no producer is interested in making another whodunit movie with virtually the same plot (the plot that Copycat copied), Kay is unable to sell the screenplay rights to her novel, and its value is thus reduced.

3. What Is Timely Registration?

We said above that copyright owners can collect statutory damages and attorneys fees if they *timely* register their work—that is, register within the time period prescribed by the Copyright Act. There are different time periods for published and unpublished works.

- within *three months* of the date of the *first* publication, or
- *before* the date the copyright infringement began.

A work is published for copyright purposes when copies are made available to the public on an unrestricted basis. (See Chapter 2, *Copyright Basics,* for detailed discussion of what constitutes publication.)

> **EXAMPLE 1:** Assume that Kay's novel in the examples above was registered by her publisher two months after it was published. Kay is then entitled to elect to receive statutory damages and attorney fees if she sues Copycat (or anyone else) for copyright infringement.

> **EXAMPLE 2:** Assume that Kay's publisher neglected to register Kay's novel. Kay finds out about this and registers it herself nine months after publication. Copycat published his copycat novel three months later. Kay is entitled to statutory damages and fees if she sues Copycat and his publisher because she registered her work before Copycat copied it.

> **EXAMPLE 3:** Assume instead that Kay's novel was never registered. After discovering Copycat's infringing novel, Kay registers her novel with the Copyright Office. If Kay sues Copycat and his publisher, she may not elect to receive statutory damages and attorney fees and costs. Reason: Kay's novel was neither registered within three months of publication nor before Copycat copied her work.

a. Published works

A published work is considered to be timely registered, entitling the copyright owner to statutory damages and attorney fees, only if it was registered:

b. Unpublished works

If an unpublished manuscript is infringed upon, its author or other copyright owner is entitled to obtain statutory damages and attorney fees from the infringer only if the work was registered *before the infringement occurred.*

> **EXAMPLE:** Anais, an internationally known artist and jet-setter, keeps a detailed diary which she has never published. The *National Inquisitor* tabloid gets its hands on a portion of the diary and publishes it without permission. If Anais sues the *Inquisitor*, she would be entitled to statutory damages and attorney fees only if she had registered the diary before the *Inquisitor* committed the infringement (published the diary).

You cannot get around this requirement by publishing the manuscript and then registering it within three months of the publication date. The three-month rule discussed above applies only if the infringement began after first publication.

4. Registration Deters Infringement

Another reason to register is that it causes the work to be indexed in the Copyright Office's records under the title and author's name. These records are open to the public and are frequently searched by persons or organizations seeking to find out whether a particular known work has been registered and, if so, who currently owns the copyright. If you have registered your work, these people may contact you and be willing to pay you a permission fee or royalty to use it. If you haven't registered, they may conclude that you're not very serious about enforcing your copyright rights. As a result, they may be inclined to use your work without asking your permission (that is, commit copyright infringement).

C. What Can and Should Be Registered

Any work containing material that is protected by copyright may be registered. A work need not consist entirely of protected material to be registrable. So long as a part of a work is protectible, it may be registered. The registration covers those portions of the work that are protected. (See Chapter 6, *What Copyright Protects.*)

1. Published Works

As a general rule, any published work of value should be registered within three months of publication. You can probably forget about registration, however, if your work is not worth copying (which is usually the case where the work will become outdated shortly after publication or where it is not especially new or creative), or if you aren't concerned about someone copying your work.

2. Unpublished Works

In deciding whether to register your unpublished work, you need to consider how many people will see it, who they are, how valuable you feel the work is and how likely it is that someone would want to copy it.

The potential for copying exists whenever you circulate a manuscript to publishers, literary agents, personal contacts and others. When you submit a manuscript to publishers or others, you have no control over how many people are going to read it.

However, don't be unduly paranoid about others stealing your work. The fact is that very few manuscripts are ever copied by publishers. It is usually easier and cheaper for a publisher to purchase the right to publish a manuscript than go to the trouble of copying it and risk an infringement suit.

Nonetheless, since registration is so easy and relatively inexpensive and the consequences of not registering can be so dire, if there is any doubt in your mind, REGISTER!

MAJOR CHANGES IN COPYRIGHT REGISTRATION ARE PENDING

As this book went to press, a bill making sweeping changes in the copyright registration rules was being considered by Congress. The bill, called the Copyright Reform Act of 1993 (H.R. 897), passed the House of Representatives in November 1993 and was pending in the Senate as of April 1994. However, Senate officials were uncertain when the Senate would vote on the act—perhaps in late 1994 or not until 1995. Proponents of the bill believe that its chances for final passage are good, but far from certain. The bill has been strongly supported by most authors' groups and the software industry, but opposed by the publishing industry.

We'll keep you apprised of what happens in the *Nolo News* (you get a free subscription if you send in your registration card) and in future editions of *The Copyright Handbook*.

The changes proposed by the Copyright Reform Act include:

- **Registration not a prerequisite to infringement suits.** First and foremost, the act does away with the requirement that a work be registered with the Copyright Office before a copyright infringement suit may be filed. Under the new law, an infringement suit may be brought whether or not a work is registered.

- **Reduced benefits of registration.** In addition, the act does away with two of the most important benefits conditional upon registration: the ability to obtain statutory damages and attorney fees in an infringement suit. Such damages and fees will be available to a plaintiff in an infringement suit regardless of whether the work was registered.

- **Simplified registration forms and procedures.** The act also requires the Copyright Office to adopt a new, simplified copyright registration form and to simplify, and in some cases eliminate, its deposit requirements. Group registration will also be expanded under the new law in order to make registration more affordable.

- **New incentives to register.** To give copyright owners an incentive to continue to register their works, the act will permit copyright owners to include information on who to contact regarding licenses and permissions on their copyright registration forms. In addition, information concerning copyright deposits will be placed into a computerized database and made available on the Internet. Presumably, this will make it easier for third parties to find out who to contact if they want permission to use or purchase a copyright owner's work.

In addition, copyright registration will continue to satisfy the Library of Congress's deposit requirements for published works. And the registration certificate will continue to receive special evidentiary weight in copyright infringement suits (see Chapter 12, Section B.1.a). Finally, registration helps provide a copyright owner with priority when a document transferring copyright rights is recorded with the Copyright Office (see Chapter 9, Section G.3).

For these reasons, it will usually be advisable for copyright owners to continue to register their published works even if the Copyright Reform Act is enacted.

Ownership of copyrights is discussed in detail in Chapter 8, *Initial Copyright Ownership,* and Chapter 9, *Transferring Copyright Ownership.* The following discussion briefly describes ownership solely for registration purposes.

1. Ownership by the Author(s)

Unless a work is a work made for hire (see below) the copyright initially belongs to the person or persons who created it.

a. Individually authored works

The copyright in a work created by a single individual is owned by that individual. An individually authored work can be registered by the author or his authorized agent (that is, someone he asks to register for him).

> **EXAMPLE:** Shelby has written a history of the Civil War. Shelby can register the book himself, or it can be registered on Shelby's behalf by his authorized agent—for example, his publisher.

b. Works made for hire

A work made for hire is a work created by an employee as part of her job, or a work that has been specially commissioned under a written work-for-hire agreement. For registration purposes, the author of a work made for hire is the writer's employer or other person for whom the work was prepared. It is normally the employer who registers a work made for hire, not the employee-writer.

> **EXAMPLE:** Bruno is a technical writer/translator employed by BigTech, Inc. His latest project was translating a manual on MS DOS into

---

> ### IDEAS ARE NOT PROTECTED BY REGISTRATION
>
> Copyright does not protect facts or ideas, only their expression in a tangible form. (See Chapter 6, *What Copyright Protects.*) This means you cannot register a book or article idea. And registering a book or article proposal, outline and/or sample chapters before submission to a publisher will not extend copyright protection to your idea.
>
> > **EXAMPLE:** Leslie writes a detailed outline and sample chapters for a proposed book on nude skydiving. She registers the outline and chapters, and then sends them to several publishers. Larry, a freelance writer, hears about Leslie's submission from an editor acquaintance at one of these publishers and decides to write a book of his own on nude skydiving. In doing so, however, Larry does not copy anything from Leslie's outline or sample chapters (indeed, he never saw them). Leslie cannot successfully sue Larry for copyright infringement for stealing her idea for a book on nude skydiving. The fact that she registered her outline and sample chapters did not extend copyright protection to the ideas they contained.

D. Who Can Register?

Anyone who owns all or part of the rights that make up a work's copyright may register that work, as can that person's authorized agent (representative). This means registration may be accomplished by:

- the author or authors of a work
- anyone who has acquired one or more of the author or authors' exclusive copyright rights, or
- the authorized agent of any of the above.

German. The manual, called *Vas Es DOS*, is a work made for hire and should be registered by BigTech, Bruno's employer.

Cross-reference

If you create a protectible work on a freelance basis for someone else, the question of ownership can be complex. Read Chapter 8, Initial Copyright Ownership, before completing the registration.

c.   Joint works

If two or more persons who are not employees create a protectible work together, the work so created is called a joint work. A joint work is co-owned by its creators and can be registered by one, some or all of the authors or by their agent.

> **EXAMPLE:** Bob, Carol, Ted and Alice decide to write a nonfiction book entitled *The New Celibacy*. They each agree to write one-quarter of the entire work and agree that they will each own 25% of the entire copyright. After it is written, *The New Celibacy* may be registered by any combination of Bob, Carol, Ted and Alice or their authorized agent.

Again, for a detailed discussion of these categories, see Chapter 8, *Initial Copyright Ownership*.

LETTING YOUR PUBLISHER REGISTER THE COPYRIGHT

Published authors usually do not register their books themselves. Indeed, if you have signed over all of your copyright rights to your publisher, there is no reason for you to register since you no longer have the right to commercially exploit the work. Your publisher should register the book. Even if you retain some of your rights, your publisher should accomplish the registration as an owner of an exclusive right or rights (such as the right to make copies and sell the book) or as your authorized agent.

However, you should check with your publisher one or two months after publication to make sure your book has been registered; especially if you're dealing with a very small and/or inexperienced publisher that may be lax about such matters. (Recall that to obtain statutory damages and attorney fees, your work must be registered within three months of publication or before the infringement begins.)

Of course, the situation is very different if you are self-publishing your work. In this situation, you must handle the registration yourself. This is also usually the case if you are paying a vanity press to publish your book.

---

2.   Registration by Publishers and Other Transferees

As discussed in Chapter 2, *Copyright Basics*, an author's copyright is really a bundle of separate, exclusive rights. These exclusive rights include the right to make copies of an original work, the right to distribute or sell the work, the right to display the work and the right to adapt—that is, make derivative works out of—the work. A copyright owner can sell or otherwise transfer all or part of his exclusive copyright rights. Indeed, this is usually how an author benefits economically from his work.

Transferees need to be concerned about registration because, if the work is not timely registered, they will not be entitled to obtain statutory damages and attorney fees if they successfully sue a person who infringes on the rights they purchased. (Again, registration is timely only if accomplished before an infringement occurs or within three months of publication.) Fortunately, transferees do not have to rely on authors to timely register. Anyone who obtains one or more of an author's exclusive rights is entitled to register the author's work.

EXAMPLE 1: In return for a 12% royalty on each copy sold, Darlene transfers to Able Publishers all of her exclusive rights to her bowling instruction guide. Able may register the book.

EXAMPLE 2: Assume instead that Darlene transfers to Able the exclusive right to sell, display and make copies of the book, but retains her other copyright rights. As a holder of some of Darlene's exclusive rights, Able is still entitled to register the book.

If only a portion of a work's copyright is transferred, it is possible that several different persons or entities qualify to register the copyright.

EXAMPLE: Bill writes a novel and grants Scrivener & Sons only the exclusive right to publish it in the United States. He also grants Repulsive Pictures the exclusive right to author and produce a screenplay based on the novel. Scrivener and Repulsive each hold one of the exclusive rights that are part of Bill's overall copyright, and Bill holds the rest. This means the novel could be registered by Bill, by Scrivener or by Repulsive.

Although several people may be entitled to register a work, normally only one registration is allowed for each version of a published work. It makes absolutely no difference who gets the job done. The single registration protects every copyright owner.

EXAMPLE: Assume that Scrivener & Sons registered Bill's novel in the example above. This means that neither Bill nor Repulsive Pictures can register it. Nor do they need to. The single registration by Scrivener covers them all—that is, they are all entitled to the benefits of registration.

Again, for a detailed discussion of the rights of copyright transferees, see Chapter 9, *Transferring Copyright Ownership.*

E. Registration As a Single Unit

A book, magazine, periodical or other work often contains many separate works of authorship that have been combined to form a unitary whole. For example, a book will normally consist of a main text written by an author or authors. But it may also contain photographs and/or artwork supplied by the author or others. It may have a dust jacket containing artwork and/or promotional copy written by someone other than the author(s) of the text. Or, if the book is a paperback, the cover may contain artwork and copy. And it may contain an introduction or other material written by someone other than the author(s) of the main text.

The question naturally arises, "Must I register each type of authorship separately or can I register everything together at the same time?"

You can register any number of *separate* works of authorship together on one application if:

- they are being published for the *first* time
- they constitute a *single unit of publication*—that is, they're sold together as a single unit with

each work an integral part of the whole unit, and

- the same person(s) created *all* the works in the unit, or the same person or entity has acquired ownership of all the copyright rights in all of the works in the unit.

Let's apply this rule to some real life situations.

1. Works Containing Photographs and/or Artwork

The artwork and/or photographs a written work contains can be registered together with the text only if:

- they have never been published before, and
- they were created by the author of the text, or the same person or entity owns the copyright to the artwork and/or photos and text.

EXAMPLE 1: Jackie is a poet and Bill a photographer. Jackie and Bill collaborate to publish a book combining Bill's photographs and Jackie's poetry. They agree to co-own the entire copyright in the work. Normally, poetry and photographs are registered separately on different application forms (see Section H, below). However, Jackie and Bill may register the entire book at the same time for one application fee on one application form since the work is a single unit of publication and the text and photos are owned by the same persons.

EXAMPLE 2: Jim and Jean agree to produce a book on how to operate a toxic waste dump. Jim writes the text and Jean provides the pictorial illustrations for the book. Jim and Jean decide that each is the sole owner of their respective contributions. The single registration rule does not apply here. The photos and text were not created by the same persons and they are not owned by the same persons: they were created and are owned separately by Jim and Jean. This means that Jim and Jean must each register their work separately, and each pay an application fee.

I SEE MANY MEDIUMS IN YOUR FUTURE.

2. Multimedia Works

For copyright registration purposes, a multimedia work is any work which, excluding its container, combines authorship in two or more media. The authorship may include text, artwork, sculpture, cinematography, photography, sounds, music or choreography. The media may include printed matter such as a book; audiovisual material such as videotape, slides, filmstrips; a phonorecord such as an audio tape or audio disk; or any machine-readable copy such as a computer disk, tape or chip. For example, a book combined with a filmstrip or audio tape would be a multimedia work. More importantly, however, written works that are combined with CD-ROM disks or other computer disks are also multimedia works; as are written works published on CD-ROMs alone along with graphics, photos, video, music, etc.

An entire multimedia work can be registered at one time on one registration form for one registration fee provided that:

- the copyright claimant is the same for all elements of the work for which copyright protection is sought, and
- all such elements are published at the same time as a single unit.

For a detailed discussion, See Chapter 14, *Electronic Publishing*.

3. Artwork, Photos and Promotional Copy on Book Dust Jackets or Covers

The artwork, photos and/or promotional copy on a book dust jacket or cover may be registered together with the text only if:

- the artwork and copy have never been published before, and
- the same person or entity owns the copyright to the text, cover art and promotional copy.

Since cover art and promotional copy is normally owned by the publisher (whether created by the publisher's employees or independent contractors hired by the publisher), these items usually can be registered together with the text of the book only if the publisher acquired all the author's rights in the text.

EXAMPLE 1: Jane Milsap writes a novel and sells all her copyright rights to Acme Press. Acme employees prepare artwork and text for the cover. The text of the novel and artwork and text for the cover can be registered together on one Form TX because Acme owns them all.

EXAMPLE 2: Bart Milsap, Jane's brother, writes a novel and grants Acme Press only the exclusive right to publish it in North America. Bart retains all his other copyright rights. Acme employees prepare artwork and text for the cover. The text of the novel and the artwork and text for the cover must be registered separately because they are separately owned. Acme may register the artwork and cover copy together on the same form. (See Section H for which form to use.)

HOW TO REGISTER ARTWORK AND PHOTOGRAPHS

If you have to register artwork or photographs separately from the main text of a written work, you must do so on Form VA. This form is nearly identical with Form TX, so refer to Section I, below, on how to fill it out. A copy of the form is included in the tear-out appendix at the end of this book.

---

4. Introductions, Prefaces, Bibliographies, Indexes and Similar Items

An introduction, preface, bibliography, index or similar material may be registered together with a work's main text only if it is being published for the first time and the person or entity that owns the copyright in the main text also owns the introduction, bibliography, index or other item.

EXAMPLE 1: Sam writes a book on the Civil War and gets the well-known Civil War expert Shelby Hand to write an introduction. Hand only gives Sam's publisher the right to use the introduction in Sam's book and retains all his other copyright rights. The introduction would have to be registered separately from the book.

EXAMPLE 2: Assume instead that Acme Press, Sam's publisher, paid Hand for all his rights in the introduction and that Acme also acquired all of Sam's copyright rights in the main text. Acme could register both the text and the introduction together as a single unit. Reason: The same entity owns the copyright in both the main text and the introduction.

5. Anthologies, Newspapers, Magazines and Other Periodicals

Anthologies, newspapers, magazines and similar works usually contain a number of separate articles, photos, artwork and other material. Each individual contribution must be registered by the person or entity that owns it. If the same person or entity owns all the contributions, only one registration is required. The anthology or magazine should also be registered once as a whole, usually by its publisher. Registration of newspapers, magazines and other periodicals is discussed in Section K, below.

REGISTERING UNPUBLISHED COLLECTIONS FOR A SINGLE APPLICATION FEE

If you have a number of unpublished works, you can register them together at one time on one application form for one $20 application fee. This is so even though the works are self-contained (that is, do not constitute a single unit of publication) and would normally be registered separately. This procedure can save you a great deal of money. Four requirements must be met:

- the same person or entity must own all the copyright rights in all the unpublished works and in the collection as a whole
- the works must be by the same author, or if they are by different authors, at least one of the authors must have contributed to each work
- the unpublished works must be assembled in an orderly form (one copy must be deposited with the Copyright Office), and
- the collection must be given a title identifying the collection as a whole.

EXAMPLE: Joe Sixpack has written 12 unpublished short stories. He collects the stories together into a binder and calls the collection *The Unpublished Stories of Joe Sixpack*. Joe may register all 12 stories together for one $20 application fee. Note: If Joe had registered each story separately it would have cost him $240— that is, 12 registrations times the $20 application fee.

6. How Many Times to Register a Single Unit of Publication

Subject to the exceptions noted below, a single unit of publication need be and can be registered only once.

a. Published works

As a general rule, a published work constituting a single unit of publication can only be registered once. If the facts stated in the registration application change after the work has been registered—for instance, the work's title is changed—an application for supplemental registration should be filed with the Copyright Office to correct them. See Chapter 5, *Correcting or Changing Copyright Notice or Registration*.

However, there are exceptions to the general rule. If someone other than the author is identified as the copyright claimant on a registration application (see Section I, below), the author may register the same work again in her own name as copyright claimant. A second registration may also be made if the prior registration was unauthorized or legally invalid—for instance, where registration was effected by someone other than the author, owner of exclusive rights or an authorized representative.

DIFFERENT EDITIONS WITH THE SAME CONTENT

It is common for the same work to be published in different editions—for example, in both a hardcover and paperback edition. Where the content of the different editions is identical, only one need be registered. This would normally be the first published edition.

EXAMPLE 1: Acme Publications publishes and promptly registers a hardcover edition of a book on car repair. One year later, Acme publishes the book in an identical paperback edition. The paperback need not be registered. The registration of the hardcover edition protects all the material the paperback contains.

EXAMPLE 2: Assume the same facts as example 1, except that the paperback has new cover art and copy. Acme should register the artwork and copy. But again, there is no need to reregister the text of the book.

If multiple identical editions of the same work are published simultaneously, again, only one registration need be made. In such cases, however, the applicant should deposit with the Copyright Office the edition that is the best edition. (See detailed discussion of deposits in Section M, below.)

b. Unpublished works

A work originally registered as unpublished may be registered again after publication, even if the published and unpublished versions are identical. Even if they are identical, it is a good idea to register the published version of a previously registered unpublished work. If you ever become involved in an infringement suit, it may be very helpful to have the published version of the book on deposit with the Copyright Office. The second registration also establishes the date of publication, which may later aid you in proving that an infringer had access to your work. (See Chapter 12, *Copyright Infringement.*)

F. Registering Derivative Works and Compilations

1. Derivative Works

A derivative work is one created by transforming or adapting previously existing material. This includes:

- new editions of previously published works, including condensed or abridged editions or editions containing new material (new chapters, for example)
- dramatizations or fictionalizations, such as screenplays or stageplays based on novels, histories, biographies or other works
- translations, and
- annotations, such as *Cliff's Notes*.

    These types of works are discussed in detail in Chapter 7, *Adaptions and Compilations.* If you're not

sure whether your work is a derivative work, read that chapter before attempting to register it.

PREEXISTING EXPRESSION SHOULD HAVE ALREADY BEEN REGISTERED

Assuming it's protectible, the preexisting expression used to create the derivative work, whether a novel, factual work or other work, should already be registered with the Copyright Office. If not, it should be registered. The preexisting expression can be registered together with the new expression if they constitute a single unit of publication and the copyright claimant is the same (see Section E, above). Otherwise, the preexisting expression should be registered separately by its owner.

---

a. When can a derivative work be registered?

For a derivative work to be registrable, the new expression created by the work's author must:

- be owned by the copyright claimant for the derivative work
- contain sufficient original authorship to be copyrightable as an independent work
- not be in the public domain in the United States
- be new—that is, not previously published, and
- not have been previously registered in unpublished form.

    EXAMPLE: Tom writes a play based on his novel. The play is a new work based on and adapted from the novel. Tom owns the play, and it has never previously been published or registered. The play can and should be registered separately, or Tom will not be entitled to statutory damages and attorney fees if he sues someone for copying those aspects of the work not already protected by the copyright in the novel.

b. Registering new editions of factual works

Authors of factual works such as scientific treatises, histories and textbooks often revise their works and publish new editions. Not all new editions can or should be registered. Look at the protected content of the various versions. If the first version you registered contains substantially the same protected content as a later version, there is no reason to register the later version; its content is protected by the initial registration. But if substantial new protectible material is added to another version, it's wise to register that version.

As a general rule, your changes are substantial enough to merit registration only if enough new expression has been added so that it is possible to tell the difference between the previous edition and the new edition. Trivial changes—such as spelling corrections—are not enough.

EXAMPLE 1: Augusta writes and publishes a college-level textbook on ancient Roman art. Two years later, she publishes a new edition of the work. The new edition is identical to the first except that Augusta corrected several spelling and punctuation errors. The Copyright Office probably will not register such a work and, indeed, there is no reason to do so since there is no new expression in the new edition that needs to be protected by registration.

EXAMPLE 2: Assume that five years later, Augusta substantially revises her book on Roman art. She adds three new chapters and makes numerous substantive changes in the other chapters. This new edition is clearly different from the original edition in a meaningful way.

Augusta should register the work to protect the changes she made to her preexisting material.

As a practical matter, there is no reason to go to the trouble and expense of registration merely to protect minor changes that have no value independent from the original work. However, if you've added considerable new material to your work that has substantial value and that someone may want to copy for its own sake, registration may be prudent.

c. Compare—more complete version published first

If two versions of a work are published at different times, and the more complete version is published first, the less complete version may not be registered. The Copyright Office will not knowingly register a claim in a work where all of the copyrightable content has previously been published.

EXAMPLE: Schooldays Publications publishes two editions of a Spanish textbook, one version is for teachers and the other for students. The teacher's edition contains all of the text and pictorial material in the student's edition, plus additional instructions, questions and answers. The teacher's edition was published one week before the student edition. The student edition may not be registered; all the material it contains is already protected by the registration of the teacher's edition.

2. Compilations

A compilation is a work created by selecting, organizing and arranging facts or data in such a way that the resulting work as a whole constitutes an original work of authorship. Examples include anthologies, bibliographies and catalogs of all types.

Some compilations are not considered to be sufficiently creative to merit copyright protection and may not be registered. Refer to Chapter 7, *Adaptions and Compilations,* for a detailed discussion of how to tell if your compilation is registrable (and ways to help make it so).

G. Four-Step Registration Process

To register, you must:
- select the appropriate registration form (Section H)
- fill out the registration form correctly (Sections I, J, K, L)
- decide how to satisfy the Copyright Office's deposit requirements (Section M), and
- place your application, deposit and appropriate fee in one package and send it to the Copyright Office (Section N).

WHERE TO GET HELP

If you have difficulty understanding any aspect of the registration process, you can get help by calling the Copyright Office at 202-707-3000 between 8:30 A.M. and 5:00 P.M. Eastern Time, Monday through Friday. An Information Specialist will be available to give you advice on selecting the proper form, filling it out and making the required deposit. Copyright Office Information Specialists are very knowledgeable and helpful; however, they are not allowed to give legal advice. If you have a particularly complex problem that calls for interpretation of the copyright laws, see a copyright attorney. (See Chapter 14, Help Beyond This Book.)

H. Selecting the Appropriate Registration Form

The Copyright Office has divided every conceivable type of copyrightable work into five classes and designated letter codes and has matching application forms for each class. Your copyright protection is in no way affected by which particular class your work falls into, but you must use the form for that class or the Copyright Office may require you to refile your application on the correct form.

1. Form TX: Nondramatic Literary Works

Form TX is the real workhorse in the Copyright Office's forms stable. It is used to register all types of written works (other than magazines and similar works) that are not intended to be performed before an audience. These are called nondramatic literary works (for copyright purposes, a literary work is any copyrightable work consisting of words). Form TX is used to register such works as:
- advertising copy
- articles and other individual contributions to newspapers, magazines, newsletters or other periodicals (but not the entire newspaper or periodical itself; see Section H.3, below)
- catalogs, directories and other compilations of information
- fiction of any length
- letters and diaries
- nonfiction of any length
- poetry
- reference books, textbooks and technical writings
- translations of works written in foreign languages, and
- written lectures, speeches, leaflets and pamphlets.

2. Form PA: Plays and Screenplays

Form PA is used to register all types of published and unpublished works prepared to be performed directly before an audience, such as plays. Form PA is also used for works intended to be performed indirectly by means of a mechanical device or process. This includes screenplays, teleplays or radio plays intended to be performed indirectly by means of a film projector, television or radio. Form PA is also used to register song lyrics with or without accompanying music. Musical compositions are also registered on this form.

Form PA is also used to register multimedia works combining text with graphics, photos, videos, sounds and so forth. See Chapter 14, *Electronic Publishing,* for detailed a discussion.

3. Form SE Series: Newspapers, Magazines and Other Periodicals

Form SE is used to register serial publications. A serial is a work that is (1) issued in successive parts; (2) logically numbered and/or dated; and (3) intended to be continued indefinitely. This includes:

- magazines and other periodicals of all types
- newspapers
- journals
- newsletters
- bulletins, and
- the minutes, journals, proceedings or transactions of societies.

The Copyright Office has created four different registration forms for serial publications—the regular Form SE, Short Form SE, Form SE/Group and Form G/DN. We discuss when to use what form and how to fill them out in Section K, below.

INDIVIDUAL CONTRIBUTIONS TO PERIODICALS REGISTERED ON FORM TX OR PA

The SE series of forms is used only to register a magazine or other serial publication as a whole. Form TX (or Form PA) must be used to register individual articles or other contributions to periodicals if the copyright is owned by someone other than the periodical.

EXAMPLE: Jane has contributed a short story to the literary journal *Serendipity*. She gave the journal the right to publish her story once, and has retained all other rights. Jane's story is a separate and independent work entitled to copyright protection in its own right. To register her story, she must use Form TX, the form for nondramatic literary works. But the copyright owners of *Serendipity* would use one of the SE series of forms to register the journal—a serial publication—as a whole.

---

4. Form GR/CP: Single Registration for a Group of Contributions to Serial Publications by a Single Author

Still another form, Form GR/CP, is used in conjunction with Form TX to register as a group previously published individual contributions to periodicals written by the same author. See discussion in Section L, below.

5. Other Forms Not Covered in This Book

There are other application forms for other types of work that we are not directly concerned with in this book:

- Form VA is used for all pictorial, graphic and sculptural works; this includes photographs, maps, charts, diagrams, technical drawings, pictorial or graphic labels and advertisements, and two- and three-dimensional works of fine, graphic and applied arts.

 Copyright tip
Form VA is nearly identical to Form TX. If you need to register photos or artwork on Form VA, refer to the discussion on Form TX in Section I, below.

- Form SR is used for phonograph records, tapes, CDs, and other "fixed" music or sounds.

6. Choosing the Proper Form for Hybrid Works

Choosing the proper application form can be tricky if your work contains material falling into two or more classes—for instance, where a book contains both a written text and photographs. You cannot and need not register twice using two forms (see Section F, above). Simply use the form most appropriate to the type of authorship that predominates in the work as a whole. The following examples may help make this clear.

EXAMPLE 1: Joe has written a travel guide to the Galapagos Islands. It contains 200 pages of text and 20 photographs taken by Joe. The text clearly predominates, so Joe should use Form TX (the form for nondramatic literary works) to register both the text and photos.

EXAMPLE 2: Kathleen has self-published a book of her photographs and written a short caption for each photo. The photos obviously predominate in the work as a whole, so Kathleen should use Form VA (the form for pictorial works) to register the photos and captions.

7. Choosing the Correct Form for Derivative Works and Compilations

If you're registering a derivative work (see Section F, above), use the form appropriate to the derivative work itself, not the original work it was based on.

EXAMPLE: Lester has written a screenplay based on his novel *Dinner With the Devil.* The novel was already registered using form TX. The screenplay derived from the novel should be registered on Form PA (the form for plays and screenplays).

All fact compilations must be registered on Form TX. A collection of works intended to be performed before a live audience—for example, an anthology of stageplays, screenplays or other works—would be registered on Form PA. All other collective works—for example, an anthology of short stories—should be registered on Form TX.

8. Where to Obtain the Forms

The tear-out appendix at the end of this book contains copies of the application forms discussed in this book. Additional forms can be obtained free of charge by calling the Copyright Office's Forms Hotline at 202-707-9100. You can call 24 hours a day (you may have an easier time getting through at night). Leave your name, mailing address and identify the type of forms you need according to the class or title—for example, Form TX or "Application for Copyright Registration for a Nondramatic Literary

Work." The Copyright Office will send up to ten copies of each form; specify how many you want. You can also obtain forms by writing to the Copyright Office at the following address:

> Information and Publication Section LM-455
> Copyright Office
> Library of Congress
> Washington, DC 20559

💡 Copyright tip

To save the U.S. taxpayer paper and printing costs, the Copyright Office encourages applicants to use photocopies of the blank application forms. However, the photocopies must be clear, on a good grade of white 8½-inch by 11-inch paper, and reproduced in two-sided copies with the top of the reverse side of the form at the same end as the top of the first side. Applications on forms not meeting these requirements will be returned by the Copyright Office.

I.   How to Complete Form TX

Form TX is for nondramatic literary works as discussed in Section H, above. Here's how to fill it out.

FILL OUT FORMS CAREFULLY AND CORRECTLY

Type your application form or use only black ink. When filling out the form, remember that it may end up being submitted in court to help prove your infringement case. If any part of it is found inaccurate, your case could suffer—perhaps greatly. Moreover, a person who intentionally lies on a copyright registration application may be fined up to $2,500.

You will find a sample filled out Form TX preceding the blank copyright forms in the appendix.

Space 1: Title Information

You must provide information about your work's title in Space 1.

Title of this work. The Copyright Office uses the title for indexing and identifying your work. If your work contains a title, fill in that wording. This should be the same title that appears on your deposit (see Section M, below). If your work is untitled, either state "untitled" or make a title up. You need not include this made-up title on your untitled work. If you're registering a work written in a foreign language, you don't have to translate the title into English.

💡 Copyright tip

Titles and other identifying phrases cannot be copyrighted. This means that registration will not prevent anyone from using the title to your work, but you may have other recourse. (See Chapter 2, *Copyright Basics.*)

Previous or alternative titles. Provide any additional titles under which someone searching for the registration might be likely to look—for example, a foreign country where the work was originally published under a different title. However, you don't need to include any additional titles known only to you or a few readers—such as working titles.

If you're registering a new version of a work under a new title that contains substantial new material, you don't need to list the old title here.

Publication as a contribution. If the work you're registering is an individual article or other contribution to a collective work such as an anthology, newspaper, magazine or other periodical, fill in the title of the publication after the words "Title Of This Work."

EXAMPLE: Kyle published an article entitled "Cave Exploration in the Andes" in *The Spelunker's Journal*. He should state: "*The Spelunker's Journal*."

In addition, if the collective work is a serial publication such as a magazine, periodical or newspaper, give the requested information about the issue of the serial in which the contribution appeared. The volume and issue numbers are usually found before the table of contents. The issue date is usually on the cover—for example: "June 1992" or "Winter 1992."

EXAMPLE: Kyle's article was published on pages 20–30 in the June 1992 issue of *The Spelunker's Journal*. Kyle looks at the journal's masthead and sees that this issue is listed as Volume 10, Number (or issue) 6, with a June 1, 1992 publication date. Kyle would state in the first line: "*The Spelunker's Journal*." In the second line, Kyle would indicate that the article appeared in Volume 10, Number 6, June 1, 1992, on pages 20–30.

Space 2: Author Information

Space 2 calls for information about the work's author or authors. Space 2 is divided into three identical subspaces, "a," "b," and "c." Subspaces b and c are filled out only if there is more than one author.

Name of author. We discussed who the author is for registration purposes in Section D, above. Reread that section if you're not sure who is the author of the work being registered. If you need still more information, read Chapter 8, *Initial Copyright Ownership* and Chapter 9, *Transferring Copyright Ownership*.

- Works *not* made for hire: Unless the work was made for hire, the person or people who created the work are the authors. Give the full name (full first, middle and last name) of the first, or only, author. (For use of anonymous or pseudonymous names, see below.)

- Works made for hire: We briefly defined works made for hire at Section D, above. If the work to be registered is a work made for hire, the author for registration purposes is the employer or person or entity that commissioned the work. The full legal name of the employer or commissioning party must be provided as the name of author instead of the name of the person who actually wrote the work.

EXAMPLE 1: Microstuff Incorporated publishes a line of computer books that are written by their in-house editorial staff. Their new title, *Computing as Therapy* was written by Ken Grant, Microstuff's senior editor. "Microstuff Incorporated" is listed in the "Name of Author" space.

EXAMPLE 2: Jane Milsap writes a chemistry textbook and transfers to Acme Press all her copyright rights. Acme employees prepare artwork and text for the cover. Jane should be listed as author of "entire text of chemistry textbook." Acme should be listed as the author of "cover artwork and text" in Space 2b; Acme is the author because the artwork and cover copy were works made for hire prepared by its employees. (Note: Had Jane retained any of her copyright rights, the cover artwork and text and the textbook would have had to have been registered separately; see Section E, above.)

The name of the employee who created the work made for hire may also be included if you want to make this part of the public record, but it is not required—for example: "Microstuff Incorporated, employer for hire of Ken Grant."

Copyright tip

Don't guess about the full legal name of a corporation, partnership or other entity. Find out the

FORM TX

For a Literary Work
UNITED STATES COPYRIGHT OFFICE

REGISTRATION NUMBER

_____

TX   TXU
EFFECTIVE DATE OF REGISTRATION

_____

Month   Day   Year

DO NOT WRITE ABOVE THIS LINE. IF YOU NEED MORE SPACE, USE A SEPARATE CONTINUATION SHEET.

1

TITLE OF THIS WORK ▼

PREVIOUS OR ALTERNATIVE TITLES ▼

PUBLICATION AS A CONTRIBUTION If this work was published as a contribution to a periodical, serial, or collection, give information about the collective work in which the contribution appeared.   **Title of Collective Work ▼**

If published in a periodical or serial give: Volume ▼   Number ▼   Issue Date ▼   On Pages ▼

2

a

NAME OF AUTHOR ▼

DATES OF BIRTH AND DEATH
Year Born ▼   Year Died ▼

Was this contribution to the work a "work made for hire"?
☐ Yes
☐ No

AUTHOR'S NATIONALITY OR DOMICILE
Name of Country
OR ⎰ Citizen of ▶ _____
    ⎱ Domiciled in▶ _____

WAS THIS AUTHOR'S CONTRIBUTION TO THE WORK
Anonymous? ☐ Yes ☐ No
Pseudonymous? ☐ Yes ☐ No
If the answer to either of these questions is "Yes," see detailed instructions.

NATURE OF AUTHORSHIP Briefly describe nature of material created by this author in which copyright is claimed. ▼

NOTE

Under the law, the "author" of a "work made for hire" is generally the employer, not the employee (see instructions). For any part of this work that was "made for hire" check "Yes" in the space provided, give the employer (or other person for whom the work was prepared) as "Author" of that part, and leave the space for dates of birth and death blank.

b

NAME OF AUTHOR ▼

DATES OF BIRTH AND DEATH
Year Born ▼   Year Died ▼

Was this contribution to the work a "work made for hire"?
☐ Yes
☐ No

AUTHOR'S NATIONALITY OR DOMICILE
Name of Country
OR ⎰ Citizen of ▶ _____
    ⎱ Domiciled in▶ _____

WAS THIS AUTHOR'S CONTRIBUTION TO THE WORK
Anonymous? ☐ Yes ☐ No
Pseudonymous? ☐ Yes ☐ No
If the answer to either of these questions is "Yes," see detailed instructions.

NATURE OF AUTHORSHIP Briefly describe nature of material created by this author in which copyright is claimed. ▼

c

NAME OF AUTHOR ▼

DATES OF BIRTH AND DEATH
Year Born ▼   Year Died ▼

Was this contribution to the work a "work made for hire"?
☐ Yes
☐ No

AUTHOR'S NATIONALITY OR DOMICILE
Name of Country
OR ⎰ Citizen of ▶ _____
    ⎱ Domiciled in▶ _____

WAS THIS AUTHOR'S CONTRIBUTION TO THE WORK
Anonymous? ☐ Yes ☐ No
Pseudonymous? ☐ Yes ☐ No
If the answer to either of these questions is "Yes," see detailed instructions.

NATURE OF AUTHORSHIP Briefly describe nature of material created by this author in which copyright is claimed. ▼

3

a
YEAR IN WHICH CREATION OF THIS WORK WAS COMPLETED   This information must be given ◀ Year in all cases.

b
DATE AND NATION OF FIRST PUBLICATION OF THIS PARTICULAR WORK
Complete this information ONLY if this work has been published.   Month ▶ _____ Day ▶ _____ Year ▶ _____ ◀ Nation

4

COPYRIGHT CLAIMANT(S) Name and address must be given even if the claimant is the same as the author given in space 2. ▼

See instructions before completing this space.

TRANSFER If the claimant(s) named here in space 4 is (are) different from the author(s) named in space 2, give a brief statement of how the claimant(s) obtained ownership of the copyright. ▼

APPLICATION RECEIVED

ONE DEPOSIT RECEIVED

TWO DEPOSITS RECEIVED

FUNDS RECEIVED

DO NOT WRITE HERE
OFFICE USE ONLY

MORE ON BACK ▶   • Complete all applicable spaces (numbers 5-11) on the reverse side of this page.
     • See detailed instructions.   • Sign the form at line 10.

DO NOT WRITE HERE
Page 1 of _____ pages

organization's full legal name and use it—for example, do not state "ABC, Inc." when the full legal name is "Acme Book Company, Incorporated." The full legal name may be found on the entity's organizing document, such as articles of incorporation, a partnership agreement or a registration certificate filed with the appropriate state official (often the "Secretary of State").

Anonymous or pseudonymous authors. An author's contribution to a work is anonymous if the author is not identified on the copies of the work. A contribution is pseudonymous if the author is identified under a fictitious name (pen name).

If the work is anonymous, you may:
- leave the name of author line blank (or state "N/A"),
- state "anonymous" on the line, or
- reveal the author's identity.

If the work is pseudonymous, you may leave the line blank; give the pseudonym and identify it as such—for instance, "Mike Danger, pseudonym" or reveal the author's name, making it clear which is the real name and which is the pseudonym—for example, "Harold Lipshitz, whose pseudonym is Mike Danger."

Of course, if the author's identity is revealed on the application, it will be a simple matter for others to discover it because the application becomes a public document available for inspection at the Copyright Office.

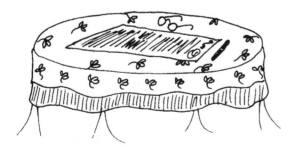

DURATION OF ANONYMOUS OR PSEUDONYMOUS WORKS

If the author of a pseudonymous or anonymous work is not identified in the Copyright Office's records, the copyright in the work lasts for a maximum of 75 years from the date of publication, or 100 years from the date of creation, whichever is less. The copyright in works by individuals in which the author is identified lasts for the life of the author plus 50 years. This could be longer than 75 years from publication, it all depends on how long the author lives. (See discussion in Chapter 10, Copyright Duration.)

If the author absolutely does not want her name revealed to anyone, the best option may be to leave the name of author line blank, or state "anonymous" or list the pseudonym without the real name. The author or her heirs can later let the Copyright Office know the author's true identity if this would extend the copyright term.

Dates of birth and death. If the author is a human being, his or her year of birth may be provided here, but this is not required (the birth year is used for identification purposes). However, if the author has died, the year of death *must* be listed unless the author was anonymous or pseudonymous. This date will determine when the copyright expires.

Leave this space blank if the author is a corporation, partnership or other organization. Corporations, partnerships and other business entities do not "die" for copyright purposes, even if they dissolve.

Was this contribution to the work a work made for hire? Check the "Yes" box if the author is a corporation, partnership or other organization. Otherwise, check the "No" box.

Author's nationality or domicile. This information must always be provided, even if the author is a business, is anonymous or used a pseudonym. An author's citizenship (nationality) and domicile could be different. An author's domicile generally is the country where she maintains her principal residence and where she intends to remain indefinitely. An author is a citizen of the country in which she was born or later moved to and became a citizen of by complying with its naturalization requirements.

EXAMPLE: Evelyn is a Canadian citizen, but she has permanent resident status and has lived year-round in Boston since 1980 and intends to remain there for the indefinite future. She is domiciled in the United States. She can state "Canada" in the citizenship blank or "U.S.A." in the domicile blank.

Copyright tip

A legal resident of the U.S. is treated the same as a citizen for copyright purposes. If you have difficulty determining whether you are domiciled in the U.S., consult an attorney. Noncitizens usually are entitled to copyright protection in the United States. (See Chapter 13, International Copyright Protection.)

Regardless of the state or states in which it is organized and does business, the citizenship of a domestic corporation, partnership or other organization should be given as "U.S.A."

Was this author's contribution to the work anonymous or pseudonymous? Check "Yes" box if the author is anonymous or used a pseudonym (pen name). Check the "No" box if the author is identified by her correct name. Don't check either box if the work was made for hire.

Nature of authorship. You must give a brief general description of the nature of the author's contribution to the work. Consider your words carefully because the Copyright Office relies on the description to determine if the work can be registered. Be sure that the description matches the work deposited with your application (deposits are discussed in Section M, below). The Copyright Office will probably send you a letter asking you to correct and resubmit your application if the "Nature of Authorship" statement(s) describes material not included in the deposit.

Entirely new works. One of the following phrases will probably adequately describe the authorship in an entirely new work. Pick the phrase that best describes the author's contribution to the particular work (or compose a better one of your own):

- "entire text" or "entire work," if the author wrote the entire work being registered
- "entire text and illustrations" (where these are being registered as a single unit; see Section E, above)
- "coauthor of entire text," if there were joint authors
- "nondramatic literary work"
- "book"
- "periodical"
- "novel"
- "poetry"
- "magazine article."

Do not list the work's title or describe the idea or concept embodied in the work (for example, "a book about skydiving"). Ideas and titles are not copyrightable. (See Chapter 6, *What Copyright Protects.*) The Copyright Office will correspond with you if your application describes your work in such terms.

Adaptions, new editions and other derivative works. If you're registering a derivative work (defined in Section F, above), describe the protectible material contributed to the work by the author. Examples of acceptable descriptions include:

- "editorial revisions," if the new material consists of editorial changes
- "editorial revisions plus additional new material" (or "Chapter 10 completely new"), if the

author made editorial changes and added new material

- "editorial revisions, annotations and other modifications"
- "Chapters 11–17," if entirely new chapters are added
- "revisions throughout, Act III completely new," if a play is revised and new material added
- "translation into English"
- "sound recording of published novel"
- "screenplay"
- "dramatization for the stage," if a play dramatizes another work such as a novel)
- "dramatization for television."

A statement such as "entire work" or "derivative work" ordinarily is not acceptable for such works. Moreover, do not describe unprotectible material added to the changed version, such as material in the public domain or copyrighted material written by others that the author obtained permission to use or used without permission under the fair use doctrine. (See Chapter 11, *Using Other Authors' Words*.)

Compilations. If you're registering a compilation (defined in Section F, above), describe both the material that has been compiled and the compilation itself. Include the terms "compilation," "selection" or "arrangement." For example:

- "Compilation and English translation," if the author translated a work into English.
- "Compilation of articles by Leroy Brown."
- "Anthology of previously published short stories."
- "Compilation of numerical data."

Copyright tip

If the Copyright Office might question whether your compilation was the product of minimal creativity, submit a letter along with your application explaining how the compilation was created. Your letter should convince the copyright examiner that minimal creativity was employed in the selection and/or arrangement of the facts, data or other items in your compilation. (See Chapter 7, *Adaptions and Compilations*.)

Information for additional authors. If there are two or three authors, go back now and fill in boxes 2b and 2c for each of them, using the above discussion as a guide. Space 2 only has enough subspaces for three authors. If the work you're registering has more than three authors, provide the required information for all the additional authors on a Copyright Office "Continuation Sheet" and clip (do not tape or staple) it to your application. There is a special continuation sheet to use with Form TX called Form TX/CON. A copy can be found in the tear-out appendix at the end of this book. You can obtain additional copies from the Copyright Office.

Space 3: Relevant Dates in Which Creation of This Work Was Completed

Fill in the year in which the work you're registering first became fixed in its final form, disregarding minor editorial changes. This year has nothing do to with publication, which may occur long after creation. Deciding what constitutes the year of creation may prove difficult if the work was created over a long period of time. Give the year in which the author completed the particular version of the work for which registration is now being sought, even if other versions exist or if further changes or additions are planned.

EXAMPLE: Martin finished writing an experimental novel in 1990. He couldn't find a publisher. He thoroughly rewrote the work in 1991 to make it more commercial, but still couldn't find a publisher. He finally self-published the original version of the novel in 1992. When he registers the book, the creation date will be 1990. This is because the particular version of the novel being registered was written in 1990.

Date and nation of first publication of this particular work. Leave this blank if an unpublished work is being registered. Publication occurs for copyright purposes when a work is made widely available to the public. (See Chapter 2, *Copyright Basics.*) Give the month, day, year and country where publication first occurred. Give only one date. If you're not sure of the exact publication date, state your best guess and make clear it is approximate—for example, "November 15, 1992 (approx.)."

Space 4: Information About Copyright Claimants

Provide the name and address of the copyright claimant(s), which must be either:

- persons or organizations that have, on or before the date the application is filed, obtained ownership of *all* the exclusive United States copyright rights that initially belonged to the author
- the author or authors of the work (including the owner of a work made for hire, if applicable), or
- the name of a person or organization that the author or owner of all U.S. copyright rights has authorized by contract to act as the claimant for copyright registration (there is no legal requirement that such contract be in writing, but it's not a bad idea). (37 C.F.R. 202.3(a)(3) (1984).)

We discuss in Chapter 2, *Copyright Basics,* the fact that under the copyright laws an author automatically holds several different exclusive rights in the work she creates—that is, the right to reproduce the work, to distribute it, to perform or publicly display it and to prepare derivative works based upon it. The author is entitled to transfer one or more—or any portion—of these rights in any way she pleases. But, if another person or organization acquires all these exclusive rights in a work, that person or organization is considered the copyright claimant for registration purposes, and the author is no longer the claimant.

EXAMPLE: Joe, an experienced mountaineer, self-publishes a pamphlet on advanced rock climbing techniques. The Colorado Rock Climbing Club purchases Joe's entire copyright in the pamphlet and republishes it. Joe never registered the pamphlet, so the club does so. The club should be listed as the copyright claimant, not Joe.

Frequently, no one owns all the exclusive rights in the work. This may occur where an author transfers fewer than all her exclusive rights to a publisher, or where a person or entity that acquired all the author's rights transfers some, but not all, of the rights to a third party. In this event, the author must be listed as the copyright claimant, even if someone else owns most of the exclusive copyright rights.

EXAMPLE 1: Assume that Joe transferred to the Rock Climbing Club only the right to publish a new edition of the pamphlet for their members and other Colorado residents. Joe retained all of his other exclusive rights. Joe is the copyright claimant.

EXAMPLE 2: Assume again that the Colorado Rock Climbing Club acquired all of Joe's exclusive rights in his pamphlet. Before the pamphlet is registered, the club transfers to the Southern California Climber's Federation the right to publish and distribute the pamphlet in California. No one now owns all the exclusive rights in the pamphlet—not Joe (who owns no rights), not the club and not the federation. When the club registers the pamphlet, Joe must be listed as the copyright claimant because he is the author and the exclusive rights are not concentrated in one pair of hands.

In the case of a work made for hire, the author is the creator's employer, or person or entity that commissioned the work under a written work-for-hire agreement (see discussion at Section D). This means the copyright claimant is either (1) the employer or commissioning party; or (2) the person or entity to whom the employer or commissioning party has transferred all of its exclusive rights in the work.

> **EXAMPLE 1:** Assume that Joe was an employee of the Colorado Rock Climbing Club and wrote the pamphlet as part of his job. The club is the copyright owner of this work made for hire, and the club should be listed as the copyright claimant.

> **EXAMPLE 2:** Assume that the club dissolved not long after Joe finished writing the pamphlet. Kate purchased all the club's exclusive rights in the pamphlet. When Kate registers the work, she should list herself as the copyright claimant.

A copyright claimant must be listed even for anonymous or pseudonymous works. You can provide the claimant's real name alone, the real name and the pseudonym, the pseudonym alone if the claimant is generally known by it or the author can authorize another person to act as the claimant (this way, the author's real name will not appear on the form).

Copyright tip
When the name listed for the claimant is different than the name of the author given in Space 2, but the two names identify one person, explain the relationship between the two names.

> **EXAMPLE:** John Smith is the author of the work he is registering, but all of the copyright rights have been transferred to his corporation, Smith Publishing Company, Inc. of which Smith is the sole owner. Smith should not just state Smith Publishing Company, Inc. Rather, he needs to explain the relationship between himself and his company-claimant—for example, "Smith Publishing Company, Inc., solely owned by John Smith."

Transfer. If the copyright claimant named just above is not the author or authors named in Space 2, give a brief general description of how ownership of the copyright was obtained. However, do not attach the transfer documents to the application.

This statement must show the copyright examiner that *all* the author's United States copyright rights have been transferred by a *written agreement* or by operation of law. Examples of acceptable transfer statements include: "By written contract," "Transfer of all rights by author," "By will," "By inheritance," "Assignment" or "By gift agreement."

Examples of *unacceptable* statements include:
- words indicating that possibly less than all the author's United States copyright rights have been transferred to the claimant—for example: "By license," "By permission" or "Transfer of right of first publication."
- statements suggesting that the person named as the claimant simply owns a copy of the work being registered, not the author's copyright rights—for example: "Author gave me this copy," "Found in attic trunk," "Author asked me to keep it for him."
- statements indicating that the named claimant has a special relationship to the author, but that do not show an actual transfer of ownership—for example: "Claimant is author's publisher," "Claimant is author's agent," or "Author is president of claimant corporation."

Again, see Chapter 9, *Transferring Copyright Ownership,* for a detailed discussion of copyright transfers.

Copyright tip
Note that the transfers space is used only to inform the Copyright Office about transfers that occurred before registration. All such transfers must be made in writing. (See Chapter 9, Section B.) If a copyright is transferred after registration, there is no need to reregister. However, although not required, it is a good idea to record (send) a copy of the trans-

EXAMINED BY	FORM TX
CHECKED BY	

☐ CORRESPONDENCE
　 Yes

FOR
COPYRIGHT
OFFICE
USE
ONLY

DO NOT WRITE ABOVE THIS LINE. IF YOU NEED MORE SPACE, USE A SEPARATE CONTINUATION SHEET.

PREVIOUS REGISTRATION Has registration for this work, or for an earlier version of this work, already been made in the Copyright Office?

☐ **Yes**　☐ **No**　If your answer is "Yes," why is another registration being sought? (Check appropriate box) ▼

a. ☐ This is the first published edition of a work previously registered in unpublished form.

b. ☐ This is the first application submitted by this author as copyright claimant.

c. ☐ This is a changed version of the work, as shown by space 6 on this application.

If your answer is "Yes," give: **Previous Registration Number** ▼　　　　**Year of Registration** ▼

5

DERIVATIVE WORK OR COMPILATION　Complete both space 6a and 6b for a derivative work; complete only 6b for a compilation.

a. Preexisting Material Identify any preexisting work or works that this work is based on or incorporates. ▼

b. Material Added to This Work Give a brief, general statement of the material that has been added to this work and in which copyright is claimed. ▼

6

See instructions
before completing
this space.

—space deleted—

7

REPRODUCTION FOR USE OF BLIND OR PHYSICALLY HANDICAPPED INDIVIDUALS A signature on this form at space 10 and a check in one of the boxes here in space 8 constitutes a non-exclusive grant of permission to the Library of Congress to reproduce and distribute solely for the blind and physically handicapped and under the conditions and limitations prescribed by the regulations of the Copyright Office: (1) copies of the work identified in space 1 of this application in Braille (or similar tactile symbols); or (2) phonorecords embodying a fixation of a reading of that work; or (3) both.

　　　　　a ☐ Copies and Phonorecords　　　　　**b** ☐ Copies Only　　　　　**c** ☐ Phonorecords Only

8

See instructions.

DEPOSIT ACCOUNT If the registration fee is to be charged to a Deposit Account established in the Copyright Office, give name and number of Account.

Name ▼　　　　　　　　　　　　　　　**Account Number** ▼

9

CORRESPONDENCE Give name and address to which correspondence about this application should be sent.　Name/Address/Apt/City/State/ZIP ▼

Be sure to
give your
daytime phone
◀ number

Area Code and Telephone Number ▶

CERTIFICATION* I, the undersigned, hereby certify that I am the

Check only one ▶ {
☐ author
☐ other copyright claimant
☐ owner of exclusive right(s)
☐ authorized agent of _____
}

of the work identified in this application and that the statements made by me in this application are correct to the best of my knowledge.

Name of author or other copyright claimant, or owner of exclusive right(s) ▲

10

Typed or printed name and date ▼ If this application gives a date of publication in space 3, do not sign and submit it before that date.

_____　date ▶ _____

☞　　Handwritten signature (X) ▼

_____

**MAIL
CERTIFI-
CATE TO**

Name ▼

Number/Street/Apartment Number ▼

City/State/ZIP ▼

**Certificate
will be
mailed in
window
envelope**

YOU MUST:
• Complete all necessary spaces
• Sign your application in space 10

**SEND ALL 3 ELEMENTS
IN THE SAME PACKAGE:**
1. Application form
2. Nonrefundable $20 filing fee in check or money order payable to *Register of Copyrights*
3. Deposit material

MAIL TO:
Register of Copyrights
Library of Congress
Washington, D.C. 20559-6000

The Copyright Office
has the authority to ad-
just fees at 5-year intervals, based on changes
in the Consumer Price
Index. The next adjust-
ment is due in 1996.
Please contact the
Copyright Office after
July 1995 to determine
the actual fee schedule.

11

*17 U.S.C. § 506(e): Any person who knowingly makes a false representation of a material fact in the application for copyright registration provided for by section 409, or in any written statement filed in connection with the application, shall be fined not more than $2,500.

July 1993—400,000　　♻ PRINTED ON RECYCLED PAPER　　　　　　　☆U.S. GOVERNMENT PRINTING OFFICE: 1993-342-582/80,020

fer document to the Copyright Office. Again, see Chapter 9, Section B.

If the author or owner of all rights has authorized another person or organization to act as the claimant, this should be indicated by including language like the following: "Pursuant to the contractual right from [author *or* owner of all U.S. copyright rights] to claim legal title to the copyright in an application for copyright registration."

Copyright tip
If there's not enough space to list all the claimants on Form TX, you can list additional claimants on the reverse side of Form TX/CON.

Space 5: Previous Registration

If all the material in the work you're registering has never been registered before, check the "No" box and skip the rest of the questions.

If all or part of the work has been previously registered, check the "Yes" box. Then, you need to check the appropriate box:

- Check the first box only if you are now registering a work you previously registered when it was unpublished.
- Check the second box only if someone other than the author was listed as the copyright claimant in Space 4 in the prior registration, and the author is now registering the work in her own name—for example, where an anonymous or pseudonymous author listed an authorized agent in Space 4, above, and now wishes to reregister in her own name.
- Check the third box only if the previously registered work has been changed, and you are registering the changed version or new edition to protect the additions or revisions.

Then provide the registration number and year of previous registration in the blanks indicated. The registration number can be found stamped on the certificate of registration. It is usually a multidigit

number preceded by the two-letter prefix of the application form used—for example, TX 012345. The Copyright Office places a small "u" following the prefix if the registered work is unpublished—for example, TXu 567890.

If you're not registering a derivative work or compilation, skip to Space 8, below. See Section F, above, if you're not sure whether your work is a derivative work or compilation.

Space 6: Description of Derivative Works or Compilations

Space 6 is completed only for derivative works or compilations. It should be completed only if the derivative work or compilation contains material that was:

- previously published
- previously registered, or
- in the public domain.

If the preexisting material in your derivative work or compilation was not published, registered or in the public domain, put "N/A" in Space 6. Technically, a work based on or adapted from preexisting unpublished expression that was never registered is a derivative work. However, for reasons of administrative convenience, the Copyright Office does not require unpublished, unregistered material to be described in Space 6.

> **EXAMPLE:** Leila writes a screenplay based on her unpublished, unregistered novel. The screenplay is a derivative work, but Leila need not complete Space 6 on Form PA when she registers the screenplay.

Preexisting material (6a). For a derivative work, identify the preexisting material that has been revised, recast, transformed or adapted—for instance, "Previously published first edition of textbook on ancient Greek history," "Public Domain

French version of *Madame Bovary*," "Previously registered unpublished manuscript."

Leave Space 6a blank if you're registering a compilation.

Material added to this work (6b). For a derivative work, describe in Space 6b the new protectible material you are registering. Often, you can simply repeat what you stated in the "Nature of Authorship" line in Space 2 (above). If the application contains more than one nature of authorship statement because there was more than one author, you'll need to combine these descriptions. Be sure you describe all the new authorship.

> **EXAMPLE:** Otto and Eva have revised their published textbook. The description of Otto's authorship in space 2 states "Revised Chapters 1–8." The description of Eva's authorship states "Added new Chapter 9." They should state in space 6b "Revised Chapters 1–8, new Chapter 9."

However, don't describe the new material in such a manner that the copyright examiner might question whether enough new material has been added to make the work registrable. For example, it's probably not wise merely to state "editorial revisions," because it is not clear from this description whether the revisions are substantial. Rather, describe the revisions—for example, "Revised forward, typographical errors deleted, new chapter heading, and new compilation of four maps."

Space 6b must be completed for all compilations. You can simply repeat in space 6b what you stated in the "Nature of Authorship" line in space 2.

Space 7:
Skip this space.

Space 8: License for Handicapped

The Library of Congress produces and distributes braille editions and recorded readings of registered works for the exclusive use of the blind and physically handicapped. If you wish to grant the Library a license to copy and/or record your work for this purpose, check one of the boxes: "a" for copies and phonorecords; "b" for copies only; or "c" for phonorecords only. Most applicants give the blind a break and check one of these boxes.

However, only a person who owns the right to reproduce and publish the work being registered can grant this license to the Library of Congress. If you're a transferee of one or more exclusive rights, but you don't own the right to reproduce and publish the work, skip this item completely.

The license is entirely voluntary and nonexclusive—it doesn't prevent you from granting anyone else a license to make braille editions or sound recordings of your work. Moreover, the Library of Congress does not copy every work to which it holds a license. You can terminate the license at any time by sending a written notice to the National Library Service for the Blind and Physically Handicapped (NLS), Library of Congress, 1291 Taylor Street NW, Washington, DC 20542.

Space 9: Deposit Account and Correspondence

Deposit Account. If you have 12 or more transactions per year with the Copyright Office, you may establish a money deposit account to which you make advance money deposits and charge your copyright fees against the account instead of sending a separate check each time. You must deposit at least $250 to open an account. For an application, obtain "Circular R5" from the Copyright Office. If you have a deposit account and wish to charge the registration fee to the account, state the account name and number.

Correspondence. Provide the name, address, area code and telephone number of the person the

Copyright Office should contact if it has questions about your application.

Copyright tip
If the registration is being made by a corporation or other entity, list the name of the person in the organization who should be contacted. The Copyright Office makes calls between 8:00 A.M. and 5:00 P.M. eastern time; so give the number or numbers where the contact person can be reached at these times.

Space 10: Certification
Check the appropriate box indicating your capacity as the person registering the work:
- Check the "author" box if you are the person (or one of several people) named in Space 2 (if there are several authors, only one need sign).
- Check the "other copyright claimant" box if you are not named in Space 2 as the author, but have acquired all the author's rights.
- Check the "owner of exclusive right(s)" box if you only own one or more—but not all—of the exclusive rights making up the entire copyright.
- Check the "authorized agent of" box if you are not signing for yourself as an individual, but as the authorized representative of the author, another person who is the copyright claimant or the owner of one or more—but not all—exclusive rights. Then state the name of the person or organization on whose behalf you're signing on the dotted line following the box.

Copyright tip
Check the "authorized agent" box if you, as an individual, are signing on behalf of a corporation, partnership or other organization that is the author, copyright claimant or holder of exclusive rights.

After checking the appropriate box, type or print your name and date in the appropriate blanks,

then sign your name on the line following "handwritten signature."

Copyright tip
If you are registering a published work, the copyright office will not accept your application if the date listed in the certification space is earlier than the date of publication shown in Space 3.

Space 11: Return mailing address
Fill in your name and the return mailing address for your copyright registration certificate in the last box on the form.

If you're registering a group of previously published articles or other individual contributions to periodicals, turn to Section L to complete Form GR/CP as well. Otherwise, skip to Section M.

J. How to Complete Form PA

Form PA is for works that are intended to be performed in public, such as plays and screenplays. (See Section H.) Form PA is virtually identical to Form TX, so we'll refer to the instructions for Form TX in Section I, above, where applicable.

Form PA is also used to register multimedia works combining text with graphics, photos, videos, sounds and so forth. See Chapter 14, *Electronic Publishing,* for a detailed discussion on how to complete Form PA when registering such works.

You will find a sample filled out Form PA in the appendix preceding the blank copyright forms.

Space 1: Title and Date of Publication
Title of this work. Follow the instructions in Section I, above.

FORM PA
For a Work of the Performing Arts
UNITED STATES COPYRIGHT OFFICE

REGISTRATION NUMBER

PA   PAU

EFFECTIVE DATE OF REGISTRATION

Month   Day   Year

DO NOT WRITE ABOVE THIS LINE. IF YOU NEED MORE SPACE, USE A SEPARATE CONTINUATION SHEET.

1

TITLE OF THIS WORK ▼

PREVIOUS OR ALTERNATIVE TITLES ▼

NATURE OF THIS WORK ▼ See instructions

2

a

NAME OF AUTHOR ▼

DATES OF BIRTH AND DEATH
Year Born ▼   Year Died ▼

Was this contribution to the work a "work made for hire"?
☐ Yes
☐ No

AUTHOR'S NATIONALITY OR DOMICILE
Name of Country
OR { Citizen of ▶_____
     Domiciled in▶_____

WAS THIS AUTHOR'S CONTRIBUTION TO THE WORK
Anonymous?   ☐ Yes ☐ No
Pseudonymous? ☐ Yes ☐ No

If the answer to either of these questions is "Yes," see detailed instructions.

NATURE OF AUTHORSHIP Briefly describe nature of material created by this author in which copyright is claimed. ▼

NOTE
Under the law, the "author" of a "work made for hire" is generally the employer, not the employee (see instructions). For any part of this work that was "made for hire" check "Yes" in the space provided, give the employer (or other person for whom the work was prepared) as "Author" of that part, and leave the space for dates of birth and death blank.

b

NAME OF AUTHOR ▼

DATES OF BIRTH AND DEATH
Year Born ▼   Year Died ▼

Was this contribution to the work a "work made for hire"?
☐ Yes
☐ No

AUTHOR'S NATIONALITY OR DOMICILE
Name of Country
OR { Citizen of ▶_____
     Domiciled in▶_____

WAS THIS AUTHOR'S CONTRIBUTION TO THE WORK
Anonymous?   ☐ Yes ☐ No
Pseudonymous? ☐ Yes ☐ No

If the answer to either of these questions is "Yes," see detailed instructions.

NATURE OF AUTHORSHIP Briefly describe nature of material created by this author in which copyright is claimed. ▼

c

NAME OF AUTHOR ▼

DATES OF BIRTH AND DEATH
Year Born ▼   Year Died ▼

Was this contribution to the work a "work made for hire"?
☐ Yes
☐ No

AUTHOR'S NATIONALITY OR DOMICILE
Name of Country
OR { Citizen of ▶_____
     Domiciled in▶_____

WAS THIS AUTHOR'S CONTRIBUTION TO THE WORK
Anonymous?   ☐ Yes ☐ No
Pseudonymous? ☐ Yes ☐ No

If the answer to either of these questions is "Yes," see detailed instructions.

NATURE OF AUTHORSHIP Briefly describe nature of material created by this author in which copyright is claimed. ▼

3

a **YEAR IN WHICH CREATION OF THIS WORK WAS COMPLETED** This information must be given ◀Year in all cases.

b **DATE AND NATION OF FIRST PUBLICATION OF THIS PARTICULAR WORK**
Complete this information ONLY if this work has been published.
Month▶_____ Day▶_____ Year▶_____
_____ ◀ Nation

4

See instructions before completing this space.

COPYRIGHT CLAIMANT(S) Name and address must be given even if the claimant is the same as the author given in space 2. ▼

TRANSFER If the claimant(s) named here in space 4 is (are) different from the author(s) named in space 2, give a brief statement of how the claimant(s) obtained ownership of the copyright. ▼

DO NOT WRITE HERE
OFFICE USE ONLY

APPLICATION RECEIVED

ONE DEPOSIT RECEIVED

TWO DEPOSITS RECEIVED

FUNDS RECEIVED

MORE ON BACK ▶ • Complete all applicable spaces (numbers 5-9) on the reverse side of this page.
• See detailed instructions.   • Sign the form at line 8.

DO NOT WRITE HERE
Page 1 of _____ pages

Previous or alternative titles. Follow the instructions in Section I, above.

Nature of this work. Give a brief description of the general nature of the work. For example: "screenplay," "television play," "drama," "musical play," "song lyrics."

Space 2: Author Information

Follow the instructions in Section I, above. Space 2 only has enough subspaces for three authors. If the work you're registering has more than three authors, provide the required information for all the additional authors on a Copyright Office "Continuation Sheet"—Form ___/CON—and clip (do not tape or staple) it to your application. A copy of Form ___/CON can be found in the tear-out appendix at the end of this book. You can obtain additional copies from the Copyright Office.

Nature of authorship. Examples of acceptable nature of authorship descriptions include:

- "entire text" or "entire work" if the author wrote the entire work being registered
- "coauthor of entire text" if there is more than one author
- "words" if the author has written song lyrics
- "revisions throughout, Act III completely new" if a play is revised and new material added.

Space 3: Relevant Dates

Follow the instructions in Section I, above.

Space 4: Copyright Claimant(s)

Follow the instructions in Section I, above. If there's not enough space to list all the claimants on Form PA, you can list additional claimants on the reverse side of Form PA/CON.

Space 5: Previous Registration

Follow the instructions in Section I, above.

Space 6: Description of Derivative Work or Compilation

Skip this item unless you are registering a derivative work or compilation. If you are, follow the instructions in Section I, above.

Space 7: Deposit Account

Follow the instructions for Space 9 in Section I, above.

Space 8: Certification

Follow the instructions for Space 10 in Section I, above.

If you're registering a group of previously published individual contributions to periodicals, turn to Section L to complete Form GR/CP as well. Otherwise, skip to Section M.

K. Registering Newspapers, Magazines and Other Periodicals: Form SE, Short Form SE, Form SE/Group, Form G/DN

1. Introduction

Newspapers, magazines and other periodicals such as newsletters and journals are normally "collective works" in which a number of individual contributions such as articles, stories, cartoons and photographs are assembled into a collective whole. Magazines and similar publications are also called serials. Both the magazine as a whole and the individual contributions are entitled to full copyright protection.

A magazine or other periodical issue is registered as a whole on one of the SE series of forms, usually by the person(s) or organization that owns the publication and/or supervises its creation. When

EXAMINED BY _____

CHECKED BY _____

☐ CORRESPONDENCE
  Yes

FORM PA

FOR
COPYRIGHT
OFFICE
USE
ONLY

DO NOT WRITE ABOVE THIS LINE. IF YOU NEED MORE SPACE, USE A SEPARATE CONTINUATION SHEET.

5

PREVIOUS REGISTRATION Has registration for this work, or for an earlier version of this work, already been made in the Copyright Office?

☐ Yes ☐ No If your answer is "Yes," why is another registration being sought? (Check appropriate box) ▼

a. ☐ This is the first published edition of a work previously registered in unpublished form.

b. ☐ This is the first application submitted by this author as copyright claimant.

c. ☐ This is a changed version of the work, as shown by space 6 on this application.

If your answer is "Yes," give: **Previous Registration Number** ▼   **Year of Registration** ▼

6

DERIVATIVE WORK OR COMPILATION Complete both space 6a & 6b for a derivative work; complete only 6b for a compilation.

a. **Preexisting Material** Identify any preexisting work or works that this work is based on or incorporates. ▼

See instructions
before completing
this space.

b. **Material Added to This Work** Give a brief, general statement of the material that has been added to this work and in which copyright is claimed.▼

7

DEPOSIT ACCOUNT If the registration fee is to be charged to a Deposit Account established in the Copyright Office, give name and number of Account.
Name ▼   **Account Number** ▼

CORRESPONDENCE Give name and address to which correspondence about this application should be sent.   Name/Address/Apt/City/State/Zip ▼

Be sure to
give your
daytime phone
◀ number.

Area Code & Telephone Number ▶

8

CERTIFICATION*   I, the undersigned, hereby certify that I am the

Check only one ▼

☐ author

☐ other copyright claimant

☐ owner of exclusive right(s)

☐ authorized agent of_____
                    Name of author or other copyright claimant, or owner of exclusive right(s) ▲

of the work identified in this application and that the statements made
by me in this application are correct to the best of my knowledge.

Typed or printed name and date ▼ If this application gives a date of publication in space 3, do not sign and submit it before that date.

                                                              date ▶

☞ Handwritten signature (X) ▼

9

MAIL CERTIFI- CATE TO

Name ▼

Number/Street/Apartment Number ▼

City/State/ZIP ▼

Certificate will be mailed in window envelope

YOU MUST:
• Complete all necessary spaces
• Sign your application in space 8

SEND ALL 3 ELEMENTS
IN THE SAME PACKAGE:
1. Application form
2. Nonrefundable $20 filing fee
   in check or money order
   payable to *Register of Copyrights*
3. Deposit material

MAIL TO:
Register of Copyrights
Library of Congress
Washington, D.C. 20559

Copyright fees are ad-
justed at 5-year inter-
vals, based on in-
creases or decreases in
the Consumer Price In-
dex. The next adjust-
ment is due in 1995.
Contact the Copyright
Office in January 1995
for the new fee sched-
ule.

* 17 U.S.C. § 506(e): Any person who knowingly makes a false representation of a material fact in the application for copyright registration provided for by section 409, or in any written statement filed in
connection with the application, shall be fined not more than $2,500.

▲ June 1992—100,000   ☆U.S. GOVERNMENT PRINTING OFFICE: 1992-312-432/60,003

a magazine or other periodical issue is registered as a whole, the registration protects:

- the revising, editing, compiling and similar efforts that went into putting the issue into final form
- any individual contributions (articles, etc.) prepared by the publication's employees or by nonemployees who signed work-for-hire agreements, and
- any individual contributions by freelancers to which the publication has purchased all rights.

If a periodical issue contains any independently authored contributions to which all of the rights have not been acquired by the publication, those contributions are not protected when the issue is registered as a whole. To protect their work, individual contributors who retain some of their rights must register separately (see Section L, below).

> **EXAMPLE:** The *Jogger's Journal* is a monthly magazine owned and published by Ededas, Inc. The July issue contains 12 articles: two articles were written by the Journal's editorial staff; two were written by freelance writers who signed work-for-hire agreements; four were written by freelancers who assigned to the journal all their rights; and three were written by freelancers who assigned to the journal only the right to publish their articles for the first time in North America. When the July issue is registered, all the material in it will be protected except for the three articles to which the journal did not acquire all rights.

a.   Four registration forms

There are four different registration forms for serial publications—Form SE, Short Form SE, Form SE/Group and Form G/DN. Which form to use depends on the nature of the magazine or other serial work you're registering. Form SE can be used to register any serial publication, but, in practice, you'll want to use it only if you cannot use the other forms because the filing fee is lower when you use those forms.

2.   Form SE/Group: Group Registration of Serials

Before 1991, each individual issue of a magazine or other serial publication had to be registered separately on Form SE. This meant that a monthly magazine had to be registered 12 times a year with 12 application fees paid. Fortunately, the Copyright Office now permits multiple issues of the same magazine to be registered together as a group for one application fee. For example, the same monthly magazine may now be registered three issues at a time on Form SE/Group. This way, registration need only be accomplished four times a year instead of twelve. Unfortunately, there are some restrictions on which periodicals may be registered together on Form SE/Group.

a.   Periodical must be a work made for hire

The magazine or other periodical must be a work made for hire. This means that the person(s) who create the periodical as a whole—that is, do the editing, compiling and similar work necessary to put the issue in its final form—must be employees of the owner of the publication or have been commissioned to do the work under a written contract. (See Chapter 8, *Initial Copyright Ownership,* for a detailed discussion of works made for hire.) Most periodicals and other serial publications are works made for hire for which the owner of the publication has hired or commissioned others to compile and edit.

> **EXAMPLE:** *Newspeak Magazine* is a weekly news magazine that is compiled and edited entirely by the publisher's editorial staff. *Newspeak*

is a work made for hire, and the weekly issues may be registered together on Form SE/Group.

However, a periodical that is independently owned and created by the same individual(s) who own it—that is, not created by employees or commissioned workers—is not a work made for hire. Such a publication may not be registered on Form SE/Group. Each issue must be separately registered on Form SE (see below).

EXAMPLE: Dr. Brown, an eminent urologist, owns, publishes, writes and edits a monthly newsletter for urologists called *Urine Analysis*. The newsletter is not a work made for hire. This means that Dr. Brown must register each newsletter issue separately on Form SE.

b. Group registration unavailable for periodicals published more than once a week or less than four times a year

You may register together two or more issues of the same periodical on Form SE/Group so long as they are published:

- no more frequently than once a week
- at least four times a year, and
- all issues being registered together were published within a 90-day period during the same calendar year.

EXAMPLE 1: Thirteen issues of *Newspeak Magazine* are published every 90 days. Instead of registering each issue separately on Form SE, up to 13 consecutive issues can be registered at the same time on Form SE/Group, so long as all the issues were published during the same calendar year—for example, the December 1992 and January and February 1993 issues could not be registered together, but the January, February and March 1993 issues could be.

EXAMPLE 2: *The Nutne Reader* is a literary magazine that is published irregularly. In 1992, one issue was published in January, another in March, another in July and another in December. The January and March issues may be registered together on Form SE/Group, since they were published within 90 days of each other. But the July and December issues must be registered separately.

c. Collective work authorship must be essentially all new

Form SE/Group may be used only if the collective work authorship—that is, the editing, compiling, revising and other work involved in creating each issue as a whole—of all the issues being registered together is essentially all new in terms of when the work was done. It's not exactly clear how recently created a periodical issue must be to qualify as essentially all new; but as an outside time limit, each issue must have been created no more than one year prior to its publication.

d. The author and copyright claimant must be the same for all issues

The author of a magazine or other periodical issue is the person(s) or organization responsible for the creation of the issue as a whole, whether it employs an editorial staff, freelance editors or uses volunteers. The author is normally the person(s) or organization that owns the publication.

To use Form SE/Group, the author of all the periodical issues being registered as a group and the copyright claimant in the issues must be the same. As discussed in Section I, above, the author of a publication is also the copyright claimant unless the author transfers all of its copyright rights to a third party. This means the author-publisher of a periodical issue would normally be the copyright claimant as well. However, if the author-publisher transferred its copyright rights to one or more of the periodical issues to a third party, those issues could not be registered on Form SE/Group.

EXAMPLE 1: *The Toxic Waste Tipster* is a monthly trade journal owned and published by a corporation called Toxic Waste Internment and Transport, Inc. (TWIT). TWIT oversees the creation of each issue through its editorial staff. TWIT is the author and copyright claimant for each issue.

EXAMPLE 2: Assume that TWIT sells the *Tipster* to the Polluters' Trade Association (PTA), effective July 1992. As of July 1, TWIT has already overseen production of all the monthly issues through September 1992. The July, August and September issues may not be registered together on Form SE/Group because, while TWIT is the author of each, the PTA owns all the copyright rights in these issues and is the copyright claimant.

e. Two complimentary subscriptions must be given to the Library of Congress

Two complimentary subscriptions for the periodical must be entered for the Library of Congress. This is in addition to the normal deposit that must be submitted with your application. (See Section M, below.) These subscriptions must continue for as long as you wish to use the group registration procedure.

The subscriptions must be mailed *separately* to:

Group Periodicals Registration
Library of Congress
Washington, DC 20540

The *first time* a magazine or other serial is submitted for group registration, a letter confirming that two complimentary subscriptions have been given to the library must be filed with the:

General Counsel
Copyright Office
Library of Congress
Department 17
Washington, DC 20540

The letter should identify the publisher, title(s), and the volume and issue numbers that begin the complimentary subscriptions.

EXAMPLE 1: The publisher of *Newspeak Magazine* decides to register three months of issues together as a group. *Newspeak* gives the Library

of Congress two free subscriptions to the magazine and sends the following letter to the Copyright Office General Counsel (this letter need only be sent once):

LETTER TO COPYRIGHT OFFICE

May 1, 1992

General Counsel
Copyright Office
Library of Congress
Department 17
Washington, DC 20540

Dear General Counsel:

The serial publication *Newspeak Magazine* has recently been submitted for group registration for the first time. This is to confirm that we have given the Library of Congress two complimentary subscriptions to *Newspeak Magazine*, commencing with Volume 52, Number 23. *Newspeak Magazine* is published by Big Brother, Inc.

Winston Smith
Newspeak Magazine
Winston Smith, Publisher

f.   How to Complete Form SE/Group

Filling out Form SE/Group is very simple.

Space 1: Title and Date of Publication
Title. Fill in the publication's complete title followed by:

- the International Standard Serial Number (ISSN) if available (see Chapter 3, *Copyright Notice*, for detailed discussion of ISSNs), and
- each issue's volume, number and issue date appearing on the copies, followed by the month, day and year of publication.

List the issues in order of publication.

No previous registration under identical title. If you have never registered the identical title before, check the box at the left.

Space 2: Author and Copyright Claimant
Name and address of the author/copyright claimant in these collective works made for hire. Give the fullest form of the author/claimant's name and mailing address. If there are joint authors and claimants, provide the names and addresses of each of them. (See Chapter 8, Initial Copyright Ownership, for discussion of joint authorship.)

For Non-U.S. works. If the issues were not published in the U.S., you must list the country of which the author is a citizen, or where she resides or state the country in which the serial was published.

Certification. The application must be signed by the copyright claimant or its duly authorized agent. Type or print this person's name after the signature.

Person to contact for correspondence about this claim. In the spaces provided, indicate the name and daytime telephone number (including area code) of the person whom the Copyright Office should contact concerning the application. Also give such person's address if it is different from the address for mailing of the certificate (below).

Deposit account. If the filing fee is to be charged against a deposit account, give the name and number of the account in the space indicated. (See Section I, above, for detailed a discussion of deposit accounts.) Otherwise, leave the space blank and forward the fee with your application.

Mail certificate to. Provide the complete address where your registration certificate should be sent. (The certificate is merely a stamped copy of your Form SE/Group.)

Reproduction for use of blind or physically handicapped individuals. If you wish to participate in the Library of Congress's special program for the blind and handicapped, check the appropriate box. (For a detailed discussion of this program, see Section I, above.)

g.   Application fee

If you don't have a deposit account with the Copyright Office, submit a check for the application fee payable to the Register of Copyrights with your application. The fee is $10 for *each* periodical issue being registered together on Form SE/Group. This means the minimum fee is $20 (at least two issues must be registered together).

3.   Form G/DN

Until recently, daily newspapers had to be registered individually on Form SE. This meant that to register an entire year's worth of issues, 365 separate registrations had to be made for $20 each. Obviously, this was very burdensome. As a result, few daily newspapers were ever registered. Fortunately, the Copyright Office amended its regulations in 1992 to permit group registration of daily newspapers. Now, an entire calendar month's worth of daily newspaper issues can be registered at one time on Form G/DN for a single $40 fee.

a.   What works qualify as daily newspapers

Any daily serial publication mainly designed to be a primary source of written information on current events (local, national or international) qualifies as a daily newspaper so long as it contains a broad range of news on all subjects and activities and is not limited to any specific subject matter. Publications such as newsletters on particular subjects and daily racing forms do not qualify as daily newspapers.

b.   Requirements for using Form G/DN

As is the case when using Form SE/Group (see Section K.2 above), Form G/DN may be used only if the newspaper is an essentially all-new collective work made for hire. Virtually all daily newspapers should be able to satisfy these requirements since they are essentially all new every day and are created by employee-reporters and editors.

In addition, the author and copyright claimant must be the same person or organization. Again, this should pose no problem because the author and claimant will normally be the owner(s) of the newspaper.

c.   An entire month's issues must be registered

To use Form G/DN, an entire calendar month of daily newspaper issues must be registered; no more and no less. This means you'll have to register 12 times a year.

d.   Microfilm deposit required

In one important respect, using Form G/DN is unique. Instead of the normal deposit of an actual copy of the work being registered, the newspaper issues must be deposited in the form of a positive, 35mm silver-halide microfilm.

If the newspaper is published in multiple editions, the last (final) edition of all the issues must be deposited. However, it is permissible (but not required) to also register and deposit earlier editions of the newspaper published the same day in a given metropolitan area. But national or regional newspaper editions distributed beyond a given metropolitan area must be registered and deposited separately.

e. Time limit for registration

The Form G/DN must be filed with the Copyright Office within three months after the publication date of the last newspaper issue included in the group.

f. Registration fee

There is a $40 registration fee when Form G/DN is used (this is twice the normal fee).

g. Filling out Form G/DN

Form G/DN is the simplest of all registration forms. Here's how to fill it out:

Space 1: Title

Identify the work being registered in Space 1 by giving the title of the newspaper, the month and year printed on the copies, the number of issues in the group, the city and state, the edition; and, if known, the ISSN number.

Space 2: Author and Copyright Claimant

Give in Space 2 the fullest form of the author and claimant's name (this will usually be the owner of the newspaper). If there are multiple owners, give all their names.

Space 3: Date of Publication

List in Space 3 the exact full date on which the first and last newspaper issues being registered were published.

Certification; correspondence; deposit account. The copyright claimant or her authorized agent must sign in the certification space; and an address and phone number of the person to be contacted about the registered issues must be provided. If the claimant has a deposit account with the Copyright Office and wants the registration fee charged to it, the "Deposit Account" space must be filled in; otherwise, leave it blank.

4. Short Form SE

A periodical issue that otherwise qualifies for group registration but cannot be registered on Form SE/Group because it is published too frequently or not frequently enough (such as a magazine published every four months), may be registered on Short Form SE instead *if*:

- the author, whether a human being or corporation or other entity, is a U.S. citizen or resides in the U.S., and
- the issue was first published in the U.S.

The advantage to using Short Form SE rather than the regular Form SE is that there is only a $10 application fee for registrations on Short Form SE, compared with a $20 fee for Form SE. Short Form SE is also easier to fill out.

Short Form SE is nearly identical to Form SE/Group. It is filled out in the same manner as Form SE/Group (above) except that only one issue is listed in Space 1 and the date of publication of the issue being registered must be provided in Space 3. If the issue was created in a different calendar year than the year of publication, the year of creation must also be given in Space 3.

5. Form SE

Periodical issues that do not qualify for group registration on Form SE/Group or Form G/DN, or for individual registration on Short Form SE must be registered individually on Form SE. This could occur, for example, where a periodical is not a work for hire.

Form SE is almost identical to Form TX discussed in Section I, above. The differences in Form SE are discussed below.

You will find a sample filled-out Form SE preceding the blank copyright forms in the appendix.

Space 1: Title

Title of this serial. Fill in the publication's complete title. Then, in the spaces provided, give the volume and issue number, the date on the issue you are submitting with the application and the frequency of publication of the serial—for instance, "ten times a year," "quarterly," "monthly," "bimonthly" or "weekly." You'll usually find this information in or near the publication's masthead.

Previous or alternative titles. Refer to Form TX, discussed in Section I, above.

Space 2: Author Information

Follow the instructions in Section I, above, with these clarifications.

Name of author. Provide the full name of the issue's author. The author is the person or organization that controls and supervises the issue's creation (see Section K.1, above). This will normally be the person or organization that owns the publication. The title of a periodical itself usually should not be listed as author because that title is usually not the owner's full legal name.

> **EXAMPLE:** *The Spelunker's Journal* is owned by the Spelunker's Society of America, a nonprofit corporation. An editor employed by the society commissions freelance writers to contribute individual articles to the journal, which the editor compiles and edits for each issue. The society is the journal's author. The society's full legal name ("Spelunker's Society of America, Incorporated") should be listed as author.

Was this contribution to the work a work made for hire? Read the discussion of when a periodical issue is a work made for hire in Section K.2, above, and check the appropriate box.

Nature of authorship. If the serial issue is a work made for hire (see Section K.2, above), it is a collective work. A collective work is a work in which individual contributions which would be copyrightable in themselves are assembled into a collective whole by an organization and its employees (Section K.1, above). If this is the case, check this box; there is no need to describe the nature of the authorship involved in creating the issue.

However, if the serial issue was independently created by an individual or individuals you must describe the nature of the authorship.

> **EXAMPLE:** Kay owns, publishes, writes and edits a newsletter on environmental law. The newsletter is not a "collective work" because Kay writes the entire content herself. Kay should not check the "collective work" box. Instead, she must describe her authorship of the newsletter. She could simply state "entire text."

If the work you're registering has more than three authors, provide the required information for all the additional authors on a Copyright Office "Continuation Sheet"—Form ___/CON—and clip it (do not tape or staple it) to your application. A copy of Form ___/CON can be found in the tear-out appendix at the end of this book. You can obtain additional copies from the Copyright Office.

Space 3: Relevant Dates

Follow the instructions on how to fill out Space 3 of Form TX in Section I, above.

FORM SE

For a Serial
UNITED STATES COPYRIGHT OFFICE

REGISTRATION NUMBER

_____ U

EFFECTIVE DATE OF REGISTRATION

Month	Day	Year

DO NOT WRITE ABOVE THIS LINE. IF YOU NEED MORE SPACE, USE A SEPARATE CONTINUATION SHEET.

1

TITLE OF THIS SERIAL ▼

Volume ▼	Number ▼	Date on Copies ▼	Frequency of Publication ▼

PREVIOUS OR ALTERNATIVE TITLES ▼

2

a

NAME OF AUTHOR ▼

DATES OF BIRTH AND DEATH
Year Born ▼   Year Died ▼

Was this contribution to the work a "work made for hire"?
☐ Yes
☐ No

AUTHOR'S NATIONALITY OR DOMICILE
Name of Country
OR { Citizen of ▶ _____
Domiciled in▶ _____

WAS THIS AUTHOR'S CONTRIBUTION TO THE WORK
Anonymous?   ☐ Yes ☐ No
Pseudonymous? ☐ Yes ☐ No

If the answer to either of these questions is "Yes," see detailed instructions.

NATURE OF AUTHORSHIP Briefly describe nature of material created by this author in which copyright is claimed. ▼
☐ Collective Work   Other:

NOTE

Under the law, the "author" of a "work made for hire" is generally the employer, not the employee (see instructions). For any part of this work that was "made for hire" check "Yes" in the space provided, give the employer (or other person for whom the work was prepared) as "Author" of that part, and leave the space for dates of birth and death blank.

b

NAME OF AUTHOR ▼

DATES OF BIRTH AND DEATH
Year Born ▼   Year Died ▼

Was this contribution to the work a "work made for hire"?
☐ Yes
☐ No

AUTHOR'S NATIONALITY OR DOMICILE
Name of Country
OR { Citizen of ▶ _____
Domiciled in▶ _____

WAS THIS AUTHOR'S CONTRIBUTION TO THE WORK
Anonymous?   ☐ Yes ☐ No
Pseudonymous? ☐ Yes ☐ No

If the answer to either of these questions is "Yes," see detailed instructions.

NATURE OF AUTHORSHIP Briefly describe nature of material created by this author in which copyright is claimed. ▼
☐ Collective Work   Other:

c

NAME OF AUTHOR ▼

DATES OF BIRTH AND DEATH
Year Born ▼   Year Died ▼

Was this contribution to the work a "work made for hire"?
☐ Yes
☐ No

AUTHOR'S NATIONALITY OR DOMICILE
Name of Country
OR { Citizen of ▶ _____
Domiciled in▶ _____

WAS THIS AUTHOR'S CONTRIBUTION TO THE WORK
Anonymous?   ☐ Yes ☐ No
Pseudonymous? ☐ Yes ☐ No

If the answer to either of these questions is "Yes," see detailed instructions.

NATURE OF AUTHORSHIP Briefly describe nature of material created by this author in which copyright is claimed. ▼
☐ Collective Work   Other:

3

a

YEAR IN WHICH CREATION OF THIS ISSUE WAS COMPLETED   This information must be given ◀Year in all cases.

b

DATE AND NATION OF FIRST PUBLICATION OF THIS PARTICULAR ISSUE
Complete this information ONLY if this work has been published.
Month▶ _____ Day▶ _____ Year▶ _____ ◀ Nation

4

COPYRIGHT CLAIMANT(S) Name and address must be given even if the claimant is the same as the author given in space 2. ▼

TRANSFER If the claimant(s) named here in space 4 is (are) different from the author(s) named in space 2, give a brief statement of how the claimant(s) obtained ownership of the copyright. ▼

See instructions before completing this space.

DO NOT WRITE HERE — OFFICE USE ONLY

APPLICATION RECEIVED

ONE DEPOSIT RECEIVED

TWO DEPOSITS RECEIVED

REMITTANCE NUMBER AND DATE

MORE ON BACK ▶ • Complete all applicable spaces (numbers 5-11) on the reverse side of this page.
• See detailed instructions.   • Sign the form at line 10.

DO NOT WRITE HERE
Page 1 of _____ pages

Space 4: Copyright Claimant

Follow the instructions on how to fill out Space 4 of Form TX in Section I, above.

Space 5: Previous Registration

Follow the instructions on how to fill out Space 5 of Form TX in Section I, above.

Space 6: Description of Derivative Work or Compilation

Leave Space 6 blank if the issue contains entirely new material appearing for the first time, such as a new issue of a periodical with all new articles. Complete Space 6 only if the issue being registered contains a substantial amount of material that was:

- previously published—for example, the *Nutne Reader* is a monthly magazine that republishes articles that previously appeared in small literary journals
- previously registered—for example, the *Nutne Reader* publishes an issue containing unpublished articles that had previously been registered, or
- in the public domain—for example, to celebrate its anniversary, the *Pacific Monthly* publishes a special issue containing, in addition to the normal articles, a facsimile of its first issue, published in 1851. The 1851 issue is in the public domain.

Derivative works and compilations are discussed in detail in Chapter 7, *Adaptions and Compilations*. Review that chapter if you're not sure whether the periodical is a derivative work, compilation or both.

Preexisting material (6a). If the serial is a derivative work, briefly describe in space 6a the preexisting material that has been recast, transformed or adapted in the issue being registered—for instance, "1990 published article by Julie Blake." Don't complete this space for compilations—for instance, a magazine consisting of unaltered, previously published articles.

Material added to this work (6b). For derivative works, briefly describe in Space 6b all of the new material contained in the serial issue—for example, "Editorial revisions," "Translation," "Additional material." If the periodical issue is a compilation, describe both the compilation itself and the material that has been compiled—for example, "Compilation of previously published journal articles."

Some serials are both derivative works and compilations. For example, an issue of the *Nutne Reader* described above consisting of previously published articles would be both a compilation and derivative work if *Nutne*'s editors made substantial editorial revisions—for instance, condensed the articles. In this event the publisher might state "Compilation of previously published articles and editorial revisions" when registering that issue of the journal.

Spaces 7–11

Follow the instructions for filling out these same spaces for Form TX in Section I, above.

e.   Application Fee

A $20 application fee must be submitted with Form SE.

L.   Registering a Group of Contributions to Periodicals: Form GR/CP

As discussed at the beginning of Section K, authors who retain some of the rights in their contributions to periodicals need to register them to obtain the benefits of registration for their work. This is so regardless of whether the publisher of the periodical registers the periodical issue as a whole on one of the SE series of forms.

EXAMINED BY	FORM SE
CHECKED BY	
☐ CORRESPONDENCE Yes	FOR COPYRIGHT OFFICE USE ONLY

DO NOT WRITE ABOVE THIS LINE. IF YOU NEED MORE SPACE, USE A SEPARATE CONTINUATION SHEET.

PREVIOUS REGISTRATION Has registration for this issue, or for an earlier version of this particular issue, already been made in the Copyright Office?

☐ Yes ☐ No If your answer is "Yes," why is another registration being sought? (Check appropriate box) ▼

a. ☐ This is the first published edition of an issue previously registered in unpublished form.

b. ☐ This is the first application submitted by this author as copyright claimant.

c. ☐ This is a changed version of this issue, as shown by space 6 on this application.

If your answer is "Yes," give: **Previous Registration Number** ▼   **Year of Registration** ▼

5

DERIVATIVE WORK OR COMPILATION Complete both space 6a and 6b for a derivative work; complete only 6b for a compilation.

a. Preexisting Material Identify any preexisting work or works that this work is based on or incorporates. ▼

b. Material Added to This Work Give a brief, general statement of the material that has been added to this work and in which copyright is claimed. ▼

6

See instructions before completing this space.

—space deleted—

7

REPRODUCTION FOR USE OF BLIND OR PHYSICALLY HANDICAPPED INDIVIDUALS A signature on this form at space 10 and a check in one of the boxes here in space 8 constitutes a non-exclusive grant of permission to the Library of Congress to reproduce and distribute solely for the blind and physically handicapped and under the conditions and limitations prescribed by the regulations of the Copyright Office: (1) copies of the work identified in space 1 of this application in Braille (or similar tactile symbols); or (2) phonorecords embodying a fixation of a reading of that work; or (3) both.

a ☐ Copies and Phonorecords   b ☐ Copies Only   c ☐ Phonorecords Only

8

See instructions.

DEPOSIT ACCOUNT If the registration fee is to be charged to a Deposit Account established in the Copyright Office, give name and number of Account.

Name ▼   **Account Number** ▼

9

CORRESPONDENCE Give name and address to which correspondence about this application should be sent.   Name/Address/Apt/City/State/ZIP ▼

Area Code and Telephone Number ▶

Be sure to give your daytime phone ◀ number

CERTIFICATION* I, the undersigned, hereby certify that I am the

Check only one ▶

☐ author
☐ other copyright claimant
☐ owner of exclusive right(s)
☐ authorized agent of _____

of the work identified in this application and that the statements made by me in this application are correct to the best of my knowledge.

Name of author or other copyright claimant, or owner of exclusive right(s) ▲

10

Typed or printed name and date ▼ If this application gives a date of publication in space 3, do not sign and submit it before that date.

_____ date ▶ _____

👉 Handwritten signature (X) ▼

MAIL CERTIFI-CATE TO

Certificate will be mailed in window envelope

Name ▼

Number/Street/Apartment Number ▼

City/State/ZIP ▼

YOU MUST:
• Complete all necessary spaces
• Sign your application in space 10

SEND ALL 3 ELEMENTS IN THE SAME PACKAGE:
1. Application form
2. Nonrefundable $20 filing fee in check or money order payable to *Register of Copyrights*
3. Deposit material

MAIL TO:
Register of Copyrights
Library of Congress
Washington, D.C. 20559-6000

The Copyright Office has the authority to adjust fees at 5-year intervals, based on changes in the Consumer Price Index. The next adjustment is due in 1996. Please contact the Copyright Office after July 1995 to determine the actual fee schedule.

11

*17 U.S.C. § 506(e): Any person who knowingly makes a false representation of a material fact in the application for copyright registration provided for by section 409, or in any written statement filed in connection with the application, shall be fined not more than $2,500.

April 1993—50,000   ☆U.S. GOVERNMENT PRINTING OFFICE: 1993-342-581/60,512

EXAMPLE: Arnie, a freelance writer, sells an article to *Newspeak Magazine*. He grants the magazine only the right to publish the article the first time in North America, and retains his other copyright rights. When the publisher of *Newspeak* registers the issue containing Arnie's article, the article will not be covered by the serial registration. Arnie must register the article himself for it to be fully protected.

You can register each article you write individually on Form TX; this form is discussed in Section I, above. However, at $20 per registration, individually registering a substantial number of articles or other periodical contributions each year can be very expensive.

Fortunately, a writer may register all of the articles he or she writes in any 12-month period as a group on one application for one $20 application fee.

1. Who Qualifies for Group Registration

For works published after March 1, 1989, a single copyright registration for a group of works can be made only if:

- all of the works are by the same author who is an individual—that is, not a work made for hire (defined in Section D, above)—or all the works are by the same coauthors
- all of the works were first published as individual contributions to periodicals (including newspapers, magazines, newsletters and journals) within any single 12-month period (not necessarily a calendar year), and
- all of the works have the same copyright claimant (see Section I, above).

WORKS PUBLISHED BEFORE MARCH 1, 1989

It's never too late to register your work. However, if any of the works to be registered were published prior to March 1, 1989, group registration is available only if each contribution as first published contained a separate copyright notice and the name of the copyright owner was exactly the same in each notice.

EXAMPLE 1: Jean published 12 short stories in various literary journals from July 1986 to 1987. She retained the copyright for all the stories. Each story contained a copyright notice listing "Jean Davis" as the copyright owner. Jean may register all twelve stories as a group at one time.

EXAMPLE 2: Assume that a copyright notice appeared on only eight of Jean's short stories. She could register those eight stories as a group but not the four stories that did not have a copyright notice. For those remaining stories, Jean would have to use four Forms TX.

2. How to Apply for Group Registration

To apply for group registration you must complete two forms: the appropriate basic application form (Form TX or Form PA), and Form GR/CP. However, you will only be required to pay a single registration fee.

a. Filling out Form TX or Form PA

You'll be using Form TX unless you're registering a group of previously published plays, screenplays, song lyrics or other dramatic works. Fill out the appropriate form following the instructions in Section I and J, above, with the following exceptions:

Space 1 (Title of this work):
State "See Form GR/CP, attached." Leave the rest of Space 1 blank.

Space 3:
Give the year of creation of the last contribution you completed. Leave blank the date and nation of first publication.

You will find sample filled-out forms preceding the blank copyright forms in the appendix.

b. How To complete Form GR/CP

Form GR/CP gives the Copyright Office some basic information about each individual article or other contribution being registered.

Part A
Identification of basic application. Check the box showing which basic application form you are using, either Form TX or Form PA.

Identification of author and claimant. Give the name of the author and the copyright claimant of all the contributions you're registering. These names should be the same as the names given in Spaces 2 and 4 of your basic application and must be the same for all the contributions being registered.

Part B
The Copyright Office prefers that you list the contributions in the order of their publication, giving the earliest first. You should also number each space consecutively in the box provided. Form GR/CP has space for 19 contributions. If you need to register more than that number, use an additional Form GR/CP.

For each article or other contribution being registered, provide the following:

Title of contribution. If the article contained a title or identifying phrase, use it. Otherwise, make up a title that identifies the particular contribution and distinguishes it from the other contributions you're registering.

Title of periodical and identifying information. Fill in the complete name of the periodical in which the article was first published. Give the volume and issue number (if any) and the issue date. Also, list the pages in the periodical issue on which the articles appeared.

Date and nation of first publication. Fill in the date and country in which the periodical issue that the article or other contribution appeared in was first published.

3. Effect of Group Registration

All of your articles or other contributions are protected by registration on the date the Copyright Office receives your application. If any of the registered articles are copied after that date, you are entitled to all the benefits of timely copyright registration (that is, statutory damages and attorney fees).

ADJUNCT APPLICATION
for
Copyright Registration for a
Group of Contributions to Periodicals

- Use this adjunct form only if your are making a single registration for a group of contributions to periodicals, and you are also filing a basic application on Form TX, Form PA, or Form VA. Follow the instructions, attached.
- Number each line in Part B consecutively. Use additional Forms GR/CP if you need more space.
- Submit this adjunct form with the basic application form. Clip (do not tape or staple) and fold all sheets together before submitting them.

⊘ **FORM GR/CP**

UNITED STATES COPYRIGHT OFFICE

REGISTRATION NUMBER

TX   PA   VA

EFFECTIVE DATE OF REGISTRATION

....
(Month)   (Day)   (Year)

FORM GR/CP RECEIVED

Page _____ of _____ pages

DO NOT WRITE ABOVE THIS LINE. FOR COPYRIGHT OFFICE USE ONLY

Ⓐ
Identification of Application

IDENTIFICATION OF BASIC APPLICATION:
- This application for copyright registration for a group of contributions to periodicals is submitted as an adjunct to an application filed on: (Check which)

☐Form TX   ☐Form PA   ☐Form VA

IDENTIFICATION OF AUTHOR AND CLAIMANT: (Give the name of the author and the name of the copyright claimant in all of the contributions listed in Part B of this form. The names should be the same as the names given in spaces 2 and 4 of the basic application.)

Name of Author: ....

Name of Copyright Claimant: ....

Ⓑ
Registration For Group of Contributions

COPYRIGHT REGISTRATION FOR A GROUP OF CONTRIBUTIONS TO PERIODICALS: (To make a single registration for a group of works by the same individual author, all first published as contributions to periodicals within a 12-month period (see instructions), give full information about each contribution. If more space is needed, use additional Forms GR/CP.)

☐ Title of Contribution: .... Title of Periodical: .... Vol..... No..... Issue Date.......... Pages.......... Date of First Publication:.......... (Month) (Day) (Year) Nation of First Publication.......... (Country)

☐ Title of Contribution: .... Title of Periodical: .... Vol..... No..... Issue Date.......... Pages.......... Date of First Publication:.......... (Month) (Day) (Year) Nation of First Publication.......... (Country)

☐ Title of Contribution: .... Title of Periodical: .... Vol..... No..... Issue Date.......... Pages.......... Date of First Publication:.......... (Month) (Day) (Year) Nation of First Publication.......... (Country)

☐ Title of Contribution: .... Title of Periodical: .... Vol..... No..... Issue Date.......... Pages.......... Date of First Publication:.......... (Month) (Day) (Year) Nation of First Publication.......... (Country)

☐ Title of Contribution: .... Title of Periodical: .... Vol..... No..... Issue Date.......... Pages.......... Date of First Publication:.......... (Month) (Day) (Year) Nation of First Publication.......... (Country)

☐ Title of Contribution: .... Title of Periodical: .... Vol..... No..... Issue Date.......... Pages.......... Date of First Publication:.......... (Month) (Day) (Year) Nation of First Publication.......... (Country)

☐ Title of Contribution: .... Title of Periodical: .... Vol..... No..... Issue Date.......... Pages.......... Date of First Publication:.......... (Month) (Day) (Year) Nation of First Publication.......... (Country)

However, if any of the contributions were copied before the registration date, you will not be entitled to statutory damages and attorney fees unless the registration was made within three months after the first publication of the contribution. (If you don't understand why, see Section B, above.) This is not nearly as confusing as it sounds. Consider these examples:

EXAMPLE 1: Percy used the group registration procedure to register ten of his published articles. The Copyright Office received Percy's application on March 15, 1992. One of Percy's articles was copied by Bob after March 15. If Percy sues Bob, he will be entitled to statutory damages and attorney fees.

EXAMPLE 2: Assume instead that Bob copied two of Percy's articles before Percy filed his group registration application on March 15. Article A was published on January 15, Article B was published in November of the preceding year. Percy is entitled to statutory damages and attorney fees for the infringement of Article A, but not for Article B. Reason: Article A was registered within three months after publication, but Article B was not.

Copyright tip

Example 2 illustrates the one drawback of group registration: If you wait more than three months after an article is published so that you can register it together with other articles for one fee, you will lose the benefits of timely registration of that article for any infringement occurring before the Copyright Office receives your application. If you feel that an article or other periodical contribution is extremely valuable, make sure that it is registered within three months of publication, even if you have to register it by itself. If you publish a large number of articles every year, you should make a group registration every three months.

M. Satisfying Copyright Office Deposit Requirements

You must submit (deposit) one or two copies of the work being registered with your application. The Copyright Office reviews your deposit to make sure that the work is copyrightable and is accurately described on your application form. Your registration only covers the material that you deposit with the Copyright Office—except where a special deposit of less than the entire work is made, such as for a multivolume encyclopedia or automated database.

1. Unpublished Works

If you're registering an unpublished work, your application must be accompanied by *one complete copy* of the work—that is, the copy must contain all the material you wish to register.

2. Published Works

Subject to the important exceptions discussed in Section 2.d, below, *two* complete copies of a published work must be deposited. This sounds quite simple, but there are some additional rules and limitations that we also discuss below.

a. Works published in two or more editions

Sometimes the same work is published simultaneously in two or more editions—for instance, in a hardcover and paperback edition, or a trade edition and a more expensively printed and bound collector's edition. Where this occurs, you must deposit the best edition of the work. The best edition is the work of the highest quality, in terms of printing and binding—for example, you would deposit a hardcover edition rather than the paperback version of a work.

If there are two hardcover versions, you would deposit the edition that is the best bound, largest in size or printed on the best paper. It's up to you to decide which edition is the best.

EXAMPLE 1: Acme Publishing Co. simultaneously publishes a novel in both paperback and hardback editions. Both editions are identical in content. The hardback is the best edition that should be deposited when the novel is registered.

EXAMPLE 2: Philip self-publishes a treatise on Byzantine art. Half the copies were printed on ordinary paper and half on archival quality paper. Philip should deposit a copy of his treatise printed on the archival quality paper; it is the "best edition."

Copyright tip

The Copyright Office publishes a circular describing in detail all the criteria used to determine what constitutes the best edition of a work. If you're in the publishing business, you may find it useful. Call or write the Copyright Office and ask for Circular R7b.

You only need to deposit the "best edition" of the work in existence at the time you register. This means if a better edition is published after you have already registered, you do not need to deposit it with the Copyright Office.

EXAMPLE: Rachel photocopies and distributes 500 copies of a collection of her poetry. She deposits two complete copies when she registers the work. To her surprise, all 500 copies are sold within a year. She decides to self-publish another edition, but this time she has the book professionally typeset and printed by offset lithography. Although the second edition of the work is of much better print quality than the first,

Rachel need not deposit it with the Copyright Office since it did not exist when she registered the work.

Make sure, however, that each of the editions has substantially the same content. If the second edition contains enough new material to be considered a new version, it must be registered separately to protect the new material. (See the discussion in Section F, above.)

b. Periodical issues

How many copies of a periodical issue need to be deposited depends on which registration form is used:

- Form SE/Group: deposit one copy of *each issue*
- Short Form SE: deposit one copy of the individual periodical
- Form SE: deposit *two copies* of the periodical issue
- Form G/DN: deposit one calendar month of daily newspaper issues on positive 35mm silver-halide microfilm

c. Registering individual contributions to periodicals and other collective works

If you are registering an individual contribution to a collective work such as a magazine or newspaper article or a contribution to an anthology, you must register one complete copy of the best edition of the entire collective work—that is, the entire magazine or anthology. Luckily, there is an exception for newspapers: instead of depositing the entire newspaper you only need to deposit the section of the paper in which your article appeared. (Imagine depositing a copy of the entire Sunday *New York Times*!)

This rule also applies to registration of a group of individual periodical contributions using Form

CR/GP—for instance, if you are registering 12 articles that appeared in 12 different journals you must deposit one complete copy of *each* journal.

d. When only one copy need be deposited

The Copyright Office permits the deposit of one, rather than two, copies of the following types of published works:

- multimedia works, see Chapter 14, *Electronic Publishing*, for a detailed discussion
- works first published outside the United States (only one copy of the first foreign edition need be deposited; it need not be the best edition)
- advertising materials (you only need to send one copy of the page in which an advertisement appeared in a periodical, not the entire periodical issue)
- lectures, sermons, speeches and addresses published separately (that is, not as part of a collection), and
- tests and test answers published separately from each other.

3. Depositing Identifying Material Instead of Copies

Depositing two complete copies of some works could prove burdensome both for the applicant and the Copyright Office. For example, you would not wish to mail, and the Copyright Office would not want to store, a 30-volume encyclopedia. Indeed, the Copyright Office will not accept any item that exceeds 96 inches in any dimension.

If your work exceeds 96 inches, you'll have to deposit identifying material rather than the entire work. For example, instead of depositing every volume of an encyclopedia that takes up ten feet of shelf-space, you might be able to submit photos of every volume. To prepare identifying material, first call the Copyright Office at 202-707-3000, describe your work and find out what type of identifying material is acceptable.

4. Library of Congress Deposit Requirements

The Library of Congress has its own deposit requirements for published works, which are separate from those of the Copyright Office. However, the library's deposit requirements are deemed satisfied when a work is registered and a deposit made with the Copyright Office. In other words, you don't have to worry about the Library of Congress if you register your work with the Copyright Office. The one exception to this rule is deposits for machine-readable works such as automated databases. The library may demand deposit of the machine-readable copies distributed after registration has been made.

If you don't register your published work with the Copyright Office, you are supposed to deposit two copies with the Library of Congress. If you don't, the library is entitled to demand that you do so and you are subject to monetary penalties if you do not comply. However, in practice this rarely happens. Contrary to popular belief, the Library of Congress does not collect copies of everything published in the United States.

N. Mailing Your Application to the Copyright Office

By now you have completed your application form and have your deposit ready to go. Make a photocopy of your application form and retain it in your records along with an exact copy of your deposit.

1. Application fee

You must submit a check or money order for the application fee payable to the Register of Copyrights. The fee is nonrefundable; it will not be returned if your application is rejected. Clip your check or money order to the application. To review, the fees are:

Form TX $20
Form PA $20
Form SE $20
Form GR/CP $20
Short Form SE $10
Form SE/Group .... $10 per issue being registered
Form G/DN $40

Copyright tip
Application fees are scheduled to rise in 1996 so call the Copyright Office at 202-707-3000 to double-check the current fees before mailing your application. Also, read the *Nolo News* for updates on fee changes. (See back of this book for information about the *Nolo News*).

2. When to Mail Your Application

If you're registering a published work, make sure that your application is not received by the Copyright Office until after the publication date listed in Space 3 of your application (see Section I, above). Reason: A published work cannot be registered prior to the date of publication.

3. Mail a Single Package to the Copyright Office

All you need to do now is put your application, deposit and check or money order for the appropriate application fee in a *single package* and mail them to:

> Register of Copyrights
> Copyright Office
> Library of Congress
> Washington, DC 20559

Be absolutely sure to mail the application, deposit and fee together in one package. If you don't, all the packages you sent will be returned by the Copyright Office. (But if you send a deposit of a published work separately, the Copyright Office will turn it over to the Library of Congress rather than return it to you, so you'll get the application and fee back, but not the deposit.)

Copyright tip
You can save on postage by mailing your deposit at the fourth-class book rate and your application form first class. This can be done even though the application and deposit are in the same package. Check with your post office for details. However, if you're getting near the end of your 90-day period to timely register a published work, make sure the Copyright Office will receive the package in time, even if you have to send the package by express mail.

4. Your Registration Is Effective When the Application Is Received

Your registration is effective on the date the Copyright Office receives all three elements: application, deposit and application fee in proper form. This is so regardless of how long it takes the Copyright Office to process the application and send you your certificate of registration. This means you don't need to worry about not being able to obtain statutory damages or attorney fees from anyone who copies your work while your application is being processed. (Remember, you can obtain such fees and damages only if the work was registered before the infringement occurred or within three months of publication; see Section B.)

EXAMPLE: Helen's cookbook is published on January 1. She sends her registration package to the Copyright Office on January 31. All the items in her package are in proper form—that is, the application form is filled out correctly and the package contains the correct deposit and $20 application fee. The Copyright Office receives her registration package on March 15. Helen receives her certificate of registration on June 15. She later discovers that Jeremy copied her work in January. If Helen sues Jeremy for copyright infringement, she will be entitled to obtain attorney fees and statutory damages. Reason: Her application was effective on the date it was received by the Copyright Office, March 15, which was within three months of publication.

HOW TO MAKE SURE THE COPYRIGHT OFFICE RECEIVED YOUR APPLICATION

The Copyright Office will not send you an acknowledgment that they received your application. The only way to know for sure that they got it is to send the application by certified or registered mail, return receipt requested. Allow three weeks for the receipt to be returned by the Post Office. The receipt will show exactly when the Copyright Office received the application.

O. Expedited Registration

A work must be registered before a copyright infringement suit may be filed (see Section B, above). You'll need to have a certified copy of your registration certificate to show the court. If you need to bring an infringement suit right away but haven't registered yet, you may request that your application be given special handling by the Copyright Office. Special handling applications are processed in five to ten days, rather than the normal four to six weeks or more.

Special handling is available only if needed for copyright litigation, to meet a contractual or publishing deadline or for some other urgent need. Special handling is not available for group registration of magazines or other periodicals on Form SE/Group—that is, you must register a periodical issue individually on Form SE to obtain special handling.

You must pay an additional $200 fee for special handling. You may complete the optional form reproduced in the tear-out appendix at the end of this book or send a letter along with your application containing the same information: why there is an urgent need for special handling; if special handling is needed for litigation; whether the case has been filed already or is pending; who the parties to the litigation are or will be; in what court the action has been or will be filed; and certification that your statements are true.

You'll need a certified copy of your registration certificate to submit to the court, so request that the Copyright Office provide you with one. There is an additional $8 fee for certified copies.

Mail the special handling form or letter, your application and deposit, and a check or money order payable to the Register of Copyrights for $228 (the $20 application fee, plus the $200 special handling fee, plus the $8 certification fee) all in one package to:

Library of Congress
Department 100
Washington, DC 20540

Write the words "Special Handling" on the outside of the envelope. But don't put the words "Copyright Office" on the envelope.

P. Dealing With the Copyright Office

The Copyright Office has an enormous workload (they handle over 700,000 applications per year) so it can take anywhere from four weeks to three months (or longer) for your application to be processed. Be patient and remember that the registration is effective on the date it is received (assuming the forms were filled out properly), not the date you actually receive your registration certificate.

The Copyright Office will eventually respond to your application in one of three ways:

- If your application is acceptable, the Copyright Office will send you a registration certificate, which is merely a copy of your application with the official Copyright Office seal, registration date and number stamped on it. Be sure to retain it for your records.
- If your application contained errors or omissions the Copyright Office believes are correctable, a copyright examiner may phone you for further information. Or he may return the application and/or deposit with a letter explaining what corrections to make.
- If the Copyright Office determines that your work cannot be registered, it will send you a letter explaining why. Neither your deposit nor fee will be returned.

1. If You Don't Hear From the Copyright Office

If you haven't heard anything from the Copyright Office 120 days after your application should have been received, write them and find out what went wrong (they may have lost the application, it may have never been received or they may be very far behind in their work). In your letter identify yourself and the copyright owner, give the date of your application and the form you used, describe the work briefly and the name of the author. If the Copyright Office cashed your check, you'll know that they did receive the application. Include a copy of the cancelled check with your letter. It will contain a number that will help the Copyright Office trace your application.

Copyright tip
You'll have to pay the Copyright Office a fee to find out about the status of your application fewer than 16 weeks after the Copyright Office received it. Call the Copyright Office at 202-707-3000 to ask about this.

2. Extent of Copyright Examiner's Review of Your Application

The Copyright Examiner will examine your deposit to see whether it constitutes copyrightable subject matter and review your application to determine whether the other legal and formal requirements for registration have been met.

a. The rule of doubt

As a matter of policy, the Copyright Office will usually register a work even if it has a reasonable doubt as to whether the work is copyrightable or the other requirements have been met. This is called the rule of doubt. The Copyright Office takes the view that determining a copyright's validity in such cases is a task for the courts. For example, the office would ordinarily register a new edition of a previously registered work under the rule of doubt, even though it had a reasonable doubt whether the edition contained enough new expression to be registrable. When registration is made under the rule of doubt, the Copyright Office will ordinarily send the applicant a letter cautioning that the claim may not be valid and stating the reason.

b. Clearly unregistrable material

The Copyright Office will refuse to register a work that is without doubt unprotectible. For example, the Copyright Office would not register a title, since titles are not copyrightable, nor would a work clearly in the public domain be registered (for instance, the King James version of the Bible) unless the applicant added protectible material to it.

c. Presence of errors or omissions

The Copyright Office will not issue a certificate if the application contains errors or omissions or is internally inconsistent or ambiguous. Here are some of the more common errors:
- failure to sign the application
- failure to pay the application fee
- failure to provide the required number of deposit copies
- failure to adequately describe nature of authorship
- deposit does not match description of nature of authorship
- nature of authorship is described by a title or identifying phrase
- failure to provide publication date
- the work made for hire box is checked, but the employer is not listed as the copyright claimant

- failure to state how ownership was transferred where copyright claimant is not the same as the author
- failure to identify adequately the material added to a new version or derivative work (Space 6b)
- date application is signed is prior to publication date in application.

The Copyright Office will ordinarily call you or send a letter asking you to fix technical errors such as these. Reread our discussion about how to complete the application forms to help you make your corrections. Send your corrected application and/or new deposit back to the Copyright Office in one package.

Be sure you respond within 120 days to any correspondence from the Copyright Office concerning your application. Otherwise, your file will be closed, your fee will not be returned to you, and you'll have to reapply by sending in a new application, deposit and fee.

3. Review of Copyright Office's Refusal to Register Application

If you think the Copyright Examiner has wrongfully refused to register your work, you may submit a written objection to the refusal and request that the Copyright Office reconsider its action. If the claim is refused after reconsideration, the head of the appropriate Examining Division section will send you written notice of the reasons for the refusal. After this, you may again request reconsideration. If the claim is refused for a third time, the Chief of the Examining Division will notify you in writing of the reasons. The Division Chief's decision constitutes the Copyright Office's final action. You may then bring a legal action to have a court review the Copyright Office's decision. In addition, you can bring a copyright infringement action notwithstanding the Copyright Office's refusal to register your work. You'll need to see a lawyer about this. (See Chapter 14, *Help Beyond This Book*.)

Q. Full Term Retention of Deposits and Other Ways to Preserve Deposits

Whether or not your application is accepted, your deposit becomes the property of the U.S. government and will never be returned to you. The Library of Congress may add the deposit to its own collection. If the Library chooses not to do so (which is usually the case), and your application is accepted, the Copyright Office will retain the deposit in its own storage facilities for five years. Due to a lack of storage space, the Copyright Office normally destroys all deposits of published works after five years. However, the Copyright Office may not destroy a deposit of an unpublished work without first making a copy of it.

1. Full Term Retention of Deposits

People sued for copyright infringement have been known to attempt to turn the tables on their accusers and claim that the accusers actually copied from them or others. Such accusations are easily disproved if the work you claim was infringed upon was deposited with the Copyright Office before the infringing work or other work the infringer claims you copied was written and/or published. In this event, you just need to submit to the court a certified copy of the deposit you made with the Copyright Office.

The Copyright Office will provide certified copies of deposits of registered works that are involved in litigation. But, of course, such copies can only be made if the Copyright Office still has the deposit. So you might be in for trouble if the infringement litigation takes place more than five years after the work was registered and the deposit has been destroyed by the Copyright Office.

If you want to protect against this possibility, you may request full term retention of your deposit. Full term retention means that the Copyright Office will retain one copy of your deposit for 75 years from the date of publication. You must request full term retention in writing and pay a $135 fee. Only the person who made the deposit, copyright owner or an authorized representative may make the request. You can make this request when you register the work or any time thereafter. There is no form for this purpose. Send a letter to the Chief, Information and Reference Division, Copyright Office, Library of Congress, Washington, DC 20559, stating that you desire full term retention of your deposit. Identify the deposit by title, author and registration number. If you request full term retention of your deposit when you make your initial registration, you must send the Copyright Office an additional copy of the deposit—that is, three copies of published works and two copies of unpublished works.

Copyright tip

There is no reason to go to the trouble and expense of having the Copyright Office retain your deposit for 75 years unless the work is very valuable and you think there is a good possibility you could end up in copyright litigation more than five years after you register it—that is, after the Copyright Office would normally destroy your deposit. Keep in mind, however, that most infringements occur relatively soon after publication. Since you can make your request for full term retention at any time, wait until four or four-and-one-half years after registration before making this decision. Things may look very different by then.

2. Mailing Deposit to Yourself

As an alternative to paying the Copyright Office for full term retention, you can mail copies of your deposit to yourself (preferably by certified mail). This way, if you later become involved in infringement litigation, you can present the package in court to help prove that your work existed in a certain form as of the date of the mailing. You must not unseal or otherwise tamper with the envelope. However, this method is not foolproof because a judge or jury might not believe that you did not tamper with the envelope (this actually happened in one case).

3. Depositing Screenplays With the Writers Guild of America

For screenplays and similar works, registration and deposit with the Writers Guild of America is actually better than full term retention by the Copyright Office. The Writers Guild is the scriptwriters' union. It represents writers primarily for the purpose of collective bargaining in the motion picture, television and radio industries. The Guild establishes guidelines regarding payment for scripts and stories and giving screen credit to authors. The Guild does not obtain employment for writers, or accept or handle material for submission to production companies. Scripts, treatments, etc., must be submitted directly to production companies or through an agent.

To help writers establish the completion date and identity of works written for the entertainment industry, the Writers Guild registers scripts deposited by writers and keeps them on file. If a dispute arises as to the authorship of the material, the Guild deposit constitutes proof that the material existed in a certain form as of the date of the deposit. You need not be a member of the Writers Guild to deposit a script with the guild (indeed, you can't join until you have sold a script or story idea or performed other writing assignments).

Copyright tip

Depositing a copy of your script with the Writers Guild is not a substitute for registration with the Copyright Office. However, the deposit will help you prove that you wrote the material deposited and when you wrote it if an authorship dispute later arises (such disputes are common in Hollywood). Moreover, many producers will not even read a script unless it has been registered with the Writers Guild.

a.   What can be deposited

The Writers Guild will accept scripts specifically intended for radio, television or theatrical motion pictures. It will also accept television series formats, step outlines and storylines. Each property must be registered separately. However, three episodes, skits or sketches for an existing television series may be deposited as a single registration.

b.   Deposit procedure

One 8½-inch by 11-inch unbound copy must be sent to the Writers Guild along with a $20 fee for non-Guild members or a $10 fee for members. Note the specific field of writing and the proper writing credits on the title page. Register under your full legal name. After receipt by the Guild, the material is sealed in a Guild registration envelope, timed, dated and assigned a registration number. A receipt is returned to the sender indicating the registration number. Place this number on your script or treatment before submitting it to a producer.

If you live west of the Mississippi River, send your deposit to: Writers Guild of America, West, Inc.,

8955 Beverly Blvd., West Hollywood, CA 90048-2541; phone 310-205-2500. If you live east of the Mississippi, send your deposit to: Writers Guild of America, East, Inc., 555 West 57th St., New York, NY 10019; phone 212-767-7800.

c.   Duration of deposit

The Guild retains the deposit for five years. You may renew the registration for an additional five years at the conclusion of the term. The Guild will return a deposit upon written request signed by the author.

R. Correcting Errors After Registration Is Completed

After registration is completed, you may later have reason to wish to correct, update or augment your registration. This is accomplished by filing an application for supplemental registration with the Copyright Office. Supplemental registration is discussed in detail in Chapter 5, *Correcting or Changing Copyright Notice or Registration*.

CHAPTER

5

Correcting or Changing Copyright Notice or Registration

Chapters 3 and 4 covered copyright notice re–quirements and registration with the Copyright Office, respectively. This chapter shows you how to cope with errors, omissions or factual changes affecting your notice or registration.

PART I: DEALING WITH ERRORS OR OMISSIONS IN COPYRIGHT NOTICE

Publishing a work without a valid copyright notice may make it more difficult to win an infringement suit or even result in loss of copyright protection; it all depends on when the publication occurred.

A. Works Published After March 1, 1989

As discussed in Chapter 3, a copyright notice is not required on any copies of a work published on or after March 1, 1989. This is so regardless of whether other copies of the same work were previously published before that date. (In this chapter, we'll refer to such copies as "Berne era" copies.) However, if a valid notice is not provided, an infringer may be able to claim innocence and escape paying you substantial damages. For this reason, if you discover that a copyright notice was omitted from your published work, make sure that one is included on all new copies that are printed. You may also wish to add notices to those copies that have already been distributed.

Chapter 3 noted that a valid copyright notice contains three elements: (1) the copyright symbol; (2) the publication date; and (3) the copyright owner's name. Since Berne era works need not have a copyright notice, errors or partial omissions in these elements will not affect the copyright's validity. But if the notice itself is deficient in one or more of these elements, a judge might allow an infringer to claim

innocence. (See discussion in Chapter, Section .C.) For this reason it is advisable for the copyright owner to make sure that errors in the notice are corrected in any subsequent printings of the work. Refer to Section B.2 below for a detailed discussion of the types of errors that invalidate a copyright notice.

B. Copies Published Between January 1, 1978 and February 28, 1989

The consequences of omission of, or errors in, the copyright notice in copies of works published between January 1, 1978 and February 28, 1989 (we'll refer to these as "decennial" copies) are much more serious than those for Berne era copies.

1. Omission of Notice Invalidates Copyright

Decennial copies must contain a valid copyright notice to be protected by copyright. However, the copyright owner will not lose her exclusive rights if any one of the following exceptions applies:

a. Exception #1: Only small number of copies distributed

Copyright protection will not be lost if the notice was omitted from no more than a "relatively small" number of copies distributed to the public. The "relatively small" criteria is deliberately vague, and left for the courts to decide on a case-by-case basis. Omission of notice from one percent or fewer of the published copies will probably satisfy the criteria. Omission of notice from more than one percent may or may not be too much, depending on the circumstances.

It is not legally necessary to cure the omission of copyright notices from a small number of copies.

However, since it is difficult to know what constitutes a small number, it is advisable to take the same corrective measures that must be employed when it is clear that more than a relatively small number of copies lack notice, as in Exception #2 below.

b.   Exception #2: Corrective measures taken to cure omission within 5 years of publication

Even if more than a small number of copies lacked a valid copyright notice, the copyright was not invalidated if, within five years after publication, the copyright owner registered the work with the Copyright Office and made a reasonable effort to add a valid notice to all copies of the work distributed after the omission was discovered.

EXAMPLE: Sam self-published a volume of poetry in 1987. However, Sam didn't know anything about copyright so he failed to register the program with the Copyright Office or include a copyright notice. In 1988, he found out about his error and decided to correct it in order to "rescue" his copyright. He registered the book with the Copyright Office and made a reasonable effort to add a notice to all copies of the book distributed after he found out about his error. By doing so, he saved his copyright in the book from entering the public domain.

Unfortunately, by the time you're reading this book it is too late for any copyright owner to rescue her copyright by doing what Sam did in the example above. This is because such corrective efforts had to be made within five years after the work was published prior to March 1, 1989. Thus, a work published on February 28, 1989 without notice entered the public domain unless corrective action was taken by February 28, 1994. Works published before February 28, 1989 entered the public domain earlier.

c.   Exception #3: Omission of notice violates written agreement

Finally, copyright protection will not be lost if the copyright owner licensed or otherwise authorized another party—for instance, a publisher—to handle her work, had a written agreement with this party requiring them to place a notice on the material when it was published, and the other party failed to do so.

Although copyright protection is not lost under these circumstances, the copyright owner cannot collect any damages from innocent infringers—that is, people who infringed the owner's copyright without knowing it due to the lack of notice. However, the copyright owner is entitled to sue the party who failed to provide the notice for any damages caused by the lack of notice. To prevent infringement from occurring in the future, the copyright owner should see to it that appropriate corrective measures are taken (Section B.3 below).

EXAMPLE: In 1987, Mavis signed a contract with Hackneyed Publications to publish her book. The contract contained a clause requiring Hackneyed to include a proper copyright notice on the book when it was published. Somehow, the notice was left off over 90% of the copies Hackneyed published in 1988. Marty copied several chapters from the book in the good faith belief that it was not copyrighted due to the lack of a copyright notice. Mavis's copyright is not invalidated due to the omission, but she won't be able to collect damages from Marty. Mavis should get her publisher to add a notice to all new copies of her book and attempt to provide proper notice to those who have purchased copies lacking notice. Mavis should also consider suing Hackneyed for the damages she otherwise could have gotten from Marty.

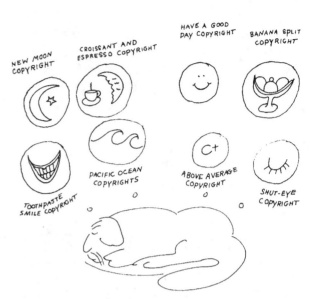

ANOTHER "NOT-GETTING-IT-RIGHT-COPYRIGHT-FRIGHT" NIGHT.

2. Types of Errors or Omissions That Invalidate a Copyright Notice

The following errors or omissions result in invalidation of the notice on decennial (and Berne era) copies. A copy with an invalid notice is treated just the same as if it has no notice at all. The corrective measures discussed in Section B.3 below need to be taken as soon as possible after these errors are discovered.

a. Omitting a required element

A copyright notice that omits any of the three required elements is invalid. This means that a notice is invalid if it:

- contains neither the copyright symbol "©," nor the words "Copyright" or "Copr."
- lacks the copyright owner's name, unless the publisher's name appears as the result of a contractual assignment by the owner (see discussion in Chapter 3, *Copyright Notice)*, or
- leaves off the year of publication.

b. Error in copyright symbol

If a copyright symbol is included in the notice but is not in the proper form, the notice will be treated as if it lacked the symbol entirely and will be invalid. This could occur, for example, if the letter "c" was not completely surrounded by a circle—for example, "(c)" was used instead of "©." However, if a notice contains both the © symbol and the word "Copyright" or "Copr.," and only one is wrong, the notice is valid in the United States.

> **EXAMPLE:** This notice would be valid in the U.S.: "(c) Copyright 1992 Carol Careless." Although, the "(c)" symbol is improper, the word "Copyright" saves the notice from being invalid. But some foreign countries do not accept use of the word "copyright" in notices, so the notice might be found invalid outside the U.S.

c. Error in publication year

A decennial copy containing a copyright notice with a publication date more than one year in the future—

that is, more than one year after the actual date of publication—is treated as if it had no notice at all. This is so even if only a small number of copies were distributed with the defective notice. The corrective measures discussed below must be taken as soon as possible after the error is discovered.

> **EXAMPLE:** Isaac's book was first published in 1987, but the copyright notice lists 1989 as the publication date. The notice is invalid.

On the other hand, where the publication date is for any year *prior* to the actual publication date, the notice's validity is not affected. However, the year stated in the notice becomes the official legal publication date for copyright duration purposes; see Chapter 10, *Copyright Duration.*

> **EXAMPLE:** Abraham's book was first published in 1978, but the copyright notice lists 1976 as the publication date. The notice is valid, but 1976 is now considered the date of publication for purposes of computing the duration of Abraham's copyright.

This rule differs for Berne era copies. A copyright notice on a Berne era copy will be invalid if the wrong year of publication is given, whether earlier or later.

> **EXAMPLE:** Sally's book was published in 1990, but her notice states 1991 as the publication date. The notice is invalid. Such errors should be corrected in later printings.

d. Errors in name

Major errors in the name in a copyright notice—using the wrong name for example—will invalidate the notice, but the validity and ownership of the copyright in a decennial copy itself is not affected (17 U.S.C. 406(a)). Minor spelling or other errors in a name in a notice do not affect the copyright's validity. Such errors are no cause for concern so long as the name is sufficient to identify the copyright owner.

> **EXAMPLE:** Misspelling John Smith's name as "John Smythe" in a copyright notice would not affect the copyright's validity or permit an infringer to claim he was misled by the notice. Errors such as these should be corrected in subsequent printings, but there is no need to take any other corrective measures.

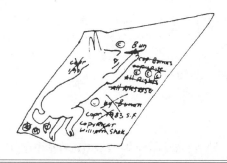

EFFECT OF ERRORS OR OMISSIONS IN COPYRIGHT NOTICE ON COPIES PUBLISHED BEFORE 1978

Subject to one very limited exception, any work published before January 1, 1978, without a valid copyright notice has entered the public domain—it is not protected by copyright. Anyone is free to use such a work in any way he wishes—for example, a publisher could publish it without paying the author a royalty. The only exception to this rule is where the copyright owner failed to provide notices on a *very few* copies by accident or mistake. In this event, the copyright owner may be allowed to enforce his copyright rights against an infringer who had actual notice of the copyright. However, this exception has rarely been successfully invoked. If you own the copyright to a work published without a notice before 1978, see a copyright lawyer to determine whether this exception might apply.

PART II: DEALING WITH ERRORS OR CHANGES AFFECTING COPYRIGHT REGISTRATION: SUPPLEMENTAL REGISTRATION

As discussed in Chapter 4, the same published work normally can only be registered once with the Copyright Office. However, a second supplemental registration may be necessary to augment your original basic registration if you later discover that you forgot something important, supplied the Copyright Office with the wrong information or if important facts have changed. A special form, Form CA, is used for this purpose. Part II of this chapter shows you when a supplemental registration is appropriate and how to accomplish it.

A. Why a Supplemental Registration Should Be Filed (When Appropriate)

If you ever become involved in copyright litigation, your registration certificate (which is simply a copy of your basic registration application form stamped and returned to you by the Copyright Office) will be submitted into evidence to prove the existence of your copyright. It could prove embarrassing, and possibly harmful to your case, if the certificate is found to contain substantial errors, is unclear or ambiguous, or if important facts have changed since you registered. For this reason, you should file a supplemental registration to correct significant errors in your certificate or to reflect important factual changes.

Also, remember that your registration is a public record. By keeping your registration accurate and up-to-date, you will make it easier for those searching the Copyright Office records to discover your work and locate you. This may result in new marketing opportunities and/or help to prevent an infringement.

1. Corrections

A supplemental registration should be filed to correct *significant* errors that occurred at the time the basic registration was made, and that were overlooked by the Copyright Office. This includes:

- identifying someone incorrectly as the author or copyright claimant of the work
- registering an unpublished work as published, or
- inaccurately stating the extent of the copyright claim.

Errors in these important facts could cast doubt upon the validity and/or duration of your copyright and will needlessly confuse and complicate copyright litigation. They will also confuse anyone searching the Copyright Office records. Correct them as soon as your discover them.

SUPPLEMENTAL REGISTRATION NOT NEEDED TO CORRECT OBVIOUS ERRORS THE COPYRIGHT OFFICE SHOULD HAVE CAUGHT

It is not necessary to file a formal supplemental registration to correct obvious errors the Copyright Office should have caught when it reviewed your application. This includes, for example, the omission of necessary information, such as the author and/or claimant's name, and obvious mistakes like listing an impossible publication date—for instance 1092. If, when you receive your registration certificate, you discover that such errors have been overlooked by the copyright examiner, simply notify the Copyright Office and the mistake will be corrected with no need for a supplemental registration and additional fee.

---

2.   Amplifications and Changes

For the same reasons discussed above, file a supplemental registration to:

- reflect important changes in facts that have occurred since the basic registration was made
- provide additional significant information that could have been provided in the original application but was not, or
- clarify or explain information in the basic registration.

a.   If you have changed your address

File a supplemental registration to change the address listed on your certificate. It is not legally necessary for you to keep your address current in the Copyright Office's records. However, by doing so you will make it easy for people who want to use your work to locate you and arrange for permission and compensation. The harder you are to locate, the more likely it is that your copyright will be infringed.

b.   If an author or copyright claimant was omitted

All the authors and copyright claimants must be listed in the registration. (See Chapter 4, Section I.)

This means a supplemental registration should be filed if an author or copyright claimant's name was omitted.

> **EXAMPLE:** Jack and Jill coauthored a children's book. Jill completed the registration form, but later discovered that she had forgotten to list Jack as a coauthor. A supplemental registration should be filed to add Jack's name.

c.   Change in claimant's name

A supplemental registration should be made where the name of the copyright claimant has changed for reasons other than a transfer of ownership.

d.   Change in title of the registered work

File a supplemental registration if you changed the title of the registered work without changing its content. However, if the content of the work is changed, a new registration will have to be made (see below).

e.   Nature of authorship needs clarification

In some cases, it is a good idea to file a supplemental registration to correct or amplify the nature of authorship statement in the original registration.

> **EXAMPLE:** Karen wrote and published a book on beekeeping in 1985. Karen never registered the book. In 1992, Karen revised and added several new chapters to her book. Karen registered this new edition with the Copyright Office. She stated "revision and chapters 9–12 added" in the nature of authorship section of her registration application. She did not complete Space 6 of the form, calling for information regarding

derivative works. This registration would only protect the new material Karen added to her book; it would not protect the preexisting material that Karen never previously registered or described in her application. Karen should file a supplemental registration to change the claim to "entire text"; she should also describe the preexisting material and new material added to this derivative work as called for in Space 6 of Form TX. (See Chapter 4, Section I.) This will ensure that all the work she did will be protected by the registration.

B. When Supplemental Registration Is Not Appropriate

Some types of errors should not be corrected by supplemental registration. And supplemental registration may not be used to reflect some types of factual changes.

1. Changes in Copyright Ownership

Supplemental registration cannot be used to notify the Copyright Office of post-registration changes in ownership of a copyright, whether by license, inheritance or other form of transfer. A special recordation procedure is used for this. (See discussion in Chapter 9, *Transferring Copyright Ownership*.)

2. Errors or Changes in Content of Registered Work

A supplemental registration cannot be filed to reflect corrections in the content of a registered work or other changes in that work. Where such changes are so substantial as to make the new work a new version, it must be registered separately and a new

deposit made. If the content changes are minor, there is no need to file a new registration since the original registration will provide adequate protection. See the detailed discussion in Chapter 4, Section F about when a new registration must be made to protect new material.

3. Errors in Copyright Notice

There is no need to file a supplemental registration where you discover and correct errors in the copyright notice as discussed in Part I of this chapter.

C. Supplemental Registration Procedure

Filing a supplemental registration is a straightforward procedure.

1. When to File

You may file a supplemental registration any time during the existence of the copyright for a work that was published or registered after January 1, 1978. However, there is a time limit for works published or registered before that date. See a copyright attorney before filing a supplemental registration for a pre-1978 published work.

2. Who Can File

After the original basic registration has been completed, a supplemental registration may be filed by:
- any author or other copyright claimant in the work
- the owner of any exclusive right in the work (See Chapter 4, Section D.), or
- the authorized agent of any of the above.

3. Completing the Application Form

Use the Copyright Office's official Form CA to file a supplemental registration. A copy of this form is contained in the tear-out appendix at the end of this book. The form contains seven parts, lettered A through G.

a. Part A: Basic instructions

Part A asks for five items of information regarding your original basic registration. This information must be the same as that which already appears on your basic registration, even if the purpose of filing Form CA is to change one of these items. Refer to your certificate of registration for this information.

Title of work. Give the title as it appears in the basic registration, including any previous or alternative titles if they appear.

Registration number. This is a six- or seven-digit number preceded by a two-letter prefix—for example, TX 1234567. It should be stamped on the upper right-hand corner of your certificate of registration (the copy of your application mailed back to you by the Copyright Office).

Registration date. Give the year when the basic registration was completed.

Name of author(s) and copyright claimant(s). Give the names of all the authors and copyright claimants exactly as they appear in the basic registration.

b. Part B: Correction

Part B should be completed only if information in the basic registration was incorrect at the time the basic registration was made (see discussion in Section A.1 above). Leave part B blank and complete part C instead if you want to add, update or clarify information rather than rectify an error. Part B asks for four items of information:

Location and nature of incorrect information. Give the line number and heading or description of the space in the basic registration where the error occurred—for example, "Line 2a... Name of Author."

Incorrect information as it appears in the basic registration. Transcribe the erroneous statement in the basic registration exactly as it appears there.

Corrected information. Give the information as it should have appeared.

Explanation of correction. If you wish, add an explanation of the error or correction.

c. Part C: Amplification

Part C should be completed if you are filing the Form CA to amplify the information in your basic registration.

Location and nature of information to be amplified. Where indicated, give the line number and heading or description of the space in the basic registration form where the information to be amplified appears.

Amplified information. Provide a statement of the added, updated or explanatory information as clearly and succinctly as possible—for example, "change nature of authorship statement from editorial revisions to entire text."

Explanation of amplification. If you wish, add an explanation of the amplification.

d. Part D: Continuation

Part D is a blank space that should be used if you do not have enough space in Part B or C.

e. Part E: Deposit account and mailing instructions

If you maintain a deposit account with the Copyright Office, identify it in Part E. Otherwise, you will need to send a nonrefundable $20 filing fee with your form. The space headed "Correspondence" should contain the name and address of the person to be consulted by the Copyright Office if there are any problems.

f.   Part F: Certification

The person making the supplemental registration must sign the application in Part F and check the appropriate box indicating her capacity—that is, author, other copyright claimant, owner of exclusive rights or authorized agent.

g.   Part G: Address for return of certificate

The address to which the Copyright Office should mail your supplemental registration certificate must be listed in Part G. Make sure the address is legible, since the certificate will be returned in a window envelope.

4.   Filing Form CA

Send the CA form to the Copyright Office along with the $20 registration fee. Make your check or money order payable to the Register of Copyrights. No deposit is necessary for a supplemental registration. Send the form and payment to:

> Register of Copyrights
> Library of Congress
> Washington, DC 20559

D. Effect of Supplemental Registration

If your application was completed correctly, the Copyright Office will assign you a new registration number and issue a certificate of supplementary registration under that number. The certificate is simply a copy of your Form CA with the new registration number, date and certification stamped on it. Be sure to keep it in your records.

The information in a supplementary registration augments, but does not supersede, that contained in the original basic registration. The basic registration is not expunged or cancelled. However, if the person who filed the supplementary registration was the copyright claimant for the original registration (or his heir or transferee), the Copyright Office will place a note referring to the supplementary registration on its records of the basic registration. This way, anyone needing information regarding the registration will know there is a supplemental registration on file if an inquiry is made regarding the work.

6

What Copyright Protects

We said in Chapter 2, *Copyright Basics,* that the copyright laws give authors and other copyright owners the exclusive right to reproduce, distribute, prepare derivative works based upon, display and perform their work. This chapter explains that these rights extend only to a work's protected expression. It is vital to clearly understand what parts of a work constitute protected expression—and therefore belong exclusively to the author or other copyright owner—and what parts are not protected at all. Those aspects of a work that are not considered protected expression are in the public domain, free for all to use.

Only works containing protected expression may be registered with the Copyright Office in the manner described in Chapter 4, *Copyright Registration.* When copyright owners sell or otherwise transfer their copyright ownership rights as described in Chapter 9, *Transferring Copyright Ownership,* what they are selling is the right to use their protected expression. And, as described in Chapter 12, *Copyright Infringement,* copyright owners have valid claims for copyright infringement against persons who use their work without permission only if it is protected expression that has been used.

A. What Copyright Protects: Tangible, Original Expression

Described at its most fundamental level, the creation of a book, article or other written work consists of selecting, from all the words in the English (or some other) language, a particular sequence of words and/or other symbols that communicate what the author wants to convey to her readers.

Subject to some important limitations we'll discuss below, copyright protects an author's particular choice of words from unauthorized use by others. But copyright protection does not end with the words an author uses. It also extends to an author's selection and arrangement of her material—that is, her choices as to what her work should contain and her arrangement of those items.

An author's particular choice of words and selection and arrangement of material is called her expression. This is all that copyright protects.

However, not all expression is protected by copyright. An author's expression is protected only if, and to the extent, it satisfies the following three fundamental requirements.

1. Requirement #1—Fixation

The most basic requirement that a person's expression must meet to qualify for copyright protection is that it must be fixed in a "tangible medium of expression." The Copyright Act is not picky about how you "fix" your expression; any medium from which your expression can be read back or heard, either directly or with the aid of a machine, will suffice. In other words, your expression will be protected if you hand write it on a piece of paper, type it on a typewriter, save it on a computer disk, dictate it into a tape recorder, act it out in front of a video camera or use any other means to preserve it.

The Copyright Act does not protect oral expressions that go unrecorded, since they aren't fixed. Likewise, copyright does not protect expression that exists in your mind but that you have not set to paper or otherwise preserved. For example, if ancient Greece had had a copyright law the same as ours, Homer's *Iliad* (which, according to tradition, Homer composed and recited in public, but never wrote down or otherwise recorded) would not have been protected by copyright.

Copyright protection begins the instant you fix your expression. There is no waiting period and it is not necessary to register with the Copyright Office (but, as discussed in Chapter 4, *Copyright Registration,* very important benefits are obtained by doing so). Copyright protects both drafts and completed works, and both published and unpublished works.

2. Requirement #2—Originality

A work consisting of expression that is written down or otherwise fixed in a tangible form is protected by copyright only if, and to the extent, it is original. But this does not mean that a written work must be novel—that is, new to the world—to be protected. For copyright purposes, a work is original if it—or at least a part of it—owes its origin to the author. A work's quality, ingenuity, aesthetic merit or uniqueness is not considered. In short, the Copyright Act does not distinguish between the Great American Novel and a six-year-old's letter to her Aunt Sally; both are entitled to copyright protection to the extent they were not copied by the author—whether consciously or unconsciously—from other works. So long as a work was independently created by its author, it is protected even if other similar works already exist.

> **EXAMPLE:** Tom, a paleontologist, spends seven years researching and writing a book advancing the theory that birds descended from dinosaurs. Unbeknownst to Tom, Jane, a paleontologist in another part of the country, has spent five years researching and writing a book of her own about the same theory. Tom and Jane never had any contact with each other or each other's work. Nevertheless, due to the similarity of the subject matter and their ideas, their books closely resemble each other. However, since they were independently created, both books are entitled to copyright protection despite the similarities.

DERIVATIVE WORKS AND COMPILATIONS

It is not necessary that an entire work be independently created by its author for it to be protectible. Copyright protects works created by adapting, transforming or combining previously existing material in new ways. These types of works are called derivative works or compilations, and are discussed in Chapter 7, *Adaptions and Compilations*. The main point to remember about derivative works and compilations here is that they aren't protected by copyright if they infringe upon a copyright in the original works.

DEAR COPYRIGHT PERSON:
I AM WRITING REGARDIN,
COPYRIGHT REGISTRATION
NO. 286 286 286 0...

PROTECTION FOR QUOTATIONS

The author of a news story, biography, history, oral history or similar work may not claim copyright ownership of statements made by others and quoted in the work. Reason: A verbatim quotation of what someone else says is not original. If the person who did the talking never writes down or otherwise fixes what he said, his words will be in the public domain.

However, a conversation reconstructed by an author from memory, rather than quoted verbatim from written notes or a recording, may be protectible by the author (not the person who made the original remarks) if some originality was involved in reconstructing the conversation (*Harris v. Miller,* 50 U.S.P.Q. 306 (S.D.N.Y. 1941).). In addition, the selection and arrangement of all the quotations in a book of quotations may be a protectible compilation, although the individual quotations are not protected (*Quinto v. Legal Times of Washington,* 506 F.Supp. 554 (D.D.C. 1981).). One or more of the individual quotations in such a book could be copied without the compiler's permission, but verbatim copying of the entire book would infringe on the compiler's copyright. (See Chapter 7, *Adaptations and Compilations* for a detailed discussion.)

---

3. Requirement #3—Minimal Creativity

Finally, a minimal amount of creativity over and above the independent creation requirement is necessary for copyright protection. Works completely lacking in creativity are denied copyright protection even if they have been independently created. However, the amount of creativity required is very slight. A work need not be novel, unique, ingenious or even any good to be sufficiently creative. All that's required is that the work be the product of a very minimal creative spark. The vast majority of written works—including catalog copy, toy instructions and third-rate poetry—make the grade.

But there are some types of works that are usually deemed to contain no creativity at all. For example, a mere listing of ingredients or contents, such as in a recipe, is considered to be completely lacking in creativity and is not protectible (but explanatory material or other original expression in a recipe or other list is protectible). Telephone directory white pages are also deemed to lack even minimal creativity. Other listings of data may also completely lack creativity; see the detailed discussion in Chapter 7, *Adaptions and Compilations.* The Copyright Office will not register such works.

4. Examples of Works Containing Protected Expression

Let's now put these three requirements—fixation, originality and minimal creativity—together by looking at a list containing examples of the types of works that commonly contain protected expression.
- advertising copy
- blank forms that convey information (see Section B.5 below)
- catalogs, directories, price lists and other compilations of information
- fiction of any length and quality
- instructions
- interviews, lectures, speeches, jokes, etc., that are fixed in a tangible medium of expression
- leaflets and pamphlets
- letters and diaries, whether or not they have any artistic merit or general interest
- magazines, newspapers, newsletters, periodicals, journals and other serial publications
- nonfiction of any length and quality
- plays
- poetry

- reference books and technical writings
- screenplays
- song lyrics, whether or not combined with music
- textbooks.

COPYRIGHT PROTECTION FOR MUSIC, MOVIES, SOUND RECORDINGS, COMPUTER SOFTWARE, PICTORIAL, GRAPHIC AND OTHER TYPES OF WORKS

This book focuses on copyright protection for works consisting wholly or primarily of words. However, copyright protects more than just words. Provided that the three fundamental requirements—fixation, originality and minimal creativity—are met, copyright protects all types of expression, including: music; pictorial, graphic and sculptural works; motion pictures and other audiovisual works; sound recordings; pantomimes and choreographic works; and architectural works (architectural drawings and blueprints and the design of actual buildings). If you're interested in copyright protection for these types of works, refer to Chapter 14, *Help Beyond This Book.*

Computer software programs and computer databases are also entitled to copyright protection. For detailed coverage of this topic, see *Software Development: A Legal Guide,* by Stephen Fishman (Nolo Press).

B. What Copyright Does Not Protect: The Boundaries of the Public Domain

Towns and cities of the 18th and 19th centuries often had a commons: a centrally located unfenced area of grassland that was free for all to use. Authors also have a commons: It's called the public domain. The public domain contains everything that is not protected by copyright and is therefore free for all to use without permission.

Without the public domain, it would be virtually impossible for anyone to write anything without committing copyright infringement. This is because new expression is not created from thin air; all authors draw on what has been written before. As one copyright expert has noted, "transformation is the essence of the authorship process. An author transforms her memories, experiences, inspirations, and influences into a new work. That work inevitably echoes expressive elements of prior works" (Litman, "The Public Domain," *39 Emory Law Journal* 965 (1990)). Without the public domain, these echoes could not exist.

1. Ideas and Copyright

Copyright only protects an author's tangible expression of her ideas, not the ideas themselves. Ideas, procedures, processes, systems, methods of operation, concepts, principles and discoveries are all in the public domain, free for all to use. In effect, they're owned by everybody. (17 U.S.C. 102(b).)

There is a good reason for this: If authors were allowed to obtain a monopoly over their ideas, the copyright laws would end up discouraging new authorship and the progress of knowledge—the two goals copyright is intended to foster.

However, although ideas are not protectible in themselves, an author's particular *selection and arrangement* of ideas may constitute protected expression. For example, an author's selection and arrangement of traits (ideas) that make up a literary character may be protected (see Section C.1 below).

PATENT LAWS PROTECT IDEAS FOR INVENTIONS

Ideas embodied in novel and non-obvious inventions can be protected under U.S. and foreign patent laws. For a detailed discussion, see *Patent It Yourself,* by David Pressman (Nolo Press).

THE UNCLEAR DEMARCATION BETWEEN IDEAS AND EXPRESSION

It's easy to say that copyright does not protect ideas, only expression, but how do you tell the difference between an unprotected idea and its protected expression? These are very fuzzy concepts and, in fact, no one has ever been able to fix an exact boundary between ideas and expression; probably nobody ever can. But after you read the following material, you should gain a better understanding of this dichotomy.

---

facts; at most, she may discover a previously unknown fact. Census-takers, for example, do not create the population figures that emerge from a census; in a sense, they copy these figures from the world around them. The Copyright Act does not protect discoveries. (17 U.S.C. 102(b).)

So, the facts contained in works such as news stories, histories, biographies and scientific treatises are not protectible. Subject to the important limitation of the merger doctrine discussed in Section 3 below, all that is protected is the author's original expression of the facts contained in such works.

COMPARE—PROTECTION OF FACTS UNDER STATE LAWS

Although facts are not protected by the Copyright Act, state laws might protect them. The Supreme Court held many years ago that state unfair competition laws that barred the misappropriation of the fruit of someone's labor prevented a newspaper from stealing the news contained in another paper (*International News Serv. v. Associated Press,* 248 U.S. 215 (1918).). In addition, trade secret laws *might* protect facts that are not disseminated to the public. However, whether protection under state law is actually available today is very unclear because the Copyright Act provides that it preempts (supersedes) state law.

---

2. Facts and Copyright

Copyright does not protect facts—whether scientific, historical, biographical or news of the day. If the first person to write about a fact had a monopoly over it, the spread of knowledge would be greatly impeded. Another reason why copyright law does not protect facts is that an author does not independently create

3. The Merger Doctrine—When Ideas, Facts and Their Expression Merge

Sometimes there is just one way, or only a few ways, to adequately express a particular idea or fact. If the first person to write about such an idea or fact could copyright his expression, he would effectively have a monopoly over that idea or fact itself—that is, no one else could write about it without his permission. The copyright law does not permit this since it would discourage authorship of new works and thereby retard the progress of knowledge. In these cases, the idea or fact and its particular expression are deemed to merge and the expression—the author's words—is either treated as if it were in the public domain or given very limited copyright protection.

The merger doctrine applies mainly to factual works such as histories, biographies and scientific treatises, rather than to works of fancy such as novels, plays and poems. This is because the ideas and facts in factual works can often be expressed only in one particular way or only in a few ways, while the ideas contained in novels and similar works can usually be expressed in a wide variety of ways.

For example, assume you wish to write an unadorned factual account of Paul Revere's famous midnight ride during the Revolutionary War. You research Revere's life and create a work containing, in part, the following sequence of words:

On April 18, 1775, the Boston minutemen learned that the British intended to march on Concord with a detachment of 700 men. Paul Revere arranged for a signal to be flashed from the steeple of the Old North Church in Boston. Two lanterns would mean that the British were coming by water, and one, by land.

The particular selection and arrangement of words in the above paragraph appears to satisfy the three requirements for copyright protection: fixation, originality and minimal creativity. Does this mean that if anyone used these three sentences without your permission they would be liable for copyright infringement? Because of the merger doctrine, the answer is probably not. This is because if anyone else wrote a brief factual account of Paul Revere's ride, it would necessarily have to contain sentences looking very much like those in your paragraph. This would be so even though the author had never read your account—there are just not many different ways to express the facts described in your paragraph. For example, how many different words can an author use to explain that one lantern meant that the British were coming by land and two by sea? The facts pretty much dictate the form of expression here.

As a result, if your paragraph were protected by copyright, nobody else could ever write a factual account of Paul Revere's ride without your permission. This the copyright law cannot permit, since it would effectively give you a monopoly over the facts concerning Paul Revere's ride. To prevent this, the facts of Paul Revere's ride and the words you used to express them would be deemed to merge. Some courts would hold that your paragraph was in the public domain, and could be copied verbatim (or used in any other way) without your permission. Other courts would not go quite this far; they would give your paragraph limited protection by holding that your paragraph was protected from unauthorized verbatim copying, but nothing else. (See *Landsberg v. Scrabble Crossword Game Player, Inc.,* 736 F.2d 485 (9th Cir. 1984); *Morrissey v. Procter & Gamble Co.,* 379 F.2d 675 (1st Cir. 1967).)

In contrast, the merger doctrine would not be applied to a work of fancy—for example, a poem—about Paul Revere's ride. Consider this:

Listen, my children, and you shall hear
Of the midnight ride of Paul Revere,
On the eighteenth of April, in Seventy-five.
Hardly a man is now alive
Who remembers that famous day and year.
He said to his friend, "if the British march
By land or sea from the town tonight,
Hold a lantern aloft in the belfry arch
Of the North Church tower as a signal light,
One, if by land, and two, if by sea.

These stanzas were written by Henry Wadsworth Longfellow over 100 years ago and are thus in the public domain because the copyright has expired—see Chapter 10, *Copyright Duration*. But let's pretend for purposes of our example that they were written just the other day.

This verse conveys almost exactly the same factual information as your paragraph above, yet the facts and expression would not be deemed to merge. Why? Because the author's words are embellished and highly distinctive. The sequence of words has not been dictated solely by the facts. Indeed, it is the unique word sequence itself, not the facts, that is the work's main attraction. No one needs to copy this particular word sequence in order to convey the same facts or to write another work of fancy about Paul Revere's ride. A person who copied even the first two lines would probably be found to have infringed on the copyright in the poem.

Copyright tip
Nonfiction writers should not get the idea that they need to start writing in poetic meter to obtain copyright protection. But, the more distinctive their words, the more protection they will receive. An elegantly written biography of Paul Revere will receive more protection than an unadorned factual account. Similarly, Loren Eiseley, Stephen J. Gould and Lewis Thomas have all written books about science whose language transcends the way their subjects are normally handled. The prose in their books receives far more protection than that of a run-of-the-mill scientific treatise. The moral is that the more effort you take to make your writing transcend the mundane and purely functional, the more copyright protection your work will receive.

4. Words, Names, Titles, Slogans, and Other Short Phrases

Individual words are always in the public domain, even if they are invented by a particular person. Names (whether of individuals, products or business organizations or groups), titles, slogans and other short phrases (for example, "I'd walk a mile for a Camel" and "No Smoking") are not protected by copyright law even if they are highly creative, novel or distinctive, and will not be registered by the Copyright Office. (37 C.F.R. 202.1(a).) However, these items—especially slogans—may be protectible under the trademark laws. (See Chapter 2, *Copyright Basics*.)

a. Titles may be protectible under state law

Although titles are not protected by the Copyright Act, they may be protected under state unfair competition laws (that is, state laws that prohibit unfair competitive business practices). Under these laws, an author may protect a title from unauthorized use if:

- the title is strongly identified in the public's mind with the author's work, and

- the author proves that the public will be confused if the title is used in another work.

This prevents a person from passing off or palming off a work on the public—that is, publishing a work with the same or similar title as a previously published, well-known work in the hope that people will buy it because they confuse it with the well-known work.

> **EXAMPLE:** A successful play called *The Gold Diggers* was made into a film entitled *Gold Diggers of Broadway*. The film's producers sued the producer of a subsequent film called *Gold Diggers of Paris* for passing off. The court held that it was unlawful for *Gold Diggers of Paris* to be marketed under that title, at least without a conspicuous disclaimer that the picture was not based on the play or the earlier picture. (*Warner Bros. Pictures, Inc. v. Majestic Pictures Corp.*, 70 F.2d 310 (2d Cir. 1934).)

5. Blank Forms

Blank forms designed solely to record information are in the public domain. The Copyright Office will not register such items. (37 C.F.R. 202.1(c).) According to the Copyright Office, this includes such items as time cards, graph paper, account books, bank checks, scorecards, address books, diaries, report forms and order forms.

However, forms that themselves convey information are protected and may be registered. The problem with this distinction is determining when a form does and does not convey protectible information. Even a true blank form—that is, a form consisting primarily of blank space to be filled in—can convey information. The columns or headings on a blank form may be interlaced with highly informative verbiage. Moreover, the configuration of columns, headings and lines may itself convey information.

The courts have been inconsistent in interpreting the blank form rule and its information

conveyance exception. Copyright protection has been denied to such items as a form prepared for television repairmen which contained spaces for lists of repairs and their costs (*M.M. Business Forms Corp. v. Uarco, Inc.*, 472 F.2d 1137 (6th Cir. 1973).); a time log chart which graphed hours in the business day on the vertical axis, and the day's project and activities on the horizontal axis (*Januz Marketing Communications, Inc. v. Doubleday & Co.* 569 F.Supp. 76 (S.D.N.Y. 1982).); and a medical "superbill" form containing spaces for patient information and lists of procedures and diagnoses to be performed by doctors (*Bibbero Systems v. Colwell Systems, Inc.*, 893 F.2d 1104 (9th Cir. 1990).).

In contrast, other courts have extended copyright protection to a form used to record medical laboratory tests (*Norton Printing Co. v. Augustana Hosp.*, 155 U.S.P.Q. 133 (N.D. Ill. 1967); recordkeeping forms with instructions (*Edwin K. Williams & Co. v. Edwin K. Williams & Co.-East*, 542 F.2d 1053 (9th Cir. 1976).); and an answer sheet for a standard multiple-choice examination, designed to be graded by an optical scanning machine (*Harcourt, Brace & World, Inc. v. Graphic Controls Corp.*, 329 F.Supp. 517 (S.D.N.Y. 1971).).

The general rule appears to be that the more word sequences (as opposed to simple headings) a form contains, the more likely it is to be protectible. Forms that contain substantial textual material—for example, insurance policies, contracts and other legal forms—are probably protectible. However, where there are only a few ways to express the facts and ideas contained in such forms, the merger doctrine might come into play to severely limit protection (see Section B.3 above). For example, one court held that insurance bond forms and indemnity agreements were protectible, but because the forms contained standard language that would have to be included in any form designed to accomplish the same purpose, only verbatim copying of the forms' exact wording would constitute infringement (*Continental Casualty Co. v. Beardsley*, 253 F.2d 702 (2d Cir. 1958).).

COMPILATIONS OF FORMS

To make things even more complicated, works consisting of forms designed solely for recording information may nevertheless be protectible as compilations if originality has been employed in selecting which items of information are to be recorded, and in the arrangement of such items. See the executive organizer (Example 2) in Chapter 7, Section B.1.

Copyright tip

If you have produced any type of form that you want protected by copyright, by all means register it with the Copyright Office. If the Copyright Office refuses to register the form, insist that they do so under their rule of doubt (see discussion in Chapter 4, *Copyright Registration*). If anyone copies the form, you will be able to sue them for copyright infringement. But be aware that a judge might decide that your form was not entitled to copyright protection after all.

6. Government Works

Government edicts such as judicial opinions, legislation, public ordinances, administrative rulings and similar official legal documents are all in the public domain. This rule applies to all levels of government—local, state and federal, and even includes foreign government edicts.

Other types of works created by United States government officers and employees as part of their jobs are also in the public domain. This includes, for example, everything published by the United States Printing Office, IRS, Copyright Office, Trademark Office and all the President's official speeches. But this rule does not apply to works by state and local

government employees; those works may be protected by copyright. For example, a state tax pamphlet or booklet on air pollution or water conservation published by a city or county may be protected.

WORKS BY FEDERAL GRANTEES

Works created for the federal government by independent contractors—that is, persons who are neither U.S. government officers nor employees—can be protected by copyright. However, the government may require these persons to sign work made for hire agreements as a condition to receiving federal money. In this event, the U.S. government, not the individual who actually wrote the work, would be considered the author of the work; this would mean that the work would be in the public domain. See Chapter 8, *Initial Copyright Ownership* for detailed discussion of work made for hire agreements.

---

7. Works in Which Copyright Protection Has Expired or Was Never Obtained

Copyright protection does not last forever. When a work's copyright protection expires, it enters the public domain and is freely available to anyone. All works first published in the United States more than 75 years ago are in the public domain. So are works published before 1964 for which the copyright owner failed to timely renew the copyright. See the detailed discussion of copyright duration and renewal in Chapter 10, *Copyright Duration*.

The public domain also includes works for which the copyright owner failed to take the necessary steps to obtain copyright protection. This may include works published before March 1, 1989, in which the copyright owner failed to include a valid copyright notice. (See detailed discussion in Chapter 3, *Copyright Notice.*)

C. Distinguishing Between Protected Expression and Material in the Public Domain: Putting It All Together

Now let's review the information we have just covered by looking at examples of protectible and public domain elements in works of fancy and factual works. Works of fancy include novels, short stories, plays, screenplays and poems. A factual work is a work of nonfiction, such as a biography, history, news story, how-to book or scientific treatise.

1. A Work of Fancy

Sue writes a novel about police work set in the South Bronx. Narrated by a rookie cop named Walker, the novel begins on her first day at the 41st Precinct station house, where she is shocked by its squalor. The book unfolds as a chronicle of police work and daily life in a violent neighborhood. Several chapters focus on specific topics, such as attacks on police officers. Throughout the book, Walker expresses compassion for those she considers the victims of the South Bronx, hopelessness regarding the prospects for basic improvement there and a sense that the officers of the 41st Precinct will continue to fight a rearguard action against lawlessness with very limited success. The book ends with her transfer to another precinct.

a. Unprotectible aspects of a work of fancy

We'll first examine those aspects of Sue's novel that are not protectible under the copyright law.

The idea to create a novel about police officers in the South Bronx. The underlying idea to create a certain type of work is always in the public domain. Thus, the fact that other authors have written many novels about police officers (including some set in the Bronx) does not preclude Sue (or anyone else) from writing another one.

The work's theme. The theme of Sue's novel—the hopelessness of the situation in the South Bronx and, by extension, all urban America—is in the public domain. Another novelist is free to express the same theme in her own words. A theme is an unprotectible idea, not a protectible expression.

The work's setting. A fictional work's setting—that is, the time and place in which the story occurs—is not protected by copyright. Anyone can write a story set in the 41st Precinct of the Bronx. But the particular words Sue used to describe this setting are protectible. For example, Sue described one vacant lot as "filled with the refuse of stunted lives; a dead place, with no colors and no smells... not even the garbage smelled." This sequence of words is protected.

The work's basic plot. A fictional work's plot—that is, the sequence of events by which Sue or any other author expresses her theme or idea—is a selection and arrangement of ideas. We know that ideas themselves are not protected, but an author's selection and arrangement of ideas does constitute protected expression to the extent that it's original—that is, independently created. Thus, Sue's plot constitutes protectible expression only to the extent it was independently created by her.

Plots are rarely protectible because there are very few independently created plots. One literary critic has noted that "authors spin their plots from a relatively small number of 'basic situations,' changing characters, reversing roles, giving modern twists to classic themes." (*The Thirty-Six Dramatic Situations*, by Polti (The Writer, Inc.).) For example, the plot of the film *The Dirty Dozen* is basically a World War II updating of *Jason and the Argonauts;* and authors have recycled the time-tested plot of boy gets girl, boy loses girl, boy gets girl back over and over again throughout the centuries. Naturally, these basic plots are all in the public domain; otherwise, it would be very difficult, if not impossible, for anyone to create a "new" work of fancy.

Independently created variations or twists on basic plots would constitute protected expression. But there aren't very many new plot twists either. For example, can you think of any variations on the boy meets girl scenario that haven't been done before?

The plot of Sue's novel may be described as follows: idealistic young person joins urban police force, is assigned to inner city, sees horrors of life there and ends up disillusioned. It's hard to see anything original in this. There are doubtless hundreds of other police stories with similar plots.

The work's scenes and situations. There are certain sequences of events, scenes, situations or details that necessarily follow from a fictional work's given theme or setting. The French call these *scènes a faire* (that which must follow a certain situation). Sue's novel includes scenes involving drunks, prostitutes, stripped cars, rats and a car chase. Any novel about police work in the South Bronx, West Oakland, East Los Angeles or any other major city would likely include such elements. Such predictable—or stock—story elements are all unprotectible ideas.

However, to the extent they are original, the particular words an author uses to describe or narrate a *scène a faire* are protected, even though the idea for the scene is not. Thus, although any author can write a police novel that includes a scene involving a high-speed car chase, he could not copy the words Sue used to describe the car chase in her novel.

The work's stock characters. Similarly, there are many standard character types that have developed in fiction over time—for example, the eccentric little old lady; the tall, silent, strong cowboy; the two-fisted, hard-drinking private detective; the streetwise fast-talking urban hustler. Since they are not original creations, these character types are not protectible; they are part of the stock of ideas that all fiction writers may draw upon. For example, one of the characters in Sue's novel is Police Sergeant Jim McCarthy, a hard-drinking fourth-generation Irish cop who's seen it all. Such a sketchily drawn stock character, commonly found in police stories, would not be protected. Any author of a police thriller is free to use such a character.

Copyright tip

Never use a well-known character—either by name or detailed description—from a copyrighted work without first consulting a copyright attorney or disguising the character to such an extent that it is not recognizable. Even if the character doesn't seem sufficiently distinctive to you to merit protection, its creator and publisher may feel quite differently and sue you for copyright infringement. Of course, you can use any character from a work in the public domain—for example, Sherlock Holmes.

PROTECTION FOR DISTINCTIVE CHARACTERS

Some courts have held that distinctively "delineated" original characters are protectible. What this appears to mean is that no one can copy the particular original combination and selection of qualities—such as personality traits, physical attributes and mode of dress—that make the character distinctive. An author's selection and combination of such distinctive qualities (ideas) is deemed to constitute protectible expression.

Unfortunately, there are no uniform standards for judging when a character is, or is not, sufficiently distinctive to be protectible. Copyright protection has been extended to such disparate characters as Tarzan, Amos & Andy, Hopalong Cassidy and E.T., and denied to Sam Spade and the Lone Ranger. Is Sam Spade any less distinctive than Hopalong Cassidy? The only general rule is that "the less developed the characters, the less they can be copyrighted." (Nichols v. Universal Pictures Corp., 45 F.2d 119 (2d Cir. 1930).) In addition, some character names may be protected under state and federal trademark laws.

The work's facts. Sue's novel is extremely well researched. She describes what police officers do and how they do it in great detail, and realistically catalogs the conditions of life in the South Bronx. Indeed, her novel is a better source of factual information on the South Bronx than many guidebooks or sociological studies. Of course, facts are not protectible, so all of the factual information contained in Sue's novel is in the public domain.

The work's writing style and individual words and phrases. Sue's novel is written in a highly unusual stream-of-consciousness style. She also invented new slang words and phrases for her characters to use. Neither Sue's style nor her new words and phrases are protectible. The original and creative word sequences in Sue's novel are protected by copyright, but a writing style itself is in the public domain, no matter how original it is. So are the individual words and short phrases a work contains, even if the author invented them. For example, the new words and phrases in George Orwell's *1984*—"newspeak," "I love big brother"—entered the public domain (and enriched our language) the moment Orwell published them.

The work's literary devices. Finally, literary devices such as the story within a story, flashbacks, the epistolary novel, prosodic forms and rhetorical devices such as alliteration are all unprotectible ideas. These and most other literary devices have been around for centuries and are all in the public domain.

b. Protected expression in a work of fancy

You may be wondering just what *is* protected by copyright law in a work of fancy. As stated in Section A above, all that is protected is the author's original expression. This includes, of course, the particular sequence of words Sue has chosen to tell her story. But her protected expression does not end there. A novel or similar work is more than just a bunch of words strewn together. To create her novel, Sue had to select, arrange and combine all the unprotected elements listed above—theme, setting, plot, characters, scenes and situations—into an integrated whole. To the extent it is original (independently created), this selection and combination also constitutes protected expression. For lack of better terms, courts sometimes call this a work's "total concept and feel" or its "overall pattern" or "fundamental essence."

2. A Factual Work

Commodore Hornblower spends 12 years researching the sinking of the H.M.S. Titanic. He scours archives in Britain and America and interviews the remaining survivors. He then writes and publishes a 500-page book describing the Titanic's voyage in minute detail. The book contains many previously unknown facts; for example, that the ship's captain actually survived the sinking and lived out his life as a circus performer under an assumed name. The book ends with a startling new interpretation of the facts: The Titanic struck the fatal iceberg because it was sailing too fast, and it was sailing too fast because there was an out-of-control fire in one of its coal bunkers—it was desperately trying to reach port before the fire destroyed the ship.

a.   Unprotectible elements of factual works

The following aspects of Hornblower's book are in the public domain:

Research. The facts that an author discovers in the course of research are in the public domain, free to all. This is so even if an author spends considerable effort conducting the research. Copyright does not protect the fruits of creative research, no matter how grueling or time-consuming the research may have been. Copyright only protects fixed, original and minimally creative expression. Thus, copyright does not protect the previously unknown facts about the Titanic's voyage that the Commodore discovered, even though it took him 12 years to discover them. Anyone is free to use these facts—for example, that the captain actually survived the sinking—in any way she wishes. But see the discussion of plagiarism in Chapter 12, *Copyright Infringement.*

Quotations from public domain materials. Hornblower included in his book numerous quotations from newspaper reports about the sinking. These reports, first published over 75 years ago, are in the public domain. Their inclusion in Hornblower's book does not revive their copyright protection. Anyone can use these quotations in a work of their own. They don't have to go back to the original sources.

Author's interpretation of facts. An author's interpretation of facts is itself a fact (or a purported fact) that is deduced from other facts. Interpretations are therefore also in the public domain. Thus, the Commodore's theory as to what caused the Titanic to hit the iceberg (the need to reach port quickly due to the coal bunker fire) is no more protectible than the fact that the Titanic hit an iceberg.

Book design. The Commodore's publisher spared no expense on his book. It is filled with photos and beautifully designed. Is the book's "look" protected by copyright? No. Book designs—that is, a book's physical and visual attributes—are considered to be unprotectible ideas. This includes the choice of typeface style and size, leading (space between lines of type), arrangement of type on pages and placement, spacing and juxtaposition of text and illustrations (46 Fed.Reg. 30651 (1981).)

b.   Protected expression in factual works

We now turn to those aspects of a factual work that are protected by copyright.

Literal expression of facts. An author's literal expression of facts is, theoretically, entitled to protection so long as it is original. Thus, anyone who copied the Commodore's words verbatim or closely paraphrased a substantial portion of the language in his book would infringe on his copyright. However, because there are often only a few ways to express the facts contained in factual works, the protection they receive may be greatly limited through application of the merger doctrine (see discussion in Section B.3 above). In addition, selected passages of Hornblower's book probably could be quoted under the fair use privilege (see discussion in Chapter 11, *Using Other Authors' Words).*

Fictional elements in factual works. Hornblower was not only a dogged researcher, but had a vivid imagination as well. He included in his book certain scenes and dialog among the Titanic's passengers and crew that seemed to him likely to have occurred but were still completely fictional. Fictional expressions in otherwise factual works are entitled to full copyright protection. However, if an author represents his work to be completely factual, he may not bring a copyright infringement suit against someone who, relying on such representations, copies a portion of it thinking it was unprotectible fact when it was really protectible fiction (*Houts v. Universal City Studios*, 603 F.Supp. 26 (C.D. Ca. 1984).).

Selection or arrangement of facts. In writing his book, the Commodore had to select which facts to write about and arrange them in a certain order. Is this selection and arrangement protected expression? If the Commodore simply arranged the facts of the Titanic's voyage and sinking in chronological order, probably not. An historical chronology is itself a fact that is in the public domain.

But what if the Commodore organized the facts contained in his book in an original nonchronological way; shouldn't that original arrangement be protected? Some courts say yes, others disagree. (Compare *Pacific & Southern Co. v. Duncan*, 744 F.2d 1490 (11th Cir. 1984) ("editorial judgment" makes a new presentation of facts an "original work of authorship") with *Hoehling v. Universal City Studios, Inc.*, 618 F.2d 972 (2d Cir. 1980) ("there cannot be any such thing as copyright in the order of presentation of the facts, nor, indeed in their selection").)

Adaptions and Compilations

When 'Omer smote 'is bloomin' lyre,
He'd eard men sing by land an' sea;
An' what he thought 'e might require,
'E went an' took—the same as me!
　　　　　　—Rudyard Kipling
　　　　　　　Barrack Room Ballads

The old saying "there's nothing new under the sun" may be the truest of all platitudes. If Kipling was right, not even the earliest authors created their works out of whole cloth. Since authorship began, authors have been borrowing and adapting what others created before them. This chapter is about works that are created by using previously existing material. It covers derivative works—works created by transforming or adapting preexisting expression—and compilations—works created by selecting and arranging preexisting material in new ways.

A. Derivative Works

If you take a molten lump of copper and add tin to it you'll end up with something new: bronze. A similar process of transformation can be used to create new works of authorship; that is, an author can take expression that already exists, add new expression to it and end up with something new— that is, a new and different work of authorship. Such works are called derivative works.

EXAMPLE: Sheila writes a screenplay based upon a novel. In doing so, she takes the novel's expression (words) and adds her own expression to it—she organizes the material into cinematic scenes, adds dialog and camera directions, and deletes prose descriptions and other material that can't be filmed. The result is a new work of authorship which can be separately protected by copyright: a screenplay that is clearly differ-

ent from the novel, yet clearly based upon, or derived from it.

Of course, all works are derivative to some extent. As Kipling declared, all authors "take" from each other. Authorship is more often than not a process of translation and recombination of previously existing ideas, facts and other elements. Rarely, if ever, does an author create a work that is entirely new. For example, writers of fiction often draw bits and pieces of their characters and plots from other fictional works they have read. The same is true of writers of factual works. For example, it's likely that any new book on the impact of the electronic media on society would be derived to some extent from Marshall McLuhan's *The Medium Is the Message* (1967).

However, a work is derivative for copyright purposes only if its author has taken a *substantial* amount of a previously existing work's *expression*. As discussed in detail in Chapter 6, *What Copyright Protects*, copyright only protects an author's expression: the words she uses and the selection and arrangement of her material, if original. Thus, a new book on the impact of the media on society would be derivative of *The Medium Is the Message* for copyright purposes only if its author copied or paraphrased substantial portions of the words McLuhan used to express his ideas.

The ideas and facts themselves are not protectible and are therefore free for anyone to use. Likewise, this year's novel about boy meets girl is not derivative of last year's novel on the same theme unless its author copied substantial portions of its expression.

How much is substantial? Enough so that the average intended reader of the work would conclude that it had been adapted from or based upon the previously existing expression.

EXAMPLE 1: Edna writes a poem about her cat. She includes one line from a poem in T.S. Eliot's cat poetry collection, *Old Possum's Book of*

Practical Cats. She probably has not used enough of Eliot's expression for her poem to be considered a derivative work of *Old Possum's Book of Practical Cats.*

EXAMPLE 2: Andrew Lloyd Webber and Trevor Nunn write a musical entitled *Cats.* The musical is based entirely on the poems in *Old Possum's Book of Practical Cats.* Here and there a word or two is altered to make the verses fit the music better, but the show is nothing more than Eliot's poems set to music. *Cats* is a derivative work of *Old Possum's Book of Practical Cats.*

1. Types of Derivative Works

There are many different types of derivative works. Let's look at those of most interest to writers in terms of the type of expression the author takes from a previously existing work and the expression she adds to it to create a new, derivative work.

a.   Editorial revisions and elaborations

Preexisting expression taken. The entire text of any preexisting work.

 New expression added. Editorial revisions and/or other new material.

> **EXAMPLE:** Dr. Blood writes a new edition of his ten-year-old textbook on heart surgery. He adds several new chapters on new surgical techniques and revises the other chapters in light of recent developments. The new edition is a derivative work based on, but designed to take the place of, the earlier edition.

b.   Fictionalizations

Preexisting expression taken. A substantial portion of the protected expression contained in a factual work (biography, history, etc.).

 New expression added. Editing, reorganization, new dialogue, descriptions and other new material needed to transform the preexisting nonfiction work into a novel, play, screenplay or other work of fiction.

> **EXAMPLE:** Art takes the nonfiction work *The Diary of Anne Frank* and transforms it into a stageplay. To do so, he deletes prose descriptions, adds new dialog, organizes the work into scenes and acts and adds new scenes and incidents that weren't in the diary. But he also retains as much of Anne Frank's expression— her words—as possible. The play is a derivative work based on the nonfiction diary.

c.   Dramatizations

Preexisting expression taken. All or substantial part of the expression in a fictional work not meant to be performed in public—that is, a short story, novel, or poem.

New expression added. Editing, reorganization, new dialogue, and other new material needed to transform the work into a work that can be performed in public—for instance, a stageplay or screenplay.

d.   Translations into a new medium

Preexisting expression taken. All or a substantial portion of the protected expression of a work in one medium—for instance, a published book.

New expression added. Transfer of the work's protected expression into a new medium.

> **EXAMPLE:** Kitty Kelly makes a sound recording of selected highlights from her unauthorized biography of Nancy Reagan. The recording is a derivative work based on the written biography.

e.   Translations into a new language

Preexisting expression taken. All the expression contained in a preexisting work.

New expression added. Translation of the work's expression into a new version in another language.

> **EXAMPLE:** Miguel translates Stephen King's latest bestseller into Spanish. To do so, he takes King's expression (the words contained in the novel) and replaces them with Spanish words. The resulting translation is a derivative work based on the original English-language novel.

f.   Abridgements and condensations of fiction or nonfiction works

Preexisting expression taken. A substantial portion of work's protectible expression.

New expression added. Editing and other revisions that transform the work into a new, shorter version.

> **EXAMPLE:** *Reader's Digest* condensed books are derivative works based on the unabridged editions of the works that are condensed.

g.   Annotations

Preexisting expression taken. All or a substantial portion of a work's protected expression.

New expression added. Notes and/or other materials that clarify the meaning of the preexisting text.

> **EXAMPLE:** The annotated version of Lewis Carroll's *Alice In Wonderland* is a derivative work prepared from the original version of *Alice*.

2.   When You Need Permission to Create a Derivative Work

One of the five exclusive copyright rights that automatically come into existence the moment an original work of authorship is written down or otherwise fixed in a tangible form is the exclusive right to prepare and distribute derivative works based on the work's protected expression. This means you cannot create and publish a derivative work by using someone else's protected expression without obtaining their permission. If you do, you violate that person's copyright and would be subject to a copyright infringement suit.

EXAMPLE: Rhonda writes a critically acclaimed novel. Rex writes a screenplay based on Rhonda's novel without obtaining her permission to do so. Rex sells the screenplay to a Hollywood studio. Rhonda has a valid claim against Rex for infringing on her right to create derivative works from her novel.

Such permission usually takes the legal form of an exclusive license to prepare a particular derivative work—for example, a screenplay—from the preexisting material. (See Chapter 9, *Transferring Copyright Ownership.*)

WHAT HAPPENS IF YOU FAIL TO GET PERMISSION?

A derivative work created without the necessary permission from the owner of the preexisting expression exists in a kind of legal limbo. The author of the derivative work cannot publish it without infringing on the copyright in the preexisting material. But nobody else can use the derivative work without its creator's permission. Absent such permission, the derivative work is essentially worthless.

EXAMPLE: Lupe translates Stephen King's latest novel into Spanish without obtaining King's permission. Lupe cannot publish the translation without infringing on King's copyright in the novel, but she still owns her translation. If Stephen King wanted to use it, he would have to get her permission.

If you intend to create a derivative work from preexisting expression that is still under copyright, be sure to get the copyright owner's permission to use the work *before* you go to the time and trouble of adapting it into a new work.

3. When You Don't Need Permission to Create a Derivative Work

In some instances, it is not necessary to seek anyone's permission to create a derivative work, and the only legal issue the author must deal with is registering the derivative work with the Copyright Office. Registration of derivative works is discussed in Chapter 4, *Copyright Registration.*

a. Author owns right to prepare derivative works from preexisting expression

An author doesn't have to get anyone's permission to create a derivative work if she owns the entire copyright in the preexisting protected expression or the right to prepare derivative works based upon it. Authors start out owning all the copyright rights in their works, including all derivative rights, but they often transfer them to publishers, film producers and others. An author cannot create a derivative work from her own work if she has transferred her derivative rights to others. (See Chapter 9, *Transferring Copyright Ownership.*)

EXAMPLE: Livia writes a novel and sells the exclusive right to prepare a screenplay based upon it to Repulsive Pictures. Livia cannot write a screenplay based upon her novel without Repulsive's permission.

b. Preexisting material in the public domain

You don't need permission to create a derivative work based on expression that is in the public domain. Public domain material belongs to the world and anyone is free to use it in any way she wishes. (See Chapter 6, *What Copyright Protects,* for a detailed discussion of the public domain.) A work may be in the public domain because it was never copyrighted or the copyright expired. The expression in such works may be used in any way without permission.

> **EXAMPLE:** You can write a screenplay based on Dicken's *Great Expectations* without obtaining anyone's permission since the novel's copyright expired long ago.

Facts and ideas are always in the public domain. For this reason, an author need not obtain permission to use the facts or ideas contained in an otherwise protected preexisting work.

> **EXAMPLE:** Shirley, a three-year-old girl, falls into a well in Texas and is rescued one week later, miraculously still alive. The entire story was reported live on CNN and extensively covered by other news media as well. Shirley's parents write a book about the episode entitled *All's Well That Ends Well.* The book contains extensive quotations from Shirley describing her experiences (primarily in baby talk). The WOLF TV Network hires Bart to write a TV movie about the event. Bart bases the teleplay on the facts contained in newspaper accounts and the CNN coverage. He also uses some of the facts contained in *All's Well That Ends Well;* but he neither quotes nor paraphrases any of the material in the book. The teleplay is not a derivative work of *All's Well That Ends Well,* and WOLF need not obtain the permission of Shirley's parents to broadcast its TV movie.

FAIR USE OF PROTECTED EXPRESSION

Even if a derivative work author uses someone else's protected expression, permission may not be required if the use constitutes a fair use. Pursuant to the fair use privilege, an author may take a *limited* amount of the protected expression in preexisting works without the copyright owner's permission. Whether or not a use is fair is determined according to the facts and circumstances of the particular case. Courts consider the purpose of the use (whether for educational or commercial purposes, for example), the nature of the preexisting expression, the amount of preexisting expression taken, and whether the use reduces the value of the copyright owner's rights in the preexisting expression. A parody of a well-known work might be one example of a derivative work that can be created without obtaining permission from the owner of the preexisting expression pursuant to the fair use privilege. Fair use is discussed in detail in Chapter 11, *Using Other Authors' Words.*

---

4. Derivative Work Doesn't Affect Existing Copyright Protection

The copyright status of preexisting expression used in a derivative work is unaffected by the derivative work. If the preexisting expression was in the public domain, it remains so and anyone else is free to use it. If the preexisting expression was protected by copyright, that copyright continues just as if the derivative work never existed.

> **EXAMPLE 1:** Jillian wants to write a screenplay based upon a novel published in 1917. She pays

the owner of the copyright in the novel to grant her the exclusive right to prepare derivative works based upon it. She writes the screenplay. She now owns the copyright to all the material she added to the preexisting material in order to adapt it into a screenplay. Her copyright in this material will last for the rest of her life plus an additional 50 years. However, the copyright in the novel itself is not extended or otherwise affected by Jillian's screenplay. The novel's copyright will expire on Dec. 31, 1992.

EXAMPLE 2: Dr. Huxley writes an updated new edition of Charles Darwin's *The Origin of Species*. The publication of the new edition does not in any way revive the copyright in *The Origin of Species*, which expired long ago. Anyone else is free to write their own updated version of Darwin's great work, or otherwise use the material in the book.

5. Registering Derivative Works

A derivative work can and should be registered with the Copyright Office. This way, if anyone infringes upon the new material that has been added to the preexisting material, the derivative work author will be able to obtain statutory damages and attorney fees in an infringement suit. (See Chapter 4, *Copyright Registration*.)

B. Compilations

A compilation is a work created by selecting, organizing and arranging previously existing material in such a way that the resulting work as a whole constitutes an original work of authorship. Compilations differ from derivative works because the author of a compilation makes no changes in the preexisting material and need not add any new material of her own. Moreover, protectible compilations can be created solely from material that is in the public domain.

1. Fact Compilations (Databases)

A protectible fact compilation is created by selecting and arranging facts or other items that are in the public domain (see Chapter 6, *What Copyright Protects* for a detailed discussion of what is and is not in the public domain).

EXAMPLE 1: Andrea, a baseball card dealer, compiles a catalog listing the 500 cards in existence she deems to be the most desirable for collectors in their order of importance. Andrea sells copies of the catalog to collectors across the country. Andrea's catalog is a protectible compilation consisting of 500 unprotectible facts—the names of 500 baseball cards.

EXAMPLE 2: Mark, an efficiency expert, takes a number of blank forms, such as a datebook and address book, and other materials in the public domain, such as a calendar, and arranges them all into a new "executive organizer." Mark's organizer is a protectible compilation consisting of unprotectible forms and calendars.

In addition to baseball card lists and executive organizers, fact compilations may include, but are not limited to, such works as automated databases (discussed in detail in Chapter 14, Section C), bibliographies, directories, price lists, and catalogs of all types.

ELECTRONIC DATABASES

Today, many extensive fact compilations are available only in electronic form. They may be accessed via on-line services like *Nexis* and *Dialog*, or are available on computer disks. Electronic databases are discussed in detail in Chapter 14, *Electronic Publishing*.

---

2. Collective Works

A compilation may also be created by selecting and arranging into a single whole work preexisting materials that are separate and independent works entitled to copyright protection in their own right. Such compilations are called collective works.

EXAMPLE: Elliot compiles an anthology of the 25 best American short stories published during the 1980s. Each story is a separate and independent work that was protected by copyright the moment it was created. However, Elliot has created a new protectible collective work by selecting and arranging the stories into a collective whole—that is, a collection of the best short stories of the 1980s.

Other examples of collective works include newspapers, magazines and other periodicals in which separately protectible articles are combined into a collective whole, and encyclopedias consisting of independently protectible articles on various topics.

FACT COMPILATION COMBINED WITH COLLECTIVE WORK

It is possible to create a compilation that includes both unprotectible facts and other items that are individually protectible.

EXAMPLE: An anthology of selected articles by various historians on ancient Sparta that also contains a bibliography listing every article written on Sparta in the 20th century.

---

3. Extent of Copyright Protection for Compilations

You may be wondering why a compilation should be protected by copyright. The author of a compilation has not written anything new. For example, how can Andrea's baseball card catalog in the example above constitute a protectible original work of authorship? Where is the originality—that is, independent creation plus minimal creativity? Andrea simply compiled a list of the names of baseball cards; none of the names on her list is individually protectible.

What makes Andrea's list protectible is the creativity and judgment she had to employ in deciding which of the thousands of baseball cards in existence belonged on her list of the 500 most desirable cards, and in deciding what order the names should appear on the list. Similarly, Elliot in the example above used creativity and judgment in selecting which of the thousands of short stories published during the 1980s belonged in his anthology of the 25 best short stories of that decade, and in deciding on the arrangement (that is, order) of the stories. It is this selection and arrangement of the material comprising a compilation that constitutes protected expression.

The copyright in a protectible fact compilation or collective work extends only to this protected expression—that is, only to the compiler's selection and arrangement of the preexisting material, not to the preexisting material itself. This is sometimes referred to as a thin copyright.

EXAMPLE: The copyright in Elliot's short story anthology extends only to Elliot's selection and arrangement of the stories in his anthology, not to the stories themselves. This means that anyone could reprint the stories contained in the collection (with the copyright owners' permission) without violating Elliot's compilation copyright. But another person could not, without Elliot's permission, publish a book of the best short stories of the 1980s using the same stories in Elliot's book, printed in the same order.

a. Raw facts in fact compilations not protected by copyright

Since the copyright in a fact compilation extends only to the compiler's selection and arrangement of the facts, the raw facts or data themselves are not protected by copyright The Supreme Court has stated that the raw facts may be copied at will and that a compiler is even free to use the facts contained in another's compilation to aid in preparing a competing compilation (*Feist Publications, Inc. v. Rural Telephone Service Co.,* 111 S.Ct. 1282 (1991)); but, as discussed above, the competing work may not feature the same selection and arrangement as the earlier compilation.

EXAMPLE: Every month, the editors of *Harper's* magazine compile the *Harper's Index;* a listing of about 40 separate facts or statistics arranged in such a way as to comment ironically on the state of the world. Here's a sample from the May 1991 *Harper's Index:*

Death rate for American personnel stationed in the Persian Gulf, per 100,000: 69

Death rate for men between the ages of 20 and 30 living in the United States, per 100,000: 104

Harper's copyright in these fact compilations extends only to the selection and arrangement of the facts, not to the facts themselves. This means that another magazine could use the individual facts contained in the *Harper's Index,* but it could not copy the arrangement of all the facts created by the *Harper's* editors. Thus, another magazine could use the statistics about death rates in the Persian Gulf War and men living in the U.S., but it could not copy the arrangement of all 40 of the statistics contained in the May 1991 *Harper's Index.*

It may seem unfair that the facts contained in a compilation gathered at great trouble and expense may be used by others without compensating the original compiler. However, recall that the purpose of copyright is to advance the progress of knowledge, not to reward authors. If the first person to compile a group of raw facts had a monopoly over them, such progress would be greatly impeded.

b. The minimal creativity requirement

A work must be the product of a minimal amount of creativity to be protected by copyright. This requirement applies to fact compilations as well as all other works. The data contained in a factual compilation need not be presented in an innovative or surprising way, but the selection and/or arrangement cannot be so mechanical or routine as to require no creativity whatsoever. If no creativity was employed in selecting or arranging the data, the compilation will not receive copyright protection.

In a landmark decision on fact compilations, the Supreme Court held that the selection and arrangement of white pages in a typical telephone directory fails to satisfy the creativity requirement and is therefore not protected by copyright. (*Feist Publications, Inc. v. Rural Telephone Service Co.*, 111 S.Ct. 1282 (1991).) There are doubtless many other types of compilations that are unprotectible for the same reason.

For example, the names, phone numbers and addresses contained in a yellow pages phone directory organized into an alphabetical list of business classifications have been found to completely lack creativity and therefore not to qualify for copyright protection. (*Bellsouth Advertising & Publishing Corp. v. Donnelley Information Publishing, Inc.*, 999 F.2d 1436 (11th Cir. 1993).)

How can you tell if your compilation makes the grade?

The *selection* of the data in a compilation will satisfy the minimal creativity test if the compiler has:
- chosen less than all of the data in a given body of relevant material, regardless of whether it is taken from one or more sources, or
- taken all of the data from several different sources and combined them to form a new work.

For example, there is no selectivity required to compile a list of *all* the people who have telephones in a given geographical area—that is, the compiler of a telephone directory need not employ any judgment in deciding who belongs in the directory.

A compiler's *arrangement* or coordination of the data in a compilation will satisfy the creativity requirement as long as the data is ordered into lists or categories that go beyond the mere mechanical grouping of data. Alphabetical, chronological or sequential listings of data are purely mechanical and do not satisfy the minimal creativity requirement. This is why the alphabetical arrangement of names in a telephone directory is not minimally creative.

Representatives of the Copyright Office have indicated that in their view the following types of compilations will usually fail to satisfy the minimal creativity requirement:

Street address directories, alumni directories, membership lists, mailing lists and subscriber lists. Where the names and addresses in these types of compilations are arranged in alphabetical or numerical order, and no selectivity was required in determining which names and addresses should be included, they would seem to contain no more creativity than telephone book white pages. Examples: an alphabetical list of all the Harvard alumni, all the members of the ACLU or all the subscribers to *Time* magazine; a mailing list in numerical order according to zip code of all persons who have contributed more than $1,000 to the Republican Party.

Parts lists. An alphabetical or numerical list of *all* the parts in a given inventory clearly fails the creativity test: If the list is exhaustive, no selectivity is required to compile it; if it is arranged in alphabetical or numerical order, no creativity is required to arrange it.

Genealogies. A genealogy (that is, a table or diagram recording a person's or family's ancestry) consisting merely of transcriptions of public records, such as census or courthouse records, or transcriptions made from headstones in a few local cemeteries, are also deemed by the Copyright Office to lack minimal creativity. On the other hand, the creativity requirement may be satisfied where the creator of a genealogy compilation uses judgment in selecting material from a number of different sources.

The Copyright Office will not register these items unless the applicant convinces the copyright examiner that a minimal amount of creativity was required to select and/or arrange the information they contain.

MAKING YOUR COMPILATION PROTECTIBLE

There are ways you can help make your compilation satisfy the minimal creativity requirement. If you must compile a list of *all* of anything, don't simply arrange your data in alphabetical, numerical or chronological order. For example, if you were compiling a bibliography of every book ever written about the Civil War, you shouldn't simply list every title alphabetically. Instead, you should employ some selectivity by breaking down your bibliography into categories—for instance, books about the causes of the war, Civil War generals, the naval war and so on. The more judgment you use in arranging your data, the more protectible your compilation.

DE MINIMIS COMPILATIONS

De minimis is Latin for trifling or insignificant. A de minimis compilation is one that contains only a few items. Even if a *de minimis* compilation meets the minimal creativity requirement, the Copyright Office will refuse to register it. The Copyright Office considers a compilation of only three items to be clearly de minimis.

COPYRIGHT OFFICE REGULATIONS

The Copyright Office has issued a regulation providing that works "consisting entirely of information that is common property containing no original authorship, such as... standard calendars, height and weight charts... schedules of sporting events and lists or tables taken from public documents or other common sources" are not protectible and may not be registered. (37 C.F.R. 202.1(d) (1984).) This is certainly true if no creativity is involved in creating such works. But, of course, a table, list or schedule would be a protectible fact compilation if the selection and arrangement of the information it contained was minimally creative.

c.   Collective works

Collective works must also meet the minimal creativity and originality requirements. If little or no selectivity and judgment is required to create a collective work, it may not be protectible. For example, an anthology consisting of ten stories in chronological order by the same author who wrote only those ten stories in her entire life would probably not be protectible because compiling such an anthology would require no selectivity or judgment.

d. Compilations containing protected expression receive greater protection

An author may add protected expression to a fact compilation or collective work. If original, such expression is protected by copyright just like any other original work of authorship. As a result, if protected expression is included throughout a compilation, it will be much more difficult and risky for users to copy the entire compilation or large chunks of it. Reason: By doing so, they would be copying not only unprotectible facts but the protected expression in the compilation as well.

> **EXAMPLE:** Robert compiles a bibliography containing the titles, authors and publishers of every book published in the United States on the Civil War (about 50,000 in all). The bibliography is simply in alphabetical order, so it probably lacks sufficient creativity to be protectible. However, Robert also includes an introduction and annotates some of the selections with explanatory notes. Both the introduction and notes constitute protected expression. Thus, if someone copied the entire bibliography they would be copying protected expression, and therefore commit copyright infringement. Of course, anyone could still copy the individual bibliographic entries so long as they left the protected expression alone.

e. Other protections for compilations

Given the limitations on copyright protection for compilations, and the fact that some compilations may not qualify for any protection at all, the owners of valuable compilations may wish to find means other than copyright to protect their work. One means might be contract restrictions similar to those employed by the owners of automated databases. For example, books containing fact compilations might be leased to users on terms similar to database licenses. The lease would provide that the user may not copy the compilation without the owner's consent. However, there are many unresolved questions about the enforceability of such contracts. For further information, you should see a qualified copyright attorney.

4. Preexisting Material in Collective Works Must Be Used Lawfully

Recall that a collective work is a compilation in which the preexisting material consists of separate and independent works that are individually protectible. If such preexisting material is in fact under copyright, it cannot be published as part of a compilation without permission from the owner of the right to reproduce the work (presumably, such permission would have to be paid for). A compilation author who publishes such preexisting material without permission infringes on the owner's copyright and invites a copyright infringement suit.

> **EXAMPLE:** Assume that Elliot (the compiler of the anthology of the 25 best short stories of the 1980s) obtained permission to republish 24 of the stories, but failed to get permission to publish a story written and owned by Tom. Tom is entitled to sue Elliot (and his publisher) for infringing on his exclusive right to reproduce his story.

Permission may take the form of a nonexclusive license to use the material in the collective work, an exclusive license or even an assignment of all rights in the material. See Chapter 9, *Transferring Copyright Ownership.*

a. Use of public domain material

No permission is necessary if the preexisting material is in the public domain. As discussed in Chapter 6, *What Copyright Protects*, public domain material is not protected by copyright; anyone can use it however she wishes.

> **EXAMPLE:** Assume that Elliot compiled an anthology of the best short stories of the 1880s (rather than the 1980s). He does not have to obtain permission to use the stories he selected. The copyright in all short stories written in the 1880s expired long ago and they are all in the public domain.

b. Use of material created by compiler

A collective work may be created from preexisting material that the collective work author created himself. For example, Elliot could create an anthology of his own best short stories. Of course, in this event the author would not need to obtain permission to use the material (assuming he still owns the copyright).

5. Copyright in Preexisting Material Unaffected by Inclusion in Collective Work

The copyright status of the preexisting material used to create a collective work is unaffected by the collective work's existence. Thus, if the preexisting material was in the public domain, it remains in the public domain. If the preexisting material was protected by copyright, such protection continues without regard to the collective work—that is, the duration of copyright protection for the preexisting material remains the same, and is unaffected by a transfer of the compiler's rights in her compilation.

> **EXAMPLE 1:** Assume again that Elliot compiles an anthology of the best short stories of the 1880s. All the stories in his anthology remain in the public domain. The fact that they were republished in Elliot's anthology does not revive the copyright in the stories.

> **EXAMPLE 2:** Assume instead that Elliot compiles an anthology of the best short stories of the 1980s. All of the stories in the anthology are protected by copyright, so Elliot had to obtain the copyright owners' permission to include the stories in his anthology. The duration of the copyrights in the stories is not affected by the fact that Elliot republished them in his anthology years after they were created. Unless Elliot purchased all or part of the copyrights in the stories, he acquired no ownership rights in them by virtue of their inclusion in his anthology.

6. Registering Compilations

Fact compilations and collective works can and should be registered. This way, if someone copies the compiler's selection and arrangement, the compiler will be able to obtain statutory damages and attorney fees in an infringement suit. (See Chapter 4, *Copyright Registration*.)

Initial Copyright Ownership

A work that satisfies the three criteria for copyright protection discussed in Chapter 6 (fixation, originality and minimal creativity) is protected automatically upon creation. At that same moment, the author (or authors) of the work becomes the initial owner(s) of the copyright in the work. This chapter is about determining who these authors—and initial owners—are.

It is important to understand who the authors/initial owners are because:

- their rights may differ, depending on the nature of their authorship
- correct identification of the authors/initial owners is required to make a valid copyright registration, and
- the nature of the authorship affects how long the copyright lasts.

There are several basic ways to author a work and thereby become its initial owner.

- An individual may independently author the work.
- An employer may pay an employee to author the work, in which case the employer is an author under the work made for hire rule.
- A person or business entity may specially commission an independent contractor to author the work under a written work made for hire contract, in which case the commissioning party becomes the author.
- Two or more individuals or entities may collaborate to become joint authors.

We discuss each of these types of authorship (and initial ownership) in turn.

A. Independent Authorship by an Individual

The individual author of a work is the initial owner of its copyright when the work made for hire doctrine doesn't apply (see Section B, below) and when there is no joint authorship (Section C, below). The individual may exercise any of her copyright rights herself. For example, she may reproduce and sell her work herself, or authorize others to do so—that is, license a publisher. She may also transfer her ownership in whole or in part to others. (See Chapter 9, *Transferring Copyright Ownership.*) An individual copyright owner can do whatever she wants with her copyright in the United States; she is accountable to no one.

IMPACT OF COMMUNITY PROPERTY LAWS ON COPYRIGHT OWNERSHIP

In states that have community property laws, property that is acquired while people are married is usually considered to belong to both spouses equally. This means that individual authors who reside in California, Idaho, Nevada, New Mexico, Arizona, Texas, Louisiana, Washington and Wisconsin may be required to share ownership of their copyrights with their spouses. (See discussion in Chapter 9, *Transferring Copyright Ownership.*)

B. Works Made for Hire

Not all works are initially owned by the person or persons who actually create them. If you create a protectible work on someone else's behalf, that person (or entity) may be considered the work's author and thereby initially own the copyright in the work, not you. These types of works are called works made for hire.

The owner of a work made for hire is considered to be the author of the work whether the owner is a human being or a business entity such as a corporation or partnership. As the author, the owner is entitled to register the work, exercise its copyright rights in the work such as publishing the work or adapting it to a different medium, permit others to exercise these rights, or sell all or part of its rights.

The actual creator of a work made for hire has no copyright rights in the work; he may not sell it, publish it, prepare a derivative work from it, or even read it in public. All he receives is whatever compensation the hiring party gives him, whether a salary or other payment.

EXAMPLE: Real estate magnate Donald Frump orders Manny, a longtime employee who serves as Donald's publicist and ghostwriter, to write his autobiography. The resulting book, entitled *The Art of the Steal*, is a worldwide bestseller. It is also a work made for hire. Donald earns $1 million in royalties and sells the film rights for another $1 million. Manny asks Donald for a 10% share of these monies, reasoning that he is entitled to them since he actually wrote the autobiography. Donald refuses, but tells Manny he'll give him a $50 a week raise. Manny can take the raise or leave it, but he is not legally entitled to any royalties from the autobiography. As far as the Copyright Act is concerned, Donald is the book's author.

Obviously, it is vitally important for all writers to understand what is and what is not a work made for hire.

1. There Are Two Different Types of Works Made for Hire

There are probably only two reasons why you or anybody else would go to the trouble of creating a protectible work for another person or entity: (1) you are that person's employee and creating the work is part of your job; or (2) a person or entity that is not your employer—a magazine for instance—asks you to create the work for payment or some other remuneration (the Copyright Act calls this specially requesting or commissioning a work).

As a result, there are two different types of works made for hire:

- Works prepared by employees within the scope of their employment, and
- Certain works prepared by nonemployees that are specially ordered or commissioned where the parties both agree in writing that the work shall be considered a work made for hire.

SOME HISTORY ABOUT WORKS MADE FOR HIRE

Before the Copyright Act took effect in 1978, no distinction was made between works created by employees as part of their job and commissioned works; both were automatically considered to be works made for hire unless the parties expressly agreed otherwise. No written work for hire agreement was ever necessary. When the 1976 Copyright Act was being drafted, organizations representing writers and other creative people strongly urged that works made for hire be limited to those created by actual employees, and that commissioned works created by nonemployees not be considered works for hire. This way, the author of a commissioned work would be the initial owner of all the rights in the work and would give to the commissioning party only those rights he expressly agreed to give up in a transfer agreement. Publishers, film producers and others strongly opposed this. A compromise was reached that was a partial victory for writers. Under the Copyright Act, commissioned works would be works made for hire only if their creators agreed in writing; and work for hire status was restricted to nine categories of commissioned works listed in Section 3, below. Works prepared by employees continued to be works for hire just as they were before.

Let's examine each type of work made for hire.

2. Works Created by Employees as Part of Their Job

A natural consequence of the employer-employee relationship is that the employer owns whatever it pays an employee to create. It's assumed that an employee agrees to this when she takes a job. For example, Ford Motor Co. doesn't have to tell persons it hires to work on its assembly lines that they won't own the cars they make or have them sign contracts to this effect. Similarly, an employer doesn't have to tell an employee that it will own copyrightable works she creates on the employer's behalf—the employee is supposed to know this without being told. For this reason, no written work for hire contract is required in the employer-employee context.

EXAMPLE: "Scoop" Jackson is hired to be a salaried reporter for the *Yakima Daily News,* which is owned by a privately held corporation. He is required to write one news story every day. These stories will be works made for hire to which the *Daily News* will own the copyright. The *Daily News* does not have to tell Scoop this and need not draw up a work for hire agreement for him to sign.

The example above is obvious, but the work made for hire rule is not limited to works written by in-house editorial staffs. The rule extends to anything written by any employee within the scope of his employment, including reports, memoranda, letters and in-house newsletters.

One problem in applying the work made for hire rule in the employer-employee context is determining:

- just who is an employee, and
- when a work is written within the scope of employment.

a. Who is an employee?

The U.S. Supreme Court has held that a person is an employee for copyright purposes if the person on whose behalf the work is done has the *right to control* the manner and means by which the work is created. It makes no difference what the parties call themselves or how they characterize their relationship. If the person on whose behalf the work is done has the requisite right of control, the person hired is an employee and any protectible work he creates within the scope of his employment is a work made for hire. It also makes no difference whether the control is actually exercised, so long as the *right* to exercise it is present. (*CCNV v. Reid,* 109 S.Ct. 2166 (1989).)

If a legal dispute results as to whether the creator of a protectible work was an employee, the courts are supposed to examine a variety of factors to determine if the requisite degree of control was present in the relationship. Many of these criteria are quite broad and there are no concrete guidelines as to how they should be applied. As a practical matter, this means that judges have great discretion in deciding who is and who isn't an employee for copyright purposes.

One recent case make clear that two factors are of prime importance:

- whether the hiring firm pays the worker's Social Security taxes, and
- whether the hiring firm provides employee benefits.

The court held that a part-time computer programmer employed by a swimming pool retailer was not the company's employee for copyright purposes and the programmer was therefore entitled to ownership of a program he wrote for the company. The court stated that the company's failure to provide the programmer with health, unemployment or life insurance benefits, or to withhold Social Security, federal or state taxes from his pay was a "*virtual admission*" that the programmer was an independent contractor. The court stressed that the company could not treat the programmer as an independent contractor for tax purposes and then turn around and claim he was an employee for copyright ownership purposes—he had to be treated the same way for both purposes. (*Aymes v. Bonelli,* 980 F.2d. 857 (2d Cir. 1992).)

In no other case has a court determined that a worker was an employee for copyright purposes where the hiring firm treated him as an independent contractor for tax purposes. *The moral is this:* If you don't pay a worker's Social Security taxes or provide him with benefits, you should assume he is an independent contractor for copyright ownership purposes.

Given the track record in the courts, you can probably safely assume that a formal salaried employee for whom you pay social security taxes and employee benefits would be considered an employee for copyright purposes. However, the rules are ambiguous and given to highly subjective interpretation. When anything short of a formal, salaried employment relationship is involved, there is always a risk it will not be deemed an employment relationship for copyright purposes. This could happen even though you treat such a worker as an employee for tax purposes.

FACTORS CONSIDERED IN DETERMINING EMPLOYEE STATUS

Here is a list of some of the factors judges are supposed to consider in determining if a person is an employee for copyright purposes. This is not an exclusive list, and no single factor is determinative:

- The skill required to do the work
- The source of tools and materials used to create the work
- The duration of the relationship
- Whether the person who pays for the work has the right to assign additional projects to the creative party
- Who determines when and how long the creative party works
- The method of payment
- Who decides what assistants will be hired, and who pays them
- Whether the work is in the ordinary line of business of the person who pays for the work
- Whether the creative party is in business for herself
- Whether the creative party receives employee benefits from the person who pays for the work
- The tax treatment of the creative party.

Copyright tip

A person who pays someone else to create a protectible work should not rely on the work made for hire rule outside the context of a formal salaried arrangement. Instead, the person should have the creator transfer to him those rights that he needs. A written agreement must be signed by both parties to accomplish this. (See Section B.6 for further discussion.)

b. When a work is created within the scope of employment

Not everything an employee writes belongs to his employer. An employee's writings and other copyrightable works are works made for hire only if they are created within the scope of employment. An employee's work is created within the scope of employment only if it:

- is the kind of work the employee is paid to perform,
- occurs substantially within work hours at the work place, and
- is performed, at least in part, to serve the employer. (*Miller v. CP Chemicals, Inc.*, 808 F.Supp. 1238 (D.S.C. 1992) (quoting *Restatement of Agency*).)

Unless an employer and employee agree otherwise, anything an employee writes outside the scope of employment is not a work made for hire. This is so even if the work arises out of the employee's activities on the employer's behalf.

EXAMPLE: Recall our intrepid reporter Scoop Jackson in the example above. Assume that Scoop writes a series of articles for the *Yakima Daily News* exposing unsafe practices in the meatpacking industry. Of course, these articles are works for hire the copyright to which is owned by Scoop's newspaper. Scoop also writes a novel on his own time about a reporter who exposes the meatpacking industry. Although the novel is based on Scoop's experiences as an employee-reporter, it is not a work for hire because it was not created within the scope of his employment—that is, his job duties as a reporter did not include writing fiction.

Works created by an employee outside the scope of employment are automatically owned by the employee. Thus, it is not legally necessary to sign an agreement to this effect. However, an agreement stating that a particular work is not created within the scope of employment can be a very good idea where arguments might later develop about what the scope of employment entails. For this reason, Scoop had his employer sign the following document before he began work on the novel:

LETTER TO THE *YAKIMA DAILY NEWS*

The *Yakima Daily News* hereby acknowledges that:

(1) Scoop Jackson is employed as a reporter for the *Daily News;*

(2) Scoop Jackson intends to write a novel, tentatively entitled *You Are What You Eat;*

(3) *You Are What You Eat* will be written by Scoop Jackson on his own time, outside the scope of his employment by the *Daily News* and shall not constitute a work made for hire; and

(4) The *Daily News* shall claim no ownership interest whatsoever in this novel.

Yakima Daily News, by _____

Date: _____

An employer and employee are free to agree that the employee will own all or part of the copyright in works she creates *within* the scope of employment. Such an agreement amounts to a transfer of copyright ownership from the employer to the employee. The employer is still considered the author of the work made for hire. To be effective, the agreement must be in writing and signed by *both* parties.

The agreement can be entered into either before or after the employee creates the work. See Chapter 9, *Transferring Copyright Ownership,* for a detailed discussion of transfer agreements.

EXAMPLE: Assume that Scoop Jackson in the example above wants to write a nonfiction book based on his articles about the meatpacking industry. Of course, these articles were works made for hire and Scoop's employer, the *Yakima Daily News,* is considered their author for copyright purposes. For this reason, only the *Daily News* has the right to create derivative works based upon them. Scoop gets the *Daily News* to agree to let him create a book from the articles. Scoop and the *News* must both sign a transfer agreement. It might look like this:

SAMPLE TRANSFER AGREEMENT

For value received, the *Yakima Daily News* hereby assigns to Scoop Jackson the exclusive right to prepare derivative works based on the series of five articles entitled "Do You Know What You're Eating?," Parts 1–5, published in the *Yakima Daily News* during April 1991.

Yakima Daily News, by _____

Date: _____

Approved and Accepted:

/s/ Scoop Jackson

Date: _____

c.   Are scholarly writings works made for hire?

Works created by professors and other scholars employed by universities, colleges and other academic institutions pose a special problem. Prior to the adoption of the current Copyright Act in 1976, virtually all courts had held that the copyrights in lecture notes, articles and books written by professors were owned by the professors themselves, not by the universities or colleges that employed them. However, the Copyright Act apparently abolished this special teacher exemption to the work made for hire rules. (*Hays v. Sony Corp. of America*, 847 F.2d 412 (7th Cir. 1988).) To determine the ownership of scholarly writings created after January 1, 1978 (the effective date of the 1976 Copyright Act), the agency law factors set out in a sidebar in Section 2.a, above, must be applied to the facts to decide whether the requisite degree of control is present.

Arguably, colleges and universities typically do not exercise sufficient control over what professors write for such writings to constitute works made for hire. Although academic institutions may "require" scholars to create scholarly works or risk not being awarded tenure and other benefits ("publish or perish"), they usually do not dictate what should be written or supervise the writing process itself. The principle of academic freedom is supposed to prevent universities from controlling the ideas expressed in scholarly writings. However, no court has yet decided this question.

As a practical matter, most academic writings have little or no economic value and it's unlikely that a college or university would claim copyright ownership in such works. However, an academic institution might claim ownership of a scholarly work that turns out to be valuable—for example, a popular textbook. Professors can protect themselves from this possibility by having their university employers sign an agreement stating that the faculty member is the sole owner of the copyright in the work in question. The faculty member must also sign the agreement.

3. Specially Ordered or Commissioned Works

We've seen above that in the employer-employee context no work for hire agreement is necessary, and any type of protectible work may be a work made for hire. In contrast, where a person or entity asks a writer who is not an employee to prepare a protectible work, that work may be a work for hire only if (1) both parties sign a work for hire agreement, *and* (2) the work is one of the types of work set out in the sidebar below.

NINE TYPES OF WORKS THAT MAY BE CONSIDERED WORKS MADE FOR HIRE BY NONEMPLOYEES

- A contribution to a collective work such as a magazine newspaper article or anthology (See Chapter 7, *Adaptions and Compilations*)
- A part of a motion picture or other audio-visual work such as a screenplay
- A translation
- Supplementary works such as forewords, afterwords, supplemental pictorial illustrations, maps, charts, editorial notes, bibliographies, appendices and indexes)
- A compilation (See Chapter 7)
- An instructional text
- A test
- Answer material for a test
- An atlas.

Works that don't fall within one of the nine categories set out in the sidebar constitute works made for hire only if created by an employee within the scope of employment as discussed in Section B.2, above.

---

a. Express work for hire contract required

A specially commissioned work constitutes a work made for hire only if the commissioning party and the creative party both sign a written contract providing that the work shall be considered a work made for hire before the work is created. The written agreement is absolutely crucial. Work for hire agreements are discussed in detail in Section C.4, below.

EXAMPLE: Steve hires Sara to write an introduction for his book. Both Sara and Steve sign a contract stating that the introduction will be a work made for hire. When Sara completes the introduction, Steve will be considered its author for copyright purposes.

SPECIAL RULES FOR CALIFORNIA

California law provides that a person who commissions a work made for hire is considered to be the employer of the creator of the work for purposes of the workers' compensation, unemployment insurance and unemployment disability insurance laws. (Cal. Labor Code Section 3351.5(c); Cal. Unemployment Insurance Code Sections 621, 686.) No one is entirely sure what impact this has on persons or entities who commission works made for hire. Neither the California courts nor state agencies have addressed the question. However, it may mean that the commissioning party has to obtain workers' compensation coverage for the creative party and might be liable for any injuries she sustains in the course of her work. It might also mean that special penalties could be assessed against a commissioning party who willfully fails to pay the creative party any monies due her after she is discharged or resigns.

These potential requirements and liabilities are one reason why it might be desirable for those commissioning work in California not to enter into a work made for hire agreement, and instead have the creator assign the desired copyright rights to the commissioning party in advance. (See discussion at Section B.5–6, below.)

b. Freelance contributions to magazines and other collective works

The term freelance writer, usually connotes a self-employed person who contributes articles to newspapers, magazines and similar publications. Although you may not naturally think of freelance articles as works made for hire, they are if the freelancer and the publication that buys the work both sign a work for hire agreement.

> **EXAMPLE:** The editor of *The Egoist Magazine* asks Gloria, a freelance writer, if she would be interested in writing an article for the magazine on nightlife in Palm Beach. Gloria says yes. The editor then sends Gloria a letter agreement to sign setting forth such terms as Gloria's compensation and the deadline for the article and its length, and stating that the article shall be a work made for hire. If Gloria signs the agreement, her article will be a work made for hire—that is, the magazine will be the author and initial owner— instead of her.

Copyright tip for publishers and editors Although the Copyright Act gives the publishers of magazines, periodicals, and other collective works the right to use work made for hire agreements with freelance writers, this doesn't mean that they should exercise this right. Many successful freelancers simply refuse to sign work for hire agreements or will demand substantial extra compensation to do so. Generally, it's wiser—and more supportive of the arts—simply to have the author assign the rights that the magazine really needs, and let her retain the others.

c. Screenplays

Screenplays are among the types of work that are considered to be made for hire if specially commissioned pursuant to a work made for hire agreement. Such agreements are commonly used in the film industry. However, the Writers Guild of America (the screenwriter's union) has entered into collective bargaining agreements with the entertainment industry providing that its members are entitled to retain certain copyright rights in their made for hire screenplays. The Writer's Guild should be consulted about this.

d. Supplemental works

An author or publisher who hires an independent contractor (that is, a nonemployee) to compile an index or bibliography, put together an appendix, take some photographs or create a few illustrations, maps or charts to supplement the text would naturally assume that she will own the copyright in the work she pays for. By now you should know that this will be true only if both parties sign a work made for hire agreement or the independent contractor signs an agreement assigning her rights in the work to the author or publisher. If they do neither, the contractor will own the copyright in the work he creates. However, the commissioning party will probably be entitled to use the work (see discussion at section B.5, below).

e. Unsolicited manuscripts are not specially commissioned works

A work is specially ordered or commissioned only if it is created at the commissioning party's request. By definition, an unsolicited manuscript is not requested and thus cannot be considered a specially ordered or commissioned work. This fact cannot be altered by contract.

> **EXAMPLE:** Archie, a beginning freelance writer, writes an article about a trip he took to Pago Pago and sends it "over the transom" to World Travel Magazine. The magazine accepts the article for publication and sends Archie a contract saying that the work will be a work made for hire. Although Archie's article comes within one of the nine categories of specially ordered works (it is a contribution to a collective work), it is not a work made for hire because it was not

written at the magazine's request. However, if Archie signs the contract, it might be considered a transfer of his copyright in the article to the magazine (see Section B.5, below).

4.   Work Made for Hire Agreements

We'll first look at work made for hire agreements with independent contractors to create specially commissioned works, and then at agreements with employees.

a.   Specially commissioned works

An agreement to specially commission a work made for hire must make clear that the work is made for hire. The words work made for hire should be used. You don't need to use a fancy contract; a memo or letter will suffice so long as both parties sign.

The work for hire agreement must be signed *before* the work is commenced to be effective. The hiring party cannot wait until after the work is finished and a final manuscript delivered to decide that the work should be a work made for hire. (*Schiller & Schmidt, Inc. v. Nordisco Corp.*, 969 F.2d 410 (7th Cir. 1992).)

> **EXAMPLE:** Nastassia writes a nonfiction book and asks Bill, a librarian, to compile an index for it. An index is a supplementary work; one of the nine categories of specially commissioned works. This means the index will be a work for hire if Nastassia and Bill both sign a work for hire agreement before Bill starts work. Nastassia could have Bill sign a letter agreement worded something like this:

SAMPLE AGREEMENT

May 1, 199X

Dear Bill:

I hereby commission you to create a two-level alphabetical index of at least 50 double-spaced typewritten pages for the book entitled *The History of Sex*. We both agree that the index shall be considered a work made for hire. You understand that I shall own all rights in the index, including but not limited to the copyright.

The index shall be completed and delivered to me by August 1, 199X. I will pay you $1,000 within 30 days after I accept the index.

Please indicate your acceptance of these terms by signing below and returning this letter to me.

Very truly yours,

Nastassia Kinsey

Nastassia Kinsey

Approved and accepted:

_____

Bill Bennett

Date: _____

---

b.   Agreements with employees

As discussed above, protectible works created by employees within the scope of their employment automatically become works made for hire. The employee's consent is not required and an express work for hire agreement is not necessary. Indeed, the employer need not even inform the employee that it will own the copyright in her creations.

However, although it is not legally required, it may be desirable in some cases to have an employee sign an agreement stating that he understands the work he's creating is a work made for hire. This will ensure that the employee understands that he has no copyright rights in the work to be created.

If you're not sure whether the creative person is an employee (as discussed above, this can be far from clear in some cases), having her sign a work for hire agreement will not make her one. But, if the work to be created falls within one of the nine categories of specially commissioned works discussed at Section B.3 above, the work will be considered a work for hire if both parties sign a work for hire agreement. If the work does not fall within one of the nine categories of specially commissioned works, don't use a work for hire agreement. The best approach in this situation is to have the creative person assign to you the rights you need in the work (see Section B.5, just below).

5. What Happens When a Work Does Not Satisfy the Work Made for Hire Requirement ?

What happens if someone hires another to create a work with the belief that it will constitute a work made for hire, but it turns out that the work for hire requirements were not satisfied? It won't be the end of the world, but the person laying out the money might be in for an unpleasant surprise.

a. The creator of the work owns the copyright

First of all, since the work is not a work for hire, its creator (or creators) is the author and initial owner of all the copyright rights.

> **EXAMPLE 1:** Mark pays Sally, a freelance photographer, to take some photographs of toxic waste dumps to supplement his treatise on toxic waste management. Sally is not Mark's employee and Sally and Mark did not sign a work for hire agreement. As a result, Sally owns the copyright in the photos. This means that Sally may sell them to others, reproduce them, create derivative works from them or otherwise exercise her copyright rights in the photos.

> **EXAMPLE 2:** Marlon, a well-known actor, pays Tom $50,000 to ghostwrite his autobiography. Tom's work could constitute work made for hire only if Tom was Marlon's employee and the work was created within the scope of employment. Assume that Marlon does not exercise sufficient control over Tom for him to be considered Marlon's employee. Who owns the copyright in Tom's work? Tom does! Tom is entitled to sell the autobiography to others, serialize it in magazines, sell it to movie producers, etc.

b. Hirer has nonexclusive license to use work

At the very least, a person who pays an author to create a protectible work has a nonexclusive license to use it as intended. This seems only fair, considering that the hiring party paid for the work. A person with a nonexclusive license in a work may use the work, but may not prevent others from using it as well. Nonexclusive licenses may be implied from the circumstances; no express agreement is required. (See detailed discussion of nonexclusive licenses in Chapter 9, *Transferring Copyright Ownership.*)

> **EXAMPLE 1:** Since Mark, from the above example, paid Sally to take the toxic waste photos for inclusion in his book, he would have a nonexclusive license to use them in the book. But this would not prevent Sally from allowing others to use the photographs in other publications.

EXAMPLE 2: Likewise, since Marlon paid Tom to write his autobiography, Marlon would have the right to publish it. But, again, this would only be a nonexclusive license. Tom could sell the autobiography to others.

c. Transfer of rights under a work made for hire contract

What happens if the creator of a protectible work signed a work for hire contract, but the requirements for work made for hire status were not satisfied? This could occur where a work for hire contract was signed by a nonemployee, but the work created did not fall within one of the nine categories of specially commissioned works. In this event, a court *might* interpret the contract as a transfer by the creator of his rights in the work to the hiring party.

EXAMPLE: Assume that Marlon in the example above had Tom sign a contract stating that the autobiography would be a work made for hire. Unfortunately for Marlon, the authorship of entire autobiographies does not come within one of the nine categories of specially commissioned works. This means that regardless of what Marlon's contract said, the work is not a work made for hire and Tom is the author and initial owner of the copyright.

POSSIBLE COURT HELP FOR A FAILED CONTRACT

It is possible that a court would interpret the work made for hire contract as a transfer by Tom to Marlon of all his copyright rights in his work. Tom would still be the initial owner and author, but Marlon would still end up owning all the copyright rights in the work—that is, he would have the exclusive right to publish it, create derivative works based upon it and so on. But it's also possible that a judge would rule the contract unenforceable and simply award Marlon a nonexclusive license.

---

d. Joint work created

If the hiring party and creative party worked together on the writing project, the work might constitute a joint work, with both parties being considered authors and initial copyright owners.

EXAMPLE: Assume that Marlon in the examples above worked with Tom in writing the autobiography, contributing not only ideas, but also writing portions of the book. Is Tom still the sole owner of the copyright in the autobiography? Probably not. The autobiography would probably constitute a joint work and would be jointly owned by Tom and Marlon. See Section C, below, for a detailed discussion of joint works.

6. Assignment of Rights as Alternative to Reliance on Work Made for Hire Rule

Hopefully, it is clear by now that relying on the work made for hire rule can be a risky proposition for the hiring party. Unless the hiring party is dealing with a conventional employee or commissioning one of the nine specially commissioned works discussed in Section B.3, above, under an express work for hire contract, he can never be absolutely sure who will end up owning the copyright in the work he pays for.

The solution to this problem is to have the creator of the work transfer all or part of her rights—whatever they are—to the hiring party. As discussed above, this may mean that the creator will still be considered the author and initial owner, but the result will be that the hiring party will end up owning the copyright.

EXAMPLE 1: Assume that Marlon, in the examples discussed in Section B.5, above, had Tom sign an agreement assigning to him all his rights in the autobiography. Marlon would become the owner of the copyright in the autobiography by virtue of the assignment agreement.

EXAMPLE 2: Similarly, had Mark, in the examples discussed in Section B.5, above, had his photographer Sally assign all her rights in the toxic waste photos to him, Mark would have owned the copyright in the photos.

An assignment must be put into effect through a written transfer agreement signed by both parties. The agreement may be signed before or after the work is created. See Chapter 9, *Transferring Copyright Ownership*, for a detailed discussion and sample form.

ASSIGNMENTS CAN BE TERMINATED AFTER 35 YEARS

One possible disadvantage of using an assignment of rights as opposed to a work made for hire agreement is that an assignment can be terminated by the author or her heirs 35 to 40 years after it is made. (See Chapter 10, *Copyright Duration*, for a detailed discussion.) However, in most cases this disadvantage is meaningless because very few works have a useful economic life of 35 years.

C. Jointly Authored Works

Things can get even more complicated when two or more individuals create a work that is not a work made for hire. Such a work is normally jointly owned by its creators—that is, each contributing author shares in the ownership of the entire work. A joint author's life is not quite as simple as that of an individual copyright owner. There may be restrictions on what each joint author can do with his or her ownership share, and joint authors must account to each other for any profits they receive from commercial exploitation of the joint work.

1. When Is a Work Jointly Authored?

A work is jointly authored automatically upon its creation if (1) two or more authors contributed material to the work; and (2) each of the authors prepared his or her contribution with the *intention* that it would be combined with the contributions of the other authors as part of a single unitary work. We'll refer to such works as joint works.

> **EXAMPLE:** Peter and Christianne agree to write a biography of Saddam Hussein together. Peter writes the chapters covering the first half of Saddam's life and Christianne writes the remainder. They combine their work to form a single biography of Saddam's entire life. The biography is a joint work by Peter and Christianne.

a. Authors' intent is controlling factor

The key to determining whether a work is a joint work is the authors' intent *at the time the work is created*. If the authors intended that their writing be absorbed or combined with other contributions into an integrated unit, the work that results is a joint work. It is not necessary that the authors work together or work at the same time. Indeed, it is not even necessary that they know each other when they create their respective contributions.

> **EXAMPLE:** Paul writes a children's story with the intention that it be combined with a number of illustrations to be created by Jean. Unfortunately, Jean dies before she can create the illustrations. Five years later, Paul meets Mary, a successful artist. Mary reads Paul's story and tells him that she would like to create the illustrations for it. Paul agrees. Mary creates the illustrations. Mary and Paul combine Paul's story and Mary's illustrations into a single integrated work—a children's book. The book is a joint work, co-owned by Mary and Paul. This is so even though Paul had never met Mary when he wrote his story and the story was written years before Mary drew her illustrations. All that matters is that when Paul and Mary created their respective contributions they intended that they be combined with other work to form an integrated whole.

b. How much material must a person contribute to be a joint author?

The respective contributions made to a joint work by its authors need not be equal in terms of quantity or quality. But, to be considered a joint author, a person must contribute more than a minimal amount of work to the finished product. For example, a person who proofreads and makes spelling corrections to a book written by another is not a joint author of that book.

c. May a joint author only contribute ideas?

Most courts require that a person's contribution consist of protectible expression—that is, actual written work—for her to be considered a joint author. A person who contributes ideas or other unprotectible items is not entitled to an ownership interest in the work's copyright unless the parties expressly agree to it, preferably in writing. (See Chapter 6, *What Copyright Protects.*)

> **EXAMPLE:** Abe and Zsa Zsa agree to collaborate on a screenplay. Abe conceives a detailed and complex plot for the screenplay, but does no writing himself. Instead, he tells Zsa Zsa the plot and Zsa Zsa uses Abe's ideas to actually write the screenplay. Most courts would hold Zsa Zsa the sole owner of the copyright in the screenplay unless she and Abe had agreed otherwise.

Copyright tip

It is always a good idea for collaborators to have a written agreement setting forth their respective interests in the work to be written. This way, if one contributor is found not to be a joint owner of the work because he did not contribute protectible expression to it, he would still be entitled (as a matter of contract law) to the ownership interest stated in the collaboration agreement. (See Section C.3. below for further discussion of collaboration agreements.)

d.   Joint authors need not be human beings

A joint author doesn't have to be a human being. A corporation, partnership or other business entity can also be a joint author.

> **EXAMPLE:** Sunnydale Farms, Incorporated, a large corporation that manufactures and sells gardening implements and seeds, agrees to coauthor a book on urban gardens with Ralph, a famous expert on roses. Ralph writes the chapters on growing flowers, while Sunnydale employees write the chapters on growing vegetables. The chapters written by Sunnydale's employees are works made for hire for which Sunnydale is considered the author. The resulting book is a joint work. The joint authors are Ralph and Sunnydale.

2.   Joint Works Compared With Derivative and Collective Works

What happens if the intent to combine contributions into an integrated whole arises *after* the contributions were created? In this event, the resulting work is not a joint work. Rather, it is either a collective work or a derivative work. It will be a collective work if the respective contributions of the authors were independently created and later simply combined into a collective whole without changing them. It will be a derivative work if the respective authors' contributions are recast, transformed or adapted to create a new work.

> **EXAMPLE 1:** Assume that Paul in the example above wrote his children's story without any intent that it be combined with illustrations. Acme Publications purchases Paul's entire copyright in the story and decides to publish it with illustrations created by Jean. The resulting work is a collective work—that is, a work in which separately protectible works are combined into a collective whole without making any internal changes to the material. (See Chapter 7, *Adaptions and Compilations*, for a detailed discussion of collective works.)

> **EXAMPLE 2:** Art writes and publishes a scientific treatise on quantum theory. Several years later, Art and his colleague Marie decide to produce an updated and expanded version of the work. This revised version of the treatise will

not be a joint work because when Art wrote his original treatise he did not intend to combine it with any other work. Rather, the revised treatise is a derivative work—that is, a work created by transforming the original treatise into a new, revised treatise. (See Chapter 7, *Adaptions and Compilations*, for a detailed discussion of derivative works.)

WHY IT IS IMPORTANT TO KNOW THE DIFFERENCE BETWEEN JOINT WORKS AND DERIVATIVE OR COLLECTIVE WORKS

Knowing the difference between a joint work and a derivative or collective work is important for these reasons:

- The copyright in a derivative work extends only to the material added to the preexisting material by the derivative work's authors.
- Contributors to a collective work own the copyright only in the material they contributed to the work.
- The authors of a joint work each share ownership in the *entire* work.

---

3. Joint Authors' Collaboration Agreement

A written collaboration agreement is not legally required to create a joint work; an oral agreement is sufficient. However, as Samuel Goldwyn supposedly once said, "an oral agreement isn't worth the paper it's printed on." It is vital that collaborators draft and sign a written agreement spelling out their rights and responsibilities. This avoids innumerable headaches later on.

A collaboration is like a marriage—no two are the same. It is not, therefore, a good idea to simply fill in the blanks on a form agreement. Rather, collaborators need to think carefully about the form their relationship should take and custom draft an agreement that suits their particular needs. Listed below are the most important points a collaboration agreement should cover. (For a detailed discussion of these issues and sample agreements, see *The Writer's Legal Companion*, by Bunnin and Beren (Addison-Wesley); and *How To Write With a Collaborator*, by Bennett and Larsen (Writer's Digest Books).)

a. Collaborators' contributions

Obviously, the collaborators need to decide what each will contribute to the work and how they will work together. Some collaborators write everything together; others work independently and then review and revise each other's first drafts. If possible, write a detailed outline or synopsis and indicate on it who will write each section. The outline should be attached to the collaboration agreement.

b. Completion date

Collaborators need to decide on a realistic deadline for completion of the work. They also need to agree on what will happen if the deadline is not met—can it be extended?

c. Quitting the collaboration

If one collaborator wants to quit the project before it is completed, can the other(s) finish it? If so, do they owe the former collaborator compensation for any work she did?

d. How is the copyright in the work to be owned?

Ownership can be divided in any way the collaborators wish. This is so regardless of the quality or quantity of their contributions. Two joint authors would each share an undivided one-half interest; three joint authors would each own a one-third interest and so forth. This is so regardless of the quantity or quality of their respective contributions.

> **EXAMPLE:** Molly, Rick and Tom agree to write a nonfiction work. Molly and Rick each agree to write 40% of the work and Tom agrees to write the remaining 20%. However, since Tom is a well-known author whose name will help sell the book, Molly and Rick agree that he will own a 50% interest in the copyright, while Molly and Rick will each own a 25% interest. Molly, Rick and Tom should sign a collaboration agreement setting forth their respective interests.

e. Authors' credit

How will the joint authors' names appear on the published work? Alphabetically or some other way?

f. Negotiations and decision-making

Do all the collaborators conduct negotiations and make important decisions together, or can one act for the others? Must they all agree to any transfers of their copyright rights?

g. Independent parties

Do the collaborators want to be partners? Partners are each individually responsible for *all* partnership debts and each partner can make agreements that are binding on the other partners. For this reason, partnerships should be entered into with caution. Most collaboration agreements contain a provision something like this: "The parties to this agreement are independent of one another. Nothing in this agreement shall be deemed to create a partnership or joint venture between them."

h. Money management

Will royalties and other income be placed in a joint account, paid to each joint author separately, or handled in some other way?

i.   Assignments

Can one collaborator substitute someone else in her place? If so, does she need the other collaborator's consent?

j.   Noncompetition clause

Do the collaborators wish to prevent each other from creating any works in the future that would compete with the joint work?

k.   Collaborators' death or disability

If a collaborator dies or becomes disabled before the work is completed, can the survivor(s) complete the work? If so, what compensation should the deceased collaborator's heirs receive?

Joint owners can agree to own the joint work as joint tenants. This means that if one of them dies, her share automatically passes to the other joint owner(s). The last surviving owner would become sole owner of the entire work. Again, such an agreement should be made part of a written collaboration agreement.

l.   Dispute resolution

How will disputes be resolved? Many collaborators agree to have a mediator or arbitrator resolve serious disagreements.

4.   Joint Authors' Rights and Duties in the Absence of a Collaboration Agreement

The drafters of the Copyright Act realized that not all joint authors would be prudent enough to enter into a written (or even oral) collaboration agreement setting forth their ownership interests, rights and duties. To avoid chaos, they made sure that the act contained provisions governing the most important aspects of the legal relationship between joint authors who fail to agree among themselves how their relationship should operate. You might think of these provisions as similar to a computer program's default settings that control the program when the user fails to make his own settings.

a.   Ownership interests

Unless they agree otherwise, joint authors each have an undivided interest in the entire work. This is basically the same as joint ownership of a house or other real estate. When a husband and wife jointly own their home they normally each own a 50% interest in the entire house—that is, they each have an undivided one-half interest. Similarly, joint authors share ownership of all five exclusive rights that make up the joint work's copyright.

b.   Right to exploit copyright

Unless they agree otherwise, each joint author has the right to exercise any or all of the five copyright rights inherent in the joint work—that is, any of the authors may reproduce and distribute the work or prepare derivative works based upon it (or display or perform it). Each author may do so without the other joint author's consent.

c.   Right to license joint work

Unless they agree otherwise, each joint author may grant third parties permission to exploit the work—on a nonexclusive basis—without the other owners' consent. This means that different authors may grant nonexclusive licenses of the same right to different persons!

EXAMPLE: Manny, Moe and Jack are joint authors of a novel. Manny gives Publisher A the nonexclusive right to publish the book in North America. Moe gives the same right to Publisher B, and Jack to Publisher C. The result, perfectly legal, is that three publishers have the right to publish the book at the same time.

Copyright tip

To avoid the kind of results illustrated in the above example, anyone who purchases an exclusive right in a joint work should require signatures by all the authors. (See Chapter 9, *Transferring Copyright Ownership*, for a detailed discussion of copyright transfers.)

d. Right to transfer ownership

Finally, unless they agree otherwise, each author of a joint work may transfer her entire ownership interest to another person without the other joint authors' consent. Such person then co-owns the work with the remaining authors. But a joint author can only transfer her particular interest, not that of any other author.

EXAMPLE: Sue, Deborah and Martin are joint authors of a college textbook. Sue decides to transfer her ownership interest to her son, Sam. Since Sue, Deborah and Martin have not agreed among themselves to restrict their transfer rights in any way, Sue may transfer her interest to Sam without Deborah's or Martin's consent (but Sue could not transfer Deborah's or Martin's ownership interests to Sam without their consent). When the transfer is completed, Sam will have all the rights Sue had as a joint author.

e. Duty to account for profits

Along with these rights, each joint author has the duty to account to the other joint owners for any profits received from his use or license of the joint work. All the joint authors are entitled to share in these profits. Unless they agree otherwise, the profits must be divided among the authors according to their proportionate interests in the joint work. (Note, however, that such profits do not include what one author gets for selling his or her share of the copyright.)

EXAMPLE: Bill and Lee are joint authors of a novel. Bill writes a screenplay based on the novel and sells it for $10,000. Lee is entitled to one-half of the $10,000.

It may not seem fair that a joint author who goes to the time and trouble of exploiting the copyright in the joint work by publishing it or creating derivative works based upon it is required to share his profits equally with the other joint authors who did nothing. This is still another reason why it's wise to enter into a collaboration agreement.

f. What happens when joint authors die?

Absent a joint tenancy agreement, a deceased joint author's heirs would acquire her share in the joint work. The other joint authors do not acquire a deceased owner's share (unless, of course, the deceased owner willed it to them, or the author died without a will and another joint author was related to her and inherited her interest under the general inheritance laws).

CHAPTER

9

Transferring Copyright Ownership

In Chapter 8, *Initial Copyright Ownership*, we discuss the rights that accompany copyright ownership. Here is a brief recap. An author automatically becomes the owner of a complete set of exclusive rights in any protected expression he or she creates. These include the right to:

- reproduce the protected expression
- distribute copies of the work to the public by sale, rental, lease or otherwise
- prepare derivative works using the protected expression (that is adapt new works from the expression), and
- perform and display the work publicly.

These rights are exclusive because only the owner of one or more particular rights that together make up copyright ownership may exercise it or permit others to do so. For example, only the owner of the right to distribute a book may sell it to the public or permit others—a publisher for instance—to do so.

With the important exception of self-publishers who reproduce and distribute their work themselves, authors normally profit from their copyrights by selling their rights to publishers or others to exploit. And, except where they publish works that are in the public domain (such as works originally published more than 75 years ago), publishers must acquire the right to reproduce and sell a work from its author or other copyright owner.

THE TERMINOLOGY OF TRANSFERS

Several different terms can be used to describe a transfer of copyright ownership rights. Many of these terms are used interchangeably and have no settled legal meaning; but here is how we'll use them in this book:

- **assignment** means a transfer of all the exclusive rights that make up a copyright
- **exclusive license** means a transfer on an exclusive basis, of one or more, but less than all, of a copyright owner's exclusive rights
- **nonexclusive license** means giving someone the right to exercise one or more of a copyright owner's rights on a nonexclusive basis. Since this does not prevent the copyright owner from giving others permission to exercise the same right or rights at the same time, it is not a transfer of copyright ownership.

Again, please remember that these definitions are only for the purposes of this discussion. In the real world it makes no difference if a transfer is called an assignment, a license, a contract, a grant of rights or is given no label. The effect of an agreement to transfer copyright ownership rights is determined according to the language it contains, not its label.

A. How Copyright Ownership Rights Are Transferred to Others

A transfer of copyright ownership rights must be in writing to be valid. There are two basic types of copyright transfers: exclusive licenses and assignments. Although these terms are often used interchangeably, there are some differences.

1. Exclusive Licenses

The term exclusive license is usually used when a copyright owner transfers one or more of her rights, but retains at least some of them.

EXAMPLE: Jane writes an article on economics and grants *The Economist's Journal* the exclusive right to publish it for the first time in the United States and Canada. Jane has granted the *Journal* an exclusive license. Only the *Journal* may publish the article for the first time in the U.S. and Canada. The *Journal* owns this right. But Jane retains the right to republish her article after it appears in the *Journal* and to include it in a book. She also retains the right to create derivative works from it (for example, to expand it into a book-length work), as well as other rights that weren't specifically transferred in the license.

A copyright owner's exclusive rights are almost infinitely divisible. That is, they can be divided and subdivided and licensed to others in just about any way imaginable. In the publishing business, the most common divisions are by language, type of media (hardcover and softcover books, magazines, film, video, audiotapes, computers, etc.), time or geography.

EXAMPLE 1: Jennifer writes a high school math textbook and sells Scrivener & Sons an exclusive license to distribute it in the United States only. She then grants MacKenzie Press an exclusive license to sell the book in Canada, and Trans-European Publishing Co. the right to sell it in all EEC (common market) countries.

EXAMPLE 2: Leo writes a biography and grants Scrivener & Sons the exclusive right to sell it in the United States in hardcover. He grants all English language rights outside the U.S. to the British publisher MacCauley & Unwin, and sells the U.S. paperback rights to Acme Press.

EXAMPLE 3: Martha writes a detective novel. She grants Hardboiled Publications, Inc. the exclusive right to sell the book in the U.S. and Canada. She then gives Repulsive Pictures the exclusive right to create and distribute a film based on her work, ABC the right to use it for a television series and Tapes Unlimited, Inc. the right to adapt it into an audiotape.

EXCLUSIVE LICENSEE'S RIGHTS

The holder of an exclusive license becomes the owner of the transferred right(s). As such, unless the exclusive license provides otherwise, she is entitled to sue anyone who infringes on that right while she owns it, and is entitled to transfer her license to others. She may also record the exclusive license with the Copyright Office; this provides many valuable benefits (see discussion in Section H, below).

---

2. Assignments

If an owner of all the exclusive rights in a copyright transfers the entire bundle of rights that make up his copyright simultaneously to a single person or entity, the transaction is usually called an assignment or sometimes an all rights transfer. An assignment must be in writing to be valid.

EXAMPLE: Otto assigns Acme Romances the entire copyright in his romance novel *Love's Lost Languor.* This means that Acme, and only Acme, may publish the work or permit others to do so, or exercise any other part of the bundle of rights that make up the copyright in the work (such as authorizing someone to adapt the book into a screenplay). Otto has relinquished these rights. For all practical purposes, Acme now owns the copyright instead of Otto.

3. Nonexclusive Licenses Do Not Transfer Copyright Ownership

As mentioned earlier, a nonexclusive license gives someone the right to exercise one or more of a copyright owner's rights, but does not prevent the copyright owner from giving others permission to exercise the same right or rights at the same time. A nonexclusive license is not a transfer of ownership; it's a form of sharing. The most common type of non-exclusive license is one granting an author permission to quote from, photocopy or otherwise use a protected work; such licenses are often called permissions. See Chapter 11, *Using Other Authors' Words,* for a detailed discussion and sample permission form.

> **EXAMPLE:** Tony, an avid parachutist, has written and self-published a pamphlet on advanced parachuting techniques. He gives the Fresno Parachuting Club permission to make 100 copies of the pamphlet and distribute them in the Fresno area. Tony retains the right to let others copy and distribute his pamphlet in Fresno (and anywhere else), or may do so himself. Tony has given the club a nonexclusive license to exercise some of his copyright rights in his pamphlet. The license is nonexclusive because the club cannot prevent Tony from letting others exercise the same rights he has granted to it.

As with exclusive licenses, nonexclusive licenses may be limited as to time, geography, media or in any other way. They can be granted orally or in writing. The much better practice, however, is to use some sort of writing; this can avoid possible misunderstandings and gives the nonexclusive licensee certain priority rights discussed in Section H.4. It is not necessary to have a formal contract filled with legalese to grant a nonexclusive license. A simple letter or memo is sufficient. Just make sure that you make clear the license is nonexclusive (use the term nonexclusive license) and spell out the terms and conditions of the license—that is, what rights are being licensed, to whom and for how long.

NONEXCLUSIVE LICENSE MAY BE IMPLIED FROM CIRCUMSTANCES

An express written or oral agreement is not always required to create a nonexclusive license. A nonexclusive license can be implied from the circumstances—that is, where the circumstances are such that a copyright owner must have intended to grant a nonexclusive license, it can be considered to exist without an actual agreement.

> **EXAMPLE:** When a person sends a letter to the editor of a newspaper or magazine, a nonexclusive license giving the publication the right to publish the letter in its letters to the editor section is implied; the newspaper or magazine need not seek the letter writer's formal permission to publish the letter.

---

4. Sales of Copies Do Not Transfer Copyright Ownership

Ownership of a copyright and ownership of a material object in which the copyrighted work is embodied—such as a book or article—are entirely separate things. This means the sale or gift of a copy or copies of a book, article or other protected work does not transfer the copyright owner's exclusive rights in the work. A copyright owner's exclusive rights can only be transferred by a written agreement. For example, a person who buys a copy of a book or manuscript owns that book or manuscript, but acquires no copyright rights in the work.

> **EXAMPLE:** Luther, an extremely wealthy and avid book collector, purchases the original manuscript of James Joyce's *Finnegan's Wake* from Joyce's estate. However, Luther does not obtain any copyright rights in the work. Although Luther owns the manuscript, he cannot reproduce and distribute it or exercise any other of the copyright owners' rights in the work without obtaining their permission.

FIRST SALE DOCTRINE

Under what is known as the first sale doctrine, once a copyright owner sells or gives away a copy or copies of a book or other physical manifestation of his copyright, he relinquishes all control over that physical copy itself. The purchaser can resell the copy without the copyright owner's permission; or, if the purchaser is a library, lend it to the public.

> **EXAMPLE:** Morris has self-published 500 copies of a book on do-it-yourself plumbing. He sells all 500 copies of the book to Joe's Hardware Store, but does not transfer any copyright rights to Joe's. Joe's is entitled to sell all 500 copies, rent them, give them away, destroy them or do anything else it wants with them. But, of course, Joe's cannot reproduce the book or exercise any of Morris's other exclusive rights without his permission.

---

5. Copyright Transfers Do Not Affect Copyright Duration

Copyright transfers do not affect the duration of the copyright, even if the entire bundle of copyright ownership rights is transferred. See Chapter 10, *Copyright Duration.* However, a transfer itself may be limited as to time; that is, it doesn't have to be for the entire duration of the copyright.

> **EXAMPLE:** Margaret grants Green Thumb Publishing the exclusive right to publish her book on gardening in the United States for 20 years. The copyright in the book will last for the rest of Margaret's life plus an additional 50 years. The transfer to Green Thumb has no effect on this. When the 20 years are up, the transferred rights will revert to Margaret or her heirs and will last for the remainder of the copyright term.

B. Rights Automatically Retained by Author After Transfer

A copyright owner who transfers her entire bundle of exclusive rights still retains some important rights.

1. Statutory Termination of Transfers After 35 Years

A potentially important right retained by authors and their families is the statutory right to terminate transfers of copyright ownership made after December 31, 1977. This includes the original grant of rights an author gives to her publisher. These statutory termination rights can never be waived or contracted away.

a. What rights can be terminated?

Any transfer of copyright rights made by a living author after December 31, 1977 may be terminated.

A transfer of a copyright by will that occurs after an author dies is not subject to statutory termination.

b. Who can exercise termination right?

This termination right may be exercised only by the author of a work; or if the author is dead when the time to terminate arrives, by the author's widow or widower, children (including illegitimate and adopted children) and grandchildren. If an author dies without leaving a surviving spouse or children or grandchildren, the termination right ceases to exist. Note that an author cannot leave her termination rights to others in a will. When an author dies, her termination rights automatically pass on to her surviving spouse and children and grandchildren, if any. The provisions in an author's will are irrelevant.

The owner of a work made for hire, whether an individual or a business entity such as a corporation, has no statutory termination rights.

EXAMPLE 1: Sam writes a book in 1992 and signs a publishing contract transferring his entire copyright to Scrivener & Sons that same year. The transfer may later be terminated by Sam or certain family members as described below.

EXAMPLE 2: Sue writes a book in 1991 and transfers her entire copyright to her boyfriend Bill by a will upon her death in 1992. This transfer may not be terminated by Sue's surviving family.

c. When can transfers be terminated?

A transfer of the right to publish (that is, reproduce and distribute) a work, may be terminated any time during a five-year period beginning either 40 years after the date of the transfer or 35 years after the date of first publication, whichever is earlier. A transfer of any other rights (for example, the right to adapt a work into a film) can be terminated any time during a five-year period beginning 35 years after the transfer was made and ending 40 years afterwards.

EXAMPLE: Kelly Stewart signs a contract with Scrivener & Sons on January 1, 1980, to write a novel, and grants Scrivener the exclusive right to publish the book in the U.S. and Canada. The novel, entitled *The Voyeur*, is not published until January 1, 1990. On January 1, 1991, Kelly sells the film rights to her novel to Repulsive Pictures. The publication rights transferred to Scrivener may be terminated by Kelly or her heirs anytime between January 1, 2020, and January 1, 2025, 40 to 45 years after the publishing contract was signed. This is earlier than 35 years after the date of actual publication of the book. The film rights transfer to Repulsive may be terminated between January 1, 2025, and January 1, 2031 (35 to 40 years after the transfer was made).

d. What happens after a transfer is terminated?

After a transfer is terminated, the terminated rights revert back to the author if he or she is still alive. If the author is dead, the rights are shared by the author's widow or widower, children and grandchildren. However, the owners of any derivative works prepared from the work may continue to distribute such works.

EXAMPLE 1: Assume that it is the year 2020. Kelly Stewart has terminated the publication rights grant she made to Scrivener & Sons in 1980. This means that Scrivener may not publish any more copies of Kelly's novel without her permission. Kelly may now resell her novel's publication rights to Scrivener or any other publisher, or self-publish her novel if she so chooses.

EXAMPLE 2: Assume that is now the year 2025. Kelly has terminated the film rights transfer she made to Repulsive Pictures back in 1991. Kelly now owns the right to make any new films based upon her novel. However, Repulsive may continue to distribute *Front Window*, a film it produced based on Kelly's novel in 1994; it just can't make any new films from the novel without Kelly's permission.

e. What is the termination procedure?

A written notice of termination complying with the statutory requirements must be sent to the owners of the rights being terminated and recorded with the Copyright Office. We won't discuss the required contents of a termination notice in detail here because the earliest such a notice may be sent is January 1, 2011 (to terminate a transfer made on January 1, 1978).

3. Filing Documents With the Copyright Office

An author or other copyright owner retains the right to file the following documents with the Copyright Office following a transfer of copyright rights:

a. Supplemental registrations

Certain types of new information or changes in the information supplied in the original registration may be supplemented by the author or other copyright owner according to the procedures discussed in Chapter 5, *Correcting or Changing Copyright Notice or Registration*, even though the author or other copyright owner no longer owns any of the copyright rights.

b. Notice regarding contractual termination or revocation of transfer

A copyright owner who transfers ownership of her copyright right(s) for a set term (for example, ten years) has the right to notify the Copyright Office when the term has expired so she can expressly reclaim her ownership on the record. Similarly, revocation is desirable when a transfer is revoked because the transferee did not abide by the terms of his license (for example, failed to sell a required number of copies) or for some other reason.

An owner in this situation should send the Copyright Office a letter along the following lines, and also have the letter recorded (see Section H, below).

SAMPLE LETTER

January 2, 199X

Dear Examiner:

My copyright registration #TX 1234657 in the textbook entitled *French For First Graders* was transferred in full to Kiddie Publications for a period of ten (10) years, commencing on January 1, 199X. This is to notify you that the transfer has terminated and I am the sole owner of copyright #TX 1234567.

Sincerely,

Jacques Paul Jones

Jacques Paul Jones

4. Moral rights

In many European and other countries an author automatically retains certain additional rights in his work. These are called moral rights (or *droits morals*). Moral rights are rights an author can never transfer to a third party because they are considered an extension of her being. Briefly, they consist of the right to proper credit or attribution whenever the work is published, to disclaim authorship of unauthorized copies, to prevent or call back distribution under certain conditions and to object to any distortion, mutilation or other modification of the author's work injurious to her reputation. The right to prevent colorization of black and white films is an example of a moral right. Moral rights are generally of most concern to visual artists.

The Berne Convention (an international copyright treaty) requires that signatory countries extend these rights to authors (see discussion in Chapter 13, *International Copyright Protection*). In 1991, Congress amended the Copyright Act to extend certain moral rights to visual artists (see Section 106A of the Copyright Act); but the U.S. has not granted similar rights to authors. The courts will have to decide whether moral rights must be granted to writers under American copyright law pursuant to the Berne Convention.

However, American courts have recognized certain types of rights that are analogous to moral rights, although they may not be referred to as such. For example any author of a work published in the U.S. retains the right to have his authorship continuously recognized on works that remain true to the original. Conversely, an author retains the right to have her name taken off a work that has been substantially changed from the original. These rights do not come from the Copyright Act, but rather from the trademark laws which prohibit misrepresentation of a product's origins. In addition, one court has held that unauthorized changes in a work that are so extensive as to impair its integrity constitute copyright infringement. (See *Gilliam v. American Broadcasting Cos.,* 538 F.2d 14 (2d Cir. 1976) (The British comedy group Monty Python obtained an injunction stopping ABC from airing Monty Python programs it had obtained a license to broadcast and had heavily edited.).)

C. Copyright Transfers Between Freelance Writers and Magazines and Other Periodicals

Now that you have a general understanding of copyright transfer law, let's see how it applies to the relationship between authors and publishers of magazines, newspapers and similar publications (often called serial publications). Since publishers' and writers' interests differ in these transactions, we'll examine them first from an author's and then from a publisher's or editor's point of view.

1. Transfers From the Writer's Point of View

a. Publishing jargon

Editors, literary agents and others in the publishing business have their own jargon to describe an author's copyright rights. An author attempting to sell an article or other contribution to a magazine, newspaper or other serial publication is likely to encounter some of the following terms:

All world rights. Transfer of all world rights or all rights means that the author assigns all of his copyright rights to the magazine or other serial publication. The publication becomes the sole copyright owner. It may publish the work anywhere in the world any number of times, syndicate it, use it in databases, create derivative works from it or permit others to do so, or do anything else it wants with it. The author may not resell the work, create derivative works from it (for example, use it as a chapter in a book) or use it in any other way without the

magazine's permission—the author no longer owns the work.

> **COMPARE—WORK MADE FOR HIRE AGREEMENTS**
>
> Magazines and other periodicals are permitted to enter into work made for hire agreements with freelance contributors. Technically, a work made for hire agreement is not a transfer of rights; rather, the employer is considered to be the author of the work. But the practical result is the same as a transfer of all rights: the magazine owns all the rights in the work. The only difference is that an author who makes an all rights assignment may terminate the assignment after 35 years and retains certain moral rights. Work made for hire agreements are discussed in Chapter 8, *Initial Copyright Ownership.* Termination of copyright transfers is discussed in Section B.1, above.

All world serial rights. A transfer of all world serial rights means that the publisher acquires an exclusive license to publish the contribution in newspapers, magazines and other serial publications throughout the world any number of times for the duration of the copyright term. The author of the article or other contribution may not resell it to any other serial publication anywhere in the world. But the author retains all his other rights—for instance, he may use it as a chapter in a book or sell it for adaptation as a movie or video.

First North American serial rights. A grant of first North American serial rights means that the magazine or other serial publication has an exclusive license to publish the work for the first time in North America (the U.S. and Canada). Once the work has been published, the author may resell it, create derivative works from it or do anything else she wants with it—she owns all the other rights in the work.

Second serial rights. A transfer of second serial rights (or reprint rights) gives a magazine, newspaper or other serial publication a *nonexclusive* license to reprint a work once after it has already appeared in another serial publication.

One-time rights. A transfer of one-time rights (also called simultaneous rights) gives the magazine or other publication the right to publish a previously unpublished work once; but, in contrast to a grant of first serial rights (above), the author may sell the work to other publications to appear at the same time. This is a nonexclusive license, rather than an ownership transfer. (See Section A.3 for discussion of nonexclusive licenses.) Newspapers often purchase one-time rights from freelance contributors.

b.   Which rights should you sell?

It is always in a writer's best interests to retain as many rights as possible. Let's examine the consequences of an all rights grant compared with a grant of first North American rights.

> **EXAMPLE 1:** George writes a short story about a six-year-old's experiences at Christmas. In 1986, he sells all his rights in the story to *Maudlin Magazine* for $750. The story appears in *Maudlin's* December 1986 issue. The story proves to be so popular that *Maudlin* reprints it every December thereafter. Not only that, every year it sells reprint rights to the story to several other magazines and newspapers throughout the country. George gets absolutely nothing from all these reprintings.

> **EXAMPLE 2:** Assume instead that George only sold Maudlin Magazine first North American serial rights to his story in 1986. After Maudlin printed the story in North America for the first

time in December 1986, it had no further rights in the story. George, and only George, could permit Maudlin or other magazines and newspapers to reprint it. The income George receives from these reprintings far exceeds the $750 he got from Maudlin for the story's initial publication.

THE REAL WORLD OF PUBLISHING PRACTICES

Traditionally, magazines and other periodicals usually only acquired North American serial rights, second serial rights or one-time publication rights. This meant that after the article appeared in the magazine, the author could resell it elsewhere. However, things are changing fast in magazine publishing. An increasing number of magazines seek to obtain all the writer's rights; or, even worse from the writer's point of view, have the writer sign a work made for hire contract under which the magazine is considered to be the work's author. A 1991 survey by the publication *Writer's Market* found that 29% of consumer magazines routinely either bought all world rights or used work for hire agreements; 41% of trade journals (that is, magazines for people in a certain business or profession) did the same. To put it mildly, writer's groups are bitterly opposed to this trend and advise freelancers never to sign work made for hire contracts.

Copyright tip

You'll often find that many magazines will initially ask for all your rights, but will be willing to take less if you negotiate with them. Don't be afraid to speak up and demand to be treated fairly.

2. Transfers From a Magazine's Point of View

If you're the editor or publisher of a magazine, periodical or similar publication, you need to obtain the rights you need from freelancers with the least amount of paperwork and the fewest headaches possible. Be aware that a written agreement is always necessary to purchase an exclusive right from a writer —for example, first North American serial rights.

If you want to be sure a freelancer's piece will appear first and/or only in your magazine, you must use a written agreement. In the absence of a written agreement, a publisher obtains only a nonexclusive license to publish a freelancer's piece in the magazine or other periodical. Thus, the author can sell it to other magazines (or use it in any other way).

Exclusive first publication rights are of most importance to publishers of national magazines. If you're publishing a newspaper or regional publication, it probably won't matter much if the same piece appears at the same time (or has already appeared) in another periodical in a different part of the country.

Most magazines, especially regional publications, are not interested in resale rights and adaptation rights (such as film rights or the right to include the piece in a book). These rights have value only if there is a market for them; usually there isn't.

You should develop a transfer agreement form. This may be in the form of a letter or a more formal looking contract. See the sources listed in Section E below for sample forms. If you're considering using a work for hire agreement, be sure to read the discussion of work made for hire in Chapter 8, *Initial Copyright Ownership*.

D. Copyright Transfers Between Writers and Book Publishers

Book publishers operate differently than magazines or newspapers.

1. Publishing Argot

The copyright rights in a book are normally divided into two categories: the primary publication rights and subsidiary (sub) rights.

a. Primary publication right

The exclusive right to publish a work in book form for the first time in the English language is sometimes called the primary right. Publishing agreements vary as to the territory to which this right extends. At a minimum, a U.S. publisher will normally want the exclusive right to publish the work in the U.S. The territory is often extended to all countries in which English is spoken; these are called all English language rights. The most expansive possible grant is all world rights—that is, the right to publish the book in all countries in all languages.

Book publishers usually obtain the exclusive right to publish a work for the full copyright term, but, in some cases, a shorter period may be involved.

HARDCOVER AND SOFTCOVER EDITIONS

In the past, publishers specialized in selling hardcover or softcover books. This meant that the right to publish a book in hardcover and softcover editions were sold separately, usually to different publishers. Typically, the hardcover edition would be published first and then the softcover rights sold at an auction at which any number of softcover publishers could bid. Today, however, many publishers sell both hardcover and softcover books. As a result, the old softcover auction isn't nearly as common as it used to be. Instead, an author's initial grant of publication rights to a publisher will often cover both hardcover and softcover editions of the book.

b. Subsidiary or sub rights

All the other copyright rights in a book are called subsidiary or sub rights. These include film, television, radio and live-stage adaptation rights; the right to publish all or part of the work in a newspaper, magazine or other periodical prior to or after book publication; book club publication rights; the right to publish the book in a foreign language or license others to do so; the right to create and distribute nondramatic audio recordings of the work; and the right to publish braille, large-type and other editions for the handicapped.

IMPORTANCE OF FOREIGN LANGUAGE RIGHTS

The right to translate and sell a book in a foreign language can be very important for some books, such as popular novels, art books and children's books. These rights are usually sold language-by-language at international book fairs (such as the Frankfurt, Germany book fair) and by international literary agents.

---

2. Transfers From an Author's Point of View

It is usually in an author's best interest to retain as many rights as possible, unless, of course, the publisher pays so much that it makes sense to assign all rights. The more bargaining power an author has, the more rights she'll likely be able to keep. However, it can make good sense to sell subsidiary rights to a publisher in return for a share of the profits (at least 50%) if the publisher is better able to market these rights than the author or the author's agent. A large full-line publisher will often know the subsidiary rights markets well and have the contacts and experience to effectively market an author's sub rights.

3. Transfers From a Book Publisher's Point of View

It is in a book publisher's best interest to demand an assignment of all rights from the author in return for a royalty and a share of the profits from the sale of the subsidiary rights listed earlier. This gives the publisher the right to sell all the subsidiary rights one by one and keep part of the profits. A 50–50 split of the profits from sub rights sales is common, but other divisions are also used.

E. Transfer Documents

Virtually all book publishers—and many magazines as well—have standard publication agreements they ask authors to sign. Such contracts usually are written by lawyers who have the publisher's best interests in mind, not the author's. If you're an author, be aware that many of the provisions in such agreements normally are subject to negotiation. The topic of author-publisher contract negotiations is beyond the scope of this book. Excellent sources on this topic include:

- *The ASJA Handbook*, by the American Society of Journalists and Authors, Inc. (This 42-page pamphlet must be obtained directly from the ASJA, 1501 Broadway, Ste. 1907, New York, NY, 10036 212-997-0947.) Contains a recommended standard letter of agreement between a freelancer and a magazine, the ASJA's code of ethics and chapters on selling books and articles.
- *A Writer's Guide to Contract Negotiations*, by Balkin (Writer's Digest Books). Written by a literary agent, this book is filled with useful tips and practical advice.
- *The Writer's Legal Companion*, by Bunnin and Beren (Addison-Wesley). A good discussion of book and magazine contracts with sample forms; also covers libel, slander and invasion of privacy issues. Warning: The material on copyright is out-of-date.

- *Business & Legal Forms for Authors & Self-Publishers*, by Crawford (Allworth Press). Contains 17 tear-out agreements for writers and self-publishers, including a book contract and collaboration agreement.

Sample contracts and useful advice on all aspects of publishing (including finding a good agent) can also be obtained from the following writers' groups:

- The Authors Guild, Inc., 330 W. 42nd St., New York, NY 10036, 212-463-5904. The Guild publishes a *Guide to the Authors Guild Trade Book Contract*, an extensively annotated sample trade book contract available only to Guild members. There is a publication requirement for membership.
- The National Writers' Union, 13 Astor Place, 7th Floor, New York, NY 10003, 212-254-0279. This national writers' organization has no publication requirement for membership. Members may

obtain sample magazine and book contracts and a pamphlet entitled *16 Points to a Better Contract.*

a. Minimum provisions transfer agreement must contain

If you encounter a situation where you need to draft your own transfer agreement, there are certain basic requirements that must be satisfied. To be valid, an exclusive license or assignment must be in writing and signed by the owner of the right(s) being transferred. However, in the case of a transfer between an employer and employee, the agreement must be signed by both parties.

A transfer agreement can take many forms. It may be a formal contract, a letter signed by an author or a signed memorandum. It makes no difference if a transfer agreement is called an assignment, a license, a contract, a grant of rights or nothing at all. The effect of the agreement is determined according to the language it contains.

Whatever a transfer agreement is called, it is important that it be accurate and complete. Listed below are the minimum provisions a transfer agreement normally must contain to be legally binding:

- The names and addresses of the copyright owner and person or entity acquiring the copyright right(s).
- A description of what rights are being transferred in what work. If the copyright owner is transferring all his rights, the following phrase may be used: "John Smith hereby transfers [or assigns] all his right, title and interest in the novel entitled *Greed* to Mary Jones for the full copyright term. If less than the entire bundle of copyright rights is being transferred, the agreement must clearly state which right(s) are involved—for example, "John Smith hereby grants Mary Jones an exclusive license to prepare a theatrical motion picture based upon the novel

entitled *Greed";* "John Smith hereby grants an exclusive license to *Business Magazine* to publish the article entitled 'Greed' for the first time in North America."

NOTARIZATION

The transferor's signature need not be notarized, but if it is, it constitutes *prima facie* (that is, very strong) proof that the agreement was signed by the copyright owner (that is, was not forged). If you want to attain this benefit, sign the document in the presence of a notary. Include the following language after the transfer agreement's signature line:

State of _____

County of _____

Before me, a notary public in and for said county, personally appeared the above named _____ who acknowledged that he/she did sign the foregoing instrument and that the same is his/her free act and deed.

In Witness Whereof, I have here unto affixed my name and official seal at _____, this ____ day of _____, 19__.

_____

Notary Public

My Commission expires _____.

Copies. You should have the transferor sign three original transfer documents—one for him, one for you and one to record with the Copyright Office.

SAMPLE AGREEMENT

Millie, a beginning freelance writer, writes an article on dog training. Desperate to sell her work, Millie grants *Dog's Life Magazine* all world rights. One year after the article is published, Millie contacts *Dog's Life* and asks them to reassign the rights in her article to her so she can use it in a book she's writing. The editor at *Dog's Life* agrees, and tells Millie to send him a transfer agreement to sign. Millie could draft something like this:

For value received, *Dog's Life Magazine*, located at 890 Fireplug Lane, New York, NY 10234, assigns to Millie Vanilly, located at 1234 Nowhere Place, Erehwon, PA 12345, its entire right, title and interest in the article entitled "Dog Do's and Don'ts," published in the November 1990 issue of *Dog's Life Magazine* at pp. 34–39.

Dog's Life Magazine, by

_____

Date: _____

Caution

This section describes the minimum provisions a transfer document must contain to be legally valid. Unlike the example, most publishing contracts contain many additional provisions that have nothing to do with copyright—for instance, provisions regarding royalties, delivery of manuscript, a warranties and indemnities clause and many others. For a discussion of these and other provisions contained in publishing contracts, refer to the sources cited in Section E, above.

F. Marriage, Divorce and Copyright Ownership

Like everybody else, writers and other copyright owners get married and get divorced. A copyright is an item of personal property that must be given to one spouse or the other, or somehow shared, upon divorce. Every state has a set of laws about how property acquired or created by married persons is owned and divided upon divorce. These laws vary greatly from state to state. This section highlights some basic principles. You'll need to consult an attorney to answer specific questions about how the laws of your state operate.

1. Copyrights as Community Property

Nine states have community property laws: Arizona, California, Idaho, Louisiana, Nevada, New Mexico, Texas, Washington and Wisconsin (in all but name). Under these laws, unless they agree otherwise, a husband and wife automatically become *joint owners* of most types of property they acquire during their marriage. Property acquired before or after marriage is separately owned.

A court in the most populous community property state—California—has held that a copyright acquired by one spouse during marriage is community property—that is, is jointly owned by both spouses. (*Marriage of Worth*, 195 Cal. App.3d 768, 241 Cal. Rptr. 135 (1987).) This means that if you are married and reside in California (or later move there), any work you have created or will create automatically would be owned jointly by you and your spouse *unless you agree otherwise* (see below). This amounts to a transfer of copyright ownership by operation of law.

EXAMPLE: Emily and Robert are married and live in California. Emily writes a novel. Unless they agree otherwise, Robert automatically ac-

quires an undivided one-half interest in the copyright the moment the work is created.

Courts in the other eight community property states have yet to consider whether copyrights are community property. No one knows whether they will follow California's lead. If you're married and reside in Arizona, Idaho, Louisiana, Nevada, New Mexico, Texas, Washington or Wisconsin, the most prudent approach is to assume that the copyright in any protectible work you create during marriage is community property. However, check with a family law or copyright lawyer familiar with the laws of your state before taking any action.

The following discussion briefly highlights the effect of according copyrights community property status in California.

a. Right to control copyrights

Normally, *either* spouse is entitled to sell community personal property (which would include a copyright) without the other's consent. But the profits from such a sale would themselves be community property (that is, jointly owned). The rule is different, however, as to gifts: neither spouse can give away community property without the other's consent. However, a special provision of California law (Civil Code Section 5125(d)) provides that a spouse who operates a business has the primary management and control of that business and its assets. In most cases, a married professional writer would probably be considered to be operating a business and would therefore have primary management and control over any work he or she creates (the business's assets).

This means that a married professional writer may transfer all or part of the copyright in a work he or she creates during marriage without his or her spouse's consent and/or signature on any contract. However, the author is legally required to give his or her spouse prior written notice of such transfers (but failure to do so only results in giving the nonauthor spouse the right to demand an accounting of the profits from the transfer).

b.   When a spouse dies

Under California law (Probate Code section 201.5), each spouse may will a one-half interest in their community property to whomever they choose; this would include, of course, their interest in any community property copyright. If a spouse dies without a will, the surviving spouse acquires all the deceased spouse's community property.

c.   Division of copyrights at divorce

When a California couple gets divorced, they are legally entitled to arrange their own property settlement, jointly dividing their property as they wish. If, however, they can't reach an agreement and submit the dispute to the court, a judge will divide the community property equally. A judge would have many options as how to divide community property copyrights—e.g., she could award all the copyrights to one spouse and give the other cash or other community property of equal value; if there were, say, ten copyrights of equal value, she could give five to one spouse and five to the other; or the judge could permit each spouse to separately administer their one-half interest in all the copyrights.

d.   Changing marital ownership of copyrights by contract

Property acquired during marriage by California residents does not *have* to be community property. Spouses are free to agree either before or during marriage that all or part of their property will be separately owned. Such an agreement must be in writing and signed by the spouse giving up his or her community property interest; in some cases, it is desirable for the spouse giving up the interest to consult a lawyer. This is something a husband and wife must discuss and decide on their own; we're not advising you to take any particular action. For detailed discussion, see *California Marriage & Divorce Law,* by Warner, Ihara and Elias (Nolo Press), Chapter 5.

2.   Equitable Distribution States

All states other than the nine community property states listed above (with the exception of Mississippi) employ equitable distribution principles when dividing property at divorce. Equitable distribution is a principle under which assets (including copyrights) acquired during marriage are divided equitably (fairly) at divorce. In theory, equitable means equal, or nearly so. In some equitable distribution states, however, if a spouse obtains a fault divorce, the guilty spouse may receive less than an equal share of the marital property. Check with a family law attorney in your state for details.

G. Recording Copyright Transfers With the Copyright Office

The Copyright Office does not make or in any way participate in transfers of copyright ownership. But the Office does *record* transfer documents after they have been signed by the parties. When a transfer document is recorded, a copy is placed in the Copyright Offices files, indexed and made available for public inspection. This is similar to what happens when a deed to a house or other real estate is recorded with a county recorder's office. Recordation of transfer documents is not mandatory, but it results in so many valuable benefits that it is almost always a good idea.

THE DIFFERENCE BETWEEN RECORDATION AND REGISTRATION

As described in detail in Chapter 4, copyright registration is a legal formality by which an author or other copyright owner fills out a registration application for a published or unpublished work and submits it to the Copyright Office along with one or two copies of the work. If the copyright examiner is satisfied that the work contains protected expression and the application is completed correctly, the work is registered—that is, assigned a registration number, indexed and filed in the Copyright Office's records. The copies are retained for five years. Recordation does not involve submitting copies of a work. Recordation simply means that the Copyright Office files a document so that it is available for public inspection. As mentioned above, this can be any document relating to copyright. It can be for a work that is published, unpublished or even not yet written. A good way to distinguish the two procedures is to remember that written works containing protected expression are registered, while contracts or other documents relating to the copyright in a work are recorded.

1. Why Record a Copyright Transfer?

Because a copyright is intangible and can be transferred simply by signing a piece of paper, it is possible for dishonest copyright owners to rip off copyright purchasers.

EXAMPLE: Carol signs a contract transferring the exclusive right to publish her novel *The Goniff*, to Scrivener & Sons. Two months later, Carol sells the same rights in the novel to Acme Press. Acme had no idea that Carol had already sold the same rights to Scrivener. Carol has sold the same property twice! As a result, if Scrivener and Acme both publish the book, they'll be competing against each other (and they'll both probably be able to sue Carol for breach of contract, fraud and other causes of action).

Recordation of transfer documents protects copyright transferees from these and other abuses by establishing the legal priorities between copyright transferees if the transferor makes overlapping or confusing grants (see Section 3, below). Recordation also establishes a public record of the contents of transfer documents. This enables prospective purchasers of copyright rights to search the Copyright Office's transfer records to make sure that the copyright seller really owns what she's selling (this is similar to the title search that a homebuyer conducts before purchasing a house). Finally, recordation of a transfer document for a registered work gives the entire world constructive notice of the transfer; constructive notice means everyone is deemed to know about the transfer, whether or not they really do.

2. What Can Be Recorded?

Any document pertaining to a copyright can be recorded with the Copyright Office. Of course, this includes any document transferring all or part of a copyright—whether it be an exclusive license or assignment. It also includes nonexclusive licenses, wills, powers of attorney in which authors or other copyright owners give others the power to act for them and other contracts dealing with a copyrighted work.

You can record a document without registering the work it pertains to, but important benefits are obtained if the work is registered. You can even record a document for a work that doesn't exist because it has yet to be written—for example, a publishing contract.

3. Effect of Recordation on Copyright Conflicts

So what happens when an unethical (or awfully forgetful) author or publisher transfers the same copyright right(s) to different persons or entities? The rules of priority for copyright transfers may be summarized as follows:

- As between two conflicting transfers of exclusive rights to a work that has been *registered with the Copyright Office*, the first transfer is always entitled to priority over the later transfer if it was recorded first.
- But even if the second transfer is recorded first, the first transfer is still entitled to protection if it's recorded *within one month* after it is signed (two months if signed outside the U.S.).
- However, if the first transfer is recorded more than one month after it's signed (or not recorded at all), the transfer that is recorded first is entitled to protection (even if it was the second one granted). (This rule does not apply if the second transfer was a gift or bequest—that is, inherited through a will.)
- But the later transfer is entitled to protection only so long as it was made in good faith and without knowledge of the earlier transfer.

A subsequent transferee will always lose out to a prior transferee who records first because such recordation gives the later transferee (and everyone one else in the world) constructive notice of the prior transfer—that is, the second transferee is deemed to know about the earlier transfer whether or not he really did. This means that the second transferee cannot claim that he recorded the later transfer without knowledge of the earlier transfer.

EXAMPLE 1: Naomi writes a novel which she registers with the Copyright Office. Naomi sells the North American publication rights to the novel to Repulsive Publications on July 1. One week later, she sells the same rights to Acme Books. Assume that Repulsive recorded its transfer agreement from Naomi on August 2. Acme records its transfer agreement on August 3. Who is entitled to publish Naomi's novel? Repulsive. The first transfer is always entitled to priority if the work has been registered and the first transfer is recorded first.

EXAMPLE 2: Assume instead that Acme records its transfer agreement from Naomi on July 10. Acme did not know about the prior transfer from Naomi to Repulsive and acted in good faith. Repulsive did not record its transfer agreement until July 30. Who has the exclusive right to publish Naomi's novel? Still Repulsive. Since Repulsive recorded its transfer agreement within 30 days of the July 1 transfer, it prevails over Acme regardless of when Acme recorded.

EXAMPLE 3: Assume the same facts as in Example 2 except that Repulsive waited until August 15 to record, while Acme recorded in good faith on July 10. Who prevails? Acme. Since Repulsive waited more than 30 days to record, the first transferee to record prevails regardless of when the transfer itself was made.

EXAMPLE 4: Assume the same facts as in Example 3, except that Acme actually knew about Naomi's prior transfer to Repulsive (Naomi told them). In this event, Repulsive would prevail regardless of when it recorded.

Copyright tip

You wouldn't buy a house or other real estate without conducting a title search. Likewise, you shouldn't spend a substantial sum to purchase all or part of a copyright without searching the Copyright Office's records to make sure the transferor owns what he's selling. See Chapter 11, Section F.2 for a discussion of how to search the Copyright Office's records. Take careful note, however, that such searches are not foolproof. As discussed above, under the priority rules, a transferee who records within one month after the transfer is signed (two months if signed abroad) has priority over all subsequent transfers even if they were recorded earlier. Thus, a person who received a transfer less than one month before you (two months if the transfer document was signed outside the U.S.) will have priority over you even if she records after you, provided that she records within one month after the transfer to her.

TRANSFERS OF UNREGISTERED WORKS

What happens if conflicting transfers are made of a work that has not been registered? Until the work is registered, no transferee has legal priority over any other transferee.

EXAMPLE: Fouad signs a contract with ABC Publications to write a college textbook on Middle Eastern politics, and assigns ABC exclusive worldwide publication rights in all languages. One week later he signs an agreement to write an identical book for XYZ Publications and assigns them worldwide publication rights. When Fouad finishes writing the book, who owns the publication rights, ABC or XYZ? They both do until the book is registered and transfer document recorded. But the first one to register and record will have priority over the other. The publisher without priority may not publish Fouad's book, but can probably sue him for breach of contract, fraud and other causes of action.

---

4. Priority When a Copyright Transfer and a Written Nonexclusive License Conflict

What happens if a copyright owner grants A a nonexclusive license to exercise some of his copyright rights, but later transfers those same rights (or all his exclusive copyright rights) to B? B now owns the rights A has a nonexclusive license to use. May A continue to rely on the nonexclusive license or must he seek a new nonexclusive license from B? Luckily for nonexclusive licensees, there is a special statute giving them priority over later conflicting transfers of ownership. As long as a nonexclusive license is (1) in writing and (2) signed by the licensor, it prevails over a conflicting transfer if:

- the license was taken before the conflicting transfer was signed, or
- the license was taken in good faith before recordation of the transfer and without notice of it.

EXAMPLE 1: Sue obtains permission from John to quote several lengthy passages from a book John has written. John signs a written nonexclusive license. A week later, John sells all his copyright rights in the book to Acme Publications. Sue may continue to quote from John's book; she need not obtain Acme's permission to do so. Her written nonexclusive license has *priority* over John's subsequent transfer to Acme.

EXAMPLE 2: Change facts: Assume that John transferred all his copyright rights in his book to Acme. However, before Acme records the transfer agreement, John grants the nonexclusive license to Sue. John does not tell Sue about the prior transfer to Acme and she knows nothing about it. Sue's nonexclusive license still has priority.

5. How to Record Transfer Documents (or Other Documents Pertaining to Copyright)

To record a document with the Copyright Office, you must complete and sign the Copyright Office "Document Cover Sheet" form and send it to the Copyright Office along with the document and recordation fee.

If the work involved hasn't already been registered with the Copyright Office, it should be at the same time the document is recorded.

a. Step 1: Complete the Document Cover Sheet

First, complete and sign the Document Cover Sheet. A copy of the form is included in the tear-out appendix to this book. You can obtain additional copies by calling the Copyright Office Forms Hotline at 202-707-9100. Here's how to fill out the form.

Space 1: Name of Parties to Document

In Space 1, you must name all the parties to the document you are recording. The document will be indexed under their names. Under "Party 1," list the name of the assignor or grantor—that is, the name of the person making a transfer of copyright rights (a work's author, for example). Under "Party 2," list the name of the assignee or grantee—that is, the name of the person receiving the transfer of copyright rights (a publisher, for example). If you don't have enough space to list all the parties involved, use a white 8 1/2-inch by 11-inch sheet of paper to list them.

Space 2: Description of Document

Check the box that best describes the document you're recording. This will usually be the first box: "Transfer of Copyright."

Space 3: Title(s) of Work(s)

List here the titles, registration numbers (if any) and authors of all the works covered by the document being recorded. Use additional white sheets if you can't fit them all in on the form.

Space 4: Completeness of Document

A document being recorded with the Copyright Office should be complete on its own terms. At a minimum, it should contain (1) the names and addresses of the copyright owner(s) and person(s) or entity acquiring the copyright right(s); and (2) a description of the rights that are being transferred. The transfer document must also be signed by the transferor. See Section E, above, for a detailed discussion.

The Copyright Office will not examine your document to see if it meets these requirements. It will be recorded whether it does or not. However, if it doesn't, it may not be legally effective.

If your document meets these requirements, check the first box in Space 4. If not, and you want it recorded anyway, check the second box instructing the Copyright Office to record it as is.

Space 5: Number of Titles in Document

List in Space 5 the number of titles covered by the document. This will determine the recordation fee.

Space 6: Fee

State the amount of the recordation fee in Space 6. The Copyright Office charges a $20 fee to record a transfer document covering one to ten titles. For additional titles, there is an added charge of $10 for each group of up to ten titles—for example, it would cost $30 to record 11–20 titles, $40 to record 21–30 titles and so forth.

DOCUMENT COVER SHEET
For Recordation of Documents
UNITED STATES COPYRIGHT OFFICE

DATE OF RECORDATION
(Assigned by Copyright Office)

_____ _____ _____
Month   Day   Year

Volume _____   Page _____

Volume _____   Page _____

DO NOT WRITE ABOVE THIS LINE.

REMITTANCE _____

To the Register of Copyrights:
Please record the accompanying original document or copy thereof.

FUNDS RECEIVED _____

1 NAME OF THE PARTY OR PARTIES TO THE DOCUMENT, AS THEY APPEAR IN THE DOCUMENT.

Party 1: _____   Party 2: _____
         (assignor, grantor, etc.)   (assignee, grantee, etc.)

_____   _____
         (address)   (address)

2 DESCRIPTION OF THE DOCUMENT:
☐ Transfer of Copyright   ☐ Termination of Transfer(s) [Section 304]   ☐ Transfer of Mask Works
☐ Security Interest   ☐ Shareware   ☐ Other _____
☐ Change of Name of Owner   ☐ Life, Identity, Death Statement [Section 302]

3 TITLE(S) OF WORK(S), REGISTRATION NUMBER(S), AUTHOR(S), AND OTHER INFORMATION TO IDENTIFY WORK.
Title   Registration Number   Author

_____   _____   _____   Additional sheet(s) attached?
_____   _____   _____   ☐ yes
_____   _____   _____   ☐ no
                                                                If so, how many? _____

4 ☐ Document is complete by its own terms.
☐ Document is not complete. Record "as is."

5 Number of titles in Document: _____

6 Amount of fee enclosed or authorized to be charged to a
Deposit Account_____ .

7 Account number _____
Account name _____

8 Date of execution and/or effective date of accompanying
document _____
          (month)   (day)   (year)

9 AFFIRMATION:* I hereby affirm to the Copyright Office that the information given on this form is a true and correct representation of the accompanying document. This affirmation will not suffice as a certification of a photocopy signature on the document.

10 CERTIFICATION:* Complete this certification if a photocopy of the original signed document is submitted in lieu of a document bearing the actual signature.
I certify under penalty of perjury under the laws of the United States of America that the accompanying document is a true copy of the original document.

_____
Signature

_____
Duly Authorized Agent of:

_____
Signature

_____
Date

_____
Date

MAIL RECORDA-TION TO:

Name▼

Number/Street/Apartment Number▼

City/State/ZIP▼

YOU MUST:
• Complete all necessary spaces
• Sign your cover sheet in space 9

SEND ALL 3 ELEMENTS
IN THE SAME PACKAGE:
1. Two copies of the Document Cover Sheet
2. Fee in check or money order payable to *Register of Copyrights*
3. Document

MAIL TO:
Documents Unit,Cataloging Division, Copyright Office, Library of Congress Washington, D.C. 20559

The Copyright Office has the authority to adjust fees at 5-year intervals, based on changes in the Consumer Price Index. The next adjustment is due in 1996. Please contact the Copyright Office after July 1995 to determine the actual fee schedule.

*Knowingly and willfully falsifying material facts on this form may result in criminal liability. 18 U.S.C.§1001.

January 1993—50,000

☆ U.S. GOVERNMENT PRINTING OFFICE: 1993–342-582/60,032

Space 7: Deposit Account

If you have a deposit account with the Copyright Office and want the fee charged to it, give the account number and name in Space 7.

Space 8: Date of Execution

State in Space 8 the date the document being recorded (not the Cover Sheet) was signed or became effective.

Space 9: Affirmation

The person submitting the document being recorded or her representative must sign where indicated in Space 9.

Space 10: Certification

You are supposed to submit one copy of the *original* transfer document *signed by the transferor.* If this is not possible, and you need to record a photocopy of the original document instead, Space 10 must be completed; otherwise, leave it blank.

To submit a photocopy in lieu of the original document, one of the parties to the document or his or her authorized representative must sign and date Space 10. By doing so, the signor certifies under penalty of perjury that the copy is a true copy of the original document.

Address

Finally, include at the bottom of the form the address where the Copyright Office should send the Certificate of Recordation.

b. Step 2: Send Your Recordation Package to the Copyright Office

You need to send all the following to the Copyright Office in one package:

- The original signed Document Cover Sheet and one copy,
- The proper recordation fee in a check or money order payable to the Register of Copyrights (unless you have a deposit account), and
- The document to be recorded.

    Send your package to:
    Documents Unit, LM-462
    Cataloging Division
    Copyright Office
    Library of Congress
    Washington, DC 20559

Within six to eight weeks, you should receive a Certificate of Recordation from the Copyright Office showing that your transfer document (or nonexclusive license) has been recorded. The original signed transfer document (or nonexclusive license) will be returned with the certificate.

Copyright Duration

Copyright protection doesn't last forever, but it lasts long enough to benefit many people besides the author, potentially including children, grandchildren, great-grandchildren, publishers, agents and other people and businesses who may have acquired an interest in the copyright.

No matter how many times a copyright is transferred, its duration does not change. The duration is determined by who the original author was and how long he or she lives; or, in some cases, by the date the work was created or first published.

When a work's copyright expires, it enters the public domain; in effect, it belongs to everybody. Anyone is free to use it without asking permission, but no one can ever own it again.

A. Works Created During or After 1978

The great divide in determining a copyright's duration is the date January 1, 1978. The copyright in works created on or after that date usually lasts for the life of the author(s) plus 50 years. Works created before that date have a very different duration.

1. Single Author Works: Life Plus 50 Years

As discussed in Chapter 2, *Copyright Basics*, copyright protection begins when a work is created—that is, when it is written down or otherwise fixed in a tangible form. Unless one of the exceptions discussed below applies, the copyright in a work created by a single individual author on or after January 1, 1978, lasts for the life of the author plus an additional 50 years. This means, at the very least, that the copyright in an individually authored work lasts 50 years. And the copyright in a work by a young author could easily last 100 years or more, depending of course on how long the author lives.

EXAMPLE 1: Bill has a fatal heart attack just as he finishes writing his epic novel on ancient Sparta. The novel's copyright will last for 50 years after Bill's death.

EXAMPLE 2: Natalie completes her own epic novel on ancient Sparta when she is 30 years old. If she ends up living to 80, the copyright in her novel will last for 100 years.

a. Drafts and uncompleted works

Copyright doesn't just protect finished works; it also protects drafts and uncompleted works. Each draft of a work created over a period of time by an individual author is protected for the life plus 50 year term. A work that is never completed is entitled to the same period of protection.

2. Works Made for Hire

As discussed in detail in Chapter 8, *Initial Copyright Ownership*, a work made for hire is a work created by an employee as part of his job or a work that is specially ordered or commissioned pursuant to a written work for hire contract. The copyright in a work made for hire lasts for 75 years from the date of its *first publication*, or 100 years from the date of its *creation*, whichever comes first. (A work is published when it is made freely available to the public; see Chapter 2, *Copyright Basics,* for a definition of publish.)

This means that if there were a 30-year delay between creation and publication, the copyright would last for 100 years; a 5-year delay would result in an 80-year term. But, if creation and publication occur within the same calendar year, as they usually do, the copyright in a work made for hire lasts for 75 years.

EXAMPLE 1: Leo, the assistant editor of *New Pathways Magazine*, writes an article for the magazine as a part of his job. The article is published just one month after he completed it. The copyright in the article will last for 75 years.

EXAMPLE 2: *New Pathways Magazine* hires Sheila, a freelance writer, to write an article on a work for hire basis under a written work for hire agreement. Shiela completes the article in 1991, but it's not published until 1993. The copyright in the article will last for 77 years.

3. Joint Author Works

As discussed in detail in Chapter 8, *Initial Copyright Ownership*, a joint work is a work authored by two or more persons on their own behalf (that is, not a work made for hire). The copyright in a joint work lasts for the life of the last surviving author plus 50 years.

EXAMPLE: Joseph Herodotus and Mary Thucydides write a history of the Persian Gulf War. Herodotus dies soon thereafter. The copyright in the work will last for the rest of Thucydides' life plus 50 more years.

If a work is created by two or more persons who work for hire, the 75- or 100-year work made for hire term discussed in Section 2, above applies.

EXAMPLE: Two editors employed by Acme Press and two employed by Scrivener & Sons jointly author a book on publishing for their employers. The book is a joint work, co-owned by Acme and Scrivener, but the work made for hire copyright term applies.

Sometimes, a work will be jointly created both by people who work for hire and people who don't. It's not exactly clear whether the life plus 50 or work for hire term should apply in these situations. The

Register of Copyrights has suggested that the life plus 50 term should apply if at least two of the work's creators did not work for hire. It's likely the courts will adopt this rule.

EXAMPLE: Acme Press has two of its editors collaborate on a book with two freelance writers. The contributions by Acme's editors are works made for hire. The contributions by the two freelancers are not works made for hire. Since two of the authors did not work for hire, the life plus 50 rule should apply according to the Register of Copyrights. That is, the copyright in the work would last for the life of the last surviving freelancer plus 50 years.

What if a work is created by one or more people who work for hire and only *one* person who does not work for hire? The Register of Copyrights suggests that in this situation whatever copyright term is longer—life plus 50 or the work for hire term—should apply.

EXAMPLE: Assume that two editors employed by Acme Press and only one freelance writer write a book together. Again, the editors' contributions are works made for hire, while the freelancer's contribution is not a work made for hire. According to the Register of Copyrights, the copyright in the book should last for the longer of the work made for hire terms or 50 years after the freelancer dies.

4. Anonymous and Pseudonymous Works

Obviously, there is no identified author with an interest in the copyright of an anonymous or pseudonymous work. This makes it impractical to measure the duration of the copyright against the life of the author. This means that, as with works made for hire, there is a copyright term of 75 years from the date of first publication of an anonymous or pseudonymous

work, or 100 years from the date of its creation, whichever comes first.

a. Changing the term to life plus 50 by making identity known to Copyright Office

If the identity of the author of an anonymous or pseudonymous work is officially made known to the Copyright Office before the 75- or 100-year term expires, the copyright term changes to the life of the author plus 50 years (the same as if the true author's name had been on the copyright to begin with). Note, however, that this won't necessarily be longer than a 75- or 100-year term; it all depends on how long the author lives after the work was published.

Any person who owns all or part of the copyright in a pseudonymous or anonymous work may notify the Copyright Office of the author's true identity. This may be done by registering the work under the author's true name or, if the work has already been registered, by filing a supplementary registration with the Copyright Office. Copyright registration is discussed in Chapter 4, supplemental registration in Chapter 5.

Alternatively, it is possible to record (file) a statement with the Copyright Office setting forth the following:

- the name of the person filing the statement
- the nature of the person's interest in the copyright
- the title of the particular work affected, and
- the copyright registration number, if known.

The Copyright Office requires payment of a $20 fee to record the statement and an extra $2 for each additional title. (See Chapter 9, *Transferring Copyright Ownership,* for a detailed discussion of how to record documents with the Copyright Office.)

EXAMPLE: Harold Lipshitz writes a detective novel under the pseudonym "Mike Danger." The book is published the same year Harold wrote it, so the copyright will last for 75 years unless Harold notifies the Copyright Office of his true identity. Harold gets to thinking: He was only 25 when he wrote the novel and his parents both lived well into their 80s so he figures his copyright would last much longer than 75 years under the normal life plus 50 years term. Harold sends the Copyright Office the following notice.

SAMPLE LETTER TO COPYRIGHT OFFICE

SAMPLE LETTER TO COPYRIGHT OFFICE

Register of Copyrights
Library of Congress
Washington, DC 20559
RE: Copyright Registration TX01234567

Dear Register:

I am writing regarding copyright registration #TX01234567, registered on 1-1-92. This work is a novel registered under the title *And Then You Die*. It is registered under the pseudonymous authorship of "Mike Danger." This is to inform you that I, Harold Lipshitz, am the author and owner of the copyright in this work. Please record this notice. A check for $20 is enclosed for the recordation fee.

Very truly yours,
Harold Lipshitz
Harold Lipshitz

Copyright tip
If an individual author is very ill or rather elderly and not likely to live 25 years after his work is published, the work would probably receive longer copyright protection under the 75-year term for anonymous or pseudonymous works or works made for hire than under the normal life plus 50 years copyright term. The copyright term would also probably last longer if the work was written with a younger collaborator—that is, the copyright would last for 50 years after the last collaborator died. Does this mean that elderly authors should write anonymously or under a pseudonym, or, if possible, characterize their works as works made for hire or write them with youthful collaborators? In most cases, no. Very few works have a useful economic life of more than 50 years. Thus, the life plus 50 term is usually more than adequate.

B. End of Calendar Year Rule

All copyright durations run until the end of the calendar year in which they would otherwise expire. For example, the copyright in a work made for hire that was first published in 1992 would expire on December 31, 2067, regardless of what month and day during 1992 it was published. Similarly, if the individual author of a work died in 1980, the copyright in the work would expire on December 31, 2030, regardless of the month and day of his death.

C. Works Created but Not Published or Registered Before January 1, 1978

With one important exception, works created before January 1, 1978, but not published or registered with the Copyright Office, are subject to the same basic copyright duration rules as those created after January 1, 1978. That is, the copyright lasts for the life of an individual author plus 50 years, or 75 or 100 years (from publication and creation, respectively) for a work made for hire or for a pseudonymous or anonymous work.

> **EXAMPLE:** Louisa, a well-known novelist, dies in 1992 leaving behind an unpublished manuscript written in 1977. The copyright in the manuscript will last until 2042 (50 years after Louisa's death).

Important Exception. Under a special provision in the copyright law, the copyright in a work that was created before January 1, 1978, but not published until after that date cannot expire before December 31, 2002, no matter when the author died. This means that everything ever written, but not published, before 1978 will remain under copyright at least until December 31, 2002. Obviously, this is a prodigious body of work. This rule has important ramifications for historians, biographers and other scholars.

EXAMPLE: Samuel, a Revolutionary War historian, finds a heretofore unknown and unpublished diary written by George Washington in 1790. Since the diary was never published (or registered with the Copyright Office), it will remain under copyright until December 31, 2002 even though Washington died in 1799. The copyright will be owned by whoever inherited Washington's papers, not Samuel. Samuel may not publish or otherwise use the diary without the copyright owner's permission, unless the use falls within the fair use privilege (see Chapter 11, *Using Other Authors' Words*).

Moreover, if such a work is published between January 1, 1978, and January 1, 2003, the copyright cannot expire before December 31, 2027. This is so regardless of when the author died. This means you can automatically extend the copyright term of such unpublished works for 25 years simply by publishing them before 2003.

EXAMPLE: Assume that George Washington's diary is published in 1991. The copyright will last until December 31, 2027.

D. Works Published or Registered Before January 1, 1978

Determining the copyright term for works created before 1978 can be a complex undertaking. Under the pre-1978 copyright law (called the Copyright Act of 1909), all eligible works enjoyed an initial copyright term of 28 years from the *date of first publication* with a proper copyright notice. Before the end of the first 28 years, they could be renewed for an additional 28-year term by filing a renewal registration with the Copyright Office. This second term is called the renewal term.

This sounds pretty simple, but things get more complicated. The renewal term for works published

before 1978 has been extended an additional 19 years to 47 years (28 + 19 = 47), for a total of 75 years of copyright protection (28 + 47 = 75).

Under the law in effect from 1909 through 1992, the renewal term was not automatic. It could be obtained only by filing a renewal registration with the Copyright Office during the 28th year after a work's publication. As you might expect, many authors failed to timely file a renewal for their work. Indeed, only about 20% of all pre-1978 published works were ever renewed.

This meant that a vast body of work entered the public domain 28 years after publication due to failure to comply with a mere technical formality. This seemed unfair to many people and as a result the law was changed in 1992. The new law made copyright renewals automatic—in other words, the 47-year renewal term was obtained whether or not a renewal registration was filed. Renewal registrations were made purely optional; but the law gives copyright owners who file renewal registrations some important benefits we'll discuss below.

⚠ **Caution**
The 1992 automatic renewal law applies only to works published between January 1, 1964 and December 31, 1977. Works published before 1964 had to be renewed during the 28th year after publication or they entered the public domain where they will forever remain.

The following subsections provide some general rules that will help you decide whether a work published prior to 1978 is still protected by copyright.

1. Works Published More Than 75 Years Ago

The copyright for any work published or registered with the Copyright Office more than 75 years ago—that is, more than 75 years before the year in which you're reading this book—has expired. This means that the work is now in the public domain. Anyone can use it without permission or payment, but no one can ever own it.

Copyright tip
To determine whether a book or other work was first published more than 75 years ago, simply look at the year shown in the work's copyright notice. This should be the same year as the year of first publication.

2. Works Published Before 1964 But Less Than 75 Years Ago

Works published less than 75 years before the year in which you're reading this book but before 1964 have already entered the public domain unless a renewal registration was timely filed with the Copyright Office by the end of the initial 28-year term. If it was, the renewal term lasts for 47 years.

> **EXAMPLE 1:** The copyright in a work that was first published in 1932, and timely renewed in 1960, lasts through the end of 2007 (75 years in all).

> **EXAMPLE 2:** The copyright in a work that was first published in 1962, but not timely renewed in 1990, expired on December 31, 1990 (the end of the initial 28-year term). The work is now in the public domain.

a. How to determine whether a renewal has been timely filed

As these examples illustrate, it is impossible to know how long the copyright in a work published between 75 years ago and 1963 will last unless you know whether a renewal registration was timely filed. When a book is reprinted after renewal, the copyright notice usually provides this information. Otherwise you'll need to research the Copyright Office's records to find out if a renewal was timely filed. There are three ways to do this:

1. Have the Copyright Office search its records for you. They charge $20 an hour for this service. Call the Reference & Bibliography Section at 202-707-6850 and ask for an estimate of how long they think your particular search will take (they usually take no more than one hour). Then, fill out the search request form located in the appendix to this book, and send it and your check in the amount of the estimate payable to the Register of Copyrights to:

    Reference & Bibliography Section, LM-451
    Copyright Office
    Library of Congress
    Washington, DC 20559

2. Have a professional search firm conduct the search for you. This will probably cost much more than having the Copyright Office do the search—fees start at about $100—but you will get much faster service. Search firms usually report back in two to ten working days, while it often takes the Copyright Office one or two months to conduct a search.

COPYRIGHT SEARCH FIRMS

There are five copyright search firms, located primarily in the Washington, DC area:

Copyright Council
2121 Crystal Dr., Ste. 704
Arlington, VA 22202
703-521-1669

Government Liaison Services, Inc.
3030 Clarendon Blvd., Ste. 209
Arlington, VA 22201
800-642-6564 or 703-524-8200

Robert G. Roomian
P.O. Box 7111
Alexandria, VA 22307
703-549-7010

Thomson & Thomson
Copyright Research Group
500 E St. S.W., Ste. 970
Washington, DC 20024
800-356-8630
(This is the largest and best-known search firm.)

XL Corporate Services
62 White St.
New York, NY 10013
800-221-2972 or 212-431-5000

---

open from 8:30 A.M. to 5:00 P.M. Monday through Friday. The *CCE* can also be found in government depository libraries throughout the country.

In addition, Copyright Office registration and renewal records made during or after 1978 are available on-line. They can be accessed via Dialog Information Services, Inc., 800-334-2564; this is a large commercial database that can be very expensive to use. The records are also available on the Internet (an enormous network of computer networks), which is much cheaper to use. Most university libraries and many public libraries have access to the Internet. The Internet "address" is "locis.loc.gov"; the password is "Copyright Information."

COPYRIGHT DURATION CHART

Date of Work	Copyright Terms
Created during or after 1978	Single term of life plus 50 years (except if anonymous or pseudonymous work or work for hire, 75 years from publication or 100 years from creation, whichever is first)
Published during 1964–1977	28-year initial term from date of publication; 47-year renewal term begins automatically; renewal registration optional
Published before 1964 but less than 75 years ago	28-year initial term from date of publication; 47-year renewal term if renewal registration was timely filed, if not, work is now in public domain
Published more than 75 years ago	The work is now in the public domain
Created but not published or registered before 1978	Single term of at least life plus 50 years, but cannot expire before 12/31/2002 (if work remains unpublished) or 12/31/2027 (if work is published by the end of 2002)

---

3. Search the Copyright Office records yourself. This entails looking up the work in the *Catalog of Copyright Entries (CCE)*. This is a monumental series of annual catalogs listing and cross-referencing every work registered and renewed by the Copyright Office. The *CCE* is available to the public at the Copyright Office, located in the James Madison Memorial Building, 101 Independence Ave. S.E., Washington, DC. The Office is

Copyright tip

Before researching a copyright renewal yourself, obtain a copy of *Researching Copyright Renewal,* by Iris J. Wildman and Rhonda Carlson. It's published by Fred B. Rothman & Co., 10368 West Centennial Rd., Littleton, CO 80127, 800-457-1986. This 85-page paperback written by two law librarians clearly explains exactly how to go about determining whether a renewal was timely filed, including how to decipher the often cryptic entries in the *Catalog of Copyright Entries.*

3. Works Published During 1964–1977

The 47-year renewal term begins automatically for works published between January 1, 1964 and December 1, 1977.

> **EXAMPLE:** Jackie published a novel in 1965. The initial 28-year copyright term for the book expired on December 31, 1993 (28 years after the year of publication). The 47-year renewal term began automatically on January 1, 1994, whether or not Jackie filed a renewal application with the Copyright Office.

However, as discussed in Section F, below, important benefits can be obtained in some cases by filing an optional renewal registration with the Copyright Office.

E. Duration of Copyright in Adaptions (Derivative Works)

As discussed in detail in Chapter 7, *Adaptions and Compilations,* a derivative work is a work that transforms or adapts previously existing material into a new work of authorship. A good example is a screenplay based on a novel. The copyright in a derivative work published before 1978 lasts for 75 years from publication if timely renewed, 28 years if

not. The copyright in a derivative work created on or after January 1, 1978, lasts for the life of the author plus 50 years, unless it's a work for hire or pseudonymous or anonymous work as discussed above. The creation of a derivative work has no effect on the duration of the copyright in the preexisting material it incorporates.

> **EXAMPLE:** Barbara writes a screenplay in 1992 based on a novel published by Art in 1980. The copyright in the novel will expire 50 years after Art dies. The copyright in the screenplay will expire 50 years after Barbara dies.

It is quite common for the copyright in the preexisting material to expire long before the copyright in a derivative work based upon it. In this event, others can use the preexisting material to create their own derivative works, or for any other purpose, without asking permission from the owner of the derivative work or anyone else. But others cannot use the material added to the preexisting work by the creator of the derivative work.

> **EXAMPLE:** Leslie purchases the right to create a play based from a novel published by Burt in 1932. She publishes the play in 1980. The copyright in the novel was timely renewed in 1960. Thus, copyright protection for the novel will last until 2007, while the copyright in Leslie's play will last for the rest of her life plus 50 years. After 2007, anyone may write their own play based upon Burt's novel, since it is in the public domain. But, in doing so, they could not copy from Leslie's play without her permission.

F. Renewal of Copyright in Pre-1978 Works

As mentioned above, it is no longer necessary to file a renewal registration with the Copyright Office to obtain a renewal term for a work published during 1964–1977. However, renewal registration is still permitted and, in some cases, important benefits can be obtained by doing so. But his does not necessarily mean you should bother renewing all pre-1978 works; and, in some instances, it may actually be advantageous not to renew.

The ins and outs of copyright renewal are perhaps the most complex and confusing aspects of the entire copyright law. We can't begin to explain them all here. Persons who might benefit from filing a copyright renewal should consult with a copyright attorney. We'll attempt to identify below just who needs to be concerned with filing copyright renewals and should therefore seek legal assistance.

a. Only valuable pre-1978 works need to be renewed

First of all, you need only worry about filing renewals for works that still have some economic value 28 years after publication or where still-valuable derivative works are based on them. The sad fact is that the majority of published works have little or no value more than 28 years after publication—either because no valuable derivative works have been based on them or because they are out of print and other authors are not seeking permission to quote from or otherwise use them. If a work published between January 1, 1964 and December 31, 1977 is now valueless, don't worry about filing a renewal. It will just be a waste of time and the $20 filing fee.

b. Living authors of still-valuable pre-1978 works

If you are the author of a still valuable work published during 1964–1977, you probably don't need to do anything about renewal. Your publisher undoubtedly owns the renewal term copyright (pre-1978 publishing agreements typically required authors to transfer their renewal term rights to the publisher). Whether you or your publisher file a renewal registration will not affect your transfer of your renewal term rights provided that you live until the beginning of the 29th year after publication. However if you're not sure whether you transferred the copyright in the renewal term to a publisher or other entity, seek legal assistance during the 28th year after publication.

c. Families of deceased authors of valuable pre-1978 works

The situation may be very different if you are the spouse, child or grandchild of a deceased author of a still-valuable pre-1978 work or one from which a still-valuable derivative work was created. In this event, regardless of any prior transfers by the author, the author's spouse and children will own the copyright in the renewal term. In addition, the filing of a copyright renewal during the 28th year after publication may block the continued exploitation of any derivative works created from the original pre-1978 work. This can be a very valuable benefit for the dead author's heirs.

> **EXAMPLE:** Larry published a short story called *Front Window* in 1967. In 1968, he sold the film rights in the story to Repulsive Pictures. The film based on the story was released in 1970 and also called *Front Window*. The film is a derivative work based on Larry's short story. Larry died in 1980. If Larry's widow and children file a renewal registration for his story during 1995 (28 years after publication) they can prevent the film from being distributed or otherwise economically exploited (for example, sold on videocassettes) during the 47-year renewal term commencing on January 1, 1996.

Such a deceased author's spouse, children and/or grandchildren should see a copyright attorney during the 28th year after publication.

d. Families of very ill authors of valuable pre-1978 works

If an author of a still-valuable pre-1978 work (or one from which valuable derivative works was created) is very ill and not likely to live to the end of the 28th year after publication, the author's heirs will benefit if the author does *not* file a copyright renewal or permit a publisher to do so on his behalf. Instead, the heirs should wait until the author dies during the 28th year after publication and file a renewal application themselves. This way, they will own the copyright in the renewal term and be able to block continued exploitation of derivative works during the renewal term. A copyright attorney should definitely be consulted no later than the beginning of the 28th year after publication in this situation.

G. Termination of Transfers of Renewal Term Rights in Pre-1978 Works

As discussed above, works first published or registered before 1978 originally had an initial 28-year copyright term and a second 28-year renewal term.

However, the renewal term was extended an additional 19 years, to 47 years, by the current Copyright Act. This means the owner(s) of the renewal term ownership rights in a pre-1978 work would enjoy 47 years of copyright protection provided the work was timely renewed.

A pre-1978 work's initial and renewal terms are considered to be completely separate. An author may transfer all or part of her copyright ownership rights during her work's renewal term. Such a transfer may be made any time before a work's renewal term actually begins. Indeed, before 1978, authors typically transferred their renewal term rights to their publishers and/or others when they first sold their work. This meant that in most cases publishers and other transferees would be entitled to the additional 19 years of copyright protection created by extending the renewal term to 47 years, not authors or their families.

The whole purpose of having a renewal term was to give authors and their families a second chance to market their work. Thus, it did not seem fair that publishers should benefit from the extra 19 years added to the renewal term. To prevent this, a special provision of the Copyright Act gives authors or certain family members the right to get back those

WHAT'S HE SO SMUG ABOUT?

I HEAR HE JUST ENTERED THE PUBLIC DOMAIN.

extra 19 years of copyright ownership by terminating pre-1978 transfers of renewal term rights.

> **EXAMPLE:** Art published a novel in 1940. His publishing contract contained a provision by which he transferred to his publisher his publication rights in the novel for the renewal term. Art's publisher timely filed a renewal application with the Copyright Office in 1968. The renewal term will last for 47 years, until 2015. However, Art or his surviving family can terminate the renewal rights transfer Art made to his publisher in 1940 and get back the publication rights in the novel for the last 19 years of the renewal term—that is, from 1996 until 2015.

1. When renewal term transfers may be terminated

A transfer of renewal rights may be terminated at any time during the five-year period beginning either 56 years from the date that the work was first published or January 1, 1978, whichever comes later. For example, a renewal rights grant for a work published in 1935 may be terminated any time between January 1, 1991 and December 31, 1996. You should think of this period as a five-year window of opportunity during which you can get back the last 19 years of copyright ownership.

2. What to Do

If you are the author of a pre-1978 work that still has value more than 50 years after publication, or the widow, widower, child or grandchild of such an author, you and/or other family members should consult a copyright attorney some time during the 54th year after publication. She'll be able to determine if a terminable transfer of renewal term copyright ownership rights was made and, if so, help you take the necessary procedural steps to terminate it.

Using Other Authors' Words

To quote is not necessarily stealing. Quotation can be vital to the fulfillment of the public-enriching goals of copyright law.

—Judge Pierre N. Leval

A. Introduction

This chapter is about using other authors' words. Sooner or later, almost all of us feel the need to quote, closely paraphrase, photocopy or otherwise use what others have written. Here are some examples:

- Nancy, a book reviewer, quotes several passages from a novel in the context of a published book review.
- Phil, an historian and biographer, quotes from several unpublished letters and diaries written by his subject.
- Regina, a freelance writer, closely paraphrases two paragraphs from the *Encyclopedia Britannica* in an article she's writing.
- Sylvia, a poet, quotes a line from a poem by T.S. Eliot in one of her own poems.
- Kay, a librarian, makes a photocopy of the library's only remaining copy of Stephen King's latest bestseller.
- Arnold, a high school teacher, makes 30 copies of a newspaper article to distribute to his class.

Some of these uses are lawful without obtaining the permission of the owner of the copyrighted material; others would constitute copyright infringement absent the copyright owner's consent. The purpose of this chapter is to enable you to know when permission is and is not required.

1. Three-Step Analysis to Determine if Permission Is Required

To determine whether you need to obtain permission to use any given item, you need to answer the following three questions. If the answer to all three is yes, you need permission; otherwise you don't.

a. Are you taking an author's expression?

You only need permission to use an author's expression—that is, the particular sequence of words an author writes down or otherwise fixes in a tangible form to express her ideas, explain facts, etc. Ideas and facts themselves are in the public domain, freely available for all to use. This idea-expression dichotomy is discussed in detail in Chapter 6, *What Copyright Protects*. Review that chapter to determine whether what you want to use is expression. If you're sure it isn't, you don't need permission to use it. If there's any doubt in your mind, however,

assume that it is expression and go on to the next question. (Of course, photocopying another author's work always constitutes a taking of that person's expression.)

b. Is the author's expression protected by copyright?

Not all expression is protected by copyright. Much is in the public domain and may be used freely without seeking anyone's permission. All expression contained in works for which copyright protection has expired is in the public domain. This includes any work published more than 75 years ago and works published before 1964 which have not been timely renewed. Review the discussion of copyright duration and renewal in Chapter 10, *Copyright Duration.*

The expression in works published before March 1, 1989 without a valid copyright notice may also be in the public domain. If the expression you want to use is in a pre-1989 work that lacks a copyright notice or whose notice doesn't look correct, review the discussion of copyright notice in Chapter 3, *Copyright Notice* and Chapter 5, *Correcting or Changing Copyright Notice or Registration.*

In addition, certain types of expression are not entitled to copyright protection at all; this includes, for example, works by U.S. Government employees, titles and short phrases and certain blank forms. (See Chapter 6, Section B for a detailed discussion.)

If the expression *is* protected by copyright, go on to the next question.

c. Does your intended use of the protected expression go beyond the bounds of fair use?

You do not need permission to use other authors' protected expression if your use constitutes a fair use. However, permission is required where the intended use of the expression goes beyond the

bounds of fair use. The fair use privilege is discussed in detail below. If, after reading that discussion, you decide that your intended use of expression protected by copyright is not a fair use, you must seek permission to use it. The mechanics of seeking permissions are discussed in Section F, below.

B. Introduction to the Fair Use Privilege

As we discussed in Chapter 1, the purpose of the copyright laws is to advance the progress of knowledge by giving authors an economic incentive to create new works. Authors and their heirs are automatically granted the exclusive right to reproduce, adapt, perform and display their works for at least 50 (and usually more) years; they are in effect, granted a monopoly over the use of their work.

However, there are situations where strict enforcement of an author's monopoly would hinder, rather than promote, the growth of knowledge. An obvious example is that of a researcher or scholar whose own work depends on the ability to refer to and quote from prior scholars' work. No author could create a new work if she were first required to repeat the research of every author who had gone before her.

Of course, scholars and researchers could be required to bargain with each copyright owner for permission to quote from or refer to prior works. But this would likely prove so onerous that many scholars would hunt for another line of work, and the progress of knowledge would be greatly impeded.

To avoid these types of results, the fair use privilege was created. Pursuant to the fair use rule, an author is permitted to make *limited* use of a prior author's work without asking permission. All authors and other copyright owners are deemed to give their automatic consent to the fair use of their work by others. The fair use privilege is perhaps the most significant limitation on a copyright owner's exclusive rights.

CODIFICATION OF FAIR USE PRIVILEGE

The fair use privilege was originally created by judges in the 19th century. It was subsequently made a part of the Copyright Act when it was enacted in 1976. Section 107 of the act provides that:

The fair use of a copyrighted work... for purposes such as criticism, comment, news reporting, teaching... scholarship, or research, is not an infringement of copyright. In determining whether the use made of a work in any particular case is a fair use the factors to be considered... include:

(1) the purpose and character of the use, including whether such use is of a commercial nature or is for nonprofit educational purposes;

(2) the nature of the copyrighted work;

(3) the amount and substantiality of the portion used in relation to the copyrighted work as a whole; and

(4) the effect of the use upon the potential market for, or value, of the copyrighted work.

C. When Is a Use a Fair Use?

Determining whether the fair use privilege applies in any given situation is not an exact scientific process. Rather, it requires a delicate balancing of all the factors discussed below. Probably the only useful rule for fair use is this variant of the golden rule: *"Take not from others to such an extent and in such a manner that you would be resentful if they so took from you."* (McDonald, "Non-infringing Uses," *9 Bull. Copyright Society 466* (1962).)

The following four factors must be considered to determine whether an intended use of an item constitutes a fair use:

- the purpose and character of the use,
- the nature of the copyrighted work,
- the amount and substantiality of the portion used, and
- the effect of the use upon the market for the copyrighted work.

Not all these factors are equally important in every case, but all are considered by the courts in deciding whether a use is fair. You should consider them all in making your own fair use analysis.

Caution
If you're not sure whether an intended use is a fair use, seek legal advice or get permission.

CAN FAIR USE APPLY WHERE PERMISSION IS DENIED?

If you ask a copyright owner for permission to use her work and she refuses, can you then use it without permission on the grounds of fair use? The Supreme Court has said yes: "If the use is otherwise fair, no permission need be sought or granted. Thus, being denied permission to use a work does not weigh against a finding of fair use." (*Campbell v. Acuff-Rose Music, Inc.*, 114 S. Ct. 1164 (1994).)

This means that even though you're certain that your intended use is fair, you can go ahead and seek permission for the use from the copyright owner because you want to avoid the possibility of expensive litigation. If the copyright owner proves to be unreasonable and withholds permission, you can then go ahead and use the material on the basis of fair use. But, of course, the copyright owner could still sue you. If the use really was fair, you would win the suit even though you had unsuccessfully sought permission.

1. The Purpose and Character of the Use

First, the purpose and character of your intended use must be considered in determining whether it is a fair use. The test here is to see whether the subsequent work merely serves as a substitute for the original or "instead adds something new, with a further purpose or different character, altering the first with new expression, meaning, or message." *(Campbell v. Acuff-Rose Music, Inc.)* The Supreme Court calls such a new work transformative.

This is a very significant factor. The more transformative a work, the less important are the other fair use factors, such as commercialism, that may weigh against a finding of fair use. Why should this be? It is because the goal of copyright to promote human knowledge is furthered by the creation of transformative works. "Such works thus lie at the heart of the fair use doctrine's guarantee of a breathing space within the confines of copyright." *(Campbell v. Acuff-Rose Music, Inc.)*

Following are very typical examples of transformative uses where preexisting expression is used to help create new and different works. These types of uses are most likely to be fair uses:

- **Criticism and comment**—for example, quoting or excerpting a work in a review or criticism for purposes of illustration or comment.
- **News reporting**—for example, summarizing an address or article, with quotations, in a news report.
- **Research and scholarship**—for example, quoting a passage in a scholarly, scientific or technical work for illustration or clarification of the author's observations.

Although not really transformative, photocopying by teachers for classroom use may also be a fair use since teaching also furthers the knowledge-enriching goals of the copyright laws (see Section D, below for a detailed discussion of photocopying).

Note that the uses listed above, with the possible exception of news reporting, are primarily for nonprofit educational purposes. Although some

money may be earned from writing a review or scholarly work, financial gain is not usually the primary motivation—disseminating information or otherwise advancing human knowledge is.

If permission were required for these socially helpful uses (presumably for a fee), it is likely that few or no reviews or scholarly works would be written; neither the authors nor publishers of works that earn such modest sums could afford to pay for the necessary permissions. (Newspapers probably could afford to pay for permissions, but requiring them to do so in all cases would inevitably impede the free flow of information, and might also violate the free press guarantees of the First Amendment of the Constitution.)

In contrast, an author and/or publisher of a work written primarily for commercial gain usually can afford to pay for permission to use other's protected expression. It also seems inherently fair to require him to do so. In the words of one court, fair use "distinguishes between a true scholar and a chiseler who infringes a work for personal profit." (*Wainwright Securities, Inc. v. Wall Street Transcript Corp.* 448 F.2d 91 (2d Cir. 1977).)

For these reasons, the fact that a work is published primarily for private commercial gain weighs against a finding of fair use. For example, using the line, "You don't need a weatherman to know which way the wind blows" (from Bob Dylan's song) in a poem published in a small literary journal would probably be a fair use; but using the same line in an advertisement for raincoats probably would not be.

However, the fact that a writer's primary motive is commercial does not always mean he can't exercise the fair use privilege. If the other fair use factors are in the writer's favor, the use may be considered a fair use. This is particularly likely where the use benefits the public by furthering the fundamental purpose of the copyright laws—the advancement of human knowledge.

EXAMPLE: The authors of an unauthorized popular biography of Howard Hughes quoted from two *Look* Magazine articles about Hughes. All three fair use rules were satisfied. Only a small number of words were quoted and the authors had provided proper attribution for the quotes. In addition, the copyright owner of the articles (who turned out to be Hughes himself) had no intention of using the articles in a book, so the use was not a competitive use. A court held that the quotations qualified as a fair use. Although the biography had been published primarily to earn a profit, it also benefited the public. The court stated that "while the Hughes biography may not be a profound work, it may well provide a valuable source of material for future biographers (if any) of Hughes or for historians or social scientists." (*Rosemont Enters. v. Random House, Inc.* 336 F.2d 303 (2nd Cir. 1966).)

It is even possible for an advertisement to constitute a fair use of protected expression if it serves the public interest as well as the advertiser's commercial interests. For example, a vacuum cleaner manufacturer was permitted to quote in an ad from a report in *Consumer Reports* comparing various vacuum cleaners (and concluding that the manufacturer's model was the best) because the ad

significantly increased the number of people exposed to the Consumers Union's evaluations. The ad served the public interest by disseminating helpful consumer information. (*Consumers Union v. General Signal Corp.*, 724 F.2d 1044 (2d Cir. 1983).) The same rationale probably applies to the widespread practice of quoting from favorable reviews in advertisements for books, films, plays, etc. However, as a general rule, you should always seek permission to quote protected material in an ad.

ATTRIBUTION DOES NOT MAKE A USE FAIR, BUT SHOULD ALWAYS BE PROVIDED

Some people have the mistaken idea that they can use any amount of material so long as they give the author credit, whether in a footnote or by mentioning the title of the book after a quotation. This is simply not true. Providing credit for a quotation will not in and of itself make the use of the quote a fair use. For example, if you quote an entire chapter from another author's book without permission, your use wouldn't be considered fair even if you give that author credit.

On the other hand, although the Copyright Act does not expressly require authors to provide attribution for quoted or paraphrased material, it is a factor that courts consider. It is likely that a judge or jury would look with disfavor on an author who attempts to pass off the words of others as his own and then has the nerve to cry "Fair use!" when he's sued for copyright infringement. They might be inclined not only to find that the use is not a fair use, but to impose particularly heavy damages in an infringement suit. If you quote someone else's work, always give that person credit. Quoting with attribution is a very good hedge against getting sued, or losing big if you are sued.

2. The Nature of the Prior Work

As we discussed in Chapter 6, *What Copyright Protects*, to preserve the free flow of information, less copyright protection is given to factual works (scholarly, technical, scientific works, etc.) than to works of fancy (novels, poems, plays, etc.). This is particularly true where there are only a few ways to express the facts or ideas in a factual work, and the idea or fact and its expression are deemed to merge (see Chapter 6, Section B). Thus, authors have more leeway in using material from factual works than from fanciful ones, especially where it's necessary to use extensive quotations to ensure the accuracy of the factual information conveyed.

a. Use of unpublished materials

The extent to which unpublished materials such as letters and diaries may be quoted without permission has been one of the most controversial copyright issues in recent years.

> **EXAMPLE:** Anthony, a well-known civil war historian, finds a letter written in 1865 by a previously unknown civil war veteran in the attic of an old house in Georgia. The unpublished letter will remain under copyright at least until the end of 2002 (see Chapter 10 for a detailed discussion of copyright duration of unpublished works). May Anthony quote from the letter in a book he's writing on the civil war without obtaining permission from the letter's copyright owners (presumably, the veteran's descendants and heirs)? The answer is maybe, maybe not.

When it comes to fair use, unpublished works are inherently different from published works. Publishing an author's expression before she has authorized it infringes upon the author's right to decide when and whether her work will be made public.

Obviously, this factor is not present with published works and the Supreme Court has held that the fact that a work is unpublished weighs heavily against a finding of fair use. (*Harper & Row v. Nation Enterprises,* 471 U.S. 539 (1985).)

This in itself was not surprising. However, in a pair of highly controversial decisions, federal courts in New York, where most major publishers are located, went much further than the Supreme Court and indicated that the unauthorized use of unpublished materials can *never* be a fair use. In the first case, (*Salinger v. Random House, Inc.* 811 F.2d 90 (1987).) a well-known literary biographer was prohibited from quoting or closely paraphrasing in a biography of J.D. Salinger from 44 unpublished letters written by Salinger which the biographer had discovered in university research libraries. In the other case, (*New Era Publications v. Henry Holt* 873 F.2d 576 (1989).) the court held that, but for a legal technicality, it would have been impermissible for an author to quote without permission from L. Ron Hubbard's unpublished writings in a highly critical Hubbard biography.

These decisions had a definite chilling effect on publishers—that is, books that quoted letters were rewritten to omit the quotations. And suits against other biographers were filed.

As you might expect, publishers, authors' groups, biographers, historians and others in the literary community were highly critical of these two decisions, arguing that they enabled the heirs of well-known figures to control how scholars and others can use their unpublished writings; effectively creating a class of widow or widower censors.

After a two-year fight, the fair use provision in the Copyright Act was amended in 1992 to make clear that the fact that a work is unpublished does not act as an absolute bar to a finding of fair use. Section 107 of the Copyright Act now states "The fact that a work is unpublished shall not itself bar a finding of fair use if such finding is made upon consideration of all... [four] fair use factors."

This amendment to the Copyright Act was intended to return the law to where it was before the controversial New York federal court decisions discussed above. The fact that a work is unpublished weighs against fair use, but it is a hurdle that can be overcome in some cases. An important case decided before the amendment became law illustrates how the law works today. In this case a biographer's unauthorized use of a modest amount of material from unpublished letters and journals by the author Richard Wright was found to be a fair use. The court held that, although the unpublished status of the material weighed against fair use, the other three fair use factors all were in the biographer's favor. (*Wright v. Warner Books, Inc.*, 953 F.2d 731 (2d Cir. 1991).)

Copyright tip

In deciding whether your unauthorized use of unpublished material could be a fair use, focus first and foremost on the impact of your use on the value of the material. J.D. Salinger's literary agent testified at trial that Salinger could earn as much as $500,000 if he published his letters. Thus, if a biographer were permitted to publish portions of his most interesting letters first, it could have cost Salinger substantial royalties. This could not be a fair use. But, you might be able to use unpublished material if would not cost the copyright owner anything. For example, quoting a few lines from a letter written by an unknown and long-dead civil war veteran might constitute a fair use where the letter itself has little or no intrinsic value to the veteran's heirs.

b. Fair use of out-of-print works

The drafters of the Copyright Act and the Supreme Court have suggested that a user may have more justification for reproducing a work without permission if it is out-of-print and unavailable for purchase through normal channels. (*Harper & Row v. Nation Enterprises* 471 U.S. 539 (1985).) Thus, most courts give users more leeway when they quote from or photocopy out-of-print works. But this does not mean that any amount of material from out-of-print works may be used without permission.

3. The Amount and Substantiality of the Portion Used

The more material you take the more likely it is that your work will serve as a substitute for the original and adversely affect the value of the copyright owner's work, making it less likely that the use can be a fair use. However, contrary to what many people believe, there is no absolute word limit for fair use. For example, it is not always okay to take one paragraph or less than 200 words. Copying 12 words from a 14 word haiku poem wouldn't be fair use. Nor would copying 200 words from a work of 300 words likely qualify as a fair use. However, copying 2,000 words from a work of 500,000 words might be fair. It all depends on the circumstances—for example, it may be permissible to quote extensively from one scientific work to ensure the accuracy of another scientific work.

The *quality* of the material you want to use must be considered as well as the quantity. The more important it is to the original work, the less likely is your use a fair use. For example, in one famous case, *The Nation* magazine obtained a copy of Gerald Ford's memoirs prior to their publication. The magazine published an article about the memoirs in which only 300 words from Ford's 200,000-word manuscript were quoted verbatim. The Supreme Court held that this was not a fair use because the material quoted, dealing with the Nixon pardon, was the "heart of the book... the most interesting and moving parts of the entire manuscript." (*Harper & Row Publishers, Inc. v. Nation Enterprises* 471 U.S. 539 (1985).)

An author of a work consisting primarily of a prior work—particularly the heart of the work, with little added or changed—will likely not be successful in invoking the fair use privilege.

Copyright tip

As a general rule, never quote more than a few successive paragraphs from a book or article, one or two lines from a poem, or take more than one graphic such as a chart, diagram or illustration. Also, be aware that although there is no legally established word limit for fair use, many publishers act as if there were one and require their authors to obtain permission to quote more then a specified number of words (ranging from 100 to 1,000 words). You should always ask your publisher about such requirements and seek to obtain any necessary permissions as soon as possible. See discussion at Section G, below.

4. The Effect of the Use on the Market for, or Value of, the Prior Work

The fourth fair use factor is the effect of the use upon the potential market for, or value, of the copyrighted work. You must consider not only the harm caused by your act of copying, but whether similar copying by others would have a substantial adverse impact on the potential market for the original work.

Since fair use is an affirmative defense to copyright infringement, it is up to the defendant—the copier—in an infringement case to show there is no harm to the potential market for the original work. This can be difficult. The more transformative the subsequent work—the more it differs from the original and is aimed at a different market—the less likely will it be deemed to adversely affect the potential market for the original.

But if you want to use an author's protected expression in a work of your own that is similar to the prior work and aimed at the same market, your intended use will probably be deemed to adversely affect the potential market for the prior work. This weighs against a finding of fair use.

EXAMPLE 1: Nick, a golf pro, writes a book on how to play golf. Not a good putter himself, he copies the chapter on putting from a how-to golf book written by Lee Trevino (one of the greatest putters in golf history). Since Nick intends for his book to compete with and hopefully supplant Trevino's, this use would likely not be a fair use, particularly given the large amount of copying. In effect, Nick is trying to use Trevino's protected expression to eat into the sales of Trevino's own book.

EXAMPLE 2: Ophelia, an historian, writes a study of women's roles in Elizabethan England. Working under extreme deadline pressure, somehow she unconsciously quotes or closely paraphrases many important passages in a groundbreaking study of the topic written by Horatio ten years before. Ophelia intends for her book to compete with and hopefully supplant Horatio's prior work. Ophelia's use of Horatio's material is likely not a fair use.

EXAMPLE 3: Suzy writes a guide to Social Security aimed at retirees. She borrows several charts and graphs from a prior work on the same subject aimed at the same market. This copying is likely not a fair use.

a. Effect of use on the market for derivative works must be considered

Since the effect of the use on the potential market for the prior work must be considered, the effect on the market for derivative works based on the original must also be analyzed. As discussed in detail in Chapter 7, *Adaptions and Compilations,* a derivative work is one that is based upon or recast from a prior work. One good example of a derivative work is a play or screenplay based on a novel. A finding that a work has a negative impact on the market for derivatives of an original work weighs against fair use.

EXAMPLE: William writes a play about a love affair between two middle-aged people in a midwestern town. Both the plot and dialog are borrowed liberally from the bestselling novel *The Bridges of Madison County*. William's copying from the novel is likely not a fair use. Even though the play will likely not affect sales of the novel itself, it probably would have a negative impact on the market for a play based on the novel, whether by the novelist himself or someone he gave permission to write such a play. In other words, William's play would negatively impact the market for derivative works based on *The Bridges of Madison County*.

D. Fair Use and the Photocopy Machine

The photocopy machine probably represents the greatest threat to copyright owners in history. With current advances in technology, it is now cheaper in many cases to photocopy an entire book than to purchase it from the publisher. Indeed, it is now possible to copy a work electronically and transfer it from one computer to hundreds of others with the push of a button.

1. Photocopying for Personal Use

The extent to which an individual may make photocopies of protected works for personal use is not entirely clear. Individual photocopying of one copy of an article from a magazine or periodical or small portion of a book for personal use—that is, not as part of a business activity—probably constitutes a fair use. Making one copy of a book or other work you already own for personal use also probably constitutes a fair use.

Making multiple copies of anything, or copying entire books or other works you get from libraries or friends to avoid having to buy them probably isn't a fair use. However, there is no practical way for copyright owners to enforce their copyright rights against individual photocopiers. There are no copyright police stationed at photocopy shops.

2. Photocopying for Commercial Use

Photocopying for commercial purposes or to promote business activities normally is not a fair use, particularly if multiple copies of a work are made. Publishers and other copyright owners are actively attempting to enforce their rights against commercial users. For example a group of seven major publishers obtained a $510,000 judgement against one duplicating business for copying excerpts from books without permission, compiling them into "course packets," and selling them to college students. (*Basic Books, Inc. v. Kinko's Graphics Corp.*, 758 F.Supp. 1522 (S.D.N.Y. 1991).)

What about photocopying scientific and technical journal articles and similar materials for research purposes? In the past, courts often held that this was a fair use, even where the research was done for a profit motive. One important reason for this judicial approach was that it was very difficult—and sometimes impossible—to obtain permissions from publishers of obscure, arcane journals. However, this is no longer the case. As discussed in detail in Section G, below, permission to photocopy over one million scientific and technical journals and other materials can be obtained easily through the Copyright Clearance Center (CCC). As a result, a federal judge in New York ruled that systematic photocopying of journal articles by the oil company Texaco for distribution to Texaco-employed researchers was not a fair use. The judge held that Texaco should have obtained permission to copy the articles through the CCC, not simply copied them without permission. (*American Geophysical Union v. Texaco, Inc.*, 802 F.Supp. 1 (S.D.N.Y. 1992).) This case is now on appeal. If it is upheld, we may see major changes in the photocopying practices of corporate and law firm libraries.

Copyright tip

Small independent newsletters and journals are particularly vulnerable to mass photocopying. Copying even a small portion of a newsletter by a profit-making user may have a significant impact on the market for the work. Newsletter and journal publishers are well aware of the problem and are fighting back. Several publishers have won substantial judgments from large corporations that have copied their works without permission. The problem is, how do publishers find out about unauthorized copying?

Here is a strategy that really worked: The publisher of the *Product Safety Letter*, a journal about product liability lawsuits distributed to law firms, placed an ad in each issue offering a $2,000 reward to persons providing conclusive evidence of unauthorized photocopying of the journal. Soon, someone at a large Washington, DC law firm notified the publisher that numerous unauthorized copies of the journal were being made for firm employ-

ees. The publisher demanded that the firm halt the copying and ultimately sued it for copyright infringement. The case was settled for an undisclosed amount and the firm stopped making the unauthorized copies.

3. Photocopying by Libraries and Archives

Fair use analysis becomes much more difficult when photocopying by libraries and archives is involved. Such institutions play a vital role in preserving and disseminating knowledge. Yet if they were permitted to engage in unfettered photocopying, the market for all written works would be reduced and authors' economic incentives to create new works would be diminished.

Congress has determined that certain types of unauthorized photocopying by libraries and archives must be permitted whether or not it would constitute a fair use under the standards discussed above. Section 108 of the Copyright Act (17 U.S.C. 108) contains highly detailed, rigid and complex rules defining the scope of this type of copying. These rules in effect give libraries and archives a special exemption from the copyright laws. We summarize the rules in the next two subsections.

a. Which libraries and archives may benefit from special exemption?

The exemption applies to all nonprofit libraries and archives—e.g., municipal libraries, university and school libraries, government archives. However, a library or archive need not be nonprofit to qualify. A library or archive owned by a profit-making enterprise or proprietary institution may qualify for the exemption so long as the photocopying itself is not commercially motivated. This means that a profit may not be earned from the photocopies themselves—for instance, they could not be sold for a profit; but the information contained in the photocopies may be used to help a company make a profit-making product. For example, the exemption might be claimed by research and development departments of chemical, pharmaceutical, automobile and oil companies; the library of a private hospital; and law and medical partnership libraries.

However, if the library or archive is not open to the general public, it must be open at least to persons doing research in the specialized field covered by the library collection who are not affiliated with the library or its owner. This requirement eliminates many libraries and archives owned by private companies that are open only to employees.

b.   When does the exemption apply?

The special exemption may be claimed only if:
- the library or archive owns the work as part of its collection
- only one copy of a work is made at a time
- no charge is made for the copying beyond the costs of making the copy, and
- the copy contains the same copyright notice that the work itself contains.

So long as these requirements are met, it is permissible for a library or archive to make an authorized photocopy of a work under the following four circumstances:

Archival reproductions of unpublished works. One unauthorized copy of any unpublished work may be made for purposes of preservation and security, or for deposit for research use in another library or archive. The copy must be in facsimile form, meaning that manuscripts may be photocopied or microfilmed, but not reproduced in machine-readable language for storage in a computer database or other information retrieval system.

Replacement of lost or damaged copy. A published work that is damaged, deteriorating, lost or stolen may also be reproduced in facsimile form. But first, the library or archives must make a reasonable effort to purchase an unused replacement at a fair price. This will always require contacting commonly known trade sources in the U.S. and, in the normal situation, the publisher or other copyright owner (if the owner can be located at the address listed in the copyright registration) or an authorized reproducing service as well.

Library user requests for articles and short excerpts. A library or archive may make one copy (it doesn't have to be a facsimile) of an article from a periodical or a small part of any other work at the request of a library user or at the request of another library on behalf of a library user, provided that:
- the copy becomes the property of the library user
- the library has no reason to believe the copy will be used for purposes other than private study, scholarship and research, and
- the library displays a copyright notice at the place where reproduction requests are accepted (for the form of this notice and other regulations regarding it, see 37 C.F.R. 201.4 (1988)).

Library user requests for entire works. A library or archive may also make a copy (it doesn't have to be a facsimile) of an entire book or periodical at a library user's request (or at the request of another library on behalf of a library user) if the library determines after reasonable investigation that a copy cannot be obtained at a reasonable price, either because the work is out-of-print or for some other reason. The same type of investigation must be conducted as for replacement of lost or damaged copies (above). In addition, the same good faith and posting requirements must be met as for reproduction of articles and short excerpts (above).

c.   No multiple copies

The library and archive exemption extends only to isolated and unrelated reproductions of a single copy. It does not authorize related or concerted reproduction of multiple copies of the same material, whether at the same time or over a period of time.

This is so whether the copies are intended for one individual or a group. For example, if a college professor instructs her class to read an article from a copyrighted journal, the school library would not be permitted to reproduce copies of the article for the class.

d. No systematic copying

Systematic copying is also prohibited. This means that a library or archives may not make copies available to other libraries or groups of users through inter-library networks and similar arrangements in such large quantities so as to enable them to substitute the copies for subscriptions or reprints which they would otherwise have purchased themselves. The National Commission on New Technological Uses for Copyrighted Works (CONTU) has developed the following guidelines as to how much copying is permissible:

- Within any calendar year, one library or archive may obtain from another library or archive not more than five copies of any factual article or articles from a single periodical published less than five years previously. The five-copy limitation applies even if each copy is of a different article or from a different issue. All that matters is that all the articles came from the same periodical and were published not more than five years before the copies are made.
- A library or archive may not obtain from another library or archive more than five copies of material other than factual periodical articles from any given work within any calendar year.
- If the requesting library or archive has on order or in its collection the item that it wants copied, but does not have the item in its possession at the time and cannot reasonably repossess it at the time, the copy made at its request will not count toward the maximum number of permissible copies.
- A library or archive may not satisfy another library's or archive's request for copies unless the request is accompanied by a representation that the request conforms with these guidelines.
- Every library or archive must keep on file each request for copies it made to other libraries or archives.

e. Photocopying beyond the scope of the exemption

Unauthorized copying that is not covered by, or goes beyond the limits of, the special exemption is permissible only if it is a fair use under the more flexible fair use factors discussed in Section C, above.

f. Photocopying by library patrons

Many libraries refuse to make copies for patrons. Instead they simply install coin-operated machines for patrons to use themselves. A library or archive is not liable for unsupervised use of photocopy machines on its premises provided that a proper warning notice is displayed. (For the form of this

notice and other regulations regarding it, see 37 C.F.R. 201.4 (1988).)

4.   Photocopying by Teachers

Photocopying by teachers for scholarly or classroom use is generally favored as a fair use because it is done for nonprofit educational purposes. However, if taken to extreme, such copying would destroy the market for educational materials. In an effort to strike a balance between the needs of teachers and publishers and authors, a set of guidelines for teacher photocopying was agreed upon by representatives of author-publisher and educational organizations and unofficially endorsed by the congressional committee that drafted the Copyright Act.

Technically, the guidelines do not have the force of law, but it is highly unlikely that any court would hold that copying by a teacher within the guidelines did not constitute a fair use.

Copyright tip

The guidelines establish *minimum* fair use standards for teachers. It is possible that teacher photocopying that exceeds the guidelines could be considered a fair use as well.

The guidelines may be summarized as follows:

a.   Single copies

A teacher may make *one copy* of the following items for purposes of scholarly research, or use in teaching or preparing to teach a class:

- a chapter from a book (but not an entire book)
- an article from a periodical or newspaper
- a short story, short essay or short poem, whether or not from a collective work such as an anthology, and
- a chart, graph, diagram, drawing, cartoon or picture from a book, periodical or newspaper.

b.   Multiple copies for classroom use

A teacher may also make multiple copies of the items listed above (not to exceed more than one copy per pupil in the course) provided that:

- the amount of material copied is sufficiently brief
- the copying is done spontaneously
- the cumulative effect test is met, and
- each copy includes a notice of copyright.

i.   Brevity

There are strict numerical limits as to how many words may be copied, but these limits may be stretched so that copies don't end with an unfinished line of a poem or an unfinished prose paragraph.

Poetry. Multiple copies may be made of a completed poem of 250 words or less that is printed on not more than two pages; and up to 250 words may be copied from longer poems.

Prose. Multiple copies may be made of a complete article, story or essay of less than 2,500 words; and excerpts up to 1,000 words or 10% of the work, whichever is less, may be copied from longer works (but 500 words may be copied from works that are between 2,500 and 4,999 words long).

Illustrations. Multiple copies for classroom use may be made of one chart, graph, diagram, drawing, cartoon or picture contained in a book or periodical issue.

Special works. The guidelines also include a category called "special works." No one is exactly sure what a special work is. However, it appears that special works include works of poetry or prose of less than 2,500 words intended for children that combine language with illustrations. Such special works may not be copied in their entirety. Only an excerpt of up to two published pages and containing not more than 10% of the words in the text may be reproduced.

ii. Spontaneity

The idea to make the copies must come from the teacher herself, not from school administrators, the board of education or any other higher authority. Moreover, the idea to make the copies and their actual classroom use must be so close together in time that it would be unreasonable to expect a timely reply to a request for permission from the publisher or copyright owner.

Copyright tip
It usually takes at least a month or two for a publisher to respond to a permission request. Thus, the spontaneity requirement will probably be met where the copies are used in class less than a month after they are made. But, of course, this rule wouldn't apply if the material is included in a curriculum prepared prior to the start of the school term.

iii. Cumulative effect of copying

Finally, the copying must not have an undue cumulative effect on the market for the copyrighted work. This test is met so long as:

- the copying is for only one course in the school where the copies are made
- not more than one short poem, article, story, essay or two excerpts from longer works are copied from the same author, nor more than three from the same anthology or other collective work or periodical volume during one class term, and
- there are no more than nine instances of such multiple copying for one course during one class term.

The limitations on the number of articles that can be copied does not apply to copying from newspapers, current news periodicals and current news sections of other periodicals.

iv. Copyright notice

A copyright notice must be included on all copies made. This can easily be accomplished by copying the page in the work where the copyright notice appears. If this is not done, the notice must be added to the copies. It should be in the exact same form as on the original work.

v. Photocopy charges

Finally, the teacher's students may not be charged more than the actual cost of making the photocopies.

c. Prohibited copying

Even if all the requirements listed above are satisfied, multiple copies may not be made to substitute for the purchase of books, publisher's reprints or periodicals; to create anthologies or compilations; or to substitute for or replace "consumable" works such as workbooks, exercises, standardized tests, test booklets and answer sheets.

In addition, the same teacher may not copy the same item from term to term. Thus, for example, it was not a fair use for a teacher to use the same photocopied materials for three successive school terms. (*Marcus v. Crowley*, 695 F.2d 1171 (9th Cir. 1983).)

E. Other Fair Uses

Fair use is not limited just to quotations and photocopying. Discussed below are some other types of uses that may be fair uses.

1. Parody

A parody is a work of fancy that ridicules another, usually well-known, work by imitating it in a comic way. Peruse the humor section of your local bookstore and you'll find many examples, such as parody versions of well-known magazines like *Cosmopolitan* (called *Catmopolitan*). Someone has even published a parody of the SAT exam called the "NSAT" (No-Sweat Aptitude Test) and a book of parody sequels to famous literary works, including titles such as *A Clockwork Tomato, 2000: A Space Iliad*, and *Satanic Reverses*.

To parody a work, it is usually necessary to use some of the original work's expression, so that readers will be able to recognize what's being parodied. However, it is rarely possible to get permission to parody or satirize someone else's work. Thus, parodies can exist only because of the fair use doctrine. Recognizing this, lower courts have historically held that parody and satire deserve substantial freedom, both as entertainment and a form of social and literary criticism.

In a much anticipated decision involving a parody of the song "Pretty Woman" by the rap group 2 Live Crew, the Supreme Court has strongly reaffirmed the view that a parody, like other comment and criticism, may be a fair use. Indeed, the court held that even a commercially distributed parody of a well-known song can constitute a fair use. To determine whether any parody is a fair use, all four fair use factors discussed in Section C above must be weighed.

The Supreme Court, in *Campbell v. Acuff-Rose Music, Inc.*, 114. S.Ct. 1164 (1994), gave specific guidance on how the fair use factors should be evaluated in a parody case.

a. Purpose and character of the use

The Supreme Court stated that the heart of any parodist's claim of fair use is that an author's pre-existing work needed to be copied in order to create a new work that, at least in part, comments on or criticizes the prior author's work. However, a self-proclaimed parodist who copies a prior work merely to get attention or to avoid the drudgery in working up something fresh has a weak claim to fair use.

Does it matter that a parody might be seen to be in bad taste? The Supreme Court said no. All that matters is that the work can reasonably be perceived to contain a parodic element—in other words, it comments on or criticizes the original work in some way. Whether a parody is in good or bad taste does not matter to fair use.

The fact that a parody was commercially motivated weighs against a finding of fair use, but is not determinative by itself.

b. The nature of the copyrighted work

As discussed in Section C above, expressive works of fancy like novels and plays are generally given greater copyright protection than more utilitarian factual works like newspaper accounts or scientific works. However, the Supreme Court stated that since parodies almost always copy publicly known expressive works, this fair use factor is not helpful "in separating the fair use sheep from the infringing goats."

c. The amount and substantiality of the portion used

To be effective, a parody must take enough material from the prior work to be able to conjure it up in the reader's or hearer's mind. To make sure the intended audience will understand the parody, the parodist usually has to copy at least some of the most distinctive or memorable features of the original work. Once enough has been taken from the original work to assure identification, how much more is reasonable to take will depend on the extent to which the work's overriding purpose and character is to parody the original. However, a parody composed primarily of an original work with little new material added is not likely to be considered a fair use.

d. Effect of the use on the market for the prior work

A finding that a parody has a detrimental affect on the market for, or value of, the original work weighs against fair use. However, the Supreme Court stated that a parody generally does not affect the market for the original work because a parody and the original usually serve different market functions. A parody is particularly unlikely to affect the market for the original where the copying is slight in relation to the parody as a whole.

But what if a parody is so scathing or critical of the original work that it harms the market for it? Does this weigh against fair use? The Supreme Court answered this question with a resounding no. Biting

criticism is not copyright infringement, even if it effectively destroys a work both artistically and commercially.

MARKET EFFECT ON DERIVATIVE WORKS MUST BE CONSIDERED

The effect of a parody on the market for derivative works based on the original must also be considered. As discussed in Chapter 7, *Adaptions and Compilations*, a derivative work is a work based on or recast from an original, such as a play or screenplay based upon a novel. The right to license derivative works is one of a copyright owner's most important rights. A parody may itself be a derivative work of the original it parodies. But the effect of a parody on the market for other parodies of the original need not be considered. This is because in the real world copyright owners hardly ever license parodies of their work. In other words, it is only necessary to consider the effect of a parody on the potential market for derivative works other than other parodies of the original. Again, where the copying is slight, the market effect on derivative works is also slight.

EXAMPLE: William writes a one-act play that parodies the best-selling novel *The Bridges of Madison County*. In deciding whether the play is a fair use, a court must consider the effect the play has on the potential market for other plays based on the novel. But the court need not consider whether the play affects the market for other parodies of the novel, since the novel's author is unlikely to license parodies of his work.

Copyright tip

Applying these fair use factors is a highly subjective exercise. One judge's fair use might be another's infringement. A parody will probably be deemed a fair use so long as:

- The parody has neither the intent nor the effect of fulfilling the demand for the original;
- The parodist does not take more of the original work than is necessary to accomplish the parody's purpose (the more recognizable the original work, the less needs to be taken to parody it); and
- The original work is at least in part an object of the parody (otherwise there would be no need to use it).

2. Calligraphy

A single copy reproduction of a copyrighted work by a calligrapher for a single client is a fair use. Likewise, a single reproduction of excerpts from a work by a student calligrapher or teacher in a learning situation would be a fair use of the copyrighted work.

3. Copying for the Blind

The making of a single braille copy or tape recording of a copyrighted work by an individual as a free service for blind persons would probably be considered a fair use. But making multiple copies or tapes for commercial purposes would not be.

F. Obtaining Permission to Use Protected Material

If you need to use another author's protected expression in a way that goes beyond the bounds of fair use as discussed above, you'll need to obtain permission from the copyright owner. Permission usually takes the form of a nonexclusive license, also called a consent-to-use license or simply a permission. Permissions should always be obtained in writing.

Most publishing contracts contain a clause making it the author's responsibility to obtain any necessary permissions. Many publishers supply their authors with their own permissions guidelines. These may state exactly when an author is expected to get a permission and contain blank permission forms the author is required to use.

You should start seeking your permissions as soon as possible because it can take several months to get them, and a publisher won't publish your book or article without them.

Copyright tip

If you need to obtain many permissions, or simply don't want to bother getting them yourself, there are private companies and individuals who obtain permissions on an author's behalf. These permissions specialists usually charge by the hour, ranging from $15 to $30 per hour or more. They are listed in the *Literary Market Place (LMP)*, a directory for the publishing business, under "Permissions." The *LMP* can be found in the reference section of many libraries. You should contact such a permissions service at least three to six months before your work is scheduled for completion.

1. Step 1: Prepare Permission Form

If your publisher has not provided you with its own permission forms to use, you'll need to prepare your own form. Usually, it is wise to seek the nonexclusive right to use the material throughout the world in all languages in all present and future editions of your book, article or other work, and also in revisions of the work. This way, you'll only need to get permission once.

Here's an example of a combination cover letter-permission agreement (nonexclusive license) you can use:

SAMPLE LETTER/PERMISSION AGREEMENT

November 20, 199X

[Name and address of publisher or copyright
owner. Direct requests to a publisher or other
entity to the Permissions Department.]

I am writing to obtain permission to use the following material from your publication: *[Accurately describe the material you want to use; including the author, title, date of publication and page numbers in which it appears (include a photocopy of the material if it would be helpful).]*

I wish to use this material in the following work: *[List the author(s), title, approximate number of pages, name of publisher, proposed date of publication and price and estimated number of copies to be initially printed.]*

I am requesting nonexclusive world rights to use this material as part of my work in all languages and for all editions and future revisions.

The material will be accompanied on publication by the following credit line (please specify):

_____

If you wish this material to be accompanied on publication by a copyright notice, please specify the form here:

_____

Other conditions, if any:

_____

If you do not control the world rights to the requested material, please specify here any additional source from whom permission must be obtained:

_____

Thank you for your prompt consideration of this request. A duplicate copy of this letter is enclosed for your convenience.

Very truly yours,

Yolanda Allende
Yolanda Allende

The above request is approved, subject to the conditions noted above.

Approved by: _____

Date: _____

2. Step 2: Find to Whom Your Permission Request Should Be Sent

Next, you'll need to find out to whom you should send your permission request form. Of course, this is the person or entity that has the right to grant the permission. The first place to contact is the permissions department of the work's publisher. The publisher may own the right to reproduce the material, or may have been given authority by the author or other copyright owner to grant permissions. If not, the publisher may forward your request to the author or her heirs (assuming they own the right to grant the permission you seek).

Copyright tip

If the publisher's address is not included in the work you wish to quote from, you may be able to find it in the *Literary Market Place* or the *Gale Directory of Publications*.

If the publisher has gone out of business or can't be located, you'll need to contact the copyright owner directly. The person or entity named in the work's copyright notice probably was the initial copyright owner, but he may have transferred his rights to somebody else. By searching the Copyright Office records, you should be able determine who the current copyright owner is and obtain an address.

You can have the Copyright Office search its records for you to determine whether the work was registered, whether any transfers of ownership were recorded and the names and addresses of the persons named in such documents (which won't necessarily be current). The Copyright Office charges $20 an hour for this service. Call the Reference & Bibliography Section at 202-707-6850 and ask for an estimate of how long they think your particular search will take. Then fill out the search request form located in the appendix to this book and send it, and your check in the amount of the estimate payable to the Register of Copyrights, to:

Reference & Bibliography Section, LM-451
Copyright Office
Library of Congress
Washington, DC 20559

Instead of having the Copyright Office conduct the search, you can have a professional search firm conduct the search for you. This will probably cost much more than having the Copyright Office do the search; fees range from $100 to $300, but you will get much faster service. Search firms usually report back in two to ten working days, while it usually takes the Copyright Office one or two months to conduct a search.

COPYRIGHT SEARCH FIRMS

There are five copyright search firms, located primarily in the Washington, DC area:

Copyright Council
2121 Crystal Dr., Ste. 704
Arlington, VA 22202
703-521-1669

Government Liaison Services, Inc.
3030 Clarendon Blvd., Ste. 209
Arlington, VA 22201
800-642-6564 or 703-524-8200

Robert G. Roomian
P.O. Box 7111
Alexandria, VA 22307
703-549-7010

Thomson & Thomson
Copyright Research Group
500 E St., S.W. Ste. 970
Washington, DC 20024
800-356-8630
(This is the largest and best-known search firm.)

XL Corporate Services
62 White St.
New York, NY 10013
800-221-2972 or 212-431-5000

Finally, you can search the Copyright Office records yourself. The Copyright Office's records are open to the public at its headquarters located in the James Madison Memorial Building, 101 Independence Ave. S.E., Washington, DC. The Office is open from 8:30 A.M. to 5:00 P.M. Monday through Friday. If you have access to a computer and modem, some of these records can be searched via the Dialog computerized database. Call 800-334-2564 for informa-

tion. The records are also available on the Internet, which is much cheaper to use. Most university libraries and many public libraries have access to the Internet. The Internet "address" is "locis.loc.gov"; the password "Copyright Information."

If you're seeking permission to use an original unpublished photo, drawing, painting or other artwork, you'll need to contact the copyright owner directly. This may be a picture agency, museum, artist or private individual who owns the reproduction rights to the work.

Send two copies of your request to the publisher's Permissions Department or to the copyright owner, and keep one copy for your files. Be sure to keep track of when you send each request and when you receive replies.

USING MATERIAL WHERE THE COPYRIGHT OWNER CAN'T BE FOUND

What happens if, after taking all the steps outlined above, you are unable to locate the copyright owner(s) and you use the material without permission? If the owner later discovers what you've done, at the very least you will be liable to him for the reasonable value of your use. If the material is not terribly valuable this won't amount to much and the owner will probably accept a small permission fee.

EXAMPLE: Arthur wants to quote 20 pages from an out-of-print zoology text in a book he's writing on aardvarks. The publisher is out of business and neither the author or her heirs can be located. Arthur decides to use the quotation anyway. One year later, he is contacted by the zoology text's copyright owner. The owner agrees to accept $200 from Arthur for retroactive permission to use the quotation.

However, if the material is quite valuable, you'll be liable for a substantial permission fee, perhaps more than you'd be able or willing to pay. Moreover, if your use caused the owner any economic loss, you'll be liable for that as well. See Chapter 12, *Copyright Infringement*, for a detailed discussion.

3. Step 3: Obtaining Responses to Your Permission Request

The copyright owner may contact you before granting permission to make sure you agree to its terms, or send you its own permission form. However, if you don't hear from the copyright owner within a reasonable period, call or send a follow-up letter. If you're dealing with a publisher or other entity, find out the name of the person to contact first.

a. Permission fees

Payment is often sought for permissions. According to *Publishers Weekly*, permission fees range from $15 to $100 per page of prose, and $5 to $25 per line of poetry. Permission to quote a song lyric, particularly a well-known one, can cost far more. A flat fee is usually charged for individual photos, illustrations, diagrams, etc.

Copyright tip

Who pays for permission depends on your publishing contract. Some publishers will agree to pay for permissions out of their own pocket, or will at least advance the fees to the author and then deduct them from the author's royalties.

4. Copyright Clearance Center

Permission to photocopy may be obtained by getting the copyright owner to sign a nonexclusive license. This is accomplished in the same way as obtaining a right-to-use license discussed above. This can be a time-consuming process. Fortunately, there is a way to legally make photocopies without going to the time and trouble of getting a nonexclusive license from the copyright owner. The Copyright Clearance Center (CCC) is a nonprofit corporation created by publishers, authors and photocopy users in 1978 to provide a more efficient means of conveying permissions and collecting fees.

The CCC does not make photocopies. Rather, it operates a centralized photocopy authorization and payment system. It works like this: Instead of tracking down a publisher or copyright owner and directly asking it for permission to photocopy (and waiting for a reply), a photocopy user can make the desired photocopies immediately and submit a standard fee directly to the CCC. The CCC will distribute the fee to the publisher.

Of course, the CCC service may only be used if the publisher of the work you want to photocopy participates in the service; thousands of publishers, both foreign and domestic, do. More than 1.5 million publications are currently covered; these include scholarly, technical, medical and trade journals, business magazines, newsletters, books, proceedings, etc. You can tell if a publication participates in the CCC service by looking it up in the CCC's *Publisher's Photo-Copy Fee Catalog,* which lists registered titles and their copying fees. In addition, publications participating in the CCC service often display a printed statement like the following, either at the bottom of the first pages of articles or just once in or near the masthead of the publication:

Permission to photocopy for internal or personal use or the internal or personal use of specific clients is granted to libraries and other users registered with the Copyright Clearance Center, Inc. (CCC), provided that the base fee of ___ per copy of the article, plus ___ per page is paid directly to CCC, 27 Congress Street, Salem, MA 01970. Special requests should be addressed to the publisher.

If you or your company make lots of photocopies every month, you can open an account with the CCC by paying an annual fee. You then periodically report those photocopies you have made from CCC-registered publications, and the CCC calculates the permissions fees and bills you. The CCC also offers an Annual Authorization Service for a flat yearly fee, which is computed on the basis of the customer's own self-conducted audit. However, you do not have to open an account to use the service.

The CCC also has an Academic Permission Service (APS) that serves as a central licensing mechanism for colleges and universities that wish to photocopy articles, portions of books and other materials to create course packets and anthologies for use by students. The APS has a printed catalog that lists publishers and titles participating in the service along with royalty fee structures, publishers' exclusions and tips for addressing publishers not participating in the APS.

For further information about this useful service, contact:

Copyright Clearance Center
27 Congress Street
Salem, MA 01970
508-744-3350 FAX: 508-741-2318

5. Acknowledgments

You should always give credit to the source of quoted or closely paraphrased material. When you obtain permission to use protected material, you should ask the copyright owner how it wants the acknowledgment worded (this request is included in the permission form above).

For a text passage complete in itself, such as a poem or graph, the full citation of the source may be followed by: "Reprinted with the publisher's permission." A credit line below a photo or illustration may read: "Courtesy of [the copyright owner—for example, the Metropolitan Museum of Art]."

Acknowledgments for quoted excerpts may be printed on the same page as the excerpt; or, if there are many quotations, they can all be collected together in an acknowledgments section at the beginning or end of the work. Here's an example of an acknowledgment that may appear at the beginning or end of a work:

Grateful acknowledgment is made to
Scrivener & Sons, Inc.
for permission to reprint from
The Plagiarist's Handbook by
Alfred E. Newman.
Copyright © 1991 by Alfred E. Newman.

Copyright Infringement: What It Is, What to Do About It, How to Avoid It

Previous chapters have discussed the steps an author or other copyright owner must take to give her work maximum protection under the copyright laws. Now we explore how these protections are enforced. This subject is referred to as copyright infringement.

When a copyright dispute arises, there are often several self-help steps a copyright owner can take. These generally amount to telling the infringer to stop the infringing activity and/or pay for the infringement. When push comes to shove, however, there is only one remedy with teeth in it. This is to ask a federal court to order the infringing activity halted and to award a judgment for damages. Because this type of litigation is procedurally complex, an attorney skilled in copyright litigation is required.

This chapter is not intended as a substitute for a good copyright attorney. Rather, its aim is to:

- help you recognize when copyright infringement has occurred
- suggest some steps an author or other copyright owner can take on her own to deal effectively with infringement without resorting to lawyers and the courts
- tell you what to expect in the event of a court action
- help you estimate what damages and other types of court relief are potentially available to you in an infringement suit
- introduce some ways to defend against infringement charges, and
- tell you how to protect yourself from infringement claims.

A. What Is Copyright Infringement?

In Chapter 2, *Copyright Basics,* we described a copyright as a bundle of five exclusive rights. These include the right to reproduce, distribute, prepare derivative works based upon, perform and display a protected work. Subject to important exceptions

discussed in Section C below, these rights cannot be exercised by anybody but the copyright owner unless the owner's permission is obtained. If copyright rights are exercised without the owner's permission, the copyright is said to be infringed.

Infringement of written works usually involves the unauthorized exercise of a copyright owner's exclusive rights to reproduce the work and prepare derivative works based on it. In plain English this means the unauthorized *copying* of the work. This chapter focuses on infringement due to copying. However, be aware that performing a play, publishing an unauthorized copy or reciting a written work in public also constitutes copyright infringement—unless the copyright owner's permission is obtained.

There are many ways to copy a written work. An infringer may copy another's work by means of a photocopy machine or other mechanical device; or he may do it the old fashioned way: by transcribing verbatim or paraphrasing protected material into a work of his own. The latter type of copying need not even be done consciously to constitute infringement. A person who unconsciously copies from memory a work he's read may be a copyright infringer; but the penalties imposed on such a person would usually be less than those for a person who consciously and willfully copied another's work. (See discussion in Section F.2, below.)

1. The Difference Between Plagiarism and Copyright Infringement

Many people believe that plagiarism and copyright infringement are the same thing. Not so: a plagiarist is a person who poses as the *originator* of words he did not write, ideas he did not conceive, and/or facts he did not discover. For purposes of plagiarism, the material stolen need not be protected by copyright. In contrast, a copyright infringer is a person who makes unauthorized use of material protected by copyright. Absent protection, there can be no infringement. Moreover, infringement can occur even though the infringer gives proper credit to the author of the protected expression. Of course, some infringers also take credit for the work they copy; they are both plagiarists and infringers.

EXAMPLE 1: Louis, a professor of French, translates a novel by the obscure 19th century French novelist Jean Valjean and publishes it under his own name. The novel is in the public domain, thus Louis has not committed copyright infringement. He is, however, a plagiarist because he has posed as the originator of the novel.

EXAMPLE 2: The publisher Scrivener & Sons publishes a paperback version of Stephen King's latest bestseller without his permission. Scrivener has infringed on King's copyright by publishing his book without permission, but has not committed plagiarism because it has not posed as the author of the book.

EXAMPLE 3: Dr. Jekyl, a biophysicist at a leading university, copies a paper written by one of his colleagues and publishes it under his own name in a scientific journal. Since the colleague's paper was protected by copyright, Dr. Jekyl is both a plagiarist and copyright infringer.

A plagiarist cannot be sued for copyright infringement if all he takes are unprotected ideas or facts, or words that are in the public domain. But, publishing contracts usually contain a provision, called a warranties and indemnities clause, by which the author promises that the work he submits to the publisher is not in the public domain. So, a plagiarist could be sued by his publisher for breach of contract or possibly fraud. And, aside from the possible legal consequences, being accused of plagiarism is usually not good for one's career. College professors and journalists have been fired because of plagiarism.

HOW TO AVOID PLAGIARISM CHARGES

To avoid charges of plagiarism, authors of scholarly works (histories, biographies, legal and scientific treatises, etc.) must always give proper credit to the sources of their ideas and facts, as well as any words they borrow. Authors of less serious works, how-to books for example, should always attribute quotations, but may not always need to give credit for ideas and facts they borrow (authors of such works should discuss this with their publishers). It is neither customary nor necessary for authors of works of fancy, such as novels and plays, to credit the sources of their inspiration, whether other works of fancy, newspaper accounts or histories. But they should, of course, give proper attribution for direct quotations.

B. How to Know Whether You Have a Valid Infringement Claim

If you come away with nothing else from this chapter, remember this: *The fact that another person's work is similar to your own does not necessarily mean that he has committed copyright infringement.* Infringement occurs only if all three requirements discussed below are present:

- ownership of a work protected by a valid copyright
- actual copying of the work by the alleged infringer (remember, this chapter focuses on infringement by copying; infringement of other exclusive copyright rights is also possible), and
- improper use of the work's protected expression by the alleged infringer.

We discuss each element below. Where it's clear you have a valid infringement claim, it may be possible to settle the matter without the aid of an attorney as discussed in Section D, below. However, if you're not sure whether you have a valid claim, get professional help. How to find a competent copyright lawyer is discussed in Chapter 15, *Help Beyond This Book.*

1. A Work Protected by Copyright

The question of infringement does not even arise unless the work allegedly infringed is protected by copyright. This means that the work must meet the three prerequisites for copyright protection discussed in detail in Chapter 6, *What Copyright Protects;* that is, the work must be:

- *fixed in a tangible medium of expression.* You cannot sue anyone for copying words you have spoken but never written down or otherwise fixed in a tangible form.
- *independently created.* The material allegedly infringed upon must have been independently created. You cannot sue someone for copying words that were copied from others.
- *minimally creative.* The work you believe has been infringed upon must have been the product of a minimal amount of creativity. You probably will not be able to successfully sue

someone for copying a recipe, an alphabetically organized directory or similar items.

a. Timely registration creates presumption of validity

So long as your work is registered within five years of the date of first publication, it is presumed to be protected by a valid copyright and the person(s) named in the registration certificate are presumed to be the copyright owners. This is one of the greatest benefits of copyright registration. It means that you do not have to go to the time and trouble of proving that your work is original (which can be very hard to prove) or that you actually wrote it. Rather, it's up to the alleged infringer to try to prove that the work was not original or that your copyright is invalid for some other reason.

2. Actual Copying by the Alleged Infringer

Second, it must be clear that the alleged infringer actually copied your work. In some cases, there may be witnesses who saw the alleged infringer copy (the infringer may have had a collaborator); or the

infringer may even admit it. However, an up-front admission of copying is unusual. More typically, copyright infringement—like adultery—usually happens behind closed doors and the participants rarely admit their involvement. For this reason, copying is usually established not through direct evidence such as witnesses or admissions, but by showing two things:

- access by the infringer, and
- that the works, or parts of them, are substantially similar.

If these are proven, copying is *inferred* because there is no other reasonable explanation for the similarities.

a. Access

To prove access, you must show that the alleged infringer had access to your work—that is, the opportunity to view it. The fact that your work has been made generally available to the public through publication is sufficient to establish access. In the case of unpublished works, however, access must be shown in different ways. One way would be to show that the alleged infringer had contact with a third person—for instance an editor—who had a copy of your manuscript in her possession. But in the absence of such contacts, you're going to have a hard time convincing anyone that the alleged infringer had access to your unpublished work.

b. Substantial similarity

Here, you must prove that your work and the work by the alleged infringer are so similar that copying must have occurred. Assuming the alleged infringer had access to your work, you must compare the similarities between your work and his to see if copying may reasonably be inferred. But keep in mind that similarity does not always mean that copying has occurred.

SIMILARITY IS NOT ALWAYS DUE TO COPYING

The late copyright attorney Alexander Lindey, in his classic study *Plagiarism and Originality* (Harper 1952), identified the following 14 causes, other than copying, why two works may be similar:

- the use, in both, of the same or similar theme
- the fact that commonplace themes carry commonplace accessories
- the use, in both works, of stereotypes or stock characters
- the fact that both employ the same well-weathered plot
- the limited number of plots generally
- the presence, in both, of hackneyed ingredients, episodes, devices, symbols and language
- the fact that both authors have drawn on the world's cultural heritage, or have cast their works in the same tradition
- the imperatives of orthodoxy and convention
- the impact of influence and imitation
- the process of evolution
- the dictates of vogue or fashion
- the fact that both authors have stolen from the same predecessor
- the fact that both have made legitimate use of the same news item, historical event or other source material, and
- the intervention of coincidence.

We would all like to think that no one else has ever had the same thoughts or feelings or dreams as we have had. But, in sad fact, this is simply not the case. We are not unique. As usual, Oscar Wilde said it best: "The brotherhood of man is not a mere poet's dream: it is a most depressing and humiliating reality." As a result, it's not only common that two or more people will have the same ideas at the same time and express them in similar ways, it's often inevitable.

To rule out the operation of factors that may give rise to similarity without copying—such as those listed in the sidebar set out above—your work and the alleged infringer's must be so similar that these factors are not a rational explanation. Courts call this level of similarity "substantial similarity."

You don't need to engage in a hypercritical textual analysis to determine whether substantial similarity exists. Simply compare both works from all angles and ask yourself whether the average reader would conclude that the author of the later-created work copied from the first.

Of course you should look for similarities in wording, but other similarities may also help establish copying. In the case of a work of fancy, such as a novel or play, compare such aspects of the works as their themes, plots, characters, settings, moods, paces and writing styles. For a factual work, such as a history or biography, similarities in the facts, structure and organization of the works may help indicate copying.

Copyright tip

Publishers of certain types of works, particularly directories and other fact compilations, sometimes deliberately insert minor errors in their work to help prove copying. If the alleged infringer's work contains the same errors, copying must have occurred.

MAKING LISTS OF SIMILARITIES

It may be helpful to draw up a list of similarities you discover between your work and another work you think might be infringing. You can then show the list to a copyright lawyer who might even have it admitted into evidence if a lawsuit results. Here's a small portion of such a list prepared by the producers of the film *Star Wars*, who claimed that their work had been copied by the creators of the television movie "Battlestar Galactica":

- The central conflict of each story is a war between the galaxy's democratic and totalitarian forces.
- In *Star Wars* the young hero's father had been a leader of the democratic forces, and the present leader of the democratic forces is a father figure to the young hero. In "Battlestar" the young hero's father is a leader of the democratic forces.
- An entire planet, central to the existence of the democratic forces, is destroyed in both stories.
- The heroine in both stories is imprisoned by the totalitarian forces.
- A friendly robot, who aids the democratic forces, is severely injured (*Star Wars*) or destroyed ("Battlestar") by the totalitarian forces.
- There is a scene in a cantina (*Star Wars*) or casino ("Battlestar"), in which musical entertainment is offered by bizarre, nonhuman creatures.

3. Improper Use of Protected Expression

The fact that the alleged infringer in all likelihood copied from your work will get you through the courthouse door, but is not enough to establish infringement. The final and most important element of infringement is that the alleged infringer has copied your work's *protected expression*. As discussed in detail in Chapter 6, *What Copyright Protects*, a work's protected expression consists of the author's independently created word sequences and the selection and arrangement of her material. Everything else, including the ideas and facts the work expresses, is in the public domain, free for all to use.

There are four levels or degrees of copying of protected expression that can constitute copyright infringement:

- verbatim copying of *all* of a work's protected expression
- verbatim copying of *part* of a work's expression
- paraphrasing a work's protected expression, and
- copying a work's total concept and feel or fundamental essence.

WHAT JUDGES AND JURIES ACTUALLY DO IN INFRINGEMENT CASES

Judges and juries normally do not engage in a hypercritical line-by-line analysis of the works in question to determine if a defendant's paraphrasing or copying of a prior work's total concept and feel constitutes infringement. Rather, they simply ask themselves whether the average intended reader of the works would regard them as substantially similar. This is not a scientific process. It's based mostly on a judge or jury's gut impressions and sense of fairness. If the judge or jury thinks that the alleged infringer has done something wrong, they will usually find him guilty of copyright infringement.

a. Verbatim copying of an entire work

The most obvious type of copyright infringement occurs when an entire book, story or article is copied verbatim (or nearly so) without the copyright owner's permission. No one can doubt that infringement has occurred when virtually every word in the alleged infringer's work is the same as yours. Indeed, when there is this much copying many courts dispense with the need to show access; instead they presume it.

EXAMPLE 1: Sally writes a short story and gives *The New Zorker* magazine permission to publish it once. Three months later, she discovers that *The Plagiarist's Review* has republished her story without asking her permission (she had retained all her other copyright rights in the story). The *Review* has clearly infringed upon Sally's copyright in her story.

EXAMPLE 2: Lou publishes a monthly newsletter on trends in the publishing world. He discovers that one of his subscribers, publisher Simon and Shyster, has been making dozens of unauthorized copies of his newsletter and circulating them to its employees. This is also verbatim copying and infringes Lou's copyright.

Fortunately, most people realize that they can't get away with copying other people's work verbatim and publishing it without permission. As a result, the type of copying in Example 1 is fairly rare, probably accounting for no more than five percent of all infringement cases. Unauthorized photocopying, however, is undoubtedly very common, but very hard to discover.

b. Partial verbatim copying

Far more common than verbatim copying of an entire work, especially where such factual works as biographies, histories and how-to books are involved, is verbatim (or near verbatim) copying of only a portion of a work's protected expression, whether a few lines, paragraphs, pages or chapters. This kind of copying constitutes copyright infringement only if a substantial amount of protected expression is taken.

How much is substantial? There is no definite answer. Verbatim copying of 300 or 400 words would usually be considered substantial enough to constitute infringement. However, it is possible for less copying to be infringement if the material taken is of great value and/or highly original. For example, infringement was found where the defendant copied 12 sentences from Martin Luther King's "I Have a Dream" speech in an advertising pamphlet for funeral accessories. (*Martin Luther King, Jr. Center for Social Change, Inc. v. American Heritage Products*, 508 F.Supp. 854 (N.D. Ga. 1981).)

c. Paraphrasing

In the infringement context, paraphrasing means making alterations in an author's words instead of copying them verbatim. Whether done consciously, to make it appear copying has not occurred, or unconsciously, paraphrasing constitutes copyright infringement if there is a substantial amount of it. If this were not so, an infringer could get away with infringement simply by making minor changes in an original work's wording.

However, this type of close paraphrasing must be contrasted with changing an author's protected expression to such an extent that there are no recognizable similarities in the prior and subsequent works' expression. In the words of one court, "copying so disguised as to be unrecognizable is not copying." (*See v. Durang*, 711 F.2d 141 (9th Cir. 1983).)

In some cases, it can be can be very difficult to tell whether a work's protected expression has been paraphrased or an alleged infringer has merely

taken the ideas and facts in the work and put them in her own words, which because of the merger doctrine (Chapter 6, *What Copyright Protects*), coincidence and others factors, happen to be similar to the prior work's. It can be difficult to predict in such cases whether a judge or jury would conclude that infringement has occurred (see the following table).

PARAPHRASING SELF-TEST

Compare the following passages taken from actual published works and decide for yourself whether the author of the second passage infringed upon the protected expression in the first passage. We'll tell you what the courts decided on the following page.

Passage in first created work	Passage in subsequent work
1. Surprisingly, the newborn is a remarkably capable organism from the moment he begins to breathe. He can see, hear, smell, and he is sensitive to pain, touch, and change in position. The only sense modality which may not be functioning immediately at birth is taste, but even this sense develops rather quickly.	From his first breath, the child is remarkably well-equipped for life. He can see, hear, smell, touch and feel pain. All his senses, except taste, are operating immediately, and even taste develops rapidly.
2. And second, he says that likely to aid comparisons this year was the surprisingly limited extent to which Fiber Division's losses shrank last year.	The second development likely to aid comparisons this year was the surprisingly limited extent to which the Fiber Division's losses shrank last year.
3. Ohm's Law is a very important law which you must learn. R = E/I where R = resistance in ohms E = pressure in volts I = current in ampheres.	Ohm early in the 19th century discovered that the ratio of the pressure to the current in a given circuit is constant. This is the fundamental law of the flow of electrical currents. R = E/I where R = resistance in ohms E = pressure in volts I = current in ampheres.
4. He looks to me like a guy who makes his wife keep a scrapbook for him.	[Salinger] had fingered [Wilkie] as the sort of fellow who makes his wife keep an album of press clippings.
5. Ellen, Julia and Rachel will be here on Tuesday; they'll stay for two days. Don't know what will happen when they get here. I'm hoping for peace and quiet.	Early in 1960, Wright wrote to Margrit de Sabloniere that Ellen, Julia and Rachel would be arriving for a two or three day visit. Wright said that he did not know what would happen when they arrived but that he was hoping for peace and quiet.
6. [A]s the Lord commanded he lifted up the rod and smote the waters of the river and all the waters that were in the river were turned to blood. And the fish that were in the river died; and the river stank; and the Egyptians could not drink the waters of the river; and there was blood throughout all the land of Egypt.	In accordance with the directive previously received from higher authority, he caused the implement to come into contact with the aquifer, whereupon a polluting effect was perceived. The consequent toxification reduced the conditions necessary for the sustenance of aquatic vertebrates below the level of continued viability. Olfactory discomfort standards were substantially exceeded, and potability declined. Social, economic and political disorientation were experienced to an unprecedented degree.

How the Courts Ruled on the Above Examples

1. Infringement. The court was probably swayed by the fact that there were over 400 examples of this type of paraphrasing from the prior work. (*Meredith Corp. v. Harper & Row, Publishers,* 378 F.Supp. 686 (S.D.N.Y. 1974).)

2. Infringement. This was just one of dozens of passages in financial reports that were closely paraphrased in a financial newspaper. (*Wainwright Sec. v. Wall Street Transcript Corp.,* 558 F.2d 91 (2d Cir. 1977).)

3. No Infringement. The court exclaimed, "how better may one express this basic principle of physics than by using the usual symbols?" (*Ricker v. General Electric Co.,* 162 F.2d 141 (2d Cir. 1947).)

4. Infringement. The author of an unauthorized biography of J.D. Salinger paraphrased these lines from an unpublished letter by Salinger. The court characterized the biographer's passage as a close paraphrase of highly original expression. (*Salinger v. Random House,* 811 F.2d 90 (2d Cir. 1987).)

5. No Infringement. The author of an unauthorized biography of Richard Wright paraphrased these lines from an unpublished letter by Wright. The court held there was no infringement because the paraphrasing constituted "straightforward factual reportage" of the "most basic and banal factual matter," not Wright's protected expression. (*Wright v. Warner Books, Inc.,* 748 F.Supp. 105 (S.D.N.Y. 1990).)

6. No Infringement. Okay, we cheated. This is a made-up example that no court has or ever could rule on. The first passage is from Exodus in the King James Version of the Old Testament, which is in the public domain. However, even if the passage was protected by copyright, it's not likely that anyone would conclude that the second passage infringed upon it. Although we would never advise anyone to write this badly, the second passage (taken from Wydick, "Plain English for Lawyers," *66 Calif. Law Review 737* (1978)) is a good example of an author's taking the facts in a prior work and putting them into his own words.

d. Copying a work's total concept and feel

The final type of copying that can constitute infringement, and the most difficult to detect and prove, is unauthorized copying of a work's total concept and feel. This type of copying is often claimed to be present in infringement cases involving such works of fancy as novels, plays and poems. This is one term courts use to describe a work's fundamental essence or overall pattern. It consists of the *totality* of all the elements an author selects and combines to form a single work of authorship. Total concept and feel includes a novelist's selection and combination of her themes, setting, stock characters, scenes, situations, literary devices, writing style and plot. This type of infringement protects an author's selection and combination of individual elements which are not separately protected by copyright. (See Chapter 6, Section C.1 for an example.)

Remember, however, that total concept and feel means just that: a work's overall pattern or fundamental essence must be copied for there to be infringement. If only a few of a work's unprotectible elements themselves are similar—for instance, stock characters, situations or plots—there is no infringement. Most authors who bring total concept and feel suits lose their cases for this reason.

A REAL LIFE EXAMPLE: Reyher published a children's story derived from an old folk tale about a child who becomes separated from her mother. To strangers, the child describes her mother as the most beautiful woman in the world. When she is finally reunited with her mother, the mother turns out to be homely in appearance. A story with an almost identical plot was subsequently published in a children's magazine. There was no verbatim copying or paraphrasing. Reyher sued the magazine for copyright infringement claiming that her story's total concept and feel had been copied. Reyher lost. The court held that although the two stories had the same plots and similar situations, they differed in almost every other way, including the setting, theme, characterization and mood. Thus the two works' total feel was not the same. (*Reyher v. Children's Television Workshop,* 433 F.2d 87 (2d Cir. 1976).)

Remember too that a work's fundamental essence or total concept or feel must be *original*— that is, independently created—to be protected. The less originality involved in selecting and combining a work's constituent elements, the less copyright protection it will receive. For example, works of fancy that are written according to tried and true formulas—for example, gothic romances, westerns, police shoot-em-ups and buddy-movies—are accorded less protection than highly original works of art containing uncommon themes, characters or plots.

C. When Copying Protected Expression Is Excused

In some cases, authors are allowed to copy other authors' protected expression without permission. This may occur through operation of the merger doctrine (legalese for situations where there are only a few ways to express an idea or fact) or where the copying constitutes a fair use of the protected expression.

1. Unavoidable Copying: The Merger Doctrine

Sometimes an author has no alternative but to copy or paraphrase another author's words. This occurs where there is just one way, or only a few ways, to adequately express a particular idea or fact. In these cases, the idea or fact and the way it's expressed are deemed to merge and the expression—the first

author's words—is given very limited copyright protection or no protection at all. The merger doctrine applies mainly to factual works such as histories, biographies and scientific treatises rather than to works of fancy such as novels, plays and poems. This is because by their very nature, facts provide their own limitation of how they can be described while the ideas present in fictional works can almost always be written in new and different ways.

As a result of the merger doctrine, in some cases verbatim copying or close paraphrasing of even a substantial number of words from a factual work may not constitute infringement. See Chapter 6, *What Copyright Protects.*

2. Fair Copying: The Fair Use Privilege

Copying of protected expression will also be excused where it constitutes a fair use of the material. The fair use privilege applies primarily in situations where an author quotes or otherwise uses a limited amount of protected expression for scholarly, educational or other nonprofit purposes. See Chapter 11, *Using Other Authors' Words.*

D. Self-Help Remedies for Copyright Infringement

Assuming you have a valid infringement claim, you may be able to obtain a satisfactory resolution of an infringement claim on your own. Depending on the circumstances, simply sending the alleged infringer and his publisher(s) (who are also liable for any infringement, see Section E.2, below) a cease and desist letter may do the trick. This sort of letter serves several functions simultaneously:

- It lets the infringer know that you believe he is infringing on your copyright.
- It establishes a date for your discovery of the infringement. This is important for purposes of

the statute of limitations on copyright infringement lawsuits discussed below.

- It tells the infringer you intend to stop him.
- It gives the alleged infringer a chance to explain his conduct and perhaps offer a satisfactory compromise before you spend a lot of money initiating a lawsuit. Even if you're sure you're right, it doesn't hurt to listen to the other person's story. In addition, by giving the infringer a chance to respond, you may find out a lot about how he plans to defend a court action if you choose to bring one.

1. Contents of a Cease and Desist Letter

A cease and desist letter should normally include:
- your name, business address and telephone number, or, if you want to protect your privacy, some way to contact you, such as a P.O. Box
- the name of your work, date of first publication and the copyright registration number if the work was registered
- the nature of the activity you believe to be an infringement of your copyright
- a demand that the infringer cease and desist from the activity and pay you for any damages you've sustained, or simply pay your damages if the infringement is not still going on, and
- a request for a response within a stated time period.

Your letter can threaten legal action, but you're probably wiser not to at this stage. The specter of imminent legal action is likely to make the other person paranoid, defensive and unwilling to cooperate. It may also send him straight to a lawyer.

When you draft your letter, remember that you may end up wanting to use it in court. Accordingly, avoid being nasty, cute, tentative or overly dramatic.

Cease and desist letters should be sent by certified mail, return receipt requested. If the infringer refuses to accept your letter, arrange to have it delivered personally by someone who isn't involved in the dispute and who'll be available to testify that the letter was delivered. You may have to hire a process server to deliver the letter if you don't know anyone who can do it for you.

a. Example 1

Sally, a freelance writer, discovers that *The Plagiarist's Review* has reprinted without her permission an article she wrote and published several years ago and to which she retains all the copyright rights. Sally sends the magazine's editor the following letter.

SAMPLE LETTER

January 1, 199X

Editor In Chief
The Plagiarist's Review
100 Copycat Lane
New York, NY 10000

Dear Sir:

I recently became aware that your magazine published in its November 199X issue an article entitled "Old Ideas In New Bottles." I originally wrote this article in January 1989 and it was first published in June 1989 in the *Potawamee Magazine*.

I own all of the rights in this article. Since I never authorized you to reprint the article in your publication, it follows that you infringed upon my copyright by doing so.

This letter is to demand that you immediately cease and desist from selling any copies of the *Plagiarist's Review* containing the infringing article. In addition, I demand to be reasonably compensated for the use of my article in the copies that have already been sold.

Please respond to this letter by January 15, 199X.

Very truly yours,

Sally Bowles
Sally Bowles

b. Example 2

James obtained his Ph.D. in French history four years ago. His Ph.D. dissertation, entitled *The French Chamber of Deputies, 1932–1940*, was microfilmed and made available to researchers in various research libraries around the country. James timely registered the dissertation with the Copyright Office. He discovers that three chapters of his dissertation have, without his permission, been copied almost verbatim in a new textbook on French history "written" by professor Coleridge and published by Copycat Press. James sends the following letter to Copycat Press and a copy to Professor Coleridge:

SAMPLE LETTER

February 28, 199X

President
Copycat Press
100 Grubstreet
Boston, MA 10001

Dear Sir:

I recently discovered that three chapters, totalling 130 pages, from my Ph.D. dissertation, entitled *The French Chamber of Deputies, 1932–1940,* have been copied nearly verbatim in your recently published title *French History Made Easy* by Professor S.T. Coleridge. Enclosed is a copy of the chapters in question along with a copy of the dissertation's title page; note the copyright notice in my name. The dissertation was registered with the Copyright Office on July 15, 199X; the registration number is TX123456.

I do not know Professor Coleridge, have never been contacted by him and never gave him or anyone else permission to use any material from my dissertation, to which I own all the copyright rights.

This letter is to demand that you immediately cease and desist from selling any copies of *French History Made Easy* containing the material from my dissertation. In addition, I demand that I be compensated for the use of my dissertation in the copies that have already been sold.

Please respond to this letter by March 15, 199X.

Very truly yours,

James C. McCarthy
James C. McCarthy

cc: Professor S.T. Coleridge
      Department of Humanities
      Esoterica College
      Marred Vista, CA 90000

2.   Responses to Cease and Desist Letters

What happens after the alleged infringer receives your letter typically depends on the nature of the infringer and the infringing conduct. Hopefully, it will be possible for you to work out a reasonable solution, such as making the infringement legal through a license under which you're paid an agreed upon fee for the use of your work (see Chapter 9, *Transferring Copyright Ownership*); and getting the infringer to stop future infringements. The fee, of course, is subject to negotiation. It should include a penalty for the inconvenience the infringer caused you—probably at least 50% more than you would have charged had the infringer asked you for permission to use your work in the first place.

Any compromise settlement should be in writing and signed by all the parties.

a.   Example 1

Sally Bowles in Example 1 above agreed to grant *The Plagiarist's Review* a retroactive nonexclusive license to publish her article. In return, the *Review* promised to print a correction in a future issue stating that she was the author of the article; it also promised to publish and pay for two new articles by Sally in upcoming issues. Sally felt that was better than just getting a one-time payment for the unauthorized use of her old article.

COMPROMISE SETTLEMENT LETTER

Felix Franklin
Editor-In-Chief
The Plagiarists Review
123 Copycat Lane
New York, NY 10000

Dear Mr. Franklin:

This letter embodies the terms of our settlement of the outstanding dispute arising from publication of the article "Old Ideas In New Bottles" in the November 199X issue of *The Plagiarist's Review:*

1. Sally Bowles hereby retroactively grants *The Plagiarist's Review* a nonexclusive license to reprint her article "Old Ideas In New Bottles" in its November 199X issue.

2. *The Plagiarist's Review* promises to print a prominently placed correction in its March 199X issue, in words approved by Sally Bowles, informing its readers that Sally Bowles was the author of the article "Old Ideas In New Bottles" than ran in the November 199X issue and that her name had been left off the article in error.

3. *The Plagiarist's Review* also promises to publish the following articles by Sally Bowles at its customary fee no later than December 199X;

   • an approximately 2,000-word article tentatively entitled "What to Do If You're Accused of Plagiarism," and

   • an article of approximately 1,500 words on the subject of marketing freelance writing.

Sally Bowles
Sally Bowles
Date: _____

Signed: _____
Felix Franklin, Editor-In-Chief
The Plagiarist's Review
Date:_____

b. Example 2

Since James, the author of the dissertation *The French Chamber of Deputies, 1932–1940* in Example 2, above, had timely registered his dissertation with the Copyright Office, he might be entitled to substantial statutory damages if the case went to court. Accordingly, Copycat Press agreed to pay James $3,000 to settle the matter (this was 50% more than James would have charged had Copycat asked him for permission to use his work in the first place). In return, James agreed to release Copycat Press from liability for infringing on his work. James was not able to reach a settlement with Professor Coleridge, who denied copying from James's dissertation. James decided to pocket the money and forget pursuing his case against Coleridge.

James sent Copycat Press the following agreement:

COMPROMISE SETTLEMENT AGREEMENT

Lisa Bagatelle
President
Copycat Press
100 Grub Street
Boston, MA 10001

Dear Ms. Bagatelle:

This letter embodies the terms of our settlement of the outstanding dispute arising from Copycat Press's publication of the book *French History Made Easy* by Professor S.T. Coleridge:

1. Copycat Press will pay James McCarthy the sum of $3,000 as compensation for the unauthorized use of material from his Ph.D. dissertation entitled *The French Chamber of Deputies, 1932–1940*.

2. Copycat Press promises not to use any of James McCarthy's work, including material from his Ph.D. dissertation, in the future without his authorization. This includes reprintings and new editions of *French History Made Easy* and other works.

3. James McCarthy agrees that this completely settles the matter in dispute between James McCarthy and Copycat Press, and releases Copycat Press from any further liability for publication of material from *The French Chamber of Deputies, 1932–1940* by Copycat Press.

James McCarthy

James McCarthy

Date: _____

Signed: _____
Lisa Bagatelle, President
Copycat Press
Date:_____

E. Overview of Copyright Infringement Lawsuits

If you can't satisfactorily resolve the matter yourself (perhaps with a short consultation with a copyright lawyer), you have two alternatives: forget about it or hire a lawyer and bring an infringement suit in federal court. The following is an overview of the nuts and bolts of a copyright infringement suit. It is intended to give you a general idea of what you can expect from copyright litigation, not as a substitute for further research or a consultation with an experienced copyright attorney. See Chapter 15, *Help Beyond This Book*, for a guide to further research and ways to find a copyright attorney.

1. Who Can Sue

A person or entity who files an infringement suit is called the plaintiff. The plaintiff must be someone who owns the copyright rights at issue, or who is entitled to receive royalties from them. This will typically be the author or the publisher to whom the author has sold some or all of her rights.

> **EXAMPLE:** Bill writes a biography of Saddam Hussein and sells his reproduction and distribution rights to Scrivener & Sons. Leslie copies a substantial portion of Bill's book in her own published biography of Saddam. Both Bill and Scrivener are entitled to sue Leslie for copyright infringement of the exclusive rights to reproduce and distribute the work.

Deciding who does and doesn't own derivative rights in a work in the context of a copyright infringement action is often complex. For example, an author may transfer film rights to one person or entity, television rights to another, and foreign language translation rights to still others. And, unless prohibited in the original transfer of rights, they may be further transferred and divided—for example,

the entity that buys the TV rights may transfer Japanese TV rights to someone else. Often, an author who transfers all or part of his derivative rights retains the right to receive part of the total fee (often a royalty) from their exploitation.

> **EXAMPLE:** Bill sells the film rights to his Hussein biography to Repulsive Pictures in return for $100,000 and a 5% share of the profits from the film. Acme Productions releases an unauthorized film based on Bill's biography. Both Bill and Repulsive may sue Acme. However, because it would get most of the recovery from a suit against Acme, Repulsive would likely carry the ball in this situation—that is, its attorneys would do most of the work and Bill would simply join along as a plaintiff.

CRIMINAL PROSECUTIONS

Willful copyright infringement is a federal crime (17 U.S.C. 506). Accordingly, the United States Attorney General has the power to prosecute infringers. A person who is convicted of infringement can be required to pay fines ranging from $10,000 to $50,000 and imprisoned for up to two years for a second offense. A convicted infringer might also be ordered to pay the copyright owner restitution. However, as a practical matter, the resources available for investigating and prosecuting this sort of crime are limited. Crimes like drug offenses, bank robberies, stock trading violations, counterfeiting and many others are given much higher priority. This means your copyright infringement case is unlikely to warrant much attention from federal authorities. For this reason, criminal trials are not discussed in this book.

2. Who Is Liable for Infringement?

Although a primary goal may be simply to stop a publisher from selling any more copies of an infringing work, you are also entitled to collect damages from those liable for the infringement. As discussed in Chapter 4, *Copyright Registration,* if you timely registered your work, you may elect to receive special statutory damages and attorney fees, which is an important right when your actual damages are very small or difficult to prove. (See Section F.2, below, for a detailed discussion of damages.)

Who may be liable for such damages and fees? Quite simply, *everybody* who participates in or contributes to copyright infringement. This may include not only the author of the infringing work, but its initial publisher and other publishers who reprint it, the publisher's printer and even the bookstores that sell the work. Such persons or entities are liable regardless of whether they actually

know that the work they published, printed or sell infringes on another person's copyright. Moreover, corporate officers and employees—such as editors employed by publishing companies—actively involved in the infringement may be held *personally liable* along with their employers. Any person who is sued for copyright infringement is called the defendant.

3. How Much Time You Have to Sue: Statute of Limitations

There are strict time limits on when copyright infringement suits may be filed. If you fail to file in time, the infringer may be able to have your suit dismissed, even though you have a strong case. In cases where you have not discovered the infringement fairly promptly after it has occurred, statute of limitations questions can be tricky. It's wise to see a knowledgeable copyright lawyer about the proper application of the limitations period to your particular case.

The general rule is that an infringement suit must be filed within three years after the date the copyright owner should reasonably have discovered the infringing act occurred. In some cases, it can reasonably take a copyright owner a long time to discover that the infringement took place, especially where the infringer attempted to conceal the act of infringement. For this reason, if more than three years have passed since the infringing work was first published, don't jump to the conclusion that your suit is barred by the statute of limitations.

EXAMPLE: In 1993, several professors at Esoterica College have Pinko's Copyshop photocopy portions of Bill's biography for inclusion in class materials for courses on Middle Eastern history. Bill doesn't discover this until 1998. If a court views the 5-year delay as reasonable, Bill will be able to bring an infringement suit against Pinkos.

MULTIPLE INFRINGEMENTS OR JUST ONE?

A factor complicating the three-year period has to do with situations in which repeated acts of infringement occur over a long period of time—for example where a book containing infringing material is sold over a period of years. Is each sale of the book a separate infringing act or are all the sales together one infringing act? Courts disagree with each other on this question.

EXAMPLE: Acme Press begins to sell a book containing infringing material in January 1985. Carl, the copyright owner, finds out about the infringement that same year but doesn't do anything about it. However, Acme continues to sell the book through January 1991, when Carl finally decides to file suit. Some courts would permit Carl to obtain damages only for the losses he incurred due to the sales that occurred within three years before he filed suit; others would permit him to recover damages from January 1985. These courts would view all the sales of the infringing works as part of one "continuing wrong." (See *Taylor v. Meirick,* 712 F.2d 1112 (7th Cir. 1983); *Gaste v. Kaiserman,* 669 F.Supp. 583 (S.D.N.Y. 1987).)

F. What You Can Get If You Win: Remedies for Copyright Infringement

Once you've proven the elements of infringement discussed in Section B above, the next step is to establish what remedies you're entitled to. The potential remedies include:

- *Injunctive relief.* This typically consists of a court order requiring the infringer to stop publishing the infringing work and destroy all remaining copies.
- *Actual damages and infringer's profits.* The plaintiff is entitled to be compensated for the value of lost sales (often difficult to prove) and for other losses resulting directly from the infringement. The plaintiff is also entitled to collect the amount of the defendant's profits from the infringement over and above the amount the plaintiff is awarded for her lost profits.
- *Statutory damages.* If the plaintiff's work was timely registered and she so chooses, she is entitled to receive special statutory damages provided in the copyright law (statute) instead of actual damages and other economic damages.
- *Attorney fees.* A copyright owner can also get attorney fees. Again, timely registration is required.

We'll examine each remedy in turn. Again, this isn't a complete description of the legal procedures involved, but is designed to give you an overview of the available remedies.

1. Injunctive Relief

An injunction is a court order telling someone to stop doing something. In a copyright infringement action, the order usually is simply for the defendant to stop the infringing activity. This is commonly a quick, effective remedy because, in many cases, it is possible to get positive action from the court long before the actual trial is held to decide who wins.

Indeed, it is possible to get a temporary restraining order (TRO) almost immediately without notifying the defendant or holding a formal court hearing. A TRO may last ten days at most. A hearing must then be held on whether the judge should issue a preliminary injunction. A preliminary injunction operates between the time it is issued and the final judgment in the case. This interim court order is available when it appears likely to a federal judge, on the basis of written documentation and a relatively brief hearing at which the lawyers for each side present their view of the dispute, that (1) the plaintiff will most likely win the suit when the trial is held, and (2) the plaintiff will suffer irreparable injury if the preliminary injunction isn't granted. Ordinarily, irreparable injury is presumed to exist where someone infringes upon a copyright owner's exclusive rights. (*Apple Computer, Inc. v. Franklin Computer Corp.,* 714 F.2d 1240 (3rd Cir. 1983).)

If the judge grants the injunction, the plaintiff must post a bond in an amount determined by the judge. If the injunction is later found to have been wrongfully granted, the defendant can collect from the bond the damages and costs he incurred due to the injunction.

Once a preliminary injunction is granted, it remains in effect pending a further determination of whether infringement occurred at the formal trial. In theory, a trial will probably be held one or two years later. In fact, the parties often fashion a settlement based on the results of the preliminary injunction hearing.

> **EXAMPLE:** In 1990, Nolo Press sued another publisher for publishing and distributing a book infringing on Nolo's title, *Dog Law,* by Mary Randolph. Nolo and Randolph were able to obtain a preliminary injunction from a federal judge barring the publisher from distributing any more copies of its book. A settlement was reached soon thereafter. The whole process took just three months from the date suit was filed.

If a settlement is not reached and a full-scale trial occurs, the same issues as those raised in the preliminary injunction hearing will be litigated in more detail. If the plaintiff again prevails, the preliminary injunction will be converted into a permanent one, either including the same terms and orders or different ones, depending on what the plaintiff proves at trial. If the plaintiff loses, the preliminary injunction (if one was granted) will be dissolved and the defendant can go back to doing what it was doing before, plus be compensated for the consequences of the lawsuit out of the bond.

2. Damages

If you win a copyright infringement suit, you usually have the right to collect money (called damages) from the infringer. As mentioned, if your work was timely registered with the Copyright Office, you will be entitled to choose between collecting actual damages and special statutory damages.

a. Actual damages and infringer's profits

Actual damages are the lost profits and/or other losses sustained as a result of the copyright infringement. In other words, actual damages are the amount of money that the plaintiff would have made but for the infringement. This may include compensation for injury to the plaintiff's reputation due to the infringement and for lost business opportunities (often difficult to prove)—for example, a lost opportunity to sign a publishing contract to write a sequel to a novel because an infringing novel hurt its sales. To obtain actual damages, the plaintiff must prove in court that the alleged losses actually occurred. Business records and witnesses (often including the plaintiff herself) must be presented to substantiate the plaintiff's actual losses.

As stated above, the plaintiff is also entitled to recover the amount of the defendant's profits from the infringement to the extent they exceed the plaintiff's recovery for her lost profits.

> **EXAMPLE:** The plaintiff is awarded $10,000 for lost sales due to the defendant's infringement.

The defendant earned $15,000 in profits from the infringement. The plaintiff is entitled to $5,000 of the defendant's profits.

To establish the defendant's profits, the plaintiff is required only to prove the infringer's gross revenue from the infringing work. The defendant's business records would usually be presented for this purpose. The defendant must then prove what its actual net profit from the infringement was—that is, the defendant must produce records or witnesses to show the amount of expenses deductible from the infringing work's gross revenues (such as printing and distribution costs) and the amount of profit, if any, attributable to the noninfringing material in the defendant's work (often difficult to prove).

b. Statutory damages

Statutory damages are set by the copyright law and require no proof of how much the loss was in monetary terms. However, as discussed in Chapter 4, *Copyright Registration*, statutory damages are only available if the work was timely registered—that is, before the infringement began or within three months of publication. Statutory damages are awarded at the judge's discretion and don't depend on having to prove a loss in any specific amount due to the infringement. Statutory damages fall within the following range:

- Absent a finding that the infringer acted either willfully or innocently, between $500 and $20,000 for all the infringements by a single infringer of a single work, no matter how many infringing acts there were. If multiple separate and independent works were infringed, statutory damages may be awarded for each work.
- If the court finds that the infringer acted *willfully*—that is, knew he had no legal right to the material he wanted, but took it anyway—it may increase the amount of statutory damages up to $100,000.

- But if the court finds that the infringer acted *innocently*—that is, he used the copyrighted material sincerely believing he had the right to do so—the judge has discretion to award as little as $200. However, if the work to which the infringer had access contained a valid copyright notice, the infringer may not claim to have acted innocently. As discussed in Chapter 3, *Copyright Notice*, this is why it is always a good idea to include a valid copyright notice on your work (even though a notice is not legally required for works published after March 1, 1989).

Because the actual damages (the owner's lost profits and other provable losses) caused by an infringement are often small, statutory damages may far exceed actual damages where the infringer acted willfully. A plaintiff who is eligible for both actual and statutory damages may choose which kind she wants to receive at any time, up to and during the trial. Your decision will depend on the facts of your particular case and should, of course, be made in conjunction with your attorney.

3. Destroying the Infringing Works

Another civil remedy for copyright infringement consists of an impound and destroy order from the court. This tells the sheriff or marshal to go to the infringer's place of business (or wherever the infringing material is located) and impound any infringing works. This can happen at any time after the suit has been filed. If the plaintiff wins, the court may order the sheriff to destroy the infringing material.

4. Attorney Fees and Costs

If your suit is successful and you timely registered your copyright, the court may also order the defendant to pay your attorney fees and other costs of going to court, such as filing fees. However, this is not required. It's up to the judge to decide whether to make such an award and how much it should be (the amount must be reasonable). The criteria some courts use to decide whether to award attorney fees include whether the defendant acted in bad faith, unreasonably or was otherwise blameworthy. Many courts will be especially likely to award fees to a plaintiff whose actions helped to advance the copyright law or defend or establish important legal principles.

The cost of bringing an infringement suit can be very high, easily tens of thousands of dollars. If for no other reason than to have the opportunity of recovering your attorney fees should you have to bring an infringement suit, you should always timely register your work with the Copyright Office.

If the plaintiff loses his suit, the court has discretion to award the defendant all or part of his attorney fees. In the past, many courts would award such fees to a defendant only if they found that the plaintiff's suit was frivolous or brought in bad faith. But these courts would not require this in making fees awards to plaintiffs. In 1994 the Supreme Court held that this approach was incorrect and that attorney fees must be awarded to plaintiffs and defendants in an evenhanded manner. In other words, the same criteria must be applied to both plaintiffs and defendants. *Fogerty v. Fantasy, Inc.*, 114 S.Ct. 1023 (1994).

G. What to Do If You're Accused of Infringement

What should you do if you're accused of copyright infringement? First, see how serious the claim is. If it's minor—for example, an author validly claims that you have quoted a bit too much of his work, used an illustration or reprinted an article without permission—the matter can usually be settled very quickly for a few hundred dollars, certainly less than $1,000. This kind of thing happens all the time in publishing. There is no need to see a lawyer (who'll probably charge you at least $150 per hour) to deal with this type of minor annoyance. Have the author sign a letter releasing you from liability in return for your payment, see Section D.2, above, for examples.

On the other hand, if you receive a letter from an author or author's attorney alleging a substantial claim—for example, that a book you're publishing to great success is an unauthorized derivative work and its sale should be halted immediately—it's probably time to find a copyright lawyer. If, even worse, you are served with a complaint (a document initiating a lawsuit), you must act quickly because you may have as little as 20 days to file an answer (response) in the appropriate court. If you don't respond in time, a judgment can be entered against you. Finding a lawyer is discussed in Chapter 15, *Help Beyond This Book*.

However, even if the case is serious, don't despair. The fact is, many infringement suits are won by the defendant, either because the plaintiff did not have a valid claim to begin with or the defendant had a good defense. This section is not a substitute for a consultation with an experienced attorney; rather, it is designed to give you an idea of some of the things you need to discuss when you see an attorney.

1. Defenses to Copyright Infringement

Even if there are substantial similarities between the plaintiff's work and your work, you will not necessarily be found guilty of infringement. The similarities may simply be the result of coincidence; in this event there is no liability. But, even direct copying from the plaintiff's work may be excused if it constitutes a fair use or there is another valid defense.

Possible defenses to an infringement action include many general legal defenses that often involve where, when and how the lawsuit was brought, who was sued, and so on. We obviously can't cover all of this here. This section is limited to outlining the major defenses that are specific to copyright infringement actions. Again, if you find yourself defending a serious copyright infringement action, retain a qualified attorney!

a. Fair use

Authors are allowed to copy other authors protected expression if the copying constitutes a fair use of the material. Fair use is a complete defense to infringement. See Chapter 11, *Using Other Authors' Words.*

b. The independent creation defense

As discussed in Chapter 6, *What Copyright Protects,* copyright protection does not prevent others from independently developing works based on the same idea or explicating the same facts. If you can convince the judge or jury that you created your work independently, not by copying from the plaintiff, you will not be held liable for infringement. In effect, you would try to prove that any similarities between your work and the plaintiff's are purely coincidental. As discussed in Section B.2, above, such coincidences are not at all uncommon.

The one sure way to show independent creation is for you to prove that your work was created before the plaintiff's. If your work was registered before the plaintiff's, this will be easy to prove.

> **EXAMPLE:** Marilyn claims that Jack turned her novel into a screenplay without her permission and sues him for infringement. Jack had deposited a copy of the allegedly infringing screenplay with the Copyright Office one year before Marilyn published her novel. Jack can prove independent creation simply by submitting a certified copy of his deposit into evidence.

In the case of unregistered works, you would have to present other evidence showing when the work was created, such as witnesses who saw you write it or dated notes and drafts.

What if the plaintiff's and your works were created at about the same time, or you can't prove when you created your work? In this event, it is very difficult, if not impossible, to prove independent creation. This is because the alleged copying need not be done consciously for the plaintiff to win. Unconscious copying also constitutes infringement (although the damages imposed may be smaller than for conscious, willful copying). Your quandary, then, is how to prove you didn't unconsciously copy from the plaintiff's work. About the best you can do in this situation is show that you created similar works in the past without copying and that you had no need to copy from plaintiff's work. The judge or jury just might believe you.

Never Assert Independent Creation or any Other Defense if It's Not True.

If your defense is based on lies, you'll most likely lose anyway and possibly anger the judge and/or jury. As a result, you could end up being far more severely punished than you otherwise might have been, and possibly prosecuted for perjury, a felony.

c. Statute of limitations

A plaintiff can't wait forever to file an infringement suit. As discussed in Section E.3 above, the statute of limitations is three years from the time the infringement should reasonably have been discovered (but applying this rule can be extremely tricky). If the plaintiff waited too long, the defendant may be able to have the case dismissed.

d. Material copied was in the public domain

If the material you allegedly copied is in the public domain, it can be used by anyone for any purpose. As discussed in detail in Chapter 6, the public domain includes:

- the ideas and facts contained in protected works
- the ideas, facts and expression contained in works that don't qualify for copyright protection because they do not constitute original, fixed, minimally creative works of authorship
- works that might otherwise qualify for protection, but are denied it, such as works by government employees, certain blank forms, titles and short phrases, and
- works for which copyright protection has expired.

Remember, however, that so long as the plaintiff's work was registered within five years after creation, it is presumed to be protected by copyright. This means that you will bear the burden of proving the work was really not protected.

e. The use was authorized

In some cases, the alleged infringer isn't an infringer, but a legal transferee. For example:

- The infringer might legitimately claim to have received a license to use the plaintiff's work, and that the work the plaintiff claims to infringe on his copyright falls within that license. Example: Author "A" orally tells author "B" he can copy his work, then later claims never to have granted the permission.
- Conflicting or confusing licenses or sublicenses are granted and the defendant claims to be the rightful owner of the right(s) in question.
- A transferee wasn't restricted in making further transfers, and transferred the copyright to individuals unknown to the original owner.

Several examples of lawful transfers are presented in Chapter 9, *Transferring Copyright Ownership*. If any of these transferees were sued they would have a good defense—that is, that their use was lawful.

f. Other defenses

Some of the other possible defenses to copyright infringement include such things as:

- the notion that if the plaintiff is guilty of some serious wrongdoing himself—for example, falsifying evidence—he cannot complain about your alleged wrongs
- the notion that the plaintiff waited so long to file suit that it would be unfair to find the defendant guilty of infringement—"It is inequitable for the owner of a copyright, with full notice of an intended infringement, to stand inactive while the proposed infringer spends large sums of money on its exploitation, and to intervene only when his speculation has proved a success. Delay under such circumstances allows the owner to speculate without risk with the other's money; he cannot possibly lose, and he may

win." (*Hass v. Leo Feist, Inc.,* 234 Fed. 105 (S.D.N.Y. 1916).)

- the idea that the copyright owner knew of your acts and expressly or impliedly consented to them.

2. Deciding Whether to Settle or Fight

If a substantial claim is involved, the decision whether to settle the case or fight it out in court should only be made after consulting an attorney who is familiar with the facts of your particular case. However, in making this decision you need to carefully weigh the following factors:

- the likelihood the plaintiff will prevail
- how much the plaintiff is likely to collect if he does win
- the costs of contesting the case, not only in terms of money, but time, embarrassment and adverse publicity, and
- how much the plaintiff is willing to settle for.

If the plaintiff clearly does not have a valid claim, you may be able to have his suit dismissed very quickly by filing what's called a summary judgment motion. Under this procedure the judge examines the plaintiff's claims and decides whether there is any possibility he could prevail if a trial were held. If not, the judge will dismiss the case. Of course, you must pay a lawyer to file a summary judgment motion, but, if successful, it will cost far less than taking the case to trial. Moreover, the court may be willing to award you all or part of your attorney fees. This is especially likely if the plaintiff's suit was clearly frivolous. See the discussion at Section F.4, above.

On the other hand, if the plaintiff does have a valid claim, paying an attorney to fight a losing battle will only compound your problems. Valid claims should be settled whenever possible. If the plaintiff was able to obtain a preliminary injunction from a federal judge, he probably has a valid claim.

3. How to Protect Yourself From Copyright Infringement Claims

The only way you can absolutely prevent others from accusing you of copyright infringement is never to write and publish anything. However there are some less drastic steps you can take to help protect yourself from infringement claims:

- First and foremost, always get permission to use other authors' protected expression unless your intended use clearly constitutes a fair use. (See Chapter 11, *Using Other Authors' Words.*) If you're not sure whether or not you need permission, consult a copyright attorney.
- Date and keep your notes and drafts; these may help you to prove that your work was created independently from the plaintiff's.
- Promptly register your finished work with the Copyright Office; registration conclusively establishes the date of creation of the material you deposited with your application; if you're extremely worried about being sued for infringement, it may even be worthwhile to register your unfinished drafts.
- If you're an editor for a magazine or publishing company, always promptly return manuscripts you reject; nothing arouses a writer's suspicions more than having a publisher keep a rejected manuscript and then later publish a similar work by another writer. If you already have another writer working on the same or similar idea, let the author of the rejected material know about it.
- Film and television producers and others in the entertainment industry who receive unsolicited submissions should either (1) have an established policy of returning unsolicited manuscripts unopened, or (2) refuse to read them unless the author signs a release absolving the reader from liability for infringement.

13

International Copyright Protection

There is no single body of international copyright law. Each country has its own copyright law that applies within its own borders. However, through a series of international treaties, almost all nations have agreed to give each other's citizens the same copyright protection they afford to their own citizens. If you take the correct procedural steps, your copyright will be protected in virtually every country in the world.

We'll first examine copyright protection outside the United States for works by American citizens or permanent residents, and then turn to copyright protection within the U.S. for foreign citizens or nationals.

A. International Protection for U.S. Citizens and Nationals

The protection afforded to written works by the U.S. copyright laws ends at the United States' borders. The extent of the protection given to work by Americans outside the U.S. is governed by international treaties. The United States and most other major industrialized countries (the Soviet Union and China excepted) have signed two overlapping treaties—the Berne Convention and the Universal Copyright Convention (U.C.C.). International copyright protection for works by U.S. citizens and permanent residents largely depends on the rights granted under these two international treaties.

1. The Berne Convention

The world's first major international copyright convention was held in Berne, Switzerland in 1886. The resulting agreement was called the Berne Convention for the Protection of Literary and Artistic Works, or the Berne Convention for short. The Berne Convention is the most important international copyright treaty, with the highest standards of protection. Most major industrialized countries (the Soviet Union and China excepted) belong to the Berne Convention. These countries include the United States (as of March 1, 1989), most of Western Europe, Japan, Canada, Mexico and Australia.

In a nutshell, Berne member countries agree that literary, artistic and scientific works, including all types of writing, are protected in the following ways.

a. Principle of national treatment

Every country that has signed the Berne Convention must give citizens or permanent residents of other Berne countries at least the same copyright protection that it affords its own nationals; this is known as national treatment. As a U.S. citizen or permanent resident, any protectible work you create or publish after March 1, 1989 (the date the U.S. joined the Berne Convention) is entitled to national treatment in every country that has signed the Berne Convention.

> **EXAMPLE:** Carl, an American citizen and resident, publishes a biography of Czar Ivan the Terrible in 1992. One year later, while browsing in a London bookstore he discovers a condensed version of his book published under another author's name by a British publisher. Since the U.S. and United Kingdom have both signed the Berne Convention, if Carl sues the British publisher and author for copyright infringement in the British courts, he will be entitled to the same treatment as any British subject who brought this suit.

b. No formalities

No formalities, such as notice and registration, may be required for basic copyright protection. However, some countries offer greater copyright protection if a copyright is registered or carries a particular type

COUNTRIES SIGNING THE BERNE CONVENTION

Argentina	Madagascar
Australia	Mali
Austria	Malta
Bahamas	Mauritania
Barbados	Mexico
Belgium	Monaco
Benin	Morocco
Brazil	Netherlands
Bulgaria	New Zealand
Cameroon	Niger
Canada	Nigeria
Central Africa Republic	Norway
Chad	Pakistan
Chile	Peru
China	Philippines
Colombia	Poland
Costa Rica	Portugal
Cyprus	Romania
Czech Republic	Rwanda
Denmark	Senegal
Fiji	Slovak Republic
Finland	South Africa
France	Spain
Gabon	Sri Lanka
Germany	Surinam
Ghana	Sweden
Greece	Switzerland
Guinea	Thailand
Hungary	Togo
Iceland	Tunisia
India	Turkey
Ireland	United Kingdom
Israel	United States
Italy	Upper Volta
Ivory Coast	Uraguay
Japan	Vatican City
Lebanon	Venezuela
Libya	Yugoslavia
Liechtenstein	Zaire
Luxembourg	Zimbabwe

of notice. For example, in Japan and Canada, registration provides a means of making your work a public record and may thus be helpful in case of an infringement action. Other countries have certain procedural requirements that must be followed before foreign works may be distributed within their borders, such as customs rules, censorship requirements or other regulations. Compliance with these types of formalities should be taken care of by a foreign agent hired by the author's publisher or the author or author's agent.

c. Minimal protections required

Every Berne country is required to offer a minimum standard of copyright protection in their own country to works first published or created by nationals of other Berne countries. This protection must include:

- copyright duration of at least the author's life plus 50 years
- the granting of moral rights to the author. Moral rights are rights an author can never transfer to a third party because they are considered an extension of her being. Briefly, they consist of the right to claim authorship, disclaim authorship of copies, to prevent or call back distribution under certain conditions, and to object to any distortion, mutilation or other modifications of the author's work injurious to her reputation. The right to prevent colorization of black and white films is an example of a moral right. Moral rights are generally of most concern to visual artists.
- some provision allowing for fair dealing or free use of copyrighted works. This includes material used in quotations for educational purposes, for reporting current events, and so

forth. (In the United States, this is called fair use, and is discussed in detail in Chapter 11, *Using Other Authors' Words.*)

APPLICATION OF BERNE CONVENTION TO WORKS CREATED BEFORE MARCH 1, 1989

As mentioned earlier, the United States was a latecomer to the Berne Convention; it did not join until March 1, 1989. The Berne Convention does not apply to a work first published in the U.S. before that date unless the work was also published in a Berne country at the same time (that is, within 30 days of each other). This is called simultaneous publication. Before 1989, American publishers commonly had their books published simultaneously in the U.S. and Canada and/or Great Britain (both Berne countries) so that they could receive the protection of the Berne Convention. This fact was usually indicated on the same page as the work's copyright notice.

---

2. The Universal Copyright Convention

The second most important international copyright treaty is the Universal Copyright Convention (U.C.C.). The United States joined the U.C.C. on September 16, 1955; it applies to all works created or originally published in the U.S. after that date. Where a country has signed both the U.C.C. and Berne Conventions, the Berne Convention has priority over the U.C.C. Since the U.S. has joined the Berne Convention, the U.C.C. is relevant to works by American nationals only (1) in countries that have signed the U.C.C. but not the Berne Convention (most notably, the Soviet Union); and (2) to works first published in the U.S. before March 1, 1989 that

were not simultaneously published in a Berne country.

The U.C.C. is very similar to the Berne Convention, with the exception that it allows member countries to require some formalities. It requires member countries to afford foreign authors and other copyright owners national treatment. The U.C.C. also requires that each signatory country provide adequate and effective protection of the rights of foreign authors and other foreign copyright owners of literary, scientific and artistic work, including writings and dramatic works. In addition, each country must:

- Offer copyright protection for at least the life of the author plus 25 years; and
- Offer the author exclusive rights to translate and reproduce her work, with the exception that if a work is not translated into the language of a U.C.C. country within seven years of the work's original publication (three years if the country is a developing country), the government of that country has the right to make a translation in that country's language. But the government has to pay the author a fair fee for the translation under a compulsory licensing system.

b. Limitation on formalities

The U.C.C. does not require member countries to dispense with formalities as a prerequisite to copyright protection. But an author or copyright owner of a work first published in one U.C.C. country can avoid complying with another U.C.C. country's formalities (registration, deposit, payment of fees, etc.) simply by placing the following copyright notice on all published copies of the work: [*Date of first publication*] © [*Your name*]. Compliance with the U.S. requirements for a valid copyright notice discussed in Chapter 3, *Copyright Notice*, also constitutes compliance with the U.C.C. notice requirement. This is one very good reason to always affix a valid copyright notice to your published work.

COUNTRIES SIGNING THE U.C.C.

Algeria	Japan
Andorra	Kampuchea (Cambodia)
Argentina	Kenya
Australia	Korea (North)
Austria	Laos
Bahamas	Lebanon
Bangladesh	Liberia
Barbados	Liechtenstein
Belgium	Luxembourg
Belize	Malawi
Brazil	Malta
Bulgaria	Mauritius
Cameroon	Mexico
Canada	Monaco
Chile	Morocco
Colombia	Netherlands
Costa Rica	New Zealand
Cuba	Nigeria
Czechoslovakia	Norway
Denmark	Pakistan
Dominican Republic	Panama
Ecuador	Paraguay
El Salvador	Peru
Fiji	Philippines
Finland	Poland
France	Portugal
Germany	Senegal
Ghana	Soviet Union
Greece	Spain
Guatemala	Sweden
Guinea	Switzerland
Haiti	Tunisia
Hungary	United Kingdom
Iceland	United States
India	Vatican City
Ireland	Venezuela
Israel	Yugoslavia
Italy	Zambia

COUNTRIES SIGNING THE U.C.C. BUT NOT THE BERNE CONVENTION

Algeria	Kenya
Andorra	Korea (North)
Bangladesh	Laos
Belize	Liberia
Cuba	Malawi
Dominican Republic	Mauritius
Ecuador	Nigeria
El Salvador	Panama
Guatemala	Paraguay
Haiti	Peru
Kampuchea	Soviet Union
(Cambodia)	Zambia

3. The Buenos Aires Convention

The Buenos Aires Convention is of little importance to U.S.-based authors because it has been substantially superseded by the Berne Convention and the U.C.C. However, there is one exception: Two South American countries who signed the Buenos Aires Convention have not signed the Berne Convention or U.C.C. These are Bolivia and Honduras. Therefore, to gain copyright protection in these countries, it's necessary to comply with the formalities of the Buenos Aires Convention. To do this, simply include the words "All Rights Reserved" in the U.C.C. copyright notice. Thus, a copyright notice that would qualify in both U.C.C. and Buenos Aires Convention countries would look like this: © [*The date of publication*] [*Your name*] All Rights Reserved.

FIRST THE WORD COPYRIGHT OR THE © SYMBOL OR COPR. THEN THE DATE, THEN YOUR NAME, THEN ALL RIGHTS RESERVED.

4. Protections in Countries Not Covered by Conventions

What about those countries that have not signed any of the three conventions discussed above? These include some potentially important markets, such as China, and countries in which copyright piracy is widespread, such as Taiwan. The United States has entered into bilateral (country to country) copyright treaties with some of these countries, including China and Taiwan. Under these treaties, works by U.S. citizens are afforded copyright protection in the country involved. In addition, many countries afford foreign authors and their works copyright protection if the foreign author's country of origin provides similar treatment. This means it is possible for your work to be protected in a country that has not signed any of the multinational conventions or entered into a bilateral copyright treaty with the U.S.

If you're interested in obtaining protection in a country that has not signed a multinational copyright convention, consult a copyright attorney or contact that country's trade representative at their U.S. embassy for more information.

5. Bringing Infringement Suits in Foreign Countries

If your work is infringed upon by a person or entity in a foreign country, the first thing to do is consult with an experienced American copyright attorney. Even if the infringement occurred in another country, you may be able to sue the infringer in the United States. In this event, an American court would apply the copyright law of the foreign country, not American law. If you have to file suit abroad, you'll need to hire a copyright attorney in the foreign country involved to represent you. Your American copyright attorney should be able to refer you to an experienced copyright lawyer in the country involved.

Before you go to the expense of filing suit, however, be sure to have your attorney explain to you what remedies (for instance, monetary damages, injunctions) you will be entitled to if the suit is successful. Remember, you'll only be entitled to the same treatment that a citizen of the country involved would receive.

Although the U.S. has been urging other nations to take copyright infringement more seriously than they have in the past, some (particularly developing) countries still do not impose meaningful penalties on infringers. This means it may not be economically worthwhile to bring infringement suits against infringers in some countries.

B. Protection in the U.S. for Non-U.S. Citizens

We now examine copyright protection in the United States from the point of view of non-U.S. citizens.

1. Protection for Nationals of Berne Countries

If you're a citizen or permanent resident (that is, a national) of a country that is a member of the Berne Convention (see list of Berne countries above), you are entitled to full copyright protection in the U.S. so long as your work was first created or published on or after March 1, 1989 (the date the U.S. joined the Berne Convention). This is true regardless of where the work was first created or published.

> **EXAMPLE 1:** Pierre, a French citizen and resident, publishes a book in 1990. Since France joined the Berne Convention in 1887, the work is entitled to protection in the U.S. pursuant to the Berne Convention.

> **EXAMPLE 2:** Assume that Pierre had previously published a book in 1985. Since this was before the U.S. joined the Berne Convention, the book could not be protected in the U.S. under that convention. Pierre would have to look to the U.C.C. for protection (see below).

2. Protection Under the U.C.C.

What if your work does not qualify for protection under the Berne Convention because it was first created or published before March 1, 1989, or because you are a citizen or permanent resident of a country that is not a member of the Berne Convention? Your published or unpublished work will still be entitled to full protection in the U.S. if your country is a member of the Universal Copyright Convention and the work is published with the proper copyright notice (see Section A.2, above). This is true regardless of where the work was first created or published.

> **EXAMPLE:** Pierre, the French citizen in Example 2 above who was not entitled to copyright protection in the U.S. for a book published in 1985, is entitled to full U.S. protection under the U.C.C. (to which France belongs) provided that his book was published with the proper copyright notice.

3. First Publication Rule

Regardless of what country you are a citizen of or permanently reside in, if your work is first (or simultaneously) published on or after March 1, 1989 in any country that is a member of the Berne Convention, you are entitled to full copyright protection in the United States under the Berne Convention. Similarly, if your work was first published with a valid copyright notice prior to March 1, 1989 (but after March 15, 1955), in a country that is a member of the U.C.C., you are entitled to full copyright protection in the U.S. pursuant to the U.C.C.

4. Protection for Nationals of Bolivia and Honduras

All citizens of Buenos Aires Convention countries are entitled to protection in the U.S. if "All Rights Reserved" is placed on their published work. As discussed in Section A.3 above, since most Buenos

Aires countries are also members of the U.C.C., this is of little practical importance except for citizens of Bolivia and Honduras (which have not joined the U.C.C.).

5. Compliance with U.S. Copyright Formalities

It is not necessary for a non-U.S. citizen to place a valid copyright notice on his published work or register it with the U.S. Copyright Office to obtain copyright protection in the U.S. Indeed, unlike the case with U.S. citizens, a non-U.S. citizen need not register her work before filing suit in the U.S. for copyright infringement. However, as discussed in Chapter 3, *Copyright Notice*, and Chapter 4, *Copyright Registration*, extremely important advantages are gained under U.S. copyright law if a published work contains a valid copyright notice and a published or unpublished work is registered with the Copyright Office. Therefore, notice and registration are strongly advised for all foreign authors.

But if your work was first published before March 1, 1989, and your copyright protection in the U.S. is based on the U.C.C., your published work must contain a valid copyright notice.

C. Marketing Your Work in Foreign Countries

If you are sharing ownership of foreign rights with your publisher, the publisher usually markets them through foreign agents with which it has established relationships and at international book fairs (the Frankfurt, Germany, book fair is the most important). If you have retained all your foreign rights and have an agent, she'll market your foreign rights through foreign subagents. If you've retained your rights and don't have an agent, you need to retain one. You can use an American agent who has contacts with foreign subagents, or directly contact agents in the particular countries in which you wish to sell your rights. The latter course will save you money since you'll only have to pay a commission to the foreign agent, not to an American agent as well. The publication *International Literary Marketplace* lists British and other foreign agents.

Electronic Publishing

According to the conventional wisdom of the day, human civilization has entered the "information age." Self-proclaimed experts assert that the printing press will soon become as obsolete as the quill pen, that the humble book will be replaced by the "information superhighway," CD-ROM disk and personal computer. This remains to be seen. Nevertheless, it is indisputable that electronic publishing is an increasingly important segment of the publishing business, and, therefore, is of increasing interest to authors and those that hire them or publish their works.

In this chapter we'll examine the special copyright questions and problems involved in the creation and exploitation of multimedia works (electronic books) and electronic databases. Then we'll look at the problem of unauthorized copying of digital works and the copyright status of electronic mail. But first, we'll try to answer the all-important question of just who controls electronic copyrights.

A. Who Controls Electronic Copyrights?

According to the National Writers' Union, many publishers are distributing author's works electronically even though their publishing contracts do not give them the right to do so. In the first case of its kind, ten freelance writers in conjunction with the National Writers' Union filed a copyright infringement suit in New York against *The New York Times*, Time Inc., Mead Data Central Corp. and others in late 1993 alleging that their works were copied and distributed on computer databases and CD-ROMs without their permission and without compensation.

This problem is undoubtedly due largely to widespread confusion on the part of publishers and authors as to who controls the electronic copyright in a work. By "electronic copyright" we mean who has the legal right to reproduce, distribute and display a work in electronic form, whether in a computer database such as Dialog or Nexis that is accessed by users via a modem over telephone lines, or on a CD-ROM disk or other magnetic media used directly in computers. To understand who owns such rights, we'll first have to review some of the fundamental rules of copyright ownership and then see how they apply in the electronic age.

1. Initial Copyright Owners' Exclusive Rights

The moment any work of authorship is created, it is automatically protected by copyright and the initial copyright owner automatically acquires a bundle of exclusive copyright rights. Exclusive means no one may exercise these rights without the copyright owner's permission. Anyone who does will be liable for copyright infringement. These exclusive rights are:

- reproduction right—that is, the right to make copies of a protected work
- distribution right—that is, the right to sell or otherwise distribute copies to the public

- right to create adaptions (or derivative works)—that is, the right to prepare new works based on the protected work, and
- performance and display rights—that is, the right to perform or display a work in public.

Publishing a work in electronic form—whether in a computer database, on a CD-ROM disk or any other means—requires the exercise of the reproduction and distribution rights, and perhaps the derivative work and display rights as well. The person or entity who controls these rights controls the electronic copyright. Now let's see who has these rights when a work is first created and who ends up with them when it is published.

2. A Work's Author Is the Initial Copyright Owner

As discussed in detail in Chapter 8, *Initial Copyright Ownership*, the exclusive rights outlined above initially belong to a work's author(s). However, for copyright purposes, the author of a work is not necessarily the person(s) who actually created it; it can be that person's employer—a corporation, for example. There are four ways a person or business entity may become an author:

- An individual may independently author the work.
- An employer (whether a person or business entity such as a corporation or partnership) may pay an employee to author the work, in which case the employer is an author under the work made for hire rule.
- A person or business entity may specially commission an independent contractor to author the work under a written work made for hire contract, in which case the commissioning party becomes the author (but this applies only to works falling within the nine work for hire categories set forth in the Copyright Act; see Chapter 8, Section B.3 for a detailed discussion).

- Two or more individuals or entities may collaborate to become joint authors, in which case they share ownership of the work's copyright.

3. Transfer of Initial Owner's Exclusive Rights

Initial copyright owners often transfer some or all of their copyright rights to others—book publishers, for example—for economic exploitation. As discussed in detail in Chapter 9, *Transferring Copyright Ownership*, there are two basic types of copyright transfers: exclusive licenses and assignments. Although these terms are often used interchangeably, there are some differences.

a. Exclusive licenses

The term exclusive license is usually used when a copyright owner transfers one or more of her rights, but retains at least some of them. The holder of an exclusive license becomes the owner of the transferred right(s). As such, unless the exclusive license provides otherwise, she is entitled to sue anyone who infringes on that right while she owns it, and is entitled to transfer her license to others. She may also record the exclusive license with the Copyright Office.

A copyright owner's exclusive rights can be divided and subdivided and transferred to others in just about any way imaginable: by geographical area, media, market segment, language, time or virtually any other way. Electronic rights can be carved out and transferred to others as well.

b. Assignments

If an owner of all the exclusive rights in a copyright transfers the entire bundle of rights that make up his copyright simultaneously to a single person or entity, the transaction is usually called an assignment or sometimes an all rights transfer. An assignment must be in writing to be valid.

4. Initial Ownership of Electronic Rights

As discussed above, a work's author will initially own all these rights, meaning that the author initially controls the electronic copyright.

a. Works created by self-employed individuals

Self-employed individuals who create written works alone or with others (the type of people we normally think of as authors) will initially own the electronic rights in their works.

> **EXAMPLE:** Sue and Al write a book on organic gardening. They are self-employed joint authors. This means they jointly own all the copyright rights in the book, including electronic rights.

b. Works made for hire

But the electronic copyright in works made for hire will be owned by the employer or hiring party. The employer or hiring party is the author for copyright purposes, not the person(s) who actually created the work. This includes:

- Works created by employees within the scope of their employment, and
- Specially commissioned works created by independent contractors under written work for hire agreements.

> **EXAMPLE 1:** Bob is employed as a reporter for *Brownnose Magazine*. The stories he writes for the magazine are works for hire to which the magazine initially owns all the rights, including electronic rights. *Brownnose* is free to transfer these rights in any way it chooses. For example, it may permit Bob's stories to be distributed on an on-line computer database like Nexis.

> **EXAMPLE 2:** *Brownnose Magazine* hires Mary, a self-employed freelance writer, to write an article. Before starting work, Mary signs an agreement stating that the article shall be a work made for hire. Although Mary is not an employee of *Brownnose*, her signing the agreement made her article a work made for hire. This means that *Brownnose* is the initial owner of all the copyright rights in the story, including electronic rights. Mary has no copyright rights.

5. Transfer of Electronic Rights by Individual Authors

With the important exception of self-publishers who reproduce and distribute their work themselves, self-employed authors normally profit from their copyrights by selling their rights to publishers and others to exploit. In today's publishing environment, such sales will typically include the transfer of some or all of the author's electronic rights.

a. Transfer of electronic rights in book publishing agreements

When an author sells a book to a publisher, the publishing contract will define which rights the publisher gets and which the author keeps, if any. Normally, the publisher will acquire the exclusive right to publish the book in print form in the U.S.; this is sometimes called the primary right. All the other rights are called subsidiary rights. These include, for example, film, television, radio, and live-stage adaptation rights, and the right to create and distribute nondramatic audio recordings of the work. The right to license a work for use in a multimedia program or other electronic publication is also a subsidiary right that is normally specifically dealt with in a modern publishing agreement.

Typically a book author will transfer some or all of her subsidiary rights to the publisher and the publisher will agree to give the author a percentage of any monies it makes from them (a 50-50 split is common). Established authors who have agents who can sell their subsidiary rights for them, often insist on retaining many of their more valuable subsidiary rights—film rights, for example. Such authors often retain the electronic rights to their work. Authors who do not have agents typically transfer all their subsidiary rights to their publisher in return for a percentage of what the publisher earns from them. This often makes sense because the publisher is better able to sell such rights than the author.

Some authors simply transfer all their copyright rights to a publisher or other entity in exchange for payment or royalties. This type of arrangement is common in academic publishing. Such all rights assignments undoubtedly include the right to reproduce and distribute the work in electronic form.

b.   Transfers of electronic rights in freelance articles

Sales of magazine and journal articles by self-employed freelance writers are usually simpler. Freelance article writers often just transfer the right to publish the article for the first time in North America (called first North American serial rights). Such a transfer probably does not include electronic rights, since this term historically has referred only to print rights. However, no court has so held; and a publisher might claim that in today's publishing environment first North American serial rights includes the right to publish an article in an electronic database or computer disk for the first time. To avoid confusion, the publishing agreement should state explicitly who owns the electronic rights.

Some freelancers transfer all their copyright rights to a publisher or sign work for hire agreements. These authors give up all their copyright rights, including electronic rights.

⚠ Copyright tip for authors

If you are concerned about ownership of electronic rights, be sure to ask your publisher, editor and/or agent about it before you sign any transfer agreement. If the publisher or other purchaser of your work wants some or all of these rights, insist that your written agreement contain a provision stating exactly which rights you're transferring, for how long and how you will be paid for them. This is the best way to avoid misunderstandings and problems in the future.

If you wish to retain ownership of all your electronic rights, seek to include in any publishing agreement you sign a clause like the following, expressly reserving such ownership to you, the author: *Author expressly reserves all electronic and digital rights in the work. Electronic and digital rights are those rights involving the transmutation of all or part of the work into forms usable in computers; including, but not limited to, those forms usable in transmission between computers and between computers and peripheral devices. Examples of how electronic and digital rights can be exploited include, but are not limited to, licensing or sale of any part of the work on CD-ROM, magnetic media such as computer diskettes, and the transmission of any part of the work through copper or optical fiber cables from a database source to an end-user.*

Detailed advice for authors on electronic rights, including sample publishing contract provisions, can be obtained from the Author's Guild and National Writers Union. See Chapter 15, *Help Beyond this Book,* for their addresses and phone numbers.

6. Ownership of Electronic Rights in Older Works

Today, publishing agreements typically include specific provisions regarding ownership of electronic rights. However, older agreements may have nothing on the subject because the technology wasn't known or anticipated at the time. In this event, it can be very difficult to tell exactly who owns the electronic rights to a work. Undoubtedly, one of the main reasons many works are apparently being published in electronic form without proper permission from the copyright owners is confusion as to exactly who owns such rights.

Court decisions vary, but as a general rule, an author of an older work who transfers all his copyright rights (his entire right, title and interest in the work) will probably be deemed to have transferred electronic rights as well. This is particularly likely where the all rights transfer includes language showing that the transfer was intended to include media that might be invented in the future—words something like the following: "I hereby transfer my entire right, title and interest in the Work in all media now known or later invented."

However, an author who transfers only some of his copyright rights and retains others, will normally be deemed to have retained his electronic rights even though they are not specifically mentioned in the agreement. This is particularly true if the contract contains an express reservation of rights—a clause like this: "All rights in the Work not specifically granted in this Agreement to the publisher are reserved to the Author."

Many older publishing agreements contain a provision granting the publisher the right to sell all or part of the work for mechanical reproduction and transmission by any then known or later devised method for information storage, reproduction and retrieval. This might be deemed to include electronic and multimedia rights, but it's far from clear.

⚠ Copyright tip
Interpreting a publishing agreement can be a tricky business. If you're not sure who owns the electronic rights in a work, seek legal assistance.

B. Multimedia Works

Multimedia works, or "electronic books," combine text with visual images (both still photos and video and film clips) and sound (including music, ordinary speech and dramatic performances). Some multimedia works consist of a printed text combined with a CD-ROM disk (the book-disk *From Alice to Ocean* is one outstanding example); others are stored only on CD-ROMs or other magnetic media. Software is usually included to enable the user to search, retrieve and manipulate the material.

Multimedia works are one of the hottest products in publishing today. However, they often present some difficult copyright problems. We'll examine below the copyright issues presented in obtaining permission to use third-party content in multimedia works. We'll also provide a detailed discussion of Copyright Office registration and deposit requirements for such works.

1.   Obtaining Permissions for Multimedia Works

Many multimedia works consist, at least in part, of preexisting materials. This poses special copyright problems. Consider this example: Scrivener & Sons, a long-established book publisher, decides to enter the electronic book market. It plans to publish a multimedia history of the Persian Gulf War on a CD-ROM disk. Scrivener wants the disk to contain a variety of preexisting materials about the Gulf War, including:

- text from several articles and books
- photos from books, magazines and other sources
- video clips from many television programs,
- music to be used as background to the images and text, and
- third party application software programs to support graphics, sound and animation.

Scrivener intends to incorporate hundreds of separate items into its multimedia package. This sounds like a fine idea for a multimedia product. However, Scrivener must overcome a substantial legal obstacle before it can publish the work: It must obtain permission to use at least some of the preexisting material. Obtaining such permission can involve tracking down many different copyright owners and negotiating licenses to use their material. This can be very time consuming and expensive. Indeed, some publishers and software developers have discovered that some multimedia works are not economically feasible in today's marketplace because the legal and licensing costs are too high.

a.   When copyright permissions are needed

Whether permission is needed to include any given item in a multimedia work depends first, of course, on who owns it. Review the discussion of ownership of electronic copyright in Section A above, and read the detailed discussions of copyright ownerships in Chapter 8, *Initial Copyright Ownership*, and Chapter 9, *Transferring Copyright Ownership*.

Generally, permission is not needed to use materials specially created for a multimedia work, whether by employees or third parties. The publisher will automatically own materials created by employees within the scope of their employment and will routinely obtain an assignment of copyright rights from nonemployees (or have them sign work made for hire agreements). For sample employment and independent contractor agreements, refer to *Software Development: A Legal Guide* by Stephen Fishman (Nolo Press).

However, permission may be needed to use *preexisting* materials created by nonemployees (or by employees before they became employees). Even in this event though, permission will not be needed if the material is (1) in the public domain, or (2) the use of the material constitutes a fair use.

We discuss the public domain in detail in Chapter 6, *What Copyright Protects*. Review that chapter and Chapter 10, *Copyright Duration*, to see if a preexisting work is in the public domain and therefore has no copyright protection.

Even if a preexisting work is protected by copyright, permission will not be needed to use it if the use constitutes a fair use. Fair use is discussed in detail in Chapter 11, *Using Other Authors' Words*. Although Chapter 11 focuses on the fair use of writings, the principles it describes are applicable to all types of protected works—graphics, music, photos, video and so forth.

If a preexisting work is protected by copyright and the intended use cannot qualify as a fair use, permission must be obtained to include it in a multimedia work.

b.   Obtaining multimedia permissions

With the notable exception of the music industry, which has had a system of rights collectives in place for many decades, obtaining permission to use copyrighted materials in a multimedia project is a difficult, time-consuming and often chaotic process.

Obtaining multimedia permissions can be especially hard because, for a variety of reasons, many copyright owners are reluctant to grant any multimedia permissions. Many copyright owners have decided not to grant multimedia permissions for the time being because the market is so new they're unsure how much such rights are worth. Others are reluctant to permit their work to be reduced to digitized form for fear they will lose control over unauthorized copying. Still others intend to launch their own multimedia ventures and don't want to help potential competitors. Some owners will grant permission, but only for exorbitant amounts of money (there are no standard rates for such permissions).

Securing a multimedia permission, then, can require a good deal of persistence, salesmanship and creative negotiating. A two-step process should be followed:

- first, find out who owns the rights that are needed,
- then, negotiate and have signed a written release or multimedia license agreement.

Refer to *Software Development: A Legal Guide* (Chapter 13) by Stephen Fishman (Nolo Press) for a detailed discussion of how to obtain permission to use text, photographs, film and video, drawings and other artwork and music. A sample multimedia license agreement is also included.

2. Copyright Registration for Multimedia Works

For all the reasons discussed in Chapter 4, *Copyright Registration*, multimedia works can and should be registered with the Copyright Office. It is always permissible to register each element of a multimedia work separately—manual, text, photos, video, etc. However, it may not be necessary to do so. An entire multimedia work can be registered at one time on one registration form for one $20 fee provided that:

- the copyright claimant is the same for all ele-

ments of the work for which copyright protection is sought, and
- all such elements are published at the same time as a single unit (excluding preexisting elements such as photos, music and video which will not be covered by the registration).

An example will help make these rules clear. Assume that Scrivener & Sons in the example in the above section has finished developing its multimedia history of the Persian Gulf War. The multimedia package consists of a CD-ROM disk containing text, photos, video and music; and a printed manual explaining how to use the CD-ROM. Scrivener is the copyright owner of the manual, which was written by its employees. Scrivener editors and work for hire freelancers also wrote some of the text on the CD-ROM. All the other material on the CD-ROM was licensed by Scrivener—that is, it obtained permission to copy and distribute it on the CD-ROM from the copyright owners. Scrivener does not own the copyright in any of these individual bits of text, photos, video or music. However, Scrivener does own a compilation copyright in the entire CD-ROM —that is, a copyright in the selection, arrangement and co-ordination of all the material on the disk, which was performed by Scrivener employees and work for hire freelancers. This selection, arrangement and coordination constitutes a work of authorship if original and minimally creative (see Section C, below).

Scrivener may register all the elements to which it claims copyright ownership—the manual, the CD-ROM text it owns and the compilation copyright covering all the CD-ROM material—on a single application for a single fee. Why? Because the copyright claimant for all the elements of the multimedia work for which protection is sought by Scrivener is the same: Scrivener; and all these elements are being published together as a single unit at the same time.

What about registering all the individual bits of text, music, photos, video that Scrivener licensed? That's the province of the copyright owner of each individual licensed item. Scrivener may not register such material since it is not the copyright claimant (owner).

MULTIMEDIA WORKS INCLUDE MORE THAN JUST CD-ROMs

For copyright registration purposes, a multimedia work includes more than works on CD-ROM disks. Rather, a multimedia work is any work which, excluding its container, combines authorship in two or more media. The authorship may include text, artwork, sculpture, cinematography, photography, sounds, music or choreography. The media may include printed matter such as a book; audiovisual material such as videotape, slides, filmstrips; a phono-record such as an audio tape or audio disk; or any machine-readable copy such as a computer disk, tape or chip. Any work combining two or more types of authorship in two or more different types of media is a multimedia work and may be registered using the procedures discussed in this section. For example, a book combined with a filmstrip or audio tape would be a multimedia work. However, since this chapter is about electronic publishing, our focus is on registering multimedia kits consisting of CD-ROM disks and written manuals.

---

a.   Which form to use

Form PA is usually used for registration of multimedia works. Form PA is used to register any multimedia work containing an audiovisual element—photos, video, film clips, etc. A multimedia work consisting solely of text is registered on Form TX. If a multimedia work does not contain any audiovisual elements, but does contain sounds in which sound-recording authorship is claimed, Form SR is used.

b.   Filling out Form PA

Form PA is virtually identical to form TX (the form used to register most types of written works). We discuss how to fill out Form TX in detail in Section I of Chapter 4, *Copyright Registration*. Following are the significant differences when registering a multimedia work on Form TX.

Space 1: Nature of This Work

State audiovisual work in the "Nature of this Work" box in Space 1.

Space 2: Name of Author

State only the name of the author(s) for the elements of the work for which copyright is claimed in this registration. If preexisting materials have been licensed from third parties, don't mention their names in Space 2. In our example above, Scrivener & Sons would be listed as the author in Space 2. The third parties from whom Scrivener licensed the material included in the work are not the authors of the work Scrivener is applying to register, and Scrivener's copyright does not cover their work.

Space 2: Nature of Authorship

The elements of the multimedia work in which original authorship is claimed should be listed here. Scrivener & Sons in our example above could state "compilation and editing of preexisting text, photographs, video clips, film clips and music plus new original text."

Or, more broadly, if you are entitled to claim copyright in an audiovisual work, artwork on computer screens and the text of a computer program, all embodied on a CD-ROM, Space 2 of your application would read: "audiovisual work, artwork on computer screens and text of computer program."

If your CD-ROM claim consists solely of an original compilation of preexisting facts and data, the authorship in Space 2 would be described as "original compilation of preexisting data." Note that this nature of authorship statement is appropriate only where the applicant claims no authorship in the preexisting data, the CD-ROM contains no computer program authorship the applicant is entitled to claim copyright in and where the work is not marketed with a print manual. In this situation, you should submit a cover letter along with your application explaining what original selection, arrangement or ordering is present—that is, explaining what work was involved in selecting and arranging the preexisting material on the CD-ROM. Such selection and arrangement must rise to the level of original authorship to be copyrightable and therefore registerable. See detailed discussion of compilation copyrights in Chapter 7, *Adaptations and Compilations.*

Space 6: Derivative Work or Compilation

If a multimedia work contains pre-existing material such as photos, video and film clips, preexisting text, or music, Space 6 must be completed. If the work contains all new material, Space 6 can be left blank Space 6a must be filled in if the multimedia work is a derivative work, it is left blank if the work is just a compilation. As discussed in detail in Chapter 7, *Adaptions and Compilations,* a derivative work is a work that is created by adapting and recasting preexisting material into a new work of authorship. Most multimedia works containing preexisting material are derivative works—the preexisting material is edited and combined with other preexisting materials and new material to form a new original work of authorship. It's not necessary to individually list every preexisting work included in the multimedia work; a general description is sufficient. For example, Scrivener in our example above could state "previously published text, film and video footage, graphics and music."

Space 6b: Material Added to This Work

Space 6b calls for a description of the new material added to the preexisting material in which copyright

is claimed. You can simply repeat what you stated in the "Nature of Authorship" box in Space 2 above.

c. Deposit requirements

The Copyright Office has imposed special deposit requirements for multimedia works. One complete copy of the best edition a multimedia work first published in the United States must be deposited with the Copyright Office. Everything that is marketed or distributed together must be deposited, whether or not you're the copyright claimant for each element. This includes:

* the ROM disk(s),
* instructional manual(s), and
* any printed version of the work that is sold with the multimedia package (for example, where a book is sold with a CD-ROM).

Multimedia works used on computers typically contain software that enables the user to operate the CD-ROM or other storage medium and access, search and retrieve the data and produce screen displays. The deposit must include identifying material for any such software in which copyright is claimed by the applicant. (But if the software is simply licensed from a third party, no such deposit is necessary.)

The deposit must consist of a printout of the program source code or object code. However, the entire program need not be deposited. Instead, the applicant may deposit a printout of the first and last 25 pages of the source code. Or, if the program contains trade secrets, the applicant has the option of depositing:

* the first and last 25 pages of source code with the portions containing trade secrets blacked out, or
* the first and last 10 pages of source code with no blacked out portions, or
* the first and last 25 pages of object code, together with any 10 or more consecutive pages of source code with no blacked out portions, or
* for programs consisting of less than 25 pages, the entire program with the trade secret portions

blacked out. For further details, see the Copyright Office brochure entitled: "Circular 61: Copyright Registration for Computer Programs."

The Copyright Office wishes multimedia applicants to inform it as to whether the operating software is part of the multimedia work, and where it is embodied—for example, on a CD-ROM disk or other medium.

The Copyright Office has experienced some difficulty in viewing a number of CD-ROM products that have been deposited because it doesn't have the proper equipment. When this occurs, the copyright examiner will require the applicant to make a supplemental deposit of identifying material. For example, it might require a supplement deposit of a video tape showing the audiovisual elements in which authorship is claimed.

C. Electronic Databases

Perhaps the most important area of electronic publishing today is the creation and economic exploitation of electronic databases. An electronic database (or automated database in Copyright Office parlance) is a body of facts, data or other information assembled into an organized format suitable for use in a computer. The variety of information contained on electronic databases is nearly endless and growing rapidly. Everything from government documents to stock quotes to magazine and journal articles can be accessed.

Many electronic databases are available on-line—the database is housed in a computer in a remote location and end-users retrieve information from the database via telephone lines or computer networks. Examples include large commercial on-line information services such as Compuserve, Lexis-Nexis-Medis and Dialog. On-line services such as these are actually collections of many databases provided by a variety of publishers and other sources. The services negotiate contracts with the owners of the databases for the right to distribute them, and pay

royalties based primarily on how much the database is used. Costs to use such services are usually based on a subscription fee plus usage charges for actual use of particular databases.

Thousands of electronic databases are also maintained by universities, research institutions, government agencies and large corporations. Many of these can be accessed via the Internet—a collection of thousands of regional, state, federal, academic and corporate computer networks operated on a nonprofit basis.

Still other electronic databases are available on CD-ROM disks or other magnetic storage media. For example, a CD-ROM database containing over 2 million patents issued by the United States Patent and Trademark Office has recently been published. The user purchases or licenses such databases directly from the publisher and uses them directly on her own computer, rather than accessing them via an on-line service or computer network. This allows the database publisher to bypass the on-line service and market its product directly to end-users.

Below, we'll look first at the nature and extent of copyright protection for such material and then show how to register an electronic database with the Copyright Office.

1. When Is the Data In Electronic Databases Protected By Copyright?

For electronic databases to be constructed, the computer must be told (programmed) where the information placed in it is stored and how that information can be retrieved upon request. Accordingly, when a database is actually constructed, it consists of:

- the data, and
- the database software—that is, the unique set of instructions that defines the way the data is to be organized, stored and retrieved.

This discussion only covers copyright protection for the data in electronic databases. To learn about protecting database software, refer to *Software Development: A Legal Guide*, by Stephen Fishman (Nolo Press).

a.   Databases are compilations or collective works

First, a little copyright law background: A database consisting of unprotectible facts or data—for instance, names and addresses or numerical data—is a fact compilation, that is, a work created by selecting, organizing and arranging previously existing material in such a way that the resulting work as a whole constitutes an original work of authorship. The individual materials contained in the database may not be entitled to copyright protection, but the selection and arrangement of the entire database may be.

A database that contains individually protectible works—for example, a full-text bibliographic database containing the full text of copyrighted articles—is a collective work. A collective work is a special type of compilation. It is a work created by selecting and arranging into a single whole work preexisting materials that are separate and independent works entitled to copyright protection in their own right. As with fact compilations, there may be copyright protection for the selection and arrangement of the materials making up a collective work.

Of course, some databases contain both protectible and unprotectible material, and are therefore both fact compilations and collective works. For a detailed discussion of copyright protection for compilations and collective works, see Chapter 7, *Adaptions and Compilations*.

b.   Originality and minimal creativity required for protection

As discussed in detail in Chapter 7, a compilation is entitled to copyright protection only where the selection, arrangement and/or coordination of the material is original and minimally creative. In a seminal decision called *Feist Publications v. Rural Telephone Service Co.*, 111 S.Ct. 1282 (1991), the U.S. Supreme Court held that one type of fact compilation—telephone book white pages—was not entitled to any copyright protection at all because absolutely no creativity was required to compile alphabetical white pages listings.

COPYRIGHT DOES NOT PROTECT HARD WORK

In the past, some courts held that copyright protected databases and other works that lacked originality and/or creativity if a substantial amount of work was involved in their creation. These courts might have protected a telephone directory, for example, if the authors had personally verified every entry. However, the Supreme Court outlawed this sweat of the brow theory in the *Feist* decision. It is now clear that the amount of work done to create a database or other work has absolutely no bearing on the degree of copyright protection it will receive. As discussed in detail in Chapter 6, *What Copyright Protects*, copyright protects only fixed, original, minimally creative expressions, not hard work.

The *Feist* decision caused great concern in the database industry because many databases would appear to involve no more creativity in their compiling than telephone book white pages. Does this mean they are not entitled to copyright protection? The answer is not entirely clear. However, database publishers should take heart from the Supreme Court statement in *Feist* that only a very minimal degree of creativity is required for copyright protection and that the vast majority of compilations should make the grade.

Nevertheless, for a database to be protected by copyright (and registrable by the Copyright Office), the selection, arrangement and/or coordination involved in its creation must rise to the level of original authorship. Databases whose creation was dictated solely by mechanical or functional considerations will likely not be protectible.

Examples of databases that likely lack copyright protection include:

- exhaustive lists or collections of all the data on a given topic—for example, an alphabetical list of all the parts contained in Ford automobiles.
- databases whose selection, arrangement and/or coordination was determined by external guidelines or rules—for example, a database containing the names and addresses of contributors to the Republican Party under 50 years of age who voted for Pat Buchanan in the 1992 presidential primaries and for Ross Perot in the general election.
- databases that are so commonplace in their parameters that a great possibility exists that someone else would arrive at the same selection—for example, a database of physicians' phone numbers, names and addresses arranged according to their medical specialties.

One of the first post-*Feist* cases dealing with electronic databases illustrates that the more "value-added" features a database publisher adds to the raw facts contained in a database, the more likely it will be copyrightable. The case involved a computerized database of state trademarks. The state trademark records were themselves in the public domain. However, the publisher added to each trademark record a code indicating the type of mark, modified the state records' description of the mark to conform to standard descriptions, divided the data into separate search fields, and added search indices to facilitate computer searches of the records. The court held that the publisher's "selection, coordination,

arrangement, enhancement, and programming of the state trademark data" satisfied the originality and creativity requirements set forth in the *Feist* decision. (*Corsearch, Inc. v. Thomson & Thomson*, Guide to Computer L. (CCH) 46,645 (S.D.N.Y. 1992).) In other words, the database qualified for copyright protection.

2. Extent of Copyright Protection

The copyright in a fact compilation extends only to the selection, coordination and arrangement of the data contained in the compilation and to any new expression the database author adds—for instance, instructions on how to use the database. The raw data itself is not protected. This is sometime called a thin copyright.

A database user may extract the individual bits of data from a fact compilation database without incurring liability for copyright infringement, but may not copy the entire database since this would involve copying the copyright owner's protected expression—that is, selection and arrangement. Thus, for example, the court held that the copyright in the state trademark database discussed above extended only to the publisher's "internally generated information and to its particular enhancements" to the state trademark records. The state trademark records themselves were not protected. Anyone could extract those records from the database and select and arrange them to create her own database without violating the publisher's copyright.

Copyright protection is greater where a database is a collective work—a work consisting of materials entitled to their own copyright protection. In this event, the database owner holds a thin copyright in the selection and arrangement of the entire database, and the items contained in the database may be protected individually. For example, each article contained in a full-text bibliographic database may be protected by copyright, as well as the database as a whole.

OTHER MEANS OF PROTECTING DATABASES

Given the limitations on copyright protection for electronic databases, and the fact that some databases are probably not even entitled to these protections, the database industry has been placing increasing reliance on the use of contracts to prevent unauthorized use of databases. For example, the owners of databases commonly require all users to sign subscription agreements in which the user promises not to reproduce the database without the owners' permission. The extent to which such agreements are enforceable—both in legal and practical terms—is unclear. This is a matter that must be discussed with an attorney knowledgeable about the database industry.

EC DATABASE DIRECTIVE

The European Economic Community (also known as the EC or Common Market) has acted to give electronic databases much greater protection in Europe than is currently available in the United States. In 1992, the EC issued a proposed directive calling on its members (most of the nations of Western Europe) to provide electronic databases with two levels of protection. First, they would be protected by copyright to the extent they constitute original works of authorship. Second, and more importantly, a new unique intellectual property right would be granted to database owners. A database creator would be able to restrict unauthorized extraction of the contents of its database for commercial purposes for a ten-year period. The directive also would impose compulsory licensing requirements on fair and nondiscriminatory terms if a publicly available database could not be independently created, collected or obtained from any other source.

What effect could this have on American database owners who do business in Europe? Not much at the moment. The protection against wrongful extraction would not be extended to database owners who are not nationals of an EC member state unless the country in which the database owner resides agrees to provide a similar right within its own borders and extends the right to EC member states. To do so, U.S. law would have to be amended to effectively overrule the *Feist* decision.

3. Registering Contents of Electronic Databases

If an electronic database is protected by copyright, it should be registered with the Copyright Office for all the reasons discussed in Chapter 4, *Copyright Registration*. Since most databases are frequently updated or revised, the Copyright Office has instituted a special group registration procedure whereby a database and all the updates or other revisions made within any three-month period may be registered in one application. This way, a database need only be registered a maximum of four times per year, rather than each time it is updated or revised.

DATABASE SOFTWARE MUST ALSO BE REGISTERED

The discussion below is only about how to register the selection and arrangement of the *contents* of a computer automated database. It does not cover registration of computer software designed to be used with databases to facilitate retrieval of the data. Software registration is beyond the scope of this book. For coverage of this topic see *Software Development: A Legal Guide*, by Stephen Fishman (Nolo Press).

---

a. Databases qualifying for group registration

To qualify for group registration, all of the following conditions must be met:
- all of the updates or revisions must be fixed or published only in machine-readable copies
- all of the updates or revisions must have been created or published within a three-month period, all within the same calendar year
- all of the updates or revisions must be owned by the same copyright claimant
- all of the updates or revisions must have the same general title, and
- the updates or revisions must be organized in a similar way.

b. Completing Form TX

Form TX must be submitted for a group database registration. Here's how to fill it out:

Space 1: Title

At the "Title of this Work" line, insert the following statement: "Group registration for automated database titled _____; published/unpublished (*choose one*) updates from _____ to _____." Give the earliest and latest dates for the updates included in the group registration. Remember, this time period must be three months or less, all within the same calendar year.

Use the "Publication as a Contribution" line to give the following information: The date (day, month, year) that is represented by the marked portions of the identifying material submitted as a deposit (see Section C, below). Also indicate the frequency with which revisions are made—for example, "daily," "weekly," "monthly."

Space 2: Author(s)

You need to give the requested information about every author who contributed any appreciable amount of protectible material to the version of the work being registered. We're talking about the compilation/collective work authorship here, not the authorship of the individual articles or other works in the database. After the words "Nature of Authorship," give a brief general statement of the nature of the particular author's contribution to the work. Examples: "updates," "revisions," "revised compilation," "revised and updated text."

Space 3: Creation and publication

Give the year in which the author(s) completed the group of updates or revisions being registered.

If the updates or revisions have been published, you must give the date (month, day, year) and nation of publication. This should be the *last* date on which revisions were added during the three-month period covered by the application. When is a database published? This is not exactly clear. For copyright purposes, publication means distributing or offering to distribute copies of a work to the public on an unrestricted basis. It is unclear whether on-line availability with or without printers for the user constitutes publication. The Copyright Office leaves it up to the copyright owners to determine whether their database has been published.

Space 4: Claimants

Follow the instructions in Chapter 4, Section I on how to complete this space.

Space 5: Previous Registration

If the database has been previously registered, check the last box and give the previous registration number and date. If more than one previous registration has been made for the database, give the number and date of any one previous registration.

Space 6: Derivative Work or Compilation

Space 6 must be completed if the updates or the database and its updates contain a substantial amount of previously published, registered or public domain material. Leave Space 6 blank if the material contained in the database and its updates is entirely new and never before registered or published.

"Preexisting Material" (Space 6a): State "previously registered material," "previously published material," or "public domain data" for a new database that has not been previously registered or published, but that contains an appreciable amount of previously registered, published or public domain material.

For a previously published or registered database that has not been revised or updated periodically, describe the preexisting material as "previ-

ously published database" or "previously registered database," or "database prior to (*earliest date represented in the present group of updates*)."

"Material Added to This Work" (Space 6b): Describe the updates or revisions or new database being registered for the first time and specify the frequency of these updates or revisions—for example, "weekly updates," "daily revisions," or "revised compilation updated monthly."

Spaces 7 & 8

Leave these spaces blank. They're not applicable to electronic databases.

Spaces 9, 10, 11: Fee, Correspondence, Certification, Return Address

Follow the instructions in Chapter 4, Section I on how to complete these spaces.

c. Deposit requirements for group registration

You must submit the following deposit with your registration application:

Identifying material: Identifying material meeting the following requirements:

- 50 representative pages of printout (or equivalent units if reproduced in microfilm) from a single-file database; or
- 50 representative complete data records (not pages) from each updated data file in a multiple-file database.

The printout or data records must be marked to show the copyrightable revisions or updates from one representative publication date (if the database is published) or from one representative creation date (if the database is unpublished) within the three-month period covered by the registration; or, alternatively, you may deposit a copy of the actual updates or revisions made on a representative date.

Descriptive statement: In addition, you must submit a brief, typed descriptive statement providing the following information:

- the title of the database
- the name and address of the copyright claimant
- the name and content of each separate file in a multiple-file database, including its subject, origin(s) of the data, and the approximate number of data records it contains
- information about the nature, location, and frequency of the changes within the database or within the separate data files in multiple-file databases and
- information about the copyright notice, if one is used, as follows:

For a machine-readable notice, transcribe the contents of the notice and indicate the manner and frequency with which it's displayed—for example, at a user's terminal only, at sign-on, continuously on terminal display or on printouts.

For a visually perceptible notice on any copies of the work (or on tape reels or containers), include a photocopy or other sample of the notice.

d. Non-group registration

If your database doesn't qualify for group registration, or for some reason you do not wish to use that procedure, simply complete Form TX in the same manner as for any other compilation. You should deposit the first and last 25 pages of a single-file database. If the database consists of separate and distinct data files, deposit one copy of 50 complete data records (not pages) from each file, or the entire file, whichever is less. You must also include a descriptive statement for a multiple-file database containing the same information described in Section C, above.

If the database is fixed in a CD-ROM, deposit one complete copy of the CD-ROM package, any instructional manual, and a printed version of the work which is fixed on the CD-ROM if such an exact print version exists. The deposit must also include any software that is included as part of the package. A print-out of the first and last 25 pages of the software source code is acceptable. If the software contains trade secrets, other deposit arrangements can be made; see the discussion in Section B.2.c, above.

D. Special Copyright Problems Posed by Digital Media

In a recent report entitled *Finding A Balance: Computer Software, Intellectual Property and the Challenge of Technological Change*, the U.S. Congress's Office of Technology Assessment identified many of the special copyright problems posed by the new digital media. The following discussion summarizes some of the OTA's findings.

1. Unauthorized Copying of Digital Information

Undoubtedly the most important problem copyright owners face when their works are reduced to digital form is unauthorized copying and distribution. Of course, this problem is not new. Ever since the perfection of the photocopy machine, books, articles and other printed works have been copied and distributed without permission from, or payment to, the copyright owners. The introduction of the fax machine has made it even easier to deliver photocopies over long distances.

However, there are important limitations on distribution of unauthorized photocopies: copy quality degrades with each generation; photocopying large amounts of work can be time-consuming, expensive and inconvenient; and a copied document is still in the same format as the original and can be easily identified as a copyrighted work.

None of these limitations exist for digital copies. Perfect digital copies can be made easily, cheaply and quickly over and over again. Digital copies do not degrade. It is easy to disguise the origins of a digital copy by making simple format changes that requires only a few keystrokes. And digital copies are easy to distribute: A copy can be posted on a computer bulletin board and easily copied by any number of users anywhere in the country or across the world.

Such unauthorized copying and distribution is, of course, copyright infringement. But this fact is of little practical use to a copyright owner when it is virtually impossible to discover that such copying has occurred.

a. Technological solutions for unauthorized copying

Some believe that a technological fix will be found to control unauthorized copying. Some progress has been made on this front. For example, University Microfilms Inc. and several universities have participated in a pilot program called BART (Billing and Royalty Tracking) to track usage of CD-ROM disks. Each page of material entered on a BART CD-ROM is encoded so that a printed record can be made each time a page is accessed and printed out. The user is billed accordingly and the copyright owner is paid a royalty. However, this system does nothing to prevent or recompense a copyright owner for unauthorized copying of the first copy that is made and paid for.

b. The use of licenses to prevent unauthorized uses of digital information

To date, the main response of copyright owners to the threat of unauthorized copying of digital works is the use of contractual restrictions on the use of such works.

For example, access to commercial databases is often limited to subscribers who sign subscription agreements. Such agreements often attempt to regulate the uses made of the data, including downloading, and may forbid the use of the database except by the subscriber.

Similarly, copies of works on CD-ROM or floppy disks are often licensed to users rather than being sold outright. This way, the first sale doctrine doesn't apply and the use of the material is made subject to the terms of the license agreement. The license may state, for example, that the user may not resell the disk, alter it, or place it on a network where more than one person can use it. Users may have to return old disks when new ones are supplied, or when the subscription period ends. Where such an agreement is actually signed by the user before purchasing the disk, it should be enforceable in court. But, where it is merely printed on the packaging a mass-marketed disk is sold in, enforceability is very questionable.

Still, as a practical matter, such contractual restrictions do not prevent unauthorized copying. Once a user has paid for a legitimate copy of something, there is no practical way to prevent him from making other unauthorized copies.

2. Unclear Copyright Status of Electronic Mail

Electronic mail has become a national and international phenomenon. Users of on-line services like Compuserve and Internet send many millions of electronic messages a year. In addition, many corporations, government agencies and universities have their own electronic mail systems. And, thousands of electronic bulletin boards of various sizes are in operation all over the world.

Most electronic mail is trivial and ephemeral in nature; the persons who create such messages probably care little and think less about copyright protection for their "works." However, some people—scholars and scientists, for example—use electronic mail to collaborate with colleagues, communicate new and important ideas and exchange drafts of works in progress. Many such people probably believe and desire that their electronic messages be protected by copyright. But are they? And, if so, how much?

As discussed in detail in Chapter 6, *What Copyright Protects*, copyright protects all original works of authorship, however trivial, the moment they are fixed in a tangible medium of expression from which they can be read or heard, with or without the aid of a machine or device. Electronic mail certainly appears to fall within this definition and should therefore be entitled to copyright protection the moment it's fixed on some permanent storage medium like a computer's hard disk. Indeed, most people would probably agree that electronic mail should be protected the same way a physical letter is. However, no court has yet ruled on this question.

Assuming electronic mail is protected by copyright, the extent and nature of such protection is far from clear. We discussed a copyright owner's exclusive rights at the beginning of this Chapter. How do they apply to electronic mail? A copyright owner has the exclusive right to reproduce, distribute and create derivative works out of her work. Does this mean that it would be copyright infringement for someone to forward an electronic message received from someone else without permission (violating the sender's exclusive reproduction and distribution rights)? What if an electronic message is modified without the sender's permission? Does this violate the sender's exclusive right to create derivative works from the message? There are no answers to these questions at the moment.

Some electronic mail is intended by the sender to be private; some is public—available to anyone with access to the on-line service, bulletin board or electronic mail system. Are public postings of electronic messages "published" for copyright purposes? The answer to this question has important ramifications. First, unauthorized use of published works is more likely to be considered a fair use than use of unpublished works.

Second, as discussed in Chapter 3, *Copyright Notice*, published works must contain a valid copyright notice or any alleged infringer can claim the infringement was innocent—that is, he didn't know the work was copyrighted. If a court buys such an innocent infringement defense, any damages awarded to the copyright owner may be drastically reduced. This may make it economically unfeasible for the author of an electronic message to file an infringement suit. Copyright notices and warnings contained on status screens when a user logs on to an on-line service or bulletin board may not serve as valid notices for all the messages contained therein. For this reason, authors of valuable electronic messages that are publicly available may wish to include copyright notices in them.

a. Computer conferences

Another problem is that many electronic mail messages are created as a part of computer conferences. Conferencing permits on-line users to communicate with each other on specific topics of mutual interest. Conferencing software on the host computer records the messages so that each participant can read what has been written by others and then add her own responses. Conferences can last a few hours or days, or go on for years. They can be limited to a few participants or be open to anyone with access to the host computer.

What exactly is the copyright status of an electronic mail conference? Are all the messages contained in a single conference a single joint work, a collective work or many separately protected works? These questions are not mere philosophic musings. The answers will determine who owns and controls the copyright in conference messages.

If a conference is viewed as simply a bunch of separately protected works, the copyright in each message will be owned by its author. Each contributor could exercise exclusive copyright rights only over the messages he or she created.

If a conference is a joint work, then it is considered to be a single work for copyright purposes. Each contributor to the conference will be deemed a joint author and own an undivided interest in the copyright. If there were 100 contributors of one message each, each would own a 1/100 interest. Each contributor would have the right to publish the whole conference (subject to accounting to the other joint authors for their pro-rata share of royalties). Each contributor would also be able to sue for infringement of any portion of the conference. See the detailed discussion of joint works in Chapter 8, *Initial Copyright Ownership*.

If a conference is deemed a collective work, each message will be separately protected; but, in addition, someone (it's unclear who) would own the copyright in the collection as a whole. See the detailed discussion of collective works in Chapter 7, *Adaptions and Compilations*.

The question of the size of the work might also be an important factor for fair use. As discussed in Chapter 12, *Using Other Authors' Words*, an important factor for determining fair use is the amount and substantiality of the material used in relation to the work as a whole. If a conference is viewed as a single joint work, taking an entire message would be taking a small part of the whole. But if each message is a separately copyrighted work, taking a whole message would be appropriation of the entire work and it would be more difficult to establish fair use.

Help Beyond This Book

opefully, this book provides a good basic background on most aspects of copyright of interest to writers. Additional general information can be obtained for free from the Copyright Office. The Copyright Office publishes a series of pamphlets (called "circulars") on many copyright topics. Various other publications can be obtained from the Superintendent of Documents of the U.S. Government Printing Office. For a complete list of these publications and ordering information, call the Copyright Office at 202-707-2100 and ask them to send you a copy of "Circular 2: Publications on Copyright." If you don't wish to call, you may write to: Information and Publication Section LM-455, Copyright Office, Library of Congress, Washington, DC 20559.

If you have any questions that aren't answered by this book, a two-step process is suggested. First, take a look at one or more intensive background resources. These may contain all the information you need. If not, access the primary copyright resources: the copyright statutes, regulations and case law.

Cross-Reference

Use *Legal Research: How to Find and Understand the Law*, by Stephen Elias (Nolo Press), or another basic legal research guide, to help you understand legal citations, use a law library and understand what you find there.

A. Intensive Background Resources

Following are some recommended intensive background resources on copyright law. You can find others in your law library's catalog.

The most authoritative source on copyright law is *Nimmer on Copyright*, a four-volume legal treatise written by the late Professor Melville B. Nimmer and updated biannually by his son David, a copyright lawyer. It is published by Matthew Bender. Most public or university law libraries have this treatise. It contains thorough discussions on virtually

every legal issue concerning U.S. and international copyright law.

Each point made by the treatise is supported by exhaustive citations to the relevant legal decisions, sections of the copyright statutes and Copyright Office regulations where appropriate. Volume 4 of *Nimmer* contains a topical index, and a detailed table of contents precedes each chapter. Volume 4 also contains a table of cases and a table of statutes. These can be used to find where *Nimmer* discusses a particular copyright decision, copyright code section or Copyright Office regulation. By using *Nimmer* you can find citations to the primary copyright materials of interest to you. You should note, however, that *Nimmer* discusses only the *law* of copyright. You will find no how to discussions. That's what you bought this book for.

Another treatise is *Copyright Principles, Law and Practice* by Paul Goldstein, a law professor at Stanford University. It is published by Little, Brown and Company. It contains particularly good discussions of copyright infringement and protection of ideas under express and implied contracts and other legal theories.

For the serious copyright student, an excellent one-volume resource is *Copyright for the Nineties* by Robert Gorman and Jane Ginsburg, published by The Michie Company (Charlottesville, VA). This is a legal casebook used to teach law students. It contains the text of virtually every important copyright court decision, the copyright law and other primary materials, excerpts from law review articles, commentary by the authors (nationally recognized authorities on copyright) and other useful materials.

An extensive discussion of copyright law is contained in *American Jurisprudence, Second Series* (Am. Jur.2d) a national legal encyclopedia that can be found in most law libraries. The article on copyright contains a detailed table of contents and the publication contains a subject matter index that you can access by looking under "Copyright."

If you are interested in copyright protection in the United States for works by foreign authors, or protection in other countries for works by Americans, the best starting point for your research is *International Copyright Protection*, edited by David Nimmer and Paul Geller and published by Matthew Bender. Unfortunately, this one-volume treatise does not contain an index.

Copyright Law Reporter. For the most recent information available on copyright, consult the *Copyright Law Reporter*, a weekly loose-leaf service published by Commerce Clearing House (CCH). It contains the full text or summaries of recent copyright-related court decisions and relevant discussions of new developments in copyright law. The first volume of the set contains easy-to-follow instructions on how to use this valuable resource.

Law Review Articles. If you have a very unusual copyright problem that is not covered by *Nimmer* or other books on copyright law, or a problem in an area in which the law has changed very recently, the best sources of available information may be articles appearing in scholarly journals called law reviews. You can find citations to all the law review articles on a particular topic by looking under "Copyright" in the *Index to Legal Periodicals* or *Current Law Index*. A key to the abbreviations used in these indexes is located at the front of each index volume. Substantial collections of law reviews are usually found only in large public law libraries or university libraries.

Forms. If you need sample agreements or other forms, consult *Lindey on Entertainment, Publishing and the Arts* by Alexander Lindey, published by Clark Boardman Co. The first volume of this four-volume work contains sample forms on every aspect of publishing.

B. Primary Source Materials on Copyright

Statutes. The primary law governing all copyrights in the United States after January 1, 1978 is the Copyright Act of 1976. The Copyright Act is located in Title 17 of the United States Code. It can be found either in United States Code Annotated (U.S.C.A.) or United States Code Service, Lawyers Edition (U.S.C.S.). The Act has also been reprinted in Volume 4 of *Nimmer on Copyright* and in the *Copyright Law Reporter*. To find a specific statute, consult either the index at the end of Title 17, or the index at the end of the entire code.

A free copy of the Copyright Act can be obtained by calling the Copyright Office forms hotline at 202-707-9100; ask for "Circular 92."

Regulations. The United States Copyright Office has issued regulations which implement the copyright statutes and establish the procedures which must be followed to register a work. These regulations can be found in Title 17 of the *Code of Federal Regulations* (CFR), a paperback service that is updated annually. The regulations can also be found in the supplement to Title 17 of the U.S.C.A., in Volume 4 of *Nimmer on Copyright* and in the *Copyright Law Reporter*.

Court decisions. There are several ways to find court decisions on a particular legal issue. As mentioned above, intensive background sources such as *Nimmer on Copyright*, the *Copyright Law Reporter* and law review articles contain many case citations. In addition, the United States Code Annotated and United States Code Service both cite and briefly summarize all the decisions relevant to each section of the Copyright Act of 1976. These are located just after each section of the act. You can also find short summaries of copyright law decisions in West Publishing Company's *Federal Practice Digest* under the term "Copyright." The digest contains a detailed table of contents and a very detailed subject matter index at the end of the set.

Case Citations. Throughout the text you'll see citations like this: *Harper & Row Publishers, Inc. v. Nation Enterprises,* 723 F.2d 195 (2d Cir. 1983). This identifies a particular legal decision and tells you where the decision may be found and read. Any case decided by a federal court of appeals is found in a series of books called the *Federal Reporter*. Older cases are contained in the first series of the *Federal*

Reporter or "F.", for short. More recent cases are contained in the second series of the *Federal Reporter*, or "F.2d" for short. To locate the *Harper & Row* case, simply find a law library that has the *Federal Reporter*, Second Series (almost all do), locate volume 723, and turn to page 195.

Opinions by the federal district courts (these are the federal trial courts) are in a series called the Federal Supplement or "F.Supp." For example, 501 F.Supp. 848 (S.D.N.Y. 1980).

Cases decided by the U.S. Supreme Court are found in three publications: United States Reports (identified as "U.S."), the Supreme Court Reporter identified as "S.Ct.") and the Supreme Court Reports, Lawyer's Edition (identified as "L.Ed."). Supreme Court case citations often refer to all three publications; for example, *Harper & Row Publishers, Inc. v. Nation Enterprises,* 471 U.S. 539, 105 S.Ct. 2230, 91 L.Ed. 405 (1985).

⚠ Caution
If you intend to do legal research yourself, be aware that interpreting statutes and cases can be difficult without legal training and a specific background in the area being researched. Before you act on anything you find in the law library, consult with a knowledgeable attorney.

C. Finding a Copyright Lawyer

Copyright law is a highly specialized field and copyright attorneys know the area better than other lawyers. If you don't know of a good copyright attorney, you may be able to find one through your publisher, literary agent or other writers you know. Writers groups are also an excellent source of referrals to copyright attorneys; some of the largest groups are listed below; many more can be found in the publication *Literary Market Place*.

INTELLECTUAL PROPERTY LAWYERS

Copyright is part of a larger specialty known as intellectual property law, which also includes patents and trademarks. Many lawyers who advertise as intellectual property lawyers can competently handle all three types of cases. But some are primarily patent attorneys who don't put much effort into the copyright side of their practice. If you are shopping for a copyright lawyer, do your best to find someone who specializes primarily in copyrights.

I READ A LOT OF BOOKS IN LAWSCHOOL - NO PROBLEM. A CONTRACT'S A CONTRACT. BY THE WAY, HOW LONG IS A COPYRIGHT THESE DAYS?

COPYRIGHT ACT CITATION GUIDE

To avoid numerous footnotes, we have not provided extensive citations to the Copyright Act in the text. Listed below are all the sections of the Copyright Act that have been discussed in this book.

Subject Matter and Scope of Copyright

Sec. 101: Legal definitions of compilation, work made for hire, derivative work and other copyright terms; works covered by Berne Convention

Sec. 102: General definition of what is protected by copyright

Sec. 103: Extent of protection for compilations and derivative works

Sec. 104: Effect of author's national origin; impact of Berne Convention

Sec. 105: No copyright in U.S. government works

Sec. 106: Copyright owners' five exclusive rights

Sec. 107: Fair use privilege

Sec. 108: Photocopying by libraries and archives

Sec. 109: First sale rule

Sec. 110: Performances and displays not constituting infringement

Copyright Ownership and Transfer

Sec. 201: General ownership provisions

Sec. 202: Ownership of copyright distinct from ownership of material object

Sec. 203: Termination of transfers and licenses

Sec. 204: Execution of transfers

Sec. 205: Recordation of transfers

Copyright Duration

Sec. 301: Copyright Act preempts other federal and state laws

Sec. 302: Post–1977 works

Sec. 303: Works created but not published before 1978

Sec. 304: Pre–1978 works

Sec. 305: Year–end termination rule

Notice, Deposit and Registration

Sec. 401: Notice requirements in general

Sec. 403: Notice for works containing U.S. government works

Sec. 404: Notice for contributions to collective works

Sec. 405: Omission of notice

Sec. 406: Error in name or date

Sec. 407: Deposit requirements

Sec. 408–410: Copyright registration

Sec. 411: Registration as prerequisite to infringement suit

Sec. 412: Registration as prerequisite to statutory damages and attorney fees

Copyright Infringement and Remedies

Sec. 501: What constitutes copyright infringement

Sec. 502– 505, Sec. 509: Remedies for infringement

Sec. 506: Criminal liability

Sec. 507: Statute of limitations on infringement suits

In addition, attorneys in many cities through-out the country operate volunteer legal aid groups that help artists and writers resolve their legal problems. These groups usually work like this: you'll generally be asked to pay a small fee ($10 to $50) to be interviewed by a paralegal or other nonattorney volunteer. If your gross household income is below a specified level (the exact amount varies among the legal aid offices), and you have a problem that requires legal assistance, you will be referred to an attorney who will represent you free of charge (except for direct out-of-pocket expenses such as filing fees, photocopying, long-distance phone calls and so forth). However, even if you earn too much to qualify for free legal assistance, these groups should be able to refer you to an experienced copyright attorney.

A state-by-state list of these groups is provided below. You don't have to use the legal aid group located nearest to where you live. If you don't qualify for free assistance from the group nearest you, a group in a different part of the country may have a higher income-eligibility requirement that you're able to meet. California Lawyers for the Arts has no means test at all. The only drawback to using these volunteer groups is that it usually takes about three to five weeks for a volunteer attorney to get around to helping you.

1. Paying an Attorney

If you don't qualify for or are unable to obtain free legal assistance, you'll quickly discover that experts don't come cheap. Most copyright attorneys charge at least $150 per hour. A 1985 survey found that the average cost of trying a copyright infringement suit in New York City ranged from $58,000 to $107,000. Costs may be lower in other parts of the country, but even so, unless you are wealthy and/or own a very valuable work, any copyright infringement action is likely to cost more than you can afford to pay out of your own pocket. However, if your work was timely registered and you win your suit, the judge has discretion to order the defendant to pay your attorney fees. The amount of such an award is completely up to the judge; the only restriction is that the award be reasonable. If you have a good case and the defendant can afford to pay such fees and damages, an attorney might agree to take your case on a contingency basis—that is, collect his fees from any damages or fees that the court ultimately awards if your suit is successful.

What about defendants in copyright infringement suits? If you are sued for infringement and prevail at trial, the judge can order the losing plaintiff to pay all or part of your attorney fees. In the past, many courts would award such fees to a defendant only if they found that the plaintiff's suit was frivolous or brought in bad faith. But these courts would not require this in making fees awards to plaintiffs. In 1994 the Supreme Court held that this approach was incorrect and that fees must be awarded to plaintiffs and defendants in an even-handed manner. In other words, the same criteria must be applied to both plaintiffs and defendants. *Fogerty v. Fantasy, Inc.*, 114 S.Ct. 1023 (1994).

The criteria some courts use to decide whether to award attorney fees to the winning side include whether the losing party's suit was frivolous or brought in bad faith; or whether the losing party otherwise acted unreasonably. Many courts will be especially likely to award fees to a prevailing party whose actions helped to advance the copyright law or defend or establish important legal principles.

Copyright and Contract Information Hotline. The New York Volunteer Lawyers for the Arts operates a hotline that authors and artists may call to obtain answers to questions on copyright and publishing contracts. The phone number is 212-977-9271; call between 9:30 A.M. and 4:30 P.M. Eastern Time, Monday through Friday.

LEGAL AID GROUPS

Arizona

Arizona Volunteer Lawyers for the Arts
2141 East Highland Avenue, #155
Phoenix, AZ 85016
602-956-7000

California

Beverly Hills Bar Association
Barristers Committee for the Arts
300 South Beverly Drive, #201
Beverly Hills, CA 90212
213-553-6644

California Lawyers for the Arts
San Francisco office
Fort Mason Center
Building C, Room 255
San Francisco, CA 94123
415-775-7200

California Lawyers for the Arts
Los Angeles office
315 W. Ninth St., Ste. 1101
Los Angeles, CA 90015
213-623-8311

San Diego Lawyers for the Arts
1205 Prospect St., Ste. 400
La Jolla, CA 92037
619-454-9696

Colorado

Colorado Lawyers for the Arts
P.O. Box 300428
Denver, CO 80203
303-892-7122

Connecticut

Connecticut Volunteer Lawyers for the Arts
277 Lawrence St.
Hartford, CT 06106
203-566-4770

District of Columbia

District of Columbia Lawyers
 Committee for the Arts
Volunteer Lawyers for the Arts, D.C.
918 Sixteenth St. N.W., Ste. 503
Washington, DC 20006
202-429-0220

Washington Area Lawyers for the Arts
1325 G Street—Lower Level
Washington, DC 20005
202-393-2826

Florida

Business Volunteers for the Arts Broward, Inc.
5900 N. Andrews Ave., Ste. 907
Fort Lauderdale, FL 33309
305-771-4131

Business Volunteers for the Arts/Miami
150 W. Flagler St., Ste. 2500
Miami, FL 33130
305-789-3590

Georgia

Georgia Volunteer Lawyers for the Arts
34 Peachtree St. N.W., Ste. 2330
Atlanta, GA 30303
404-525-6046

Illinois

Lawyers for the Creative Arts
213 W. Institute Pl., Ste. 411
Chicago, IL 60610
312-944-ARTS

Kansas

Kansas Register of Lawyers for the Arts
c/o Susan J. Whitfield-Lungren, Esq.
202 S. Second St., P.O. Box 48
Lindsborg, KS 67456
913-227-3575

Kentucky

Arts & Cultural Council
161 N. Mill St.
Lexington, KY 40507
606-255-2951

Fund for the Arts
623 W. Main St.
Louisville, KY 40202
502-582-0100

Louisiana

Louisiana Volunteer Lawyersfor the Arts
c/o Arts Council of New Orleans
821 Gravier St., Ste. 600
New Orleans, LA 70112
504-523-1465

Maine

Maine Volunteer Lawyers for the Arts
Maine Arts Commission
55 Capitol St.
State House Station 25
Augusta, ME 04333
207-289-2724

Maryland

Maryland Lawyers for the Arts
The Belvedere Hotel
One E. Chast St., Ste. 1118
Baltimore, MD 21202-2526
301-752-1633

Massachusetts

Arts Extension Service
University of Massachusetts
Division of Continuing Education
Amherst, MA 01003
413-545-2360

Volunteer Lawyers for the Arts of
   Massachusetts, Inc.
8 Park Plaza, Rm. 2240
Boston, MA 02116
617-523-1764

Minnesota

Minnesota Volunteer Lawyers for the Arts
c/o Fred Rosenblatt, Esq., Pres.
150 S. 5th St., Ste. 2300
Minneapolis, MN 55402
612-335-1500

Resources and Counseling for the Arts
429 Landmark Center
75 West 5th St.
St. Paul, MN 55102
612-292-3206

Missouri

St. Louis Volunteer Lawyers & Accountants
   for the Arts
3540 Washington Ave.
St. Louis, MO 63103
314-652-2410

Montana

Montana Volunteer Lawyers
    for the Arts
c/o Joan Jonkel, Esq.
P.O. Box 59807
Missoula, MT 59807
406-721-1835

New Jersey

Volunteer Lawyers for the Arts
    of New Jersey
15 Roszel Rd.
Princeton, NJ 08540
609-951-0800

New York

Volunteer Lawyers for the Arts
1285 Avenue of the Americas, 3rd Floor
New York, NY 10019
212-977-9271

Volunteer Lawyers for the
    Arts Program
Albany League of Arts
19 Clinton Ave.
Albany, NY 12207
518-449-5380

Huntington Arts Council
213 Main St.
Huntington, NY 11743
516-271-8423

North Carolina

North Carolina Volunteer Lawyers
    for the Arts
P.O. Box 831
Raleigh, NC 27601
919-755-2100

Ohio

Volunteer Lawyers and Accountants
    for the Arts
c/o Cleveland Bar Association
113 St. Clair Ave.
Cleveland, OH 44114-1253
216-696-3525

Toledo Volunteer Lawyers for the Arts
421-A N. Michigan St.
Toledo, OH 43624
419-243-3125

Oklahoma

Oklahoma Accountants and Lawyers
    for the Arts
3000 Pershing Blvd.
Oklahoma City, OK 73107
405-948-6400

Oregon

Northwest Lawyers and Artists, Inc.
330 Pacific Building
520 Yamhill
Portland, OR 97204
503-224-1901

Pennsylvania

Philadelphia Volunteer Lawyers for the Arts
251 S. 18th St.
Philadelphia, PA 19103
215-545-3385

Rhode Island

Ocean State Lawyers for the Arts
P.O. Box 19
Saunderstown, RI 02874
401-789-5686

South Dakota

South Dakota Arts Council
108 W. Eleventh St.
Sioux Falls, SD 57102-0788
605-339-6646

Texas

Austin Lawyers and Accountants
   for the Arts
P.O. Box 2577
Austin, TX 78768
512-476-7573

Texas Accountants and Lawyers
   for the Arts
5151 Belt Line Rd., #1005
Dallas, TX 75240
214-701-8275

Texas Accountants and Lawyers
   for the Arts
1540 Sul Ross
Houston, TX 77006
713-526-4876

Utah

Utah Lawyers for the Arts
570 S. Main St., #1600
Salt Lake City, UT 84144
801-482-5373

Washington

Washington Lawyers for the Arts
1331 Third Ave., #512
Seattle, WA 98101
206-223-0502

Writers' Groups

American Society of Journalists and Authors
1501 Broadway, Ste. 1907
New York, NY 10036
212-997-0947

The Author's Guild
243 W. 44th St.
New York, NY 10036
212-398-0838

The Dramatists Guild
234 W. 34th St.
New York, NY 10036
212-398-9366

The Freelance Editorial Association
Box 835
Cambridge, MA 02238
617-729-8164

National Writers Union
13 Astor Place, 7th Floor
New York, NY 10003
212-254-0279

The Society of Professional Journalists
53 W. Jackson Blvd., Ste. 731
Chicago, IL 60604
317-653-3333

Writers Guild of America East
555 W. 57th St.
New York, NY 10019
212-245-6180

Writers Guild of America West
8955 Beverly Blvd.
West Hollywood, CA 90048
213-550-1000

Appendix

Sample Forms

1. Single unpublished work (a novel); single author

2. Single published work; single author; photos registered separately by photographer

3. Single published work; five joint authors; publisher acquired all copyrights

4. Single work made for hire; previously published under another title and revised; a derivative work

5. Published book; derivative work based on previously published article; joint authors: one the author of the text, the other the photographer; text and photos registered together as a single unit of publication

6. Single published work; publisher acquired all rights in text; text and work for hire cover art and copy registered together as a single unit of publication

7. Published compilation (anthology); publisher registers for the authors

8. Single author; contribution to collective work

9. Group of contributions to periodicals in a 12-month period; a single author

10. Original screenplay by a single author

11. Unpublished song lyric; single author

12. Three monthly issues of a monthly magazine registered as a group on Form SE/Group

13. Single magazine issue

14. Single issue of a magazine published three times a year; single author; not a work made for hire

Blank Forms

- Form TX

- Form PA

- Form SE

- Short Form SE

- Form SE/Group

- Form G/DN

- Form VA

- Request for Special Handling

- Form TX/CON (Continuation Sheet for Form TX)

- Form _____ /CON (Continuation Sheet for Application Forms)

- Form CA

- Form GR/CP (Adjunction Application for Copyright Registration for a Group of Contributions to Periodicals)

- Search Request Form

- Document Cover Sheet

FORM TX
UNITED STATES COPYRIGHT OFFICE

REGISTRATION NUMBER

TX   TXU

EFFECTIVE DATE OF REGISTRATION

Month   Day   Year

DO NOT WRITE ABOVE THIS LINE. IF YOU NEED MORE SPACE, USE A SEPARATE CONTINUATION SHEET.

1 TITLE OF THIS WORK ▼

A Fish Story

PREVIOUS OR ALTERNATIVE TITLES ▼

PUBLICATION AS A CONTRIBUTION If this work was published as a contribution to a periodical, serial, or collection, give information about the
collective work in which the contribution appeared.   Title of Collective Work ▼

If published in a periodical or serial give: Volume ▼   Number ▼   Issue Date ▼   On Pages ▼

2 NAME OF AUTHOR ▼
a Felix Flounder

Was this contribution to the work a
"work made for hire"?
☐ Yes
☒ No

AUTHOR'S NATIONALITY OR DOMICILE
Name of Country
OR { Citizen of ▶ U.S.A.
     Domiciled in ▶

DATES OF BIRTH AND DEATH
Year Born ▼ Year Died ▼
1955

WAS THIS AUTHOR'S CONTRIBUTION TO
THE WORK
Anonymous?   ☐ Yes ☒ No
Pseudonymous? ☐ Yes ☒ No
If the answer to either
of these questions is
"Yes," see detailed
instructions.

NATURE OF AUTHORSHIP Briefly describe nature of the material created by this author in which copyright is claimed. ▼
Entire text of unpublished novel

NOTE
Under the law, the "author" of a "work made for hire" is generally the employer, not the employee (see instructions). For any part of this work that was "made for hire" check "Yes" in the space provided, give the employer (or other person for whom the work was prepared) as "Author" of that part, and leave the space for dates of birth and death blank.

NAME OF AUTHOR ▼
b

Was this contribution to the work a
"work made for hire"?
☐ Yes
☐ No

AUTHOR'S NATIONALITY OR DOMICILE
Name of country
OR { Citizen of ▶
     Domiciled in ▶

DATES OF BIRTH AND DEATH
Year Born ▼ Year Died ▼

WAS THIS AUTHOR'S CONTRIBUTION TO
THE WORK
Anonymous?   ☐ Yes ☐ No
Pseudonymous? ☐ Yes ☐ No
If the answer to either
of these questions is
"Yes," see detailed
instructions.

NATURE OF AUTHORSHIP Briefly describe nature of the material created by this author in which copyright is claimed. ▼

NAME OF AUTHOR ▼
c

Was this contribution to the work a
"work made for hire"?
☐ Yes
☐ No

AUTHOR'S NATIONALITY OR DOMICILE
Name of country
OR { Citizen of ▶
     Domiciled in ▶

DATES OF BIRTH AND DEATH
Year Born ▼ Year Died ▼

WAS THIS AUTHOR'S CONTRIBUTION TO
THE WORK
Anonymous?   ☐ Yes ☐ No
Pseudonymous? ☐ Yes ☐ No
If the answer to either
of these questions is
"Yes," see detailed
instructions.

NATURE OF AUTHORSHIP Briefly describe nature of the material created by this author in which copyright is claimed. ▼

3 YEAR IN WHICH CREATION OF THIS
a WORK WAS COMPLETED This information
  1992   ◀ Year must be given
             in all cases.

DATE AND NATION OF FIRST PUBLICATION OF THIS PARTICULAR WORK
b Complete this information Month ▶   Day ▶   Year ▶
   ONLY if this work
   has been published.   ◀ Nation

4 COPYRIGHT CLAIMANT(S) Name and address must be given even if the claimant is the
same as the author given in space 2. ▼
Felix Flounder
1000 Bonito Way
Tampa, FL 10000

APPLICATION RECEIVED

ONE DEPOSIT RECEIVED

TWO DEPOSITS RECEIVED

REMITTANCE NUMBER AND DATE

TRANSFER If the claimant(s) named here in space 4 are different from the author(s) named
in space 2, give a brief statement of how the claimant(s) obtained ownership of the copyright. ▼

MORE ON BACK ▶   • Complete all applicable spaces (numbers 5-11) on the reverse side of this page.
                 • See detailed instructions.   • Sign the form at line 10.

DO NOT WRITE HERE
Page 1 of ____ pages

(continuation side)

EXAMINED BY

CHECKED BY

☐ CORRESPONDENCE
  Yes

FOR
COPYRIGHT
OFFICE
USE
ONLY

FORM TX

DO NOT WRITE ABOVE THIS LINE. IF YOU NEED MORE SPACE, USE A SEPARATE CONTINUATION SHEET.

5 PREVIOUS REGISTRATION Has registration for this work, or for an earlier version of this work, already been made in the Copyright Office?
☐ Yes ☒ No If your answer is "Yes," why is another registration being sought? (Check appropriate box) ▼
☐ This is the first published edition of a work previously registered in unpublished form.
☐ This is the first application submitted by this author as copyright claimant.
☐ This is a changed version of the work, as shown by space 6 on this application.
If your answer is "Yes," give: Previous Registration Number ▼   Year of Registration ▼

6 DERIVATIVE WORK OR COMPILATION Complete both space 6a & 6b for a derivative work; complete only 6b for a compilation.
a. Preexisting Material Identify any preexisting work or works that this work is based on or incorporates. ▼

b. Material Added to This Work Give a brief, general statement of the material that has been added to this work and in which copyright is claimed. ▼

7 — space deleted —

8 REPRODUCTION FOR USE OF BLIND OR PHYSICALLY HANDICAPPED INDIVIDUALS   A signature on this form at space 10, and a
check in one of the boxes here in space 8, constitutes a non-exclusive grant of permission to the Library of Congress to reproduce and distribute solely for the blind
and physically handicapped and under the conditions and limitations prescribed by the regulations of the Copyright Office: (1) copies of the work identified in space
1 of this application in Braille (or similar tactile symbols); or (2) phonorecords embodying a fixation of a reading of that work; or (3) both.
a ☒ Copies and Phonorecords   b ☐ Copies Only   c ☐ Phonorecords Only

9 DEPOSIT ACCOUNT If the registration fee is to be charged to a Deposit Account established in the Copyright Office, give name and number of Account.
Name ▼   Account Number ▼

CORRESPONDENCE Give name and address to which correspondence about this application should be sent.   Name/Address/Apt/City/State/Zip ▼
Felix Flounder
1000 Bonito Way
Tampa, FL 10000
                              Area Code & Telephone Number ▶ (813) 123-4567

10 CERTIFICATION* I, the undersigned, hereby certify that I am the
Check one ▶
☒ author
☐ other copyright claimant
☐ owner of exclusive right(s)
☐ authorized agent of
  Name of author or other copyright claimant, or owner of exclusive right(s) ▲

of the work identified in this application and that the statements made
by me in this application are correct to the best of my knowledge.

Typed or printed name and date ▼ If this application gives a date of publication in space 3, do not sign and submit it before that date.
Felix Flounder   date ▶ May 1, 1992

Handwritten signature (X) ▼

11 MAIL
CERTIFI-
CATE TO

Name ▼
Felix Flounder
Number/Street/Apartment Number ▼
1000 Bonito Way
City/State/ZIP ▼
Tampa, FL 10000

Certificate
will be
mailed in
window
envelope

• Complete all necessary spaces
• Sign your application in space 10

SEND ALL 3 ELEMENTS
IN THE SAME PACKAGE:
1. Application form
2. Nonrefundable $20 filing fee
   in check or money order
   payable to Register of Copyrights
3. Deposit material

Register of Copyrights
Library of Congress
Washington, D.C. 20559

* 17 U.S.C. § 506(e): Any person who knowingly makes a false representation of a material fact in the application for copyright registration provided for by section 409, or in any written statement filed in
connection with the application, shall be fined not more than $2,500.

February 1991—200,000   ☆U.S. GOVERNMENT PRINTING OFFICE: 1991—282-170/20,010

FORM TX
UNITED STATES COPYRIGHT OFFICE

REGISTRATION NUMBER

TX   TXU

EFFECTIVE DATE OF REGISTRATION

Month   Day   Year

DO NOT WRITE ABOVE THIS LINE. IF YOU NEED MORE SPACE, USE A SEPARATE CONTINUATION SHEET

1 TITLE OF THIS WORK ▼

All About Everything

PREVIOUS OR ALTERNATIVE TITLES ▼

PUBLICATION AS A CONTRIBUTION If this work was published as a contribution to a periodical, serial, or collection, give information about the collective work in which the contribution appeared. Title of Collective Work ▼

If published in a periodical or serial give: Volume ▼   Number ▼   Issue Date ▼   On Pages ▼

2 NAME OF AUTHOR ▼

a Jane Doe

DATES OF BIRTH AND DEATH
Year Born ▼ 1955   Year Died ▼

Was this contribution to the work a "work made for hire"?
☐ Yes ☒ No

AUTHOR'S NATIONALITY OR DOMICILE
Name of country
OR { Citizen of ▶ U.S.A.
{ Domiciled in ▶

WAS THIS AUTHOR'S CONTRIBUTION TO THE WORK
Anonymous? ☐ Yes ☒ No
Pseudonymous? ☐ Yes ☒ No
If the answer to either of these questions is "Yes," see detailed instructions.

NATURE OF AUTHORSHIP Briefly describe nature of the material created by this author in which copyright is claimed. ▼
Entire Text

NOTE
Under the law, the "author" of a "work made for hire" is generally the employer, not the employee (see instructions). For any part of this work that was "made for hire" check "Yes" in the space provided, give the employer (or other person for whom the work was prepared) as "Author" of that part, and leave the space for dates of birth and death blank.

NAME OF AUTHOR ▼

b

DATES OF BIRTH AND DEATH
Year Born ▼   Year Died ▼

Was this contribution to the work a "work made for hire"?
☐ Yes ☐ No

AUTHOR'S NATIONALITY OR DOMICILE
Name of country
OR { Citizen of ▶
{ Domiciled in ▶

WAS THIS AUTHOR'S CONTRIBUTION TO THE WORK
Anonymous? ☐ Yes ☐ No
Pseudonymous? ☐ Yes ☐ No

NATURE OF AUTHORSHIP Briefly describe nature of the material created by this author in which copyright is claimed. ▼

NAME OF AUTHOR ▼

c

DATES OF BIRTH AND DEATH
Year Born ▼   Year Died ▼

Was this contribution to the work a "work made for hire"?
☐ Yes ☐ No

AUTHOR'S NATIONALITY OR DOMICILE
Name of country
OR { Citizen of ▶
{ Domiciled in ▶

WAS THIS AUTHOR'S CONTRIBUTION TO THE WORK
Anonymous? ☐ Yes ☐ No
Pseudonymous? ☐ Yes ☐ No

NATURE OF AUTHORSHIP Briefly describe nature of the material created by this author in which copyright is claimed. ▼

3 YEAR IN WHICH CREATION OF THIS WORK WAS COMPLETED This information must be given Year 1992 ◄ in all cases.

DATE AND NATION OF FIRST PUBLICATION OF THIS PARTICULAR WORK
Complete this information ONLY if this work has been published. Month ▶ May Day ▶ 1 Year ▶ 1992 Nation ▶ U.S.A.

4 COPYRIGHT CLAIMANT(S) Name and address must be given even if the claimant is the same as the author given in space 2.▼

Jane Doe
123 Any Street
Anytown, KS 30000

APPLICATION RECEIVED

ONE DEPOSIT RECEIVED

TWO DEPOSITS RECEIVED

REMITTANCE NUMBER AND DATE

TRANSFER If the claimant(s) named here in space 4 are different from the author(s) named in space 2, give a brief statement of how the claimant(s) obtained ownership of the copyright.▼

MORE ON BACK ▶ • Complete all applicable spaces (numbers 5-11) on the reverse side of this page.
• See detailed instructions. • Sign the form at line 10.

DO NOT WRITE HERE
Page 1 of ____ pages

DO NOT WRITE ABOVE THIS LINE. IF YOU NEED MORE SPACE, USE A SEPARATE CONTINUATION SHEET.

5 PREVIOUS REGISTRATION Has registration for this work, or for an earlier version of this work, already been made in the Copyright Office?
☐ Yes ☒ No If your answer is "Yes," why is another registration being sought? (Check appropriate box) ▼
☐ This is the first published edition of a work previously registered in unpublished form.
☐ This is the first application submitted by this author as copyright claimant.
☐ This is a changed version of the work, as shown by space 6 on this application.
If your answer is "Yes," give: Previous Registration Number ▼   Year of Registration ▼

6 DERIVATIVE WORK OR COMPILATION Complete both space 6a & 6b for a derivative work; complete only 6b for a compilation.
a. Preexisting Material Identify any preexisting work or works that this work is based on or incorporates. ▼

b. Material Added to This Work Give a brief, general statement of the material that has been added to this work and in which copyright is claimed. ▼

—space deleted—

7

8 REPRODUCTION FOR USE OF BLIND OR PHYSICALLY HANDICAPPED INDIVIDUALS A signature on this form at space 10, and a check in one of the boxes here in space 8, constitutes a non-exclusive grant of permission to the Library of Congress to reproduce and distribute solely for the blind and physically handicapped and under the conditions and limitations prescribed by the regulations of the Copyright Office: (1) copies of the work identified in space 1 of this application in Braille (or similar tactile symbols); or (2) phonorecords embodying a fixation of a reading of that work; or (3) both.
a ☒ Copies and Phonorecords   b ☐ Copies Only   c ☐ Phonorecords Only

9 DEPOSIT ACCOUNT If the registration fee is to be charged to a Deposit Account established in the Copyright Office, give name and number of Account.
Name ▼   Account Number ▼

CORRESPONDENCE Give name and address to which correspondence about this application should be sent. Name/Address/Apt/City/State/Zip ▼
Jane Doe
123 Any St.
Anytown, KS 30000

Area Code & Telephone Number ▶ (913) 123-4567

10 CERTIFICATION* I, the undersigned, hereby certify that I am the
Check one { ☒ author
{ ☐ other copyright claimant
{ ☐ owner of exclusive right(s)
{ ☐ authorized agent of ____
Name of author or other copyright claimant, or owner of exclusive right(s) ▲
of the work identified in this application and that the statements made by me in this application are correct to the best of my knowledge.

Typed or printed name and date ▼ If this application gives a date of publication in space 3, do not sign and submit it before that date.
Jane Doe   date ▶ July 1, 1992

Handwritten signature (X) ▼
Jane Doe

11 MAIL CERTIFICATE TO
Name ▼
Jane Doe
Number/Street/Apartment Number ▼
123 Any St.
City/State/ZIP ▼
Anytown, KS 30000

Certificate will be mailed in window envelope

SEND ALL 3 ELEMENTS IN THE SAME PACKAGE:
• Complete all necessary spaces
• Sign your application in space 10
1. Application form
2. Nonrefundable $20 filing fee in check or money order payable to Register of Copyrights
3. Deposit material
MAIL TO:
Register of Copyrights
Library of Congress
Washington, D.C. 20559

FOR COPYRIGHT OFFICE USE ONLY

EXAMINED BY

CHECKED BY

CORRESPONDENCE
☐ Yes

DO NOT WRITE HERE

* 17 U.S.C. § 506(e): Any person who knowingly makes a false representation of a material fact in the application for copyright registration provided for by section 409, or in any written statement filed in connection with the application, shall be fined not more than $2,500.

February 1991—200,000   ☆U.S. GOVERNMENT PRINTING OFFICE: 1991—282-170/20,010

FORM VA

UNITED STATES COPYRIGHT OFFICE

REGISTRATION NUMBER

VA   VAU

EFFECTIVE DATE OF REGISTRATION

Month   Day   Year

DO NOT WRITE ABOVE THIS LINE. IF YOU NEED MORE SPACE, USE A SEPARATE CONTINUATION SHEET.

1

TITLE OF THIS WORK ▼

All About Everything

PREVIOUS OR ALTERNATIVE TITLES ▼

NATURE OF THIS WORK ▼ See instructions

Photographs

PUBLICATION AS A CONTRIBUTION If this work was published as a contribution to a periodical, serial, or collection, give information about the collective work in which the contribution appeared. **Title of Collective Work ▼**

If published in a periodical or serial give: **Volume ▼**   **Number ▼**   **Issue Date ▼**   **On Pages ▼**

2

a   **NAME OF AUTHOR ▼**

Mike Minolta

Was this contribution to the work a "work made for hire"?
☐ Yes
☒ No

AUTHOR'S NATIONALITY OR DOMICILE
Name of Country
OR { Citizen of ▶ U.S.A.
     Domiciled in ▶

DATES OF BIRTH AND DEATH
Year Born ▼ Year Died ▼
1940

WAS THIS AUTHOR'S CONTRIBUTION TO THE WORK
Anonymous?   ☐ Yes ☒ No
Pseudonymous? ☐ Yes ☒ No
If the answer to either of these questions is "Yes," see detailed instructions.

NATURE OF AUTHORSHIP Check appropriate boxes(es). **See Instructions**
☐ 3-Dimensional sculpture   ☐ Map   ☐ Technical drawing
☐ 2-Dimensional artwork   ☒ Photograph   ☐ Text
☐ Reproduction of work of art ☐ Jewelry design ☐ Architectural work
☐ Design on sheetlike material

NOTE
Under the law, the "author" of a "work made for hire" is generally the employer, not the employee (see instructions). For any part of this work that was "made for hire" check "Yes" in the space provided, give the employer (or other person for whom the work was prepared) as "Author" of that part, and leave the space for dates of birth and death blank.

b   **NAME OF AUTHOR ▼**

Was this contribution to the work a "work made for hire"?
☐ Yes
☐ No

AUTHOR'S NATIONALITY OR DOMICILE
Name of Country
OR { Citizen of ▶
     Domiciled in ▶

DATES OF BIRTH AND DEATH
Year Born ▼ Year Died ▼

WAS THIS AUTHOR'S CONTRIBUTION TO THE WORK
Anonymous?   ☐ Yes ☐ No
Pseudonymous? ☐ Yes ☐ No
If the answer to either of these questions is "Yes," see detailed instructions.

NATURE OF AUTHORSHIP Check appropriate boxes(es). See instructions
☐ 3-Dimensional sculpture   ☐ Map   ☐ Technical drawing
☐ 2-Dimensional artwork   ☐ Photograph   ☐ Text
☐ Reproduction of work of art ☐ Jewelry design ☐ Architectural work
☐ Design on sheetlike material

3

a **YEAR IN WHICH CREATION OF THIS WORK WAS COMPLETED** This information must be given ◀Year in all cases.
1992

b **DATE AND NATION OF FIRST PUBLICATION OF THIS PARTICULAR WORK** Complete this information ONLY if this work has been published.
Month ▶ May   Day ▶ 1   Year ▶ 1992
Nation ▶ U.S.A.

4

COPYRIGHT CLAIMANT(S) Name and address must be given even if the claimant is the same as the author given in space 2. ▼

Mike Minolta
100 Grant St.
Chicago, IL 50000

TRANSFER If the claimant(s) named here in space 4 are different from the author(s) named in space 2, give a brief statement of how the claimant(s) obtained ownership of the copyright. ▼

See instructions before completing this space.

DO NOT WRITE HERE

OFFICE USE ONLY	
APPLICATION RECEIVED	
ONE DEPOSIT RECEIVED	
TWO DEPOSITS RECEIVED	
REMITTANCE NUMBER AND DATE	

MORE ON BACK ▶ • Complete all applicable spaces (numbers 5-9) on the reverse side of this page.
• See detailed instructions.   • Sign the form at line 8.

DO NOT WRITE HERE

Page 1 of ____ pages

FORM VA

EXAMINED BY

CHECKED BY

CORRESPONDENCE
☐ Yes

FOR COPYRIGHT OFFICE USE ONLY

DO NOT WRITE ABOVE THIS LINE. IF YOU NEED MORE SPACE, USE A SEPARATE CONTINUATION SHEET.

5

PREVIOUS REGISTRATION Has registration for this work, or for an earlier version of this work, already been made in the Copyright Office?
☐ Yes ☒ No   If your answer is "Yes," why is another registration being sought? (Check appropriate box) ▼
a. ☐ This is the first published edition of a work previously registered in unpublished form.
b. ☐ This is the first application submitted by this author as copyright claimant.
c. ☐ This is a changed version of the work, as shown by space 6 on this application.
If your answer is "Yes," give: **Previous Registration Number ▼**   **Year of Registration ▼**

6

DERIVATIVE WORK OR COMPILATION Complete both space 6a & 6b for a derivative work; complete only 6b for a compilation.
a. **Preexisting Material** Identify any preexisting work or works that this work is based on or incorporates. ▼

b. **Material Added to This Work** Give a brief, general statement of the material that has been added to this work and in which copyright is claimed. ▼

See instructions before completing this space.

7

DEPOSIT ACCOUNT If the registration fee is to be charged to a Deposit Account established in the Copyright Office, give name and number of Account.
Name ▼   **Account Number ▼**

CORRESPONDENCE Give name and address to which correspondence about this application should be sent.   Name/Address/Apt/City/State/Zip ▼

Mike Minolta
100 Grant St.
Chicago, IL 50000

Area Code & Telephone Number ▶

8

CERTIFICATION* I, the undersigned, hereby certify that I am the
Check only one ▼
☒ author
☐ other copyright claimant
☐ owner of exclusive right(s)
☐ authorized agent of _____
Name of author or other copyright claimant, or owner of exclusive right(s) ▲

of the work identified in this application and that the statements made by me in this application are correct to the best of my knowledge.

Typed or printed name and date ▼ If this application gives a date of publication in space 3, do not sign and submit it before that date.
Mike Minolta   date ▶ July 1, 1992

Handwritten signature (X) ▼
Mike Minolta

Be sure to give your daytime phone number ▼

9

MAIL CERTIFICATE TO

Certificate will be mailed in window envelope

Name ▼
Mike Minolta
Number/Street/Apartment Number ▼
100 Grant St.
City/State/ZIP ▼
Chicago, IL 50000

• Complete all necessary spaces
• Sign your application in space 8

SEND ALL 3 ELEMENTS IN THE SAME PACKAGE:
1. Application form
2. Nonrefundable $20 filing fee in check or money order payable to Register of Copyrights
3. Deposit material

Register of Copyrights
Library of Congress
Washington, D.C. 20559

*17 U.S.C. § 506(e): Any person who knowingly makes a false representation of a material fact in the application for copyright registration provided for by section 409, or in any written statement filed in connection with the application, shall be fined not more than $2,500.

May 1991—150,000   ☆U.S. GOVERNMENT PRINTING OFFICE: 1991-282-170/20,018

FORM TX
UNITED STATES COPYRIGHT OFFICE

REGISTRATION NUMBER

TX ___ TXU

EFFECTIVE DATE OF REGISTRATION

Month ___ Day ___ Year

DO NOT WRITE ABOVE THIS LINE. IF YOU NEED MORE SPACE, USE A SEPARATE CONTINUATION SHEET.

1 TITLE OF THIS WORK ▼

The History of Music

PREVIOUS OR ALTERNATIVE TITLES ▼

PUBLICATION AS A CONTRIBUTION If this work was published as a contribution to a periodical, serial, or collection, give information about the collective work in which the contribution appeared.   Title of Collective Work ▼

If published in a periodical or serial give: Volume ▼   Number ▼   Issue Date ▼   On Pages ▼

2 NAME OF AUTHOR ▼
a Peter Piccolo

Was this contribution to the work a "work made for hire"?
☐ Yes   ☒ No

DATES OF BIRTH AND DEATH
Year Born ▼ 1940   Year Died ▼

AUTHOR'S NATIONALITY OR DOMICILE
Name of Country
OR { Citizen of ▶ U.S.A.
Domiciled in ▶

WAS THIS AUTHOR'S CONTRIBUTION TO THE WORK
Anonymous?   ☐ Yes   ☒ No
Pseudonymous?   ☐ Yes   ☒ No
If the answer to either of these questions is "Yes," see detailed instructions.

NATURE OF AUTHORSHIP Briefly describe nature of the material created by this author in which copyright is claimed. ▼
Wrote chapters 1-4

NOTE
Under the law, the "author" of a "work made for hire" is generally the employer, not the employee (see instructions). For any part of this work that was "made for hire" check "Yes" in the space provided, give the employer (or other person for whom the work was prepared) as "Author" of that part, and leave the space for dates of birth and death blank.

NAME OF AUTHOR ▼
b Vicky Viola

Was this contribution to the work a "work made for hire"?
☐ Yes   ☒ No

DATES OF BIRTH AND DEATH
Year Born ▼ 1950   Year Died ▼

AUTHOR'S NATIONALITY OR DOMICILE
Name of Country
OR { Citizen of ▶ U.S.A.
Domiciled in ▶

WAS THIS AUTHOR'S CONTRIBUTION TO THE WORK
Anonymous?   ☐ Yes   ☒ No
Pseudonymous?   ☐ Yes   ☒ No
If the answer to either of these questions is "Yes," see detailed instructions.

NATURE OF AUTHORSHIP Briefly describe nature of the material created by this author in which copyright is claimed. ▼
Wrote chapters 5-10

NAME OF AUTHOR ▼
c Mary Maestro

Was this contribution to the work a "work made for hire"?
☐ Yes   ☒ No

DATES OF BIRTH AND DEATH
Year Born ▼ 1960   Year Died ▼

AUTHOR'S NATIONALITY OR DOMICILE
Name of Country
OR { Citizen of ▶ U.S.A.
Domiciled in ▶

WAS THIS AUTHOR'S CONTRIBUTION TO THE WORK
Anonymous?   ☐ Yes   ☒ No
Pseudonymous?   ☐ Yes   ☒ No
If the answer to either of these questions is "Yes," see detailed instructions.

NATURE OF AUTHORSHIP Briefly describe nature of the material created by this author in which copyright is claimed. ▼
Wrote chapters 11-15

3a YEAR IN WHICH CREATION OF THIS WORK WAS COMPLETED This information must be given ONLY if this work has been published.
1992 ◀ Year   In all cases.

b DATE AND NATION OF FIRST PUBLICATION OF THIS PARTICULAR WORK
Month ▶ April   Day ▶ 15   Year ▶ 1992
U.S.A. ◀ Nation

4 COPYRIGHT CLAIMANT(S) Name and address must be given even if the claimant is the same as the author given in space 2. ▼
Scrivener & Sons Publishing Co., Inc
12345 Park Ave.
New York, N.Y. 10000

TRANSFER If the claimant(s) named here in space 4 are different from the author(s) named in space 2, give a brief statement of how the claimant(s) obtained ownership of the copyright. ▼
By written contract

APPLICATION RECEIVED
ONE DEPOSIT RECEIVED
TWO DEPOSITS RECEIVED
REMITTANCE NUMBER AND DATE

DO NOT WRITE HERE
OFFICE USE ONLY

MORE ON BACK ▶ • Complete all applicable spaces (numbers 5-11) on the reverse side of this page.
• See detailed instructions.   • Sign the form at line 10.

DO NOT WRITE HERE
Page 1 of ___ pages

FOR COPYRIGHT OFFICE USE ONLY

EXAMINED BY
CHECKED BY
☐ CORRESPONDENCE Yes

FORM TX

DO NOT WRITE ABOVE THIS LINE. IF YOU NEED MORE SPACE, USE A SEPARATE CONTINUATION SHEET.

5 PREVIOUS REGISTRATION Has registration for this work, or for an earlier version of this work, already been made in the Copyright Office?
☐ Yes   ☒ No If your answer is "Yes," why is another registration being sought? (Check appropriate box) ▼
☐ This is the first published edition of a work previously registered in unpublished form.
☐ This is the first application submitted by this author as copyright claimant.
☐ This is a changed version of the work, as shown by space 6 on this application.
If your answer is "Yes," give: Previous Registration Number ▼   Year of Registration ▼

6 DERIVATIVE WORK OR COMPILATION Complete both space 6a & 6b for a derivative work; complete only 6b for a compilation.
a. Preexisting Material Identify any preexisting work or works that this work is based on or incorporates. ▼

b. Material Added to This Work Give a brief, general statement of the material that has been added to this work and in which copyright is claimed. ▼

7 —space deleted—

8 REPRODUCTION FOR USE OF BLIND OR PHYSICALLY HANDICAPPED INDIVIDUALS A signature on this form at space 10, and a check in one of the boxes here in space 8, constitutes a non-exclusive grant of permission to the Library of Congress to reproduce and distribute solely for the blind and physically handicapped and under the conditions and limitations prescribed by the regulations of the Copyright Office: (1) copies of the work identified in space 1 of this application in Braille (or similar tactile symbols); or (2) phonorecords embodying a fixation of a reading of that work; or (3) both.
a ☒ Copies and Phonorecords   b ☐ Copies Only   c ☐ Phonorecords Only

9 DEPOSIT ACCOUNT If the registration fee is to be charged to a Deposit Account established in the Copyright Office, give name and number of Account.
Name ▼   Account Number ▼

CORRESPONDENCE Give name and address to which correspondence about this application should be sent.   Name/Address/Apt/City/State/Zip ▼
Scrivener & Sons Publishing Co., Inc.
12345 Park Ave.
New York, N.Y. 10000
Area Code & Telephone Number ▶ (212) 123-4567

10 CERTIFICATION* I, the undersigned, hereby certify that I am the
Check one ▶
☐ author
☐ other copyright claimant
☐ owner of exclusive right(s)
☒ authorized agent of Scrivener & Sons Publishing
Name of author or other copyright claimant, or owner of exclusive right(s) ▲

of the work identified in this application and that the statements made by me in this application are correct to the best of my knowledge.

Typed or printed name and date ▼ If this application gives a date of publication in space 3, do not sign and submit it before that date.
Maxwell Perkins   date ▶ May 1, 1992

Handwritten signature (X) ▼

11 MAIL CERTIFICATE TO
Name ▼
Scrivener & Sons Publishing Co.
Number/Street/Apartment Number ▼
12345 Park Ave.
City/State/ZIP ▼
New York, N.Y. 10000

Certificate will be mailed in window envelope

• Complete all necessary spaces
• Sign your application in space 10

SEND ALL 3 ELEMENTS IN THE SAME PACKAGE
1. Application form
2. Nonrefundable $20 filing fee in check or money order payable to Register of Copyrights
3. Deposit material

MAIL TO:
Register of Copyrights
Library of Congress
Washington, D.C. 20559

* 17 U.S.C. § 506(e): Any person who knowingly makes a false representation of a material fact in the application for copyright registration provided for by section 409, or in any written statement filed in connection with the application, shall be fined not more than $2,500.

February 1991—200,000   ☆U.S. GOVERNMENT PRINTING OFFICE: 1991—282-170/20,010

CONTINUATION SHEET FOR FORM TX

FORM TX/CON
UNITED STATES COPYRIGHT OFFICE

- If at all possible, try to fit the information called for into the spaces provided on Form TX.
- If you do not have space enough for all of the information you need to give on Form TX, use this continuation sheet and submit it with Form TX.
- If you submit this continuation sheet, clip (do not tape or staple) it to Form TX and fold the two together before submitting it.
- **PART A** of this sheet is intended to identify the basic application. **PART B** is a continuation of Space 2. **PART C** (on the reverse side of this sheet) is for the continuation of Spaces 1, 4, 6, or 7. The other spaces on Form TX call for specific items of information, and should not need continuation.

REGISTRATION NUMBER

| TX | TXU |

EFFECTIVE DATE OF REGISTRATION

(Month) (Day) (Year)

CONTINUATION SHEET RECEIVED

Page _____ of _____ pages

(A) **Identification of Application**

IDENTIFICATION OF CONTINUATION SHEET: This sheet is a continuation of the application for copyright registration on Form TX, submitted for the following work:

- **TITLE:** (Give the title as given under the heading "Title of this Work" in Space 1 of Form TX.)
  The History of Music

- **NAME(S) AND ADDRESS(ES) OF COPYRIGHT CLAIMANT(S):** (Give the name and address of at least one copyright claimant as given in Space 4 of Form TX.)
  Scrivener & Son Publishing Co., 12345 Park Ave., New York, NY 10000

(B) **Continuation of Space 2**

☒ **NAME OF AUTHOR:** Ted Timpani

DATES OF BIRTH AND DEATH:
Born 1955 Died _____
(Year) (Year)

Was this author's contribution to the work a "work made for hire"? Yes _____ No X

AUTHOR'S NATIONALITY OR DOMICILE:
Citizen of U.S.A. } or { Domiciled in _____
(Name of Country) (Name of Country)

WAS THIS AUTHOR'S CONTRIBUTION TO THE WORK:
Anonymous? Yes _____ No X
Pseudonymous? Yes _____ No X
If the answer to either of these questions is "Yes," see detailed instructions attached.

AUTHOR OF: (Briefly describe nature of this author's contribution)
Chapter 16

☒ **NAME OF AUTHOR:** George Eastman

DATES OF BIRTH AND DEATH:
Born 1945 Died _____
(Year) (Year)

Was this author's contribution to the work a "work made for hire"? Yes _____ No X

AUTHOR'S NATIONALITY OR DOMICILE:
Citizen of U.S.A. } or { Domiciled in _____
(Name of Country) (Name of Country)

WAS THIS AUTHOR'S CONTRIBUTION TO THE WORK:
Anonymous? Yes _____ No X
Pseudonymous? Yes _____ No X
If the answer to either of these questions is "Yes," see detailed instructions attached.

AUTHOR OF: (Briefly describe nature of this author's contribution)
Illustrations

☐ **NAME OF AUTHOR:**

DATES OF BIRTH AND DEATH:
Born _____ Died _____
(Year) (Year)

Was this author's contribution to the work a "work made for hire"? Yes _____ No _____

AUTHOR'S NATIONALITY OR DOMICILE:
Citizen of _____ } or { Domiciled in _____
(Name of Country) (Name of Country)

WAS THIS AUTHOR'S CONTRIBUTION TO THE WORK:
Anonymous? Yes _____ No _____
Pseudonymous? Yes _____ No _____
If the answer to either of these questions is "Yes," see detailed instructions attached.

AUTHOR OF: (Briefly describe nature of this author's contribution)

☐ **NAME OF AUTHOR:**

DATES OF BIRTH AND DEATH:
Born _____ Died _____
(Year) (Year)

Was this author's contribution to the work a "work made for hire"? Yes _____ No _____

AUTHOR'S NATIONALITY OR DOMICILE:
Citizen of _____ } or { Domiciled in _____
(Name of Country) (Name of Country)

WAS THIS AUTHOR'S CONTRIBUTION TO THE WORK:
Anonymous? Yes _____ No _____
Pseudonymous? Yes _____ No _____
If the answer to either of these questions is "Yes," see detailed instructions attached.

AUTHOR OF: (Briefly describe nature of this author's contribution)

☐ **NAME OF AUTHOR:**

DATES OF BIRTH AND DEATH:
Born _____ Died _____
(Year) (Year)

Was this author's contribution to the work a "work made for hire"? Yes _____ No _____

AUTHOR'S NATIONALITY OR DOMICILE:
Citizen of _____ } or { Domiciled in _____
(Name of Country) (Name of Country)

WAS THIS AUTHOR'S CONTRIBUTION TO THE WORK:
Anonymous? Yes _____ No _____
Pseudonymous? Yes _____ No _____
If the answer to either of these questions is "Yes," see detailed instructions attached.

AUTHOR OF: (Briefly describe nature of this author's contribution)

Use the reverse side of this sheet if you need more space for:
- *Further continuation of Space 2*
- *Continuation of Spaces 1, 4, 6, or 7 of Form TX*

(B) **Continuation of Space 2**

☐ **NAME OF AUTHOR:**

DATES OF BIRTH AND DEATH:
Born _____ Died _____
(Year) (Year)

Was this author's contribution to the work a "work made for hire"? Yes _____ No _____

AUTHOR'S NATIONALITY OR DOMICILE:
Citizen of _____ } or { Domiciled in _____
(Name of Country) (Name of Country)

WAS THIS AUTHOR'S CONTRIBUTION TO THE WORK:
Anonymous? Yes _____ No _____
Pseudonymous? Yes _____ No _____
If the answer to either of these questions is "Yes," see detailed instructions attached.

AUTHOR OF: (Briefly describe nature of this author's contribution)

☐ **NAME OF AUTHOR:**

DATES OF BIRTH AND DEATH:
Born _____ Died _____
(Year) (Year)

Was this author's contribution to the work a "work made for hire"? Yes _____ No _____

AUTHOR'S NATIONALITY OR DOMICILE:
Citizen of _____ } or { Domiciled in _____
(Name of Country) (Name of Country)

WAS THIS AUTHOR'S CONTRIBUTION TO THE WORK:
Anonymous? Yes _____ No _____
Pseudonymous? Yes _____ No _____
If the answer to either of these questions is "Yes," see detailed instructions attached.

AUTHOR OF: (Briefly describe nature of this author's contribution)

☐ **NAME OF AUTHOR:**

DATES OF BIRTH AND DEATH:
Born _____ Died _____
(Year) (Year)

Was this author's contribution to the work a "work made for hire"? Yes _____ No _____

AUTHOR'S NATIONALITY OR DOMICILE:
Citizen of _____ } or { Domiciled in _____
(Name of Country) (Name of Country)

WAS THIS AUTHOR'S CONTRIBUTION TO THE WORK:
Anonymous? Yes _____ No _____
Pseudonymous? Yes _____ No _____
If the answer to either of these questions is "Yes," see detailed instructions attached.

AUTHOR OF: (Briefly describe nature of this author's contribution)

☐ **NAME OF AUTHOR:**

DATES OF BIRTH AND DEATH:
Born _____ Died _____
(Year) (Year)

Was this author's contribution to the work a "work made for hire"? Yes _____ No _____

AUTHOR'S NATIONALITY OR DOMICILE:
Citizen of _____ } or { Domiciled in _____
(Name of Country) (Name of Country)

WAS THIS AUTHOR'S CONTRIBUTION TO THE WORK:
Anonymous? Yes _____ No _____
Pseudonymous? Yes _____ No _____
If the answer to either of these questions is "Yes," see detailed instructions attached.

AUTHOR OF: (Briefly describe nature of this author's contribution)

(C) **Continuation of other Spaces**

CONTINUATION OF (Check which): ☐ Space 1 ☐ Space 4 ☐ Space 6 ☐ Space 7

August 1987—12,000

☆U.S. GOVERNMENT PRINTING OFFICE: 1987:181—531/60,008

FORM TX
UNITED STATES COPYRIGHT OFFICE

REGISTRATION NUMBER

TX   TXU

EFFECTIVE DATE OF REGISTRATION

Month   Day   Year

DO NOT WRITE ABOVE THIS LINE. IF YOU NEED MORE SPACE, USE A SEPARATE CONTINUATION SHEET.

1
TITLE OF THIS WORK ▼
What Is DOS?

PREVIOUS OR ALTERNATIVE TITLES ▼
DOS For Everyone

PUBLICATION AS A CONTRIBUTION If this work was published as a contribution to a periodical, serial, or collection, give information about the collective work in which the contribution appeared. Title of Collective Work ▼

If published in a periodical or serial give: Volume ▼   Number ▼   Issue Date ▼   On Pages ▼

2
NAME OF AUTHOR ▼
a Acme Press

Was this contribution to the work a "work made for hire"?
☒ Yes
☐ No

AUTHOR'S NATIONALITY OR DOMICILE
Name of Country
OR { Citizen of ▶ U.S.A.
Domiciled in ▶

DATES OF BIRTH AND DEATH
Year Born ▼   Year Died ▼

WAS THIS AUTHOR'S CONTRIBUTION TO THE WORK
Anonymous?   ☐ Yes ☒ No
Pseudonymous? ☐ Yes ☒ No
If the answer to either of these questions is "Yes," see detailed instructions.

NATURE OF AUTHORSHIP Briefly describe nature of the material created by this author in which copyright is claimed. ▼
Entire text

NAME OF AUTHOR ▼
b

Was this contribution to the work a "work made for hire"?
☐ Yes
☐ No

AUTHOR'S NATIONALITY OR DOMICILE
Name of Country
OR { Citizen of ▶
Domiciled in ▶

DATES OF BIRTH AND DEATH
Year Born ▼   Year Died ▼

WAS THIS AUTHOR'S CONTRIBUTION TO THE WORK
Anonymous?   ☐ Yes ☐ No
Pseudonymous? ☐ Yes ☐ No
If the answer to either of these questions is "Yes," see detailed instructions.

NATURE OF AUTHORSHIP Briefly describe nature of the material created by this author in which copyright is claimed. ▼

NAME OF AUTHOR ▼
c

Was this contribution to the work a "work made for hire"?
☐ Yes
☐ No

AUTHOR'S NATIONALITY OR DOMICILE
Name of Country
OR { Citizen of ▶
Domiciled in ▶

DATES OF BIRTH AND DEATH
Year Born ▼   Year Died ▼

WAS THIS AUTHOR'S CONTRIBUTION TO THE WORK
Anonymous?   ☐ Yes ☐ No
Pseudonymous? ☐ Yes ☐ No
If the answer to either of these questions is "Yes," see detailed instructions.

NATURE OF AUTHORSHIP Briefly describe nature of the material created by this author in which copyright is claimed. ▼

NOTE
Under the law, the "author" of a "work made for hire" is generally the employer, not the employee (see instructions). For any part of this work that was "made for hire" check "Yes" in the space provided, give the employer (or other person for whom the work was prepared) as "Author" of that part, and leave the space for dates of birth and death blank.

3
YEAR IN WHICH CREATION OF THIS WORK WAS COMPLETED This information must be given in all cases.
1992 ◀ Year

DATE AND NATION OF FIRST PUBLICATION OF THIS PARTICULAR WORK
Complete this information ONLY if this work has been published.
Month ▶ April Day ▶ 15 Year ▶ 1992
Nation ▶ U.S.A.

4
COPYRIGHT CLAIMANT(S) Name and address must be given even if the claimant is the same as the author given in space 2.▼
Acme Press
1234 Computer Rd.
Silicon Valley, CA 90000

APPLICATION RECEIVED

ONE DEPOSIT RECEIVED

TWO DEPOSITS RECEIVED

REMITTANCE NUMBER AND DATE

DO NOT WRITE HERE
OFFICE USE ONLY

TRANSFER If the claimant(s) named here in space 4 are different from the author(s) named in space 2, give a brief statement of how the claimant(s) obtained ownership of the copyright. ▼

MORE ON BACK ▶ • Complete all applicable spaces (numbers 5–11) on the reverse side of this page.
• See detailed instructions.   • Sign the form at line 10.

DO NOT WRITE HERE
Page 1 of _____ pages

EXAMINED BY

CHECKED BY

☐ CORRESPONDENCE
Yes

FOR
COPYRIGHT
OFFICE
USE
ONLY

FORM TX

DO NOT WRITE ABOVE THIS LINE. IF YOU NEED MORE SPACE, USE A SEPARATE CONTINUATION SHEET.

5
PREVIOUS REGISTRATION Has registration for this work, or for an earlier version of this work, already been made in the Copyright Office?
☒ Yes ☐ No If your answer is "Yes," why is another registration being sought? (Check appropriate box) ▼
☐ This is the first published edition of a work previously registered in unpublished form.
☐ This is the first application submitted by this author as copyright claimant.
☒ This is a changed version of the work, as shown by space 6 on this application.
If your answer is "Yes," give: Previous Registration Number ▼ Year of Registration ▼
TX-123456   1990

6
DERIVATIVE WORK OR COMPILATION Complete both space 6a & 6b for a derivative work; complete only 6b for a compilation.
a. Preexisting Material Identify any preexisting work or works that this work is based on or incorporates. ▼
First edition of work, published under title "Dos For Everyone"

b. Material Added to This Work Give a brief, general statement of the material that has been added to this work and in which copyright is claimed. ▼
Revised chapters 1-8, chapter 9 entirely new

7
—space deleted—

8
REPRODUCTION FOR USE OF BLIND OR PHYSICALLY HANDICAPPED INDIVIDUALS A signature on this form at space 10, and a check in one of the boxes here in space 8, constitutes a non-exclusive grant of permission to the Library of Congress to reproduce and distribute solely for the blind and physically handicapped and under the conditions and limitations prescribed by the regulations of the Copyright Office: (1) copies of the work identified in space 1 of this application in Braille (or similar tactile symbols); or (2) phonorecords embodying a fixation of a reading of that work; or (3) both.
a ☒ Copies and Phonorecords   b ☐ Copies Only   c ☐ Phonorecords Only

9
DEPOSIT ACCOUNT If the registration fee is to be charged to a Deposit Account established in the Copyright Office, give name and number of Account.
Name ▼   Account Number ▼

CORRESPONDENCE Give name and address to which correspondence about this application should be sent. Name/Address/Apt/City/State/Zip ▼
Acme Press
1234 Computer Rd.
Silicon Valley, CA 90000
Area Code & Telephone Number ▶ (510) 123-4567

10
CERTIFICATION* I, the undersigned, hereby certify that I am the
Check one ▶
☐ author
☐ other copyright claimant
☐ owner of exclusive right(s)
☒ authorized agent of Acme Press
Name of author or other copyright claimant, or owner of exclusive right(s) ▲

of the work identified in this application and that the statements made by me in this application are correct to the best of my knowledge.

Typed or printed name and date ▼ If this application gives a date of publication in space 3, do not sign and submit it before that date.
Susan Succubus   date ▶ May 1, 1992

Handwritten signature (X) ▼

11
MAIL CERTIFICATE TO
Certificate will be mailed in window envelope

Name ▼
Acme Press
Number/Street/Apartment Number ▼
1234 Computer Rd.
City/State/ZIP ▼
Silicon Valley, CA 90000

• Complete all necessary spaces
• Sign your application in space 10

SEND ALL ELEMENTS IN THE SAME PACKAGE
1. Application form
2. Nonrefundable $20 filing fee in check or money order payable to Register of Copyrights
3. Deposit material

Register of Copyrights
Library of Congress
Washington, D.C. 20559

*17 U.S.C. § 506(e): Any person who knowingly makes a false representation of a material fact in the application for copyright registration provided for by section 409, or in any written statement filed in connection with the application, shall be fined not more than $2,500.

February 1991—200,000   ☆U.S. GOVERNMENT PRINTING OFFICE: 1991—282-170/20,010

FORM TX
UNITED STATES COPYRIGHT OFFICE

REGISTRATION NUMBER

TX   TXU

EFFECTIVE DATE OF REGISTRATION

Month   Day   Year

DO NOT WRITE ABOVE THIS LINE. IF YOU NEED MORE SPACE, USE A SEPARATE CONTINUATION SHEET.

1 TITLE OF THIS WORK ▼

The Sex Life of the Gnu

PREVIOUS OR ALTERNATIVE TITLES ▼

What the Gnu Knew

PUBLICATION AS A CONTRIBUTION If this work was published as a contribution to a periodical, serial, or collection, give information about the collective work in which the contribution appeared.   Title of Collective Work ▼

If published in a periodical or serial give: Volume ▼   Number ▼   Issue Date ▼   On Pages ▼

2 NAME OF AUTHOR ▼
a   Nastassia Kinsey

Was this contribution to the work a "work made for hire"? □ Yes ☒ No

AUTHOR'S NATIONALITY OR DOMICILE
Name of Country
Citizen of ▶ U.S.A.
Domiciled in ▶

DATES OF BIRTH AND DEATH
Year Born ▼ 1960   Year Died ▼

WAS THIS AUTHOR'S CONTRIBUTION TO THE WORK
Anonymous? □ Yes ☒ No
Pseudonymous? □ Yes ☒ No
If the answer to either of these questions is "Yes," see detailed instructions.

NATURE OF AUTHORSHIP Briefly describe nature of the material created by this author in which copyright is claimed. ▼
Entire text

NAME OF AUTHOR ▼
b   George Eastman

Was this contribution to the work a "work made for hire"? □ Yes ☒ No

AUTHOR'S NATIONALITY OR DOMICILE
Name of Country
Citizen of ▶ U.S.A.
Domiciled in ▶

DATES OF BIRTH AND DEATH
Year Born ▼ 1950   Year Died ▼

WAS THIS AUTHOR'S CONTRIBUTION TO THE WORK
Anonymous? □ Yes ☒ No
Pseudonymous? □ Yes ☒ No

NATURE OF AUTHORSHIP Briefly describe nature of the material created by this author in which copyright is claimed. ▼
Photographs

NAME OF AUTHOR ▼
c

Was this contribution to the work a "work made for hire"? □ Yes □ No

AUTHOR'S NATIONALITY OR DOMICILE
Name of Country
Citizen of ▶
Domiciled in ▶

DATES OF BIRTH AND DEATH
Year Born ▼   Year Died ▼

WAS THIS AUTHOR'S CONTRIBUTION TO THE WORK
Anonymous? □ Yes □ No
Pseudonymous? □ Yes □ No

NATURE OF AUTHORSHIP Briefly describe nature of the material created by this author in which copyright is claimed. ▼

3 YEAR IN WHICH CREATION OF THIS WORK WAS COMPLETED
This information must be given in all cases.
1992 ◀ Year

DATE AND NATION OF FIRST PUBLICATION OF THIS PARTICULAR WORK
Complete this information ONLY if this work has been published.
Month ▶ May   Day ▶ 1   Year ▶ 1992
Nation ▶ U.S.A.

4 COPYRIGHT CLAIMANT(S) Name and address must be given even if the claimant is the same as the author given in space 2. ▼
Nastassia Kinsey
100 Tenth St.
New York, NY 10000

George Eastman
123 Kodak St.
Rochester, NY 12345

APPLICATION RECEIVED

ONE DEPOSIT RECEIVED

TWO DEPOSITS RECEIVED

REMITTANCE NUMBER AND DATE

DO NOT WRITE HERE   OFFICE USE ONLY

TRANSFER If the claimant(s) named here in space 4 are different from the author(s) named in space 2, give a brief statement of how the claimant(s) obtained ownership of the copyright. ▼

MORE ON BACK ▶
• Complete all applicable spaces (numbers 5-11) on the reverse side of this page.
• See detailed instructions.
• Sign the form at line 10.

DO NOT WRITE HERE   Page 1 of ____ pages

EXAMINED BY

CHECKED BY

□ CORRESPONDENCE Yes

FORM TX

FOR COPYRIGHT OFFICE USE ONLY

DO NOT WRITE ABOVE THIS LINE. IF YOU NEED MORE SPACE, USE A SEPARATE CONTINUATION SHEET.

5 PREVIOUS REGISTRATION Has registration for this work, or for an earlier version of this work, already been made in the Copyright Office?
□ Yes ☒ No If your answer is "Yes," why is another registration being sought? (Check appropriate box) ▼
□ a. This is the first published edition of a work previously registered in unpublished form.
□ b. This is the first application submitted by this author as copyright claimant.
□ c. This is a changed version of the work, as shown by space 6 on this application.
If your answer is "Yes," give: Previous Registration Number ▼   Year of Registration ▼

6 DERIVATIVE WORK OR COMPILATION Complete both space 6a & 6b for a derivative work; complete only 6b for a compilation.
a. Preexisting Material Identify any preexisting work or works that this work is based on or incorporates. ▼
What the Gnu Knew (an article in International Geographic, vol. 60, no. 1)

b. Material Added to This Work Give a brief, general statement of the material that has been added to this work and in which copyright is claimed. ▼
Text has been substantially revised and expanded, 50 new photographs

—space deleted—

8 REPRODUCTION FOR USE OF BLIND OR PHYSICALLY HANDICAPPED INDIVIDUALS   A signature on this form at space 10, and a check in one of the boxes here in space 8, constitutes a non-exclusive grant of permission to the Library of Congress to reproduce and distribute solely for the blind and physically handicapped and under the conditions and limitations prescribed by the regulations of the Copyright Office: (1) copies of the work identified in space 1 of this application in Braille (or similar tactile symbols); or (2) phonorecords embodying a fixation of a reading of that work; or (3) both.
a □ Copies and Phonorecords   b □ Copies Only   c □ Phonorecords Only

9 DEPOSIT ACCOUNT If the registration fee is to be charged to a Deposit Account established in the Copyright Office, give name and number of Account.
Name ▼   Account Number ▼

CORRESPONDENCE Give name and address to which correspondence about this application should be sent.   Name/Address/Apt/City/State/Zip ▼
Nastassia Kinsey and George Eastman
100 Tenth St.
New York, NY 10000
Area Code & Telephone Number ▶ (212) 123-4567

10 CERTIFICATION* I, the undersigned, hereby certify that I am the
Check one ▶
☒ author
□ other copyright claimant
□ owner of exclusive right(s)
□ authorized agent of _____
Name of author or other copyright claimant, or owner of exclusive right(s) ▲

of the work identified in this application and that the statements made by me in this application are correct to the best of my knowledge.

Typed or printed name and date ▼ If this application gives a date of publication in space 3, do not sign and submit it before that date.
Nastassia Kinsey   date ▶ June 1, 1992

Handwritten signature (X) ▼
Nastassia Kinsey

11 MAIL CERTIFI-CATE TO
Name ▼
Nastassia Kinsey
Number/Street/Apartment Number ▼
100 Tenth St.
City/State/ZIP ▼
New York, NY 10000

Certificate will be mailed in window envelope

• Complete all necessary spaces
• Sign your application in space 10

1. Application form
2. Nonrefundable $20 filing fee in check or money order payable to Register of Copyrights
3. Deposit material

MAIL TO
Register of Copyrights
Library of Congress
Washington, D.C. 20559

* 17 U.S.C. § 506(e): Any person who knowingly makes a false representation of a material fact in the application for copyright registration provided for by section 409, or in any written statement filed in connection with the application, shall be fined not more than $2,500.

February 1991—200,000   ☆U.S. GOVERNMENT PRINTING OFFICE: 1991—282-170/20,010

FORM TX
UNITED STATES COPYRIGHT OFFICE

REGISTRATION NUMBER

TX   TXU

EFFECTIVE DATE OF REGISTRATION

Month   Day   Year

DO NOT WRITE ABOVE THIS LINE. IF YOU NEED MORE SPACE, USE A SEPARATE CONTINUATION SHEET.

1 TITLE OF THIS WORK ▼

The Plagiarist's Handbook

PREVIOUS OR ALTERNATIVE TITLES ▼

PUBLICATION AS A CONTRIBUTION If this work was published as a contribution to a periodical, serial, or collection, give information about the collective work in which the contribution appeared.   Title of Collective Work ▼

If published in a periodical or serial give: Volume ▼   Number ▼   Issue Date ▼   On Pages ▼

2 NAME OF AUTHOR ▼

a Charles C. Copycat

DATES OF BIRTH AND DEATH
Year Born ▼ 1955   Year Died ▼

Was this contribution to the work a
"work made for hire"?
☐ Yes
☒ No

AUTHOR'S NATIONALITY OR DOMICILE
Name of Country
OR { Citizen of ▶ U.S.A.
     { Domiciled in ▶

WAS THIS AUTHOR'S CONTRIBUTION TO THE WORK
Anonymous? ☐ Yes ☒ No
Pseudonymous? ☐ Yes ☒ No
If the answer to either of these questions is "Yes," see detailed instructions.

NATURE OF AUTHORSHIP Briefly describe nature of the material created by this author in which copyright is claimed. ▼

Entire text

NOTE

Under the law, the "author" of a "work made for hire" is generally the employer, not the employee (see instructions). For any part of this work that was "made for hire" check "Yes" in the space provided, give the employer (or other person for whom the work was prepared) as "Author" of that part, and leave the space for dates of birth and death blank.

NAME OF AUTHOR ▼

b Acme Press

DATES OF BIRTH AND DEATH
Year Born ▼   Year Died ▼

Was this contribution to the work a
"work made for hire"?
☒ Yes
☐ No

AUTHOR'S NATIONALITY OR DOMICILE
Name of Country
OR { Citizen of ▶ U.S.A.
     { Domiciled in ▶

WAS THIS AUTHOR'S CONTRIBUTION TO THE WORK
Anonymous? ☐ Yes ☒ No
Pseudonymous? ☐ Yes ☒ No
If the answer to either of these questions is "Yes," see detailed instructions.

NATURE OF AUTHORSHIP Briefly describe nature of the material created by this author in which copyright is claimed. ▼

Cover artwork and copy

NAME OF AUTHOR ▼

c

DATES OF BIRTH AND DEATH
Year Born ▼   Year Died ▼

Was this contribution to the work a
"work made for hire"?
☐ Yes
☐ No

AUTHOR'S NATIONALITY OR DOMICILE
Name of Country
OR { Citizen of ▶
     { Domiciled in ▶

WAS THIS AUTHOR'S CONTRIBUTION TO THE WORK
Anonymous? ☐ Yes ☐ No
Pseudonymous? ☐ Yes ☐ No
If the answer to either of these questions is "Yes," see detailed instructions.

NATURE OF AUTHORSHIP Briefly describe nature of the material created by this author in which copyright is claimed. ▼

3 YEAR IN WHICH CREATION OF THIS WORK WAS COMPLETED This information must be given in all cases.
a 1992 ◀ Year

DATE AND NATION OF FIRST PUBLICATION OF THIS PARTICULAR WORK
Complete this information Month ▶ May Day ▶ 1 Year ▶ 1992
ONLY if this work has been published.
b Nation ▶ U.S.A.

4 COPYRIGHT CLAIMANT(S) Name and address must be given even if the claimant is the same as the author given in space 2 ▼

Acme Press
1000 Summit Drive
Phoenix, AZ 80000

APPLICATION RECEIVED

ONE DEPOSIT RECEIVED

TWO DEPOSITS RECEIVED

REMITTANCE NUMBER AND DATE

DO NOT WRITE HERE

OFFICE USE ONLY

TRANSFER If the claimant(s) named here in space 4 are different from the author(s) named in space 2, give a brief statement of how the claimant(s) obtained ownership of the copyright. ▼

Written transfer of all right, title and interest

MORE ON BACK ▶ • Complete all applicable spaces (numbers 5-11) on the reverse side of this page.
• See detailed instructions.
• Sign the form at line 10.

See instructions before completing this space.

Page 1 of ___ pages

FORM TX

FOR COPYRIGHT OFFICE USE ONLY

EXAMINED BY

CHECKED BY

☐ CORRESPONDENCE
  Yes

DO NOT WRITE ABOVE THIS LINE. IF YOU NEED MORE SPACE, USE A SEPARATE CONTINUATION SHEET.

5 PREVIOUS REGISTRATION Has registration for this work, or for an earlier version of this work, already been made in the Copyright Office?
☐ Yes ☒ No If your answer is "Yes," why is another registration being sought? (Check appropriate box) ▼
☐ This is the first published edition of a work previously registered in unpublished form.
☐ This is the first application submitted by this author as copyright claimant.
☐ This is a changed version of the work, as shown by space 6 on this application.
If your answer is "Yes," give: Previous Registration Number ▼   Year of Registration ▼

6 DERIVATIVE WORK OR COMPILATION Complete both space 6a & 6b for a derivative work; complete only 6b for a compilation.
a. Preexisting Material Identify any preexisting work or works that this work is based on or incorporates. ▼

b. Material Added to This Work Give a brief, general statement of the material that has been added to this work and in which copyright is claimed. ▼

See instructions before completing this space.

7 —space deleted—

8 REPRODUCTION FOR USE OF BLIND OR PHYSICALLY HANDICAPPED INDIVIDUALS   A signature on this form at space 10, and a check in one of the boxes here in space 8, constitutes a non-exclusive grant of permission to the Library of Congress to reproduce and distribute solely for the blind and physically handicapped and under the conditions and limitations prescribed by the regulations of the Copyright Office: (1) copies of the work identified in space 1 of this application in Braille (or similar tactile symbols); or (2) phonorecords embodying a fixation of a reading of that work; or (3) both.
a ☒ Copies and Phonorecords   b ☐ Copies Only   c ☐ Phonorecords Only   See instructions.

9 DEPOSIT ACCOUNT If the registration fee is to be charged to a Deposit Account established in the Copyright Office, give name and number of Account.
Name ▼   Account Number ▼

CORRESPONDENCE Give name and address to which correspondence about this application should be sent. Name/Address/Apt/City/State/Zip ▼

Acme Press
1000 Summit Drive
Phoenix, AZ 80000

Area Code & Telephone Number ▶ (602) 666-6666

Be sure to give your daytime phone ▼ number

10 CERTIFICATION* I, the undersigned, hereby certify that I am the
Check one ▶
☐ author
☐ other copyright claimant
☐ owner of exclusive right(s)
☒ authorized agent of   Acme Press
                          Name of author or other copyright claimant, or owner of exclusive right(s) ▲

of the work identified in this application and that the statements made by me in this application are correct to the best of my knowledge.

Typed or printed name and date ▼ If this application gives a date of publication in space 3, do not sign and submit it before that date.

Chandler Bartlett   date ▶ July 1, 1992

Handwritten signature (X) ▼

Chandler Bartlett

11 MAIL CERTIFI-CATE TO

Name ▼
Acme Press
Number/Street/Apartment Number ▼
1000 Summit Drive
City/State/ZIP ▼
Phoenix, AZ 80000

Certificate will be mailed in window envelope

• Complete all necessary spaces
• Sign your application in space 10

SEND ALL 3 ELEMENTS IN THE SAME PACKAGE:
1. Application form
2. Nonrefundable $20 filing fee in check or money order payable to Register of Copyrights
3. Deposit material

MAIL TO: Register of Copyrights
Library of Congress
Washington, D.C. 20559

February 1991—200,000   ☆U.S. GOVERNMENT PRINTING OFFICE: 1991—282-170/20,010

FORM TX
UNITED STATES COPYRIGHT OFFICE

REGISTRATION NUMBER

TX   TXU

EFFECTIVE DATE OF REGISTRATION

Month   Day   Year

DO NOT WRITE ABOVE THIS LINE. IF YOU NEED MORE SPACE, USE A SEPARATE CONTINUATION SHEET.

1 TITLE OF THIS WORK ▼

The Best Short Stories of 1992

PREVIOUS OR ALTERNATIVE TITLES ▼

PUBLICATION AS A CONTRIBUTION If this work was published as a contribution to a periodical, serial, or collection, give information about the collective work in which the contribution appeared.   Title of Collective Work ▼

If published in a periodical or serial give: Volume ▼   Number ▼   Issue Date ▼   On Pages ▼

2 NAME OF AUTHOR ▼

a Alan Allenby

DATES OF BIRTH AND DEATH
Year Born ▼ 1950   Year Died ▼

Was this contribution to the work a "work made for hire"?
☐ Yes
☒ No

AUTHOR'S NATIONALITY OR DOMICILE
Name of Country
OR { Citizen of ▶ U.S.A.
Domiciled in ▶

WAS THIS AUTHOR'S CONTRIBUTION TO THE WORK
Anonymous? ☐ Yes ☒ No
Pseudonymous? ☐ Yes ☒ No
If the answer to either of these questions is "Yes," see detailed instructions.

NOTE
Under the law, the "author" of a "work made for hire" is generally the employer, not the employee (see instructions). For any part of this work that was "made for hire" check "Yes" in the space provided, give the employer (or other person for whom the work was prepared) as "Author" of that part, and leave the space for dates of birth and death blank.

NATURE OF AUTHORSHIP Briefly describe nature of the material created by this author in which copyright is claimed. ▼
Anthology of previously published short stories

b NAME OF AUTHOR ▼

DATES OF BIRTH AND DEATH
Year Born ▼   Year Died ▼

Was this contribution to the work a "work made for hire"?
☐ Yes
☐ No

AUTHOR'S NATIONALITY OR DOMICILE
Name of Country
OR { Citizen of ▶
Domiciled in ▶

WAS THIS AUTHOR'S CONTRIBUTION TO THE WORK
Anonymous? ☐ Yes ☐ No
Pseudonymous? ☐ Yes ☐ No
If the answer to either of these questions is "Yes," see detailed instructions.

NATURE OF AUTHORSHIP Briefly describe nature of the material created by this author in which copyright is claimed. ▼

c NAME OF AUTHOR ▼

DATES OF BIRTH AND DEATH
Year Born ▼   Year Died ▼

Was this contribution to the work a "work made for hire"?
☐ Yes
☐ No

AUTHOR'S NATIONALITY OR DOMICILE
Name of Country
OR { Citizen of ▶
Domiciled in ▶

WAS THIS AUTHOR'S CONTRIBUTION TO THE WORK
Anonymous? ☐ Yes ☐ No
Pseudonymous? ☐ Yes ☐ No
If the answer to either of these questions is "Yes," see detailed instructions.

NATURE OF AUTHORSHIP Briefly describe nature of the material created by this author in which copyright is claimed. ▼

3 YEAR IN WHICH CREATION OF THIS WORK WAS COMPLETED This information must be given in all cases.
a 1992 ◀ Year

DATE AND NATION OF FIRST PUBLICATION OF THIS PARTICULAR WORK
Complete this information ONLY if this work has been published.
b Month ▶ May   Day ▶ 1   Year ▶ 1992
U.S.A. ◀ Nation

4 COPYRIGHT CLAIMANT(S) Name and address must be given even if the claimant is the same as the author given in space 2.▼

Allen Allenby
1000 Allen Street
Allentown, PA 20000

TRANSFER If the claimant(s) named here in space 4 are different from the author(s) named in space 2, give a brief statement of how the claimant(s) obtained ownership of the copyright. ▼

APPLICATION RECEIVED

ONE DEPOSIT RECEIVED

TWO DEPOSITS RECEIVED

REMITTANCE NUMBER AND DATE

DO NOT WRITE HERE
OFFICE USE ONLY

MORE ON BACK ▶ • Complete all applicable spaces (numbers 5-11) on the reverse side of this page.
• See detailed instructions.   • Sign the form at line 10.

DO NOT WRITE HERE
Page 1 of ____ pages

FORM TX

EXAMINED BY

CHECKED BY

CORRESPONDENCE
☐ Yes

FOR COPYRIGHT OFFICE USE ONLY

DO NOT WRITE ABOVE THIS LINE. IF YOU NEED MORE SPACE, USE A SEPARATE CONTINUATION SHEET.

5 PREVIOUS REGISTRATION Has registration for this work, or for an earlier version of this work, already been made in the Copyright Office?
☐ Yes ☐ No If your answer is "Yes," why is another registration being sought? (Check appropriate box) ▼
☐ This is the first published edition of a work previously registered in unpublished form.
☐ This is the first application submitted by this author as copyright claimant.
☐ This is a changed version of the work, as shown by space 6 on this application.
If your answer is "Yes," give: Previous Registration Number ▼   Year of Registration ▼

6 DERIVATIVE WORK OR COMPILATION Complete both space 6a & 6b for a derivative work; complete only 6b for a compilation.
a. Preexisting Material Identify any preexisting work or works that this work is based on or incorporates. ▼

b. Material Added to This Work Give a brief, general statement of the material that has been added to this work and in which copyright is claimed. ▼
Anthology of previously published short stories

7 — space deleted —

8 REPRODUCTION FOR USE OF BLIND OR PHYSICALLY HANDICAPPED INDIVIDUALS   A signature on this form at space 10, and a check in one of the boxes here in space 8, constitutes a non-exclusive grant of permission to the Library of Congress to reproduce and distribute solely for the blind and physically handicapped and under the conditions and limitations prescribed by the regulations of the Copyright Office: (1) copies of the work identified in space 1 of this application in Braille (or similar tactile symbols); or (2) phonorecords embodying a fixation of a reading of that work; or (3) both.
a ☒ Copies and Phonorecords   b ☐ Copies Only   c ☐ Phonorecords Only

9 DEPOSIT ACCOUNT If the registration fee is to be charged to a Deposit Account established in the Copyright Office, give name and number of Account.
Name ▼   Account Number ▼

CORRESPONDENCE Give name and address to which correspondence about this application should be sent. Name/Address/Apt/City/State/Zip ▼
John Smith, Acme Press
10 Grub Street
Boston, MA 01234

Area Code & Telephone Number ▶ (617) 123-4567

10 CERTIFICATION* I, the undersigned, hereby certify that I am the
Check one ▶
☐ author
☐ other copyright claimant
☐ owner of exclusive rights)
☒ authorized agent of Alan Allenby
Name of author or other copyright claimant, or owner of exclusive right(s) ▲

of the work identified in this application and that the statements made by me in this application are correct to the best of my knowledge.

Typed or printed name and date ▼ If this application gives a date of publication in space 3, do not sign and submit it before that date.
John Smith   date ▶ June 1, 1992

Handwritten signature (X) ▼
John Smith

11 MAIL CERTIFICATE TO
Name ▼
John Smith, c/o Acme Press
Number/Street/Apartment Number ▼
10 Grub Street
City/State/ZIP ▼
Boston, MA 01234

Certificate will be mailed in window envelope

Be sure to give your daytime phone number.

Complete all necessary spaces
• Sign your application in space 10
SEND ALL 3 ELEMENTS IN THE SAME PACKAGE
1. Application form
2. Nonrefundable $20 filing fee in check or money order payable to Register of Copyrights
3. Deposit material
MAIL TO: Register of Copyrights, Library of Congress, Washington, D.C. 20559

*17 U.S.C. § 506(e): Any person who knowingly makes a false representation of a material fact in the application for copyright registration provided for by section 409, or in any written statement filed in connection with the application, shall be fined not more than $2,500.

February 1991—200,000

☆U.S. GOVERNMENT PRINTING OFFICE: 1991—282-170/20,010

8. Single author; contribution to collective work

FORM TX
UNITED STATES COPYRIGHT OFFICE

REGISTRATION NUMBER

_____ TX _____ TXU

EFFECTIVE DATE OF REGISTRATION

Month _____ Day _____ Year _____

DO NOT WRITE ABOVE THIS LINE. IF YOU NEED MORE SPACE, USE A SEPARATE CONTINUATION SHEET.

1 **TITLE OF THIS WORK ▼**
The Red-Faced Killer

PREVIOUS OR ALTERNATIVE TITLES ▼
N/A

PUBLICATION AS A CONTRIBUTION If this work was published as a contribution to a periodical, serial, or collection, give information about the collective work in which the contribution appeared. **Title of Collective Work ▼**
Mysteries Unlimited

If published in a periodical or serial give: **Volume ▼** 12 **Number ▼** 3 **Issue Date ▼** March 1992 **On Pages ▼** 31-50, 63-65

2 **NAME OF AUTHOR ▼**
a   Kay Hurst
DATES OF BIRTH AND DEATH
Year Born ▼ 1941 **Year Died ▼**

Was this contribution to the work a "work made for hire"? □ Yes ☒ No
AUTHOR'S NATIONALITY OR DOMICILE
Name of Country
OR { Citizen of ▶ U.S.A.
Domiciled in ▶

WAS THIS AUTHOR'S CONTRIBUTION TO THE WORK
Anonymous? □ Yes ☒ No
Pseudonymous? □ Yes ☒ No
If the answer to either of these questions is "Yes," see detailed instructions.

NATURE OF AUTHORSHIP Briefly describe nature of the material created by this author in which copyright is claimed. ▼
Entire text of short story

NOTE
Under the law, the "author" of a "work made for hire" is generally the employer, not the employee (see instructions). For any part of this work that was "made for hire" check "Yes" in the space provided, give the employer (or other person for whom the work was prepared) as "Author" of that part, and leave the space for dates of birth and death blank.

b   **NAME OF AUTHOR ▼**
DATES OF BIRTH AND DEATH
Year Born ▼ **Year Died ▼**

Was this contribution to the work a "work made for hire"? □ Yes □ No
AUTHOR'S NATIONALITY OR DOMICILE
Name of Country
OR { Citizen of ▶
Domiciled in ▶

WAS THIS AUTHOR'S CONTRIBUTION TO THE WORK
Anonymous? □ Yes □ No
Pseudonymous? □ Yes □ No
If the answer to either of these questions is "Yes," see detailed instructions.

NATURE OF AUTHORSHIP Briefly describe nature of the material created by this author in which copyright is claimed. ▼

c   **NAME OF AUTHOR ▼**
DATES OF BIRTH AND DEATH
Year Born ▼ **Year Died ▼**

Was this contribution to the work a "work made for hire"? □ Yes □ No
AUTHOR'S NATIONALITY OR DOMICILE
Name of Country
OR { Citizen of ▶
Domiciled in ▶

WAS THIS AUTHOR'S CONTRIBUTION TO THE WORK
Anonymous? □ Yes □ No
Pseudonymous? □ Yes □ No
If the answer to either of these questions is "Yes," see detailed instructions.

NATURE OF AUTHORSHIP Briefly describe nature of the material created by this author in which copyright is claimed. ▼

3 **a** **YEAR IN WHICH CREATION OF THIS WORK WAS COMPLETED** This information must be given **Year** 1991 in all cases.

b **DATE AND NATION OF FIRST PUBLICATION OF THIS PARTICULAR WORK** Complete this information ONLY if this work has been published. **Month ▶** March **Day ▶** 1 **Year ▶** 1992 **Nation** U.S.A.

4 **COPYRIGHT CLAIMANT(S)** Name and address must be given even if the claimant is the same as the author given in space 2. ▼
Kay Hurst
2400 Great Lakes Way
Detroit, MI 48219

APPLICATION RECEIVED
ONE DEPOSIT RECEIVED
TWO DEPOSITS RECEIVED
REMITTANCE NUMBER AND DATE

TRANSFER If the claimant(s) named here in space 4 are different from the author(s) named in space 2, give a brief statement of how the claimant(s) obtained ownership of the copyright. ▼

MORE ON BACK ▶ • Complete all applicable spaces (numbers 5-11) on the reverse side of this page. • See detailed instructions. • Sign the form at line 10.

DO NOT WRITE HERE
Page 1 of _____ pages

FORM TX

FOR COPYRIGHT OFFICE USE ONLY

EXAMINED BY
CHECKED BY
□ CORRESPONDENCE Yes

DO NOT WRITE ABOVE THIS LINE. IF YOU NEED MORE SPACE, USE A SEPARATE CONTINUATION SHEET.

5 **PREVIOUS REGISTRATION** Has registration for this work, or for an earlier version of this work, already been made in the Copyright Office?
□ Yes ☒ No If your answer is "Yes," why is another registration being sought? (Check appropriate box) ▼
□ This is the first published edition of a work previously registered in unpublished form.
□ This is the first application submitted by this author as copyright claimant.
□ This is a changed version of the work, as shown by space 6 on this application.
If your answer is "Yes," give: **Previous Registration Number ▼** **Year of Registration ▼**

6 **DERIVATIVE WORK OR COMPILATION** Complete both space 6a & 6b for a derivative work; complete only 6b for a compilation.
a. **Preexisting Material** Identify any preexisting work or works that this work is based on or incorporates. ▼

b. **Material Added to This Work** Give a brief, general statement of the material that has been added to this work and in which copyright is claimed. ▼

7 —space deleted—

8 **REPRODUCTION FOR USE OF BLIND OR PHYSICALLY HANDICAPPED INDIVIDUALS** A signature on this form at space 10, and a check in one of the boxes here in space 8, constitutes a non-exclusive grant of permission to the Library of Congress to reproduce and distribute solely for the blind and physically handicapped and under the conditions and limitations prescribed by the regulations of the Copyright Office: (1) copies of the work identified in space 1 of this application in Braille or similar tactile symbols); or (2) phonorecords embodying a fixation of a reading of that work; or (3) both.
a ☒ Copies and Phonorecords   b □ Copies Only   c □ Phonorecords Only

9 **DEPOSIT ACCOUNT** If the registration fee is to be charged to a Deposit Account established in the Copyright Office, give name and number of Account.
Name ▼ **Account Number ▼**

CORRESPONDENCE Give name and address to which correspondence about this application should be sent. Name/Address/Apt/City/State/Zip ▼
Kay Hurst
2400 Great Lakes Way
Detroit, MI 48219
Area Code & Telephone Number ▶ (333) 123-4567

10 **CERTIFICATION*** I, the undersigned, hereby certify that I am the
Check one ▶ ☒ author
□ other copyright claimant
□ owner of exclusive right(s)
□ authorized agent of _____
Name of author or other copyright claimant, or owner of exclusive right(s) ▲

of the work identified in this application and that the statements made by me in this application are correct to the best of my knowledge.

Typed or printed name and date ▼ If this application gives a date of publication in space 3, do not sign and submit it before that date.
Kay Hurst **date ▶** April 21, 1992

✍ **Handwritten signature (X) ▼**
Kay Hurst

11 **MAIL CERTIFI-CATE TO**
Certificate will be mailed in window envelope
Name ▼ Kay Hurst
Number/Street/Apartment Number ▼ 2400 Great Lakes Way
City/State/ZIP ▼ Detroit, MI 48219

YOU MUST:
• Complete all necessary spaces
• Sign your application in space 10

SEND ALL 3 ELEMENTS IN THE SAME PACKAGE:
1. Application form
2. Nonrefundable $20 filing fee in check or money order payable to Register of Copyrights
3. Deposit material

MAIL TO:
Register of Copyrights
Library of Congress
Washington, D.C. 20559

* 17 U.S.C. § 506(e): Any person who knowingly makes a false representation of a material fact in the application for copyright registration provided for by section 409, or in any written statement filed in connection with the application, shall be fined not more than $2,500.

February 1991—200,000

☆U.S. GOVERNMENT PRINTING OFFICE: 1991—282-170/20,010

FORM TX
UNITED STATES COPYRIGHT OFFICE

REGISTRATION NUMBER

TX   TXU

EFFECTIVE DATE OF REGISTRATION

Month   Day   Year

DO NOT WRITE ABOVE THIS LINE. IF YOU NEED MORE SPACE, USE A SEPARATE CONTINUATION SHEET.

1 TITLE OF THIS WORK ▼

See Form GR/CP attached

PREVIOUS OR ALTERNATIVE TITLES ▼

PUBLICATION AS A CONTRIBUTION If this work was published as a contribution to a periodical, serial, or collection, give information about the collective work in which the contribution appeared. Title of Collective Work ▼

If published in a periodical or serial give: Volume ▼   Number ▼   Issue Date ▼   On Pages ▼

2 NAME OF AUTHOR ▼

a Kay Hurst

DATES OF BIRTH AND DEATH
Year Born ▼   Year Died ▼
1941

Was this contribution to the work a "work made for hire"?
☐ Yes
☒ No

AUTHOR'S NATIONALITY OR DOMICILE
Name of Country
OR { Citizen of ▶ U.S.A.
Domiciled in ▶

WAS THIS AUTHOR'S CONTRIBUTION TO THE WORK
Anonymous?   ☐ Yes ☒ No
Pseudonymous?   ☐ Yes ☒ No
If the answer to either of these questions is "Yes," see detailed instructions.

NATURE OF AUTHORSHIP Briefly describe nature of the material created by this author in which copyright is claimed. ▼
Entire text of short stories

b NAME OF AUTHOR ▼

DATES OF BIRTH AND DEATH
Year Born ▼   Year Died ▼

Was this contribution to the work a "work made for hire"?
☐ Yes
☐ No

AUTHOR'S NATIONALITY OR DOMICILE
Name of Country
OR { Citizen of ▶
Domiciled in ▶

WAS THIS AUTHOR'S CONTRIBUTION TO THE WORK
Anonymous?   ☐ Yes ☐ No
Pseudonymous?   ☐ Yes ☐ No

NATURE OF AUTHORSHIP Briefly describe nature of the material created by this author in which copyright is claimed. ▼

c NAME OF AUTHOR ▼

DATES OF BIRTH AND DEATH
Year Born ▼   Year Died ▼

Was this contribution to the work a "work made for hire"?
☐ Yes
☐ No

AUTHOR'S NATIONALITY OR DOMICILE
Name of Country
OR { Citizen of ▶
Domiciled in ▶

WAS THIS AUTHOR'S CONTRIBUTION TO THE WORK
Anonymous?   ☐ Yes ☐ No
Pseudonymous?   ☐ Yes ☐ No

NATURE OF AUTHORSHIP Briefly describe nature of the material created by this author in which copyright is claimed. ▼

3 YEAR IN WHICH CREATION OF THIS WORK WAS COMPLETED This information must be given in all cases.
1993 ◀ Year

DATE AND NATION OF FIRST PUBLICATION OF THIS PARTICULAR WORK
Complete this information ONLY if this work has been published.
Month ▶   Day ▶   Year ▶   Nation

4 COPYRIGHT CLAIMANT(S) Name and address must be given even if the claimant is the same as the author given in space 2. ▼

Kay Hurst
2400 Great Lakes Way
Detroit, MI 48219

TRANSFER If the claimant(s) named here in space 4 are different from the author(s) named in space 2, give a brief statement of how the claimant(s) obtained ownership of the copyright. ▼

APPLICATION RECEIVED
ONE DEPOSIT RECEIVED
TWO DEPOSITS RECEIVED
REMITTANCE NUMBER AND DATE

MORE ON BACK ▶ • Complete all applicable spaces (numbers 5-11) on the reverse side of this page.
• See detailed instructions.   • Sign the form at line 10.

DO NOT WRITE HERE
Page 1 of ___ pages

EXAMINED BY   FORM TX

CHECKED BY

☐ CORRESPONDENCE
☐ Yes

FOR COPYRIGHT OFFICE USE ONLY

DO NOT WRITE ABOVE THIS LINE. IF YOU NEED MORE SPACE, USE A SEPARATE CONTINUATION SHEET.

5 PREVIOUS REGISTRATION Has registration for this work, or for an earlier version of this work, already been made in the Copyright Office?
☐ Yes ☒ No If your answer is "Yes," why is another registration being sought? (Check appropriate box) ▼
a. ☐ This is the first published edition of a work previously registered in unpublished form.
b. ☐ This is the first application submitted by this author as copyright claimant.
c. ☐ This is a changed version of the work, as shown by space 6 on this application.
If your answer is "Yes," give: Previous Registration Number ▼   Year of Registration ▼

6 DERIVATIVE WORK OR COMPILATION Complete both space 6a & 6b for a derivative work; complete only 6b for a compilation.
a. Preexisting Material Identify any preexisting work or works that this work is based on or incorporates. ▼

b. Material Added to This Work Give a brief, general statement of the material that has been added to this work and in which copyright is claimed. ▼

7 —space deleted—

8 REPRODUCTION FOR USE OF BLIND OR PHYSICALLY HANDICAPPED INDIVIDUALS A signature on this form at space 10, and a check in one of the boxes here in space 8, constitutes a non-exclusive grant of permission to the Library of Congress to reproduce and distribute solely for the blind and physically handicapped and under the conditions and limitations prescribed by the regulations of the Copyright Office: (1) copies of the work identified in space 1 of this application in Braille (or similar tactile symbols); or (2) phonorecords embodying a fixation of a reading of that work; or (3) both.
a ☒ Copies and Phonorecords   b ☐ Copies Only   c ☐ Phonorecords Only

9 DEPOSIT ACCOUNT If the registration fee is to be charged to a Deposit Account established in the Copyright Office, give name and number of Account.
Name ▼   Account Number ▼

CORRESPONDENCE Give name and address to which correspondence about this application should be sent. Name/Address/Apt/City/State/Zip ▼
Kay Hurst
2400 Great Lakes Way
Detroit, MI 48219
Area Code & Telephone Number ▶ (777) 777-7777

10 CERTIFICATION* I, the undersigned, hereby certify that I am the
Check one ▶
☒ author
☐ other copyright claimant
☐ owner of exclusive right(s)
☐ authorized agent of ___
Name of author or other copyright claimant, or owner of exclusive right(s) ▲

of the work identified in this application and that the statements made by me in this application are correct to the best of my knowledge.

Typed or printed name and date ▼ If this application gives a date of publication in space 3, do not sign and submit it before that date.
Kay Hurst   date▶ May 1, 1993

Handwritten signature (X) ▼
Kay Hurst

11 MAIL CERTIFICATE TO
Certificate will be mailed in window envelope

Name ▼
Kay Hurst
Number/Street/Apartment Number ▼
2400 Great Lakes Way
City/State/ZIP ▼
Detroit, MI 48219

• Complete all necessary spaces
• Sign your application in space 10

1. Application form
2. Nonrefundable $20 filing fee in check or money order payable to Register of Copyrights
3. Deposit material

Register of Copyrights
Library of Congress
Washington, D.C. 20559

* 17 U.S.C. § 506(e): Any person who knowingly makes a false representation of a material fact in the application for copyright registration provided for by section 409, or in any written statement filed in connection with the application, shall be fined not more than $2,500.

February 1991—200,000   ☆U.S. GOVERNMENT PRINTING OFFICE: 1991—282-170/20,010

ADJUNCT APPLICATION
for
Copyright Registration for a Group of Contributions to Periodicals

FORM GR/CP
UNITED STATES COPYRIGHT OFFICE

REGISTRATION NUMBER

TX   PA   VA

EFFECTIVE DATE OF REGISTRATION

....
(Month)   (Day)   (Year)

FORM GR/CP RECEIVED

Page _____ of _____ pages

- Use this adjunct form only if your are making a single registration for a group of contributions to periodicals, and you are also filing a basic application on Form TX, Form PA, or Form VA. Follow the instructions, attached.
- Number each line in Part B consecutively. Use additional Forms GR/CP if you need more space.
- Submit this adjunct form with the basic application form. Clip (do not tape or staple) and fold all sheets together before submitting them.

DO NOT WRITE ABOVE THIS LINE. FOR COPYRIGHT OFFICE USE ONLY

A Identification of Application

IDENTIFICATION OF BASIC APPLICATION:
• This application for copyright registration for a group of contributions to periodicals is submitted as an adjunct to an application filed on:
(Check which)

☒ Form TX   ☐ Form PA   ☐ Form VA

IDENTIFICATION OF AUTHOR AND CLAIMANT: (Give the name of the author and the name of the copyright claimant in all of the contributions listed in Part B of this form. The names should be the same as the names given in spaces 2 and 4 of the basic application.)

Name of Author: Kay Hurst

Name of Copyright Claimant: Kay Hurst

B Registration For Group of Contributions

COPYRIGHT REGISTRATION FOR A GROUP OF CONTRIBUTIONS TO PERIODICALS: (To make a single registration for a group of works by the same individual author, all first published as contributions to periodicals within a 12-month period (see instructions), give full information about each contribution. If more space is needed, use additional Forms GR/CP.)

1. Title of Contribution: The Green-Nosed Killer
   Title of Periodical: Mysteries Unlimited   Vol. 11   No. 6   Issue Date 6/92   Pages 18-34
   Date of First Publication: June   15   1992   Nation of First Publication U.S.A.
   (Month) (Day) (Year)   (Country)

2. Title of Contribution: The Red-Nosed Killer
   Title of Periodical: Mysteries Unlimited   Vol. 11   No. 8   Issue Date 8/92   Pages 3-28
   Date of First Publication: August   12   1992   Nation of First Publication U.S.A.
   (Month) (Day) (Year)   (Country)

3. Title of Contribution: The Black-Nosed Killer
   Title of Periodical: Mystery Digest   Vol. 81   No. 1   Issue Date 1/93   Pages 94-116
   Date of First Publication: January   15   1993   Nation of First Publication U.S.A.
   (Month) (Day) (Year)   (Country)

4. Title of Contribution: The Noseless Killer
   Title of Periodical: The Mystery Magazine   Vol. 28   No. 4   Issue Date 4/93   Pages 80-101
   Date of First Publication: April   1   1993   Nation of First Publication U.S.A.
   (Month) (Day) (Year)   (Country)

☐ Title of Contribution:
   Title of Periodical: Vol.   No.   Issue Date   Pages
   Date of First Publication: Nation of First Publication
   (Month) (Day) (Year)   (Country)

☐ Title of Contribution:
   Title of Periodical: Vol.   No.   Issue Date   Pages
   Date of First Publication: Nation of First Publication
   (Month) (Day) (Year)   (Country)

☐ Title of Contribution:
   Title of Periodical: Vol.   No.   Issue Date   Pages
   Date of First Publication: Nation of First Publication
   (Month) (Day) (Year)   (Country)

FOR COPYRIGHT OFFICE USE ONLY

B Continued

DO NOT WRITE ABOVE THIS LINE. FOR COPYRIGHT OFFICE USE ONLY

☐ Title of Contribution:
   Title of Periodical: Vol.   No.   Issue Date   Pages
   Date of First Publication: Nation of First Publication
   (Month) (Day) (Year)   (Country)

☐ Title of Contribution:
   Title of Periodical: Vol.   No.   Issue Date   Pages
   Date of First Publication: Nation of First Publication
   (Month) (Day) (Year)   (Country)

☐ Title of Contribution:
   Title of Periodical: Vol.   No.   Issue Date   Pages
   Date of First Publication: Nation of First Publication
   (Month) (Day) (Year)   (Country)

☐ Title of Contribution:
   Title of Periodical: Vol.   No.   Issue Date   Pages
   Date of First Publication: Nation of First Publication
   (Month) (Day) (Year)   (Country)

☐ Title of Contribution:
   Title of Periodical: Vol.   No.   Issue Date   Pages
   Date of First Publication: Nation of First Publication
   (Month) (Day) (Year)   (Country)

☐ Title of Contribution:
   Title of Periodical: Vol.   No.   Issue Date   Pages
   Date of First Publication: Nation of First Publication
   (Month) (Day) (Year)   (Country)

☐ Title of Contribution:
   Title of Periodical: Vol.   No.   Issue Date   Pages
   Date of First Publication: Nation of First Publication
   (Month) (Day) (Year)   (Country)

☐ Title of Contribution:
   Title of Periodical: Vol.   No.   Issue Date   Pages
   Date of First Publication: Nation of First Publication
   (Month) (Day) (Year)   (Country)

☐ Title of Contribution:
   Title of Periodical: Vol.   No.   Issue Date   Pages
   Date of First Publication: Nation of First Publication
   (Month) (Day) (Year)   (Country)

☐ Title of Contribution:
   Title of Periodical: Vol.   No.   Issue Date   Pages
   Date of First Publication: Nation of First Publication
   (Month) (Day) (Year)   (Country)

☐ Title of Contribution:
   Title of Periodical: Vol.   No.   Issue Date   Pages
   Date of First Publication: Nation of First Publication
   (Month) (Day) (Year)   (Country)

☐ Title of Contribution:
   Title of Periodical: Vol.   No.   Issue Date   Pages
   Date of First Publication: Nation of First Publication
   (Month) (Day) (Year)   (Country)

June 1989—20,000   U.S. GOVERNMENT PRINTING OFFICE: 1989—241-428/80,025

FORM PA
UNITED STATES COPYRIGHT OFFICE

REGISTRATION NUMBER

PA / PAU

EFFECTIVE DATE OF REGISTRATION

Month — Day — Year

DO NOT WRITE ABOVE THIS LINE. IF YOU NEED MORE SPACE, USE A SEPARATE CONTINUATION SHEET.

1 TITLE OF THIS WORK ▼

And Then You Die

PREVIOUS OR ALTERNATIVE TITLES ▼

NATURE OF THIS WORK ▼ See instructions

Screenplay

2 NAME OF AUTHOR ▼

a David Griffith

DATES OF BIRTH AND DEATH
Year Born ▼ 1935   Year Died ▼

Was this contribution to the work a "work made for hire"?
☐ Yes
☒ No

AUTHOR'S NATIONALITY OR DOMICILE
Name of Country
OR { Citizen of ▶ U.S.A.
     Domiciled in ▶

WAS THIS AUTHOR'S CONTRIBUTION TO THE WORK
Anonymous?   ☐ Yes ☒ No
Pseudonymous? ☐ Yes ☒ No
If the answer to either of these questions is "Yes," see detailed instructions.

NATURE OF AUTHORSHIP Briefly describe nature of the material created by this author in which copyright is claimed. ▼
Entire text

NOTE
Under the law, the "author" of a "work made for hire" is generally the employer, not the employee (see instructions). For any part of this work that was "made for hire" check "Yes" in the space provided, give the employer (or other person for whom the work was prepared) as "Author" of that part, and leave the space for dates of birth and death blank.

b NAME OF AUTHOR ▼

DATES OF BIRTH AND DEATH
Year Born ▼   Year Died ▼

Was this contribution to the work a "work made for hire"?
☐ Yes
☐ No

AUTHOR'S NATIONALITY OR DOMICILE
Name of Country
OR { Citizen of ▶
     Domiciled in ▶

WAS THIS AUTHOR'S CONTRIBUTION TO THE WORK
Anonymous?   ☐ Yes ☐ No
Pseudonymous? ☐ Yes ☐ No
If the answer to either of these questions is "Yes," see detailed instructions.

NATURE OF AUTHORSHIP Briefly describe nature of the material created by this author in which copyright is claimed. ▼

c NAME OF AUTHOR ▼

DATES OF BIRTH AND DEATH
Year Born ▼   Year Died ▼

Was this contribution to the work a "work made for hire"?
☐ Yes
☐ No

AUTHOR'S NATIONALITY OR DOMICILE
Name of Country
OR { Citizen of ▶
     Domiciled in ▶

WAS THIS AUTHOR'S CONTRIBUTION TO THE WORK
Anonymous?   ☐ Yes ☐ No
Pseudonymous? ☐ Yes ☐ No
If the answer to either of these questions is "Yes," see detailed instructions.

NATURE OF AUTHORSHIP Briefly describe nature of the material created by this author in which copyright is claimed. ▼

3 YEAR IN WHICH CREATION OF THIS WORK WAS COMPLETED This information must be given in all cases.
1992 ◀ Year

DATE AND NATION OF FIRST PUBLICATION OF THIS PARTICULAR WORK
Complete this information ONLY if this work has been published.
Month ▶ Day ▶ Year ▶ Nation

4 COPYRIGHT CLAIMANT(S) Name and address must be given even if the claimant is the same as the author given in space 2.▼

David Griffith
666 Hollywood Blvd.
Hollywood, CA 90000

See instructions before completing this space.

TRANSFER If the claimant(s) named here in space 4 are different from the author(s) named in space 2, give a brief statement of how the claimant(s) obtained ownership of the copyright. ▼

MORE ON BACK ▶ • Complete all applicable spaces (numbers 5-9) on the reverse side of this page. • See detailed instructions. • Sign the form at line 8.

DO NOT WRITE HERE
Page 1 of ___ pages

OFFICE USE ONLY
APPLICATION RECEIVED
ONE DEPOSIT RECEIVED
TWO DEPOSITS RECEIVED
REMITTANCE NUMBER AND DATE

FORM PA

EXAMINED BY

CHECKED BY

CORRESPONDENCE
☐ Yes

FOR COPYRIGHT OFFICE USE ONLY

DO NOT WRITE ABOVE THIS LINE. IF YOU NEED MORE SPACE, USE A SEPARATE CONTINUATION SHEET.

5 PREVIOUS REGISTRATION Has registration for this work, or for an earlier version of this work, already been made in the Copyright Office?
☐ Yes ☒ No If your answer is "Yes," why is another registration being sought? (Check appropriate box) ▼
a. ☐ This is the first published edition of a work previously registered in unpublished form.
b. ☐ This is the first application submitted by this author as copyright claimant.
c. ☐ This is a changed version of the work, as shown by space 6 on this application.
If your answer is "Yes," give: Previous Registration Number ▼   Year of Registration ▼

6 DERIVATIVE WORK OR COMPILATION Complete both space 6a & 6b for a derivative work; complete only 6b for a compilation.
a. Preexisting Material Identify any preexisting work or works that this work is based on or incorporates. ▼

See instructions before completing this space.

b. Material Added to This Work Give a brief, general statement of the material that has been added to this work and in which copyright is claimed. ▼

7 DEPOSIT ACCOUNT If the registration fee is to be charged to a Deposit Account established in the Copyright Office, give name and number of Account.
Name ▼   Account Number ▼

CORRESPONDENCE Give name and address to which correspondence about this application should be sent. Name/Address/Apt/City/State/Zip ▼
David Griffith
666 Hollywood Blvd.
Hollywood, CA 90000

Area Code & Telephone Number ▶ (213) 666-6666

Be sure to give your daytime phone ▶ number

8 CERTIFICATION* I, the undersigned, hereby certify that I am the
Check only one ▼
☒ author
☐ other copyright claimant
☐ owner of exclusive right(s)
☐ authorized agent of _____
Name of author or other copyright claimant, or owner of exclusive right(s) ▲

of the work identified in this application and that the statements made by me in this application are correct to the best of my knowledge.

Typed or printed name and date ▼ If this application gives a date of publication in space 3, do not sign and submit it before that date.
David Griffith   date ▶ May 1, 1992

Handwritten signature (X) ▼
David Griffith

9 MAIL CERTIFICATE TO

Certificate will be mailed in window envelope

Name ▼
David Griffith
Number/Street/Apartment Number ▼
666 Hollywood Blvd.
City/State/ZIP ▼
Hollywood, CA 90000

• Complete all necessary spaces
• Sign your application in space 8

SEND ALL 3 ELEMENTS IN THE SAME PACKAGE
1. Application form
2. Nonrefundable $20 filing fee in check or money order payable to Register of Copyrights
3. Deposit material

MAIL TO:
Register of Copyrights
Library of Congress
Washington, D.C. 20559

* 17 U.S.C. § 506(e): Any person who knowingly makes a false representation of a material fact in the application for copyright registration provided for by section 409, or in any written statement filed in connection with the application, shall be fined not more than $2,500.

▲ February 1991—200,000

✩U.S. GOVERNMENT PRINTING OFFICE: 1991- 282-17/20,011

11. Unpublished song lyric; single author

DO NOT WRITE ABOVE THIS LINE. IF YOU NEED MORE SPACE, USE A SEPARATE CONTINUATION SHEET.

1

TITLE OF THIS WORK ▼

Why Did You Tell Me You Loved Me When You Really Loved My Pick-up

PREVIOUS OR ALTERNATIVE TITLES ▼

Shoo-Be-Do-Be-Doo

NATURE OF THIS WORK ▼ See instructions

Song lyric

2

a NAME OF AUTHOR ▼

Hank Hutchins, Jr.

Was this contribution to the work a "work made for hire"?
☐ Yes   ☒ No

DATES OF BIRTH AND DEATH
Year Born ▼   Year Died ▼

AUTHOR'S NATIONALITY OR DOMICILE
Name of country
OR { Citizen of ▶ U.S.A.
     Domiciled in ▶ _____

WAS THIS AUTHOR'S CONTRIBUTION TO THE WORK
Anonymous?   ☐ Yes   ☒ No
Pseudonymous?   ☐ Yes   ☒ No
If the answer to either of these questions is "Yes," see detailed instructions

NATURE OF AUTHORSHIP Briefly describe nature of the material created by this author in which copyright is claimed. ▼

words

b NAME OF AUTHOR ▼

Was this contribution to the work a "work made for hire"?
☐ Yes   ☐ No

DATES OF BIRTH AND DEATH
Year Born ▼   Year Died ▼

AUTHOR'S NATIONALITY OR DOMICILE
Name of country
OR { Citizen of ▶ _____
     Domiciled in ▶ _____

WAS THIS AUTHOR'S CONTRIBUTION TO THE WORK
Anonymous?   ☐ Yes   ☐ No
Pseudonymous?   ☐ Yes   ☐ No

NATURE OF AUTHORSHIP Briefly describe nature of the material created by this author in which copyright is claimed. ▼

c NAME OF AUTHOR ▼

Was this contribution to the work a "work made for hire"?
☐ Yes   ☐ No

DATES OF BIRTH AND DEATH
Year Born ▼   Year Died ▼

AUTHOR'S NATIONALITY OR DOMICILE
Name of country
OR { Citizen of ▶ _____
     Domiciled in ▶ _____

WAS THIS AUTHOR'S CONTRIBUTION TO THE WORK
Anonymous?   ☐ Yes   ☐ No
Pseudonymous?   ☐ Yes   ☐ No

NATURE OF AUTHORSHIP Briefly describe nature of the material created by this author in which copyright is claimed. ▼

NOTE
Under the law, the "author" of a "work made for hire" is generally the employer, not the employee (see instructions). For any part of this work that was "made for hire" check "Yes" in the space provided, give the employer (or other person for whom the work was prepared) as "Author" of that part, and leave the space for dates of birth and death blank.

3

a YEAR IN WHICH CREATION OF THIS WORK WAS COMPLETED This information must be given in all cases.
◀ Year   1992

b DATE AND NATION OF FIRST PUBLICATION OF THIS PARTICULAR WORK
Complete this information ONLY if this work has been published.
Month ▶ _____ Day ▶ _____ Year ▶ _____ ◀ Nation

4

COPYRIGHT CLAIMANT(S) Name and address must be given even if the claimant is the same as the author given in space 2. ▼

Hank Hutchins, Jr.
1000 Country Road
Graceland, TN 20000

TRANSFER If the claimant(s) named here in space 4 are different from the author(s) named in space 2, give a brief statement of how the claimant(s) obtained ownership of the copyright. ▼

See instructions before completing this space.

APPLICATION RECEIVED

ONE DEPOSIT RECEIVED

TWO DEPOSITS RECEIVED

REMITTANCE NUMBER AND DATE

DO NOT WRITE HERE
OFFICE USE ONLY

MORE ON BACK ▶ • Complete all applicable spaces (numbers 5-9) on the reverse side of this page.
• See detailed instructions.   • Sign the form at line 8.

DO NOT WRITE HERE
Page 1 of ____ pages

---

5 EXAMINED BY

CHECKED BY

CORRESPONDENCE
☐ Yes

FOR COPYRIGHT OFFICE USE ONLY

DO NOT WRITE ABOVE THIS LINE. IF YOU NEED MORE SPACE, USE A SEPARATE CONTINUATION SHEET.

PREVIOUS REGISTRATION Has registration for this work, or for an earlier version of this work, already been made in the Copyright Office?
☐ Yes   ☒ No   If your answer is "Yes," why is another registration being sought? (Check appropriate box) ▼
a. ☐ This is the first published edition of a work previously registered in unpublished form.
b. ☐ This is the first application submitted by this author as copyright claimant.
c. ☐ This is a changed version of the work, as shown by space 6 on this application.
If your answer is "Yes," give: Previous Registration Number ▼   Year of Registration ▼

6

DERIVATIVE WORK OR COMPILATION Complete both space 6a & 6b for a derivative work; complete only 6b for a compilation.
a. Preexisting Material   Identify any preexisting work or works that this work is based on or incorporates. ▼

See instructions before completing this space.

b. Material Added to This Work   Give a brief, general statement of the material that has been added to this work and in which copyright is claimed. ▼

7

DEPOSIT ACCOUNT If the registration fee is to be charged to a Deposit Account established in the Copyright Office, give name and number of Account.
Name ▼   Account Number ▼

CORRESPONDENCE Give name and address to which correspondence about this application should be sent.   Name/Address/Apt/City/State/Zip ▼

Hank Hutchins, Jr.
1000 Country Road
Graceland, TN 2000

Area Code & Telephone Number ▶ (444) 444-4444

Be sure to give your daytime phone number

8

CERTIFICATION* I, the undersigned, hereby certify that I am the
Check only one ▼
☒ author
☐ other copyright claimant
☐ owner of exclusive right(s)
☐ authorized agent of _____
Name of author or other copyright claimant, or owner of exclusive right(s) ▲

of the work identified in this application and that the statements made by me in this application are correct to the best of my knowledge.

Typed or printed name and date ▼ If this application gives a date of publication in space 3, do not sign and submit it before that date.
Hank Hutchins, Jr.   date ▶ Sept. 1, 199

Handwritten signature (X) ▼
Hank Hutchins, Jr.

9

MAIL CERTIFICATE TO

Name ▼
Hank Hutchins, Jr.
Number/Street/Apartment Number ▼
1000 Country Road
City/State/ZIP ▼
Graceland, TN 20000

Certificate will be mailed in window envelope

YOU MUST:
• Complete all necessary spaces
• Sign your application in space 8

SEND ALL 3 ELEMENTS IN THE SAME PACKAGE:
1. Application form
2. Nonrefundable $20 filing fee in check or money order payable to Register of Copyrights
3. Deposit material

MAIL TO:
Register of Copyrights
Library of Congress
Washington, D.C. 20559

12. Three monthly issues of a monthly magazine registered as a group on Form SE/Group

FORM SE/GROUP
UNITED STATES COPYRIGHT OFFICE

REGISTRATION NUMBER

EFFECTIVE DATE OF REGISTRATION
(Assigned by Copyright Office)

Month	Day	Year

APPLICATION RECEIVED

ONE DEPOSIT RECEIVED

EXAMINED BY   CORRESPONDENCE ☐

DO NOT WRITE ABOVE THIS LINE.

1

List in order of publication

No previous registration under identical title ☐

TITLE ▼

The Toxic Waste Tipster

ISSN▼

12345678

	Volume▼	Number▼	Issue date on copies▼	Month, day and year of publication ▼
1.	VIII	1	January 1992	January 4, 1992
2.	VIII	2	February 1992	February 3, 1992
3.	VIII	3	March 1992	March 2, 1992
4.				
5.				
6.				
7.				
8.				
9.				
10.				
11.				
12.				
13.				
14.				

2

NAME AND ADDRESS OF THE AUTHOR/COPYRIGHT CLAIMANT IN THESE COLLECTIVE WORKS MADE FOR HIRE

Toxic Waste Internment & Transport, Inc.
P.O. Box P-U
New York, NY 10012

FOR NON-U.S. WORKS: Author's citizenship ▼   Domicile ▼   Nation of publication ▼

CERTIFICATION*:   I, the undersigned, hereby certify that I am the copyright claimant or the authorized agent of the copyright claimant of the works identified in this application, that all the conditions specified in the instructions on the back of this form are met, that I have deposited two complimentary subscription copies with the Library of Congress, and that the statements made by me in this application are correct to the best of my knowledge.

Signature (X) _____   Typed or printed name John Durtt

PERSON TO CONTACT FOR CORRESPONDENCE ABOUT THIS CLAIM
Name▶ John Durtt
Daytime telephone number▶ (212) 123-4567
Address (if other than given below) ▶ _____

DEPOSIT ACCOUNT
Account number▶ _____
Name of account▶ _____

MAIL CERTIFICATE TO

Certificate will be mailed in window envelope

Name▼
Toxic Waste Internment & Transport, Inc.

Number/Street/Apartment Number▼
P.O. Box P-U

City/State/ZIP▼
New York, NY 10012

REPRODUCTION FOR USE OF BLIND OR PHYSICALLY HANDICAPPED INDIVIDUALS
a ☒ Copies and Phonorecords
b ☐ Copies Only
c ☐ Phonorecords Only

MAIL TO
Register of Copyrights
Library of Congress
Washington, D.C. 20559

*17 U.S.C. §506(e): Any person who knowingly makes a false representation of a material fact in the application for copyright registration provided for by section 409, or in any written statement filed in connection with the application, shall be fined not more than $2,500.

April 1991—100,000

☆ U.S. GOVERNMENT PRINTING OFFICE: 1991–282-170/20,016

13. Single magazine issue

SHORT FORM SE ⊘
UNITED STATES COPYRIGHT OFFICE

REGISTRATION NUMBER

EFFECTIVE DATE OF REGISTRATION
(Assigned by Copyright Office)

Month	Day	Year

APPLICATION RECEIVED

ONE DEPOSIT RECEIVED

TWO DEPOSITS RECEIVED

EXAMINED BY

CORRESPONDENCE ☐

DO NOT WRITE ABOVE THIS LINE.

1 TITLE OF THIS SERIAL AS IT APPEARS ON THE COPY

The Toxic Waste Tipster

Volume▼	Number▼	Date on Copies▼	ISSN▼
VIII	12	December 1992	12345678

2 NAME AND ADDRESS OF THE AUTHOR AND COPYRIGHT CLAIMANT IN THIS COLLECTIVE WORK MADE FOR HIRE

Toxic Waste Internment & Transport, Incorporated
P.O. Box P-U
New York, NY 10012

3 DATE OF PUBLICATION OF THIS PARTICULAR ISSUE

Month▼	Day▼	Year▼
January	2	1993

YEAR IN WHICH CREATION OF THIS ISSUE WAS COMPLETED (IF EARLIER THAN THE YEAR OF PUBLICATION): Year▼ 1992

CERTIFICATION*: I, the undersigned, hereby certify that I am the copyright claimant or the authorized agent of the copyright claimant of the work identified in this application, that all the conditions specified in the instructions on the back of this form are met, and that the statements made by me in this application are correct to the best of my knowledge.

Handwritten signature (X) _____

Typed or printed name of signer __John Durtt__

PERSON TO CONTACT FOR CORRESPONDENCE ABOUT THIS CLAIM
Name▶ John Durtt
Daytime telephone number▶ (212) 123-4567
Address (if other than given below) ▶ _____

DEPOSIT ACCOUNT
Account number▶ _____
Name of account▶ _____

MAIL CERTIFICATE TO

Name▼ Toxic Waste Internment & Transport, Inc.
Number/Street/Apartment Number▼ P.O. Box P-U
City/State/ZIP▼ New York, NY 10012

Certificate will be mailed in window envelope

YOU MUST
• Complete all necessary spaces
• Sign your application
SEND ALL 3 ELEMENTS IN THE SAME PACKAGE
1. Application form
2. Nonrefundable $10.00 filing fee in check or money order payable to *Register of Copyrights*
3. Deposit material
MAIL TO
Register of Copyrights
Library of Congress
Washington, D.C. 20559

*17 U.S.C. §506(e): Any person who knowingly makes a false representation of a material fact in the application for copyright registration provided for by section 409, or in any written statement filed in connection with the application, shall be fined not more than $2,500.

March 1990—50,000

☆U.S. GOVERNMENT PRINTING OFFICE: 1990–262-308/13

14. Single issue of a magazine published three times a year; single author; not a work made for hire

FORM SE
UNITED STATES COPYRIGHT OFFICE

REGISTRATION NUMBER

_____

U

EFFECTIVE DATE OF REGISTRATION

Month _____ Day _____ Year _____

DO NOT WRITE ABOVE THIS LINE. IF YOU NEED MORE SPACE, USE A SEPARATE CONTINUATION SHEET.

1 TITLE OF THIS SERIAL ▼

Urine Analysis: The Urologist's Journal

Volume ▼	Number ▼	Date on Copies ▼	Frequency of Publication ▼
17	2	May 1992	3 times per year

PREVIOUS OR ALTERNATIVE TITLES ▼

2 NAME OF AUTHOR ▼

a Dr. Lou Brown

DATES OF BIRTH AND DEATH
Year Born ▼ 1935   Year Died ▼

Was this contribution to the work a "work made for hire"?
☐ Yes   ☒ No

AUTHOR'S NATIONALITY OR DOMICILE
Name of Country
OR { Citizen of ▶ U.S.A.
     Domiciled in ▶

WAS THIS AUTHOR'S CONTRIBUTION TO THE WORK
Anonymous? ☐ Yes ☒ No
Pseudonymous? ☐ Yes ☒ No
If the answer to either of these questions is "Yes," see detailed instructions.

NATURE OF AUTHORSHIP   Briefly describe nature of the material created by this author in which copyright is claimed. ▼
☐ Collective Work   Other: Entire text

NOTE
Under the law, the "author" of a "work made for hire" is generally the employer, not the employee (see instructions). For any part of this work that was "made for hire" check "Yes" in the space provided, give the employer (or other person for whom the work was prepared) as "Author" of that part, and leave the space for dates of birth and death blank.

b NAME OF AUTHOR ▼

DATES OF BIRTH AND DEATH
Year Born ▼   Year Died ▼

Was this contribution to the work a "work made for hire"?
☐ Yes
☐ No

AUTHOR'S NATIONALITY OR DOMICILE
Name of Country
OR { Citizen of ▶
     Domiciled in ▶

WAS THIS AUTHOR'S CONTRIBUTION TO THE WORK
Anonymous? ☐ Yes ☐ No
Pseudonymous? ☐ Yes ☐ No
If the answer to either of these questions is "Yes," see detailed instructions.

NATURE OF AUTHORSHIP   Briefly describe nature of the material created by this author in which copyright is claimed. ▼
☐ Collective Work   Other:

c NAME OF AUTHOR ▼

DATES OF BIRTH AND DEATH
Year Born ▼   Year Died ▼

Was this contribution to the work a "work made for hire"?
☐ Yes
☐ No

AUTHOR'S NATIONALITY OR DOMICILE
Name of Country
OR { Citizen of ▶
     Domiciled in ▶

WAS THIS AUTHOR'S CONTRIBUTION TO THE WORK
Anonymous? ☐ Yes ☐ No
Pseudonymous? ☐ Yes ☐ No
If the answer to either of these questions is "Yes," see detailed instructions.

NATURE OF AUTHORSHIP   Briefly describe nature of the material created by this author in which copyright is claimed. ▼
☐ Collective Work   Other:

3 YEAR IN WHICH CREATION OF THIS ISSUE WAS COMPLETED   This information must be given in all cases.
a 1992 ◀ Year

DATE AND NATION OF FIRST PUBLICATION OF THIS PARTICULAR ISSUE
Complete this information ONLY if this work has been published.
Month ▶ May   Day ▶ 1   Year ▶ 1992
Nation ▶ U.S.A.

4 COPYRIGHT CLAIMANT(S) Name and address must be given even if the claimant is the same as the author given in space 2. ▼

Dr. Lou Brown
123 Colonic Highway
Runnymeade, VA 40000

APPLICATION RECEIVED
ONE DEPOSIT RECEIVED
TWO DEPOSITS RECEIVED
REMITTANCE NUMBER AND DATE

(DO NOT WRITE HERE / OFFICE USE ONLY)

TRANSFER If the claimant(s) named here in space 4 are different from the author(s) named in space 2, give a brief statement of how the claimant(s) obtained ownership of the copyright. ▼

MORE ON BACK ▶ • Complete all applicable spaces (numbers 5-11) on the reverse side of this page.
• See detailed instructions. • Sign the form at line 10

DO NOT WRITE HERE
Page 1 of _____ pages

See instructions before completing this space.

EXAMINED BY

CHECKED BY

☐ CORRESPONDENCE
Yes

FOR COPYRIGHT OFFICE USE ONLY

FORM SE

DO NOT WRITE ABOVE THIS LINE. IF YOU NEED MORE SPACE, USE A SEPARATE CONTINUATION SHEET.

5 PREVIOUS REGISTRATION   Has registration for this issue, or for an earlier version of this particular issue, already been made in the Copyright Office?
☐ Yes   ☒ No   If your answer is "Yes," why is another registration being sought? (Check appropriate box) ▼
a. ☐ This is the first published version of an issue previously registered in unpublished form.
b. ☐ This is the first application submitted by this author as copyright claimant.
c. ☐ This is a changed version of this issue, as shown by space 6 on this application.
If your answer is "Yes," give: Previous Registration Number ▼   Year of Registration ▼

6 DERIVATIVE WORK OR COMPILATION   Complete both space 6a & 6b for a derivative work; complete only 6b for a compilation.
a. Preexisting Material   Identify any preexisting work or works that this work is based on or incorporates. ▼

b. Material Added to This Work   Give a brief, general statement of the material that has been added to this work and in which copyright is claimed. ▼

7 —space deleted—

8 REPRODUCTION FOR USE OF BLIND OR PHYSICALLY HANDICAPPED INDIVIDUALS   A signature on this form at space 10, and a check in one of the boxes here in space 8, constitutes a non-exclusive grant of permission to the Library of Congress to reproduce and distribute solely for the blind and physically handicapped and under the conditions and limitations prescribed by the regulations of the Copyright Office: (1) copies of the work identified in space 1 of this application in Braille (or similar tactile symbols); or (2) phonorecords embodying a fixation of a reading of that work; or (3) both.
a ☒ Copies and Phonorecords   **b** ☐ Copies Only   **c** ☐ Phonorecords Only

See instructions.

9 DEPOSIT ACCOUNT   If the registration fee is to be charged to a Deposit Account established in the Copyright Office, give name and number of Account.
Name ▼   Account Number ▼

CORRESPONDENCE   Give name and address to which correspondence about this application should be sent.   Name/Address/Apt/City/State/Zip ▼
Dr. Lou Brown
123 Colonic Highway
Runnymeade, VA 40000
Area Code & Telephone Number ▶ (804) 123-4567

10 CERTIFICATION*   I, the undersigned, hereby certify that I am the
Check one ▶
☒ author
☐ other copyright claimant
☐ owner of exclusive right(s)
☐ authorized agent of _____
Name of author or other copyright claimant, or owner of exclusive right(s) ▲

of the work identified in this application and that the statements made by me in this application are correct to the best of my knowledge.

Typed or printed name and date ▼ If this application gives a date of publication in space 3, do not sign and submit it before that date.
Dr. Lou Brown   date ▶ July 1, 1992

Handwritten signature (X) ▼
Dr. Lou Brown

Be sure to give your daytime phone ◀ number

11
MAIL CERTIFICATE TO

Certificate will be mailed in window envelope

Name ▼
Dr. Lou Brown
Number/Street/Apartment Number ▼
123 Colonic Highway
City/State/ZIP ▼
Runnymeade, VA 40000

YOU MUST:
• Complete all necessary spaces
• Sign your application in space 10

SEND ALL 3 ELEMENTS IN THE SAME PACKAGE:
1. Application form
2. Non-refundable $10 filing fee in check or money order payable to Register of Copyrights
3. Deposit material

MAIL TO:
Register of Copyrights
Library of Congress
Washington, D.C. 20559

* 17 U.S.C. § 506(e): Any person who knowingly makes a false representation of a material fact in the application for copyright registration provided for by section 409, or in any written statement filed in connection with the application, shall be fined not more than $2,500.

October 1990—8,000   ☆U.S. GOVERNMENT PRINTING OFFICE: 1990—282-170/20,004

See instructions before completing this space.

FORM TX

For a Literary Work
UNITED STATES COPYRIGHT OFFICE

REGISTRATION NUMBER

_____

TX   TXU

EFFECTIVE DATE OF REGISTRATION

_____

Month   Day   Year

DO NOT WRITE ABOVE THIS LINE. IF YOU NEED MORE SPACE, USE A SEPARATE CONTINUATION SHEET.

TITLE OF THIS WORK ▼

PREVIOUS OR ALTERNATIVE TITLES ▼

PUBLICATION AS A CONTRIBUTION If this work was published as a contribution to a periodical, serial, or collection, give information about the collective work in which the contribution appeared.   **Title of Collective Work ▼**

If published in a periodical or serial give: **Volume ▼**   **Number ▼**   **Issue Date ▼**   **On Pages ▼**

---

a

NAME OF AUTHOR ▼

DATES OF BIRTH AND DEATH
Year Born ▼   Year Died ▼

Was this contribution to the work a "work made for hire"?
☐ Yes
☐ No

AUTHOR'S NATIONALITY OR DOMICILE
Name of Country
OR { Citizen of ▶ _____
Domiciled in ▶ _____

WAS THIS AUTHOR'S CONTRIBUTION TO THE WORK
Anonymous?   ☐ Yes   ☐ No
Pseudonymous?   ☐ Yes   ☐ No
If the answer to either of these questions is "Yes," see detailed instructions.

NATURE OF AUTHORSHIP Briefly describe nature of material created by this author in which copyright is claimed. ▼

---

b

NAME OF AUTHOR ▼

DATES OF BIRTH AND DEATH
Year Born ▼   Year Died ▼

Was this contribution to the work a "work made for hire"?
☐ Yes
☐ No

AUTHOR'S NATIONALITY OR DOMICILE
Name of Country
OR { Citizen of ▶ _____
Domiciled in ▶ _____

WAS THIS AUTHOR'S CONTRIBUTION TO THE WORK
Anonymous?   ☐ Yes   ☐ No
Pseudonymous?   ☐ Yes   ☐ No
If the answer to either of these questions is "Yes," see detailed instructions.

NATURE OF AUTHORSHIP Briefly describe nature of material created by this author in which copyright is claimed. ▼

---

c

NAME OF AUTHOR ▼

DATES OF BIRTH AND DEATH
Year Born ▼   Year Died ▼

Was this contribution to the work a "work made for hire"?
☐ Yes
☐ No

AUTHOR'S NATIONALITY OR DOMICILE
Name of Country
OR { Citizen of ▶ _____
Domiciled in ▶ _____

WAS THIS AUTHOR'S CONTRIBUTION TO THE WORK
Anonymous?   ☐ Yes   ☐ No
Pseudonymous?   ☐ Yes   ☐ No
If the answer to either of these questions is "Yes," see detailed instructions.

NATURE OF AUTHORSHIP Briefly describe nature of material created by this author in which copyright is claimed. ▼

---

a **YEAR IN WHICH CREATION OF THIS WORK WAS COMPLETED** _This information must be given in all cases._ ◀ Year

b **DATE AND NATION OF FIRST PUBLICATION OF THIS PARTICULAR WORK** _Complete this information ONLY if this work has been published._ Month ▶ _____ Day ▶ _____ Year ▶ _____ ◀ Nation

---

COPYRIGHT CLAIMANT(S) Name and address must be given even if the claimant is the same as the author given in space 2. ▼

TRANSFER If the claimant(s) named here in space 4 is (are) different from the author(s) named in space 2, give a brief statement of how the claimant(s) obtained ownership of the copyright. ▼

DO NOT WRITE HERE
OFFICE USE ONLY

APPLICATION RECEIVED

ONE DEPOSIT RECEIVED

TWO DEPOSITS RECEIVED

REMITTANCE NUMBER AND DATE

MORE ON BACK ▶   • Complete all applicable spaces (numbers 5-11) on the reverse side of this page.
   • See detailed instructions.   • Sign the form at line 10.

DO NOT WRITE HERE

Page 1 of _____ pages

DO NOT WRITE ABOVE THIS LINE. IF YOU NEED MORE SPACE, USE A SEPARATE CONTINUATION SHEET.

PREVIOUS REGISTRATION Has registration for this work, or for an earlier version of this work, already been made in the Copyright Office?

☐ Yes ☐ No If your answer is "Yes," why is another registration being sought? (Check appropriate box) ▼

a. ☐ This is the first published edition of a work previously registered in unpublished form.

b. ☐ This is the first application submitted by this author as copyright claimant.

c. ☐ This is a changed version of the work, as shown by space 6 on this application.

If your answer is "Yes," give: **Previous Registration Number** ▼   **Year of Registration** ▼

DERIVATIVE WORK OR COMPILATION Complete both space 6a and 6b for a derivative work; complete only 6b for a compilation.
a. Preexisting Material Identify any preexisting work or works that this work is based on or incorporates. ▼

b. Material Added to This Work Give a brief, general statement of the material that has been added to this work and in which copyright is claimed. ▼

See in
before
this sp

—space deleted—

REPRODUCTION FOR USE OF BLIND OR PHYSICALLY HANDICAPPED INDIVIDUALS A signature on this form at space 10 and a check in one of the boxes here in space 8 constitutes a non-exclusive grant of permission to the Library of Congress to reproduce and distribute solely for the blind and physically handicapped and under the conditions and limitations prescribed by the regulations of the Copyright Office: (1) copies of the work identified in space 1 of this application in Braille (or similar tactile symbols); or (2) phonorecords embodying a fixation of a reading of that work; or (3) both.

a ☐ Copies and Phonorecords   b ☐ Copies Only   c ☐ Phonorecords Only   See

DEPOSIT ACCOUNT If the registration fee is to be charged to a Deposit Account established in the Copyright Office, give name and number of Account.
Name ▼   **Account Number** ▼

CORRESPONDENCE Give name and address to which correspondence about this application should be sent.   Name/Address/Apt/City/State/ZIP ▼

Be
giv
day
◄ nur

Area Code and Telephone Number ▶

CERTIFICATION* I, the undersigned, hereby certify that I am the

Check only one ▶ {
☐ author
☐ other copyright claimant
☐ owner of exclusive right(s)
☐ authorized agent of _____

of the work identified in this application and that the statements made by me in this application are correct to the best of my knowledge.

Name of author or other copyright claimant, or owner of exclusive right(s) ▲

Typed or printed name and date ▼ If this application gives a date of publication in space 3, do not sign and submit it before that date.

date ▶ _____

☞ **Handwritten signature (X)** ▼

MAIL CERTIFI-CATE TO

Name ▼

Number/Street/Apartment Number ▼

City/State/ZIP ▼

Certificate will be mailed in window envelope

The Copy
has the au
just fees a
vals, base
in the Co
Index. Th
ment is e
Please
Copyright
July 1995
the actual

*17 U.S.C. § 506(e): Any person who knowingly makes a false representation of a material fact in the application for copyright registration provided for by section 409, or in any written statement filed in with the application, shall be fined not more than $2,500.

February 1993—100,000   ☆U.S. GOVERNMENT PRINTING OFFICE: 1993-342

FORM PA

For a Work of the Performing Arts
UNITED STATES COPYRIGHT OFFICE

REGISTRATION NUMBER

PA   PAU

EFFECTIVE DATE OF REGISTRATION

_____ _____ _____
Month   Day   Year

DO NOT WRITE ABOVE THIS LINE. IF YOU NEED MORE SPACE, USE A SEPARATE CONTINUATION SHEET.

TITLE OF THIS WORK ▼

PREVIOUS OR ALTERNATIVE TITLES ▼

NATURE OF THIS WORK ▼ See instructions

2

a

NAME OF AUTHOR ▼

DATES OF BIRTH AND DEATH
Year Born ▼   Year Died ▼

Was this contribution to the work a "work made for hire"?
☐ Yes
☐ No

AUTHOR'S NATIONALITY OR DOMICILE
Name of Country
OR { Citizen of ▶_____
     Domiciled in ▶_____

WAS THIS AUTHOR'S CONTRIBUTION TO THE WORK
Anonymous? ☐ Yes ☐ No
Pseudonymous? ☐ Yes ☐ No

If the answer to either of these questions is "Yes," see detailed instructions.

NATURE OF AUTHORSHIP Briefly describe nature of material created by this author in which copyright is claimed. ▼

NOTE

Under the law, the "author" of a "work made for hire" is generally the employer, not the employee (see instructions). For any part of this work that was "made for hire" check "Yes" in the space provided, give the employer (or other person for whom the work was prepared) as "author" of that part, and leave the space for dates of birth and death blank.

b

NAME OF AUTHOR ▼

DATES OF BIRTH AND DEATH
Year Born ▼   Year Died ▼

Was this contribution to the work a "work made for hire"?
☐ Yes
☐ No

AUTHOR'S NATIONALITY OR DOMICILE
Name of Country
OR { Citizen of ▶_____
     Domiciled in ▶_____

WAS THIS AUTHOR'S CONTRIBUTION TO THE WORK
Anonymous? ☐ Yes ☐ No
Pseudonymous? ☐ Yes ☐ No

If the answer to either of these questions is "Yes," see detailed instructions.

NATURE OF AUTHORSHIP Briefly describe nature of material created by this author in which copyright is claimed. ▼

c

NAME OF AUTHOR ▼

DATES OF BIRTH AND DEATH
Year Born ▼   Year Died ▼

Was this contribution to the work a "work made for hire"?
☐ Yes
☐ No

AUTHOR'S NATIONALITY OR DOMICILE
Name of Country
OR { Citizen of ▶_____
     Domiciled in ▶_____

WAS THIS AUTHOR'S CONTRIBUTION TO THE WORK
Anonymous? ☐ Yes ☐ No
Pseudonymous? ☐ Yes ☐ No

If the answer to either of these questions is "Yes," see detailed instructions.

NATURE OF AUTHORSHIP Briefly describe nature of material created by this author in which copyright is claimed. ▼

3

a **YEAR IN WHICH CREATION OF THIS WORK WAS COMPLETED** This information must be given in all cases.
◀ Year

b **DATE AND NATION OF FIRST PUBLICATION OF THIS PARTICULAR WORK**
Complete this information ONLY if this work has been published.
Month ▶ _____ Day ▶ _____ Year ▶ _____ ◀ Nation

4

COPYRIGHT CLAIMANT(S) Name and address must be given even if the claimant is the same as the author given in space 2. ▼

TRANSFER If the claimant(s) named here in space 4 is (are) different from the author(s) named in space 2, give a brief statement of how the claimant(s) obtained ownership of the copyright. ▼

See instructions before completing this space.

DO NOT WRITE HERE OFFICE USE ONLY

APPLICATION RECEIVED

ONE DEPOSIT RECEIVED

TWO DEPOSITS RECEIVED

FUNDS RECEIVED

MORE ON BACK ▶ • Complete all applicable spaces (numbers 5-9) on the reverse side of this page.
• See detailed instructions.   • Sign the form at line 8.

DO NOT WRITE HER[E]

Page 1 of _____ pag[e]

DO NOT WRITE ABOVE THIS LINE. IF YOU NEED MORE SPACE, USE A SEPARATE CONTINUATION SHEET.

PREVIOUS REGISTRATION Has registration for this work, or for an earlier version of this work, already been made in the Copyright Office?

☐ Yes ☐ No If your answer is "Yes," why is another registration being sought? (Check appropriate box) ▼

a. ☐ This is the first published edition of a work previously registered in unpublished form.

b. ☐ This is the first application submitted by this author as copyright claimant.

c. ☐ This is a changed version of the work, as shown by space 6 on this application.

If your answer is "Yes," give: **Previous Registration Number** ▼   **Year of Registration** ▼

DERIVATIVE WORK OR COMPILATION Complete both space 6a and 6b for a derivative work; complete only 6b for a compilation.

a. **Preexisting Material** Identify any preexisting work or works that this work is based on or incorporates. ▼

See ins
before c
this spa

b. **Material Added to This Work** Give a brief, general statement of the material that has been added to this work and in which copyright is claimed. ▼

DEPOSIT ACCOUNT If the registration fee is to be charged to a Deposit Account established in the Copyright Office, give name and number of Account.
Name ▼   **Account Number** ▼

CORRESPONDENCE Give name and address to which correspondence about this application should be sent.   Name/Address/Apt/City/State/ZIP ▼

Area Code and Telephone Number ▶

Be s
give y
dayti
◀ numb

CERTIFICATION* I, the undersigned, hereby certify that I am the

Check only one ▼

☐ author

☐ other copyright claimant

☐ owner of exclusive right(s)

☐ authorized agent of _____
   Name of author or other copyright claimant, or owner of exclusive right(s) ▲

of the work identified in this application and that the statements made
by me in this application are correct to the best of my knowledge.

Typed or printed name and date ▼ If this application gives a date of publication in space 3, do not sign and submit it before that date.

_____   **date** ▶ _____

☞ **Handwritten signature (X)** ▼

MAIL CERTIFI-CATE TO

Name ▼

Number/Street/Apartment Number ▼

Certificate will be mailed in window envelope

City/State/ZIP ▼

FORM SE

For a Serial
UNITED STATES COPYRIGHT OFFICE

REGISTRATION NUMBER

U

EFFECTIVE DATE OF REGISTRATION

Month Day Year

DO NOT WRITE ABOVE THIS LINE. IF YOU NEED MORE SPACE, USE A SEPARATE CONTINUATION SHEET.

TITLE OF THIS SERIAL ▼

Volume ▼ **Number ▼** **Date on Copies ▼** **Frequency of Publication ▼**

PREVIOUS OR ALTERNATIVE TITLES ▼

a **NAME OF AUTHOR ▼**

DATES OF BIRTH AND DEATH Year Born ▼ Year Died ▼

Was this contribution to the work a "work made for hire"? ☐ Yes ☐ No

AUTHOR'S NATIONALITY OR DOMICILE Name of Country
OR { Citizen of ▶ / Domiciled in ▶

WAS THIS AUTHOR'S CONTRIBUTION TO THE WORK
Anonymous? ☐ Yes ☐ No
Pseudonymous? ☐ Yes ☐ No
If the answer to either of these questions is "Yes," see detailed instructions.

NATURE OF AUTHORSHIP Briefly describe nature of material created by this author in which copyright is claimed. ▼
☐ **Collective Work** Other:

b **NAME OF AUTHOR ▼**

DATES OF BIRTH AND DEATH Year Born ▼ Year Died ▼

Was this contribution to the work a "work made for hire"? ☐ Yes ☐ No

AUTHOR'S NATIONALITY OR DOMICILE Name of Country
OR { Citizen of ▶ / Domiciled in ▶

WAS THIS AUTHOR'S CONTRIBUTION TO THE WORK
Anonymous? ☐ Yes ☐ No
Pseudonymous? ☐ Yes ☐ No
If the answer to either of these questions is "Yes," see detailed instructions.

NATURE OF AUTHORSHIP Briefly describe nature of material created by this author in which copyright is claimed. ▼
☐ **Collective Work** Other:

c **NAME OF AUTHOR ▼**

DATES OF BIRTH AND DEATH Year Born ▼ Year Died ▼

Was this contribution to the work a "work made for hire"? ☐ Yes ☐ No

AUTHOR'S NATIONALITY OR DOMICILE Name of Country
OR { Citizen of ▶ / Domiciled in ▶

WAS THIS AUTHOR'S CONTRIBUTION TO THE WORK
Anonymous? ☐ Yes ☐ No
Pseudonymous? ☐ Yes ☐ No
If the answer to either of these questions is "Yes," see detailed instructions.

NATURE OF AUTHORSHIP Briefly describe nature of material created by this author in which copyright is claimed. ▼
☐ **Collective Work** Other:

TE
law,
r" of a
le for
nerally
yer, not
yee
uc-
any
s work
made
heck
he
vided,
(or
son for
work
ared) as
of that
leave
for
birth and
nk.

a **YEAR IN WHICH CREATION OF THIS ISSUE WAS COMPLETED** **This information must be given in all cases.** ◀ Year

b **DATE AND NATION OF FIRST PUBLICATION OF THIS PARTICULAR ISSUE**
Complete this information ONLY if this work has been published. Month ▶ Day ▶ Year ▶ ◀ Nation

COPYRIGHT CLAIMANT(S) Name and address must be given even if the claimant is the same as the author given in space 2. ▼

TRANSFER If the claimant(s) named here in space 4 is (are) different from the author(s) named in space 2, give a brief statement of how the claimant(s) obtained ownership of the copyright. ▼

uctions
mpleting
e.

DO NOT WRITE HERE OFFICE USE ONLY
APPLICATION RECEIVED
ONE DEPOSIT RECEIVED
TWO DEPOSITS RECEIVED
REMITTANCE NUMBER AND DATE

MORE ON BACK ▶
- Complete all applicable spaces (numbers 5-11) on the reverse side of this page.
- See detailed instructions.
- Sign the form at line 10.

DO NOT WRITE HERE

Page 1 of ______ pages

DO NOT WRITE ABOVE THIS LINE. IF YOU NEED MORE SPACE, USE A SEPARATE CONTINUATION SHEET.

PREVIOUS REGISTRATION Has registration for this issue, or for an earlier version of this particular issue, already been made in the Copyright Office?

☐ **Yes** ☐ **No** If your answer is "Yes," why is another registration being sought? (Check appropriate box) ▼

a. ☐ This is the first published edition of an issue previously registered in unpublished form.

b. ☐ This is the first application submitted by this author as copyright claimant.

c. ☐ This is a changed version of this issue, as shown by space 6 on this application.

If your answer is "Yes," give: **Previous Registration Number ▼**   **Year of Registration ▼**

DERIVATIVE WORK OR COMPILATION Complete both space 6a and 6b for a derivative work; complete only 6b for a compilation.
a. Preexisting Material Identify any preexisting work or works that this work is based on or incorporates. ▼

b. Material Added to This Work Give a brief, general statement of the material that has been added to this work and in which copyright is claimed. ▼

See ins
before c
this spa

—space deleted—

REPRODUCTION FOR USE OF BLIND OR PHYSICALLY HANDICAPPED INDIVIDUALS A signature on this form at space 10 and a check in one of the boxes here in space 8 constitutes a non-exclusive grant of permission to the Library of Congress to reproduce and distribute solely for the blind and physically handicapped and under the conditions and limitations prescribed by the regulations of the Copyright Office: (1) copies of the work identified in space 1 of this application in Braille (or similar tactile symbols); or (2) phonorecords embodying a fixation of a reading of that work; or (3) both.

    a ☐ Copies and Phonorecords   **b** ☐ Copies Only   **c** ☐ Phonorecords Only   See ins

DEPOSIT ACCOUNT If the registration fee is to be charged to a Deposit Account established in the Copyright Office, give name and number of Account.
Name ▼   **Account Number ▼**

CORRESPONDENCE Give name and address to which correspondence about this application should be sent.   Name/Address/Apt/City/State/ZIP ▼

Be su
give y
daytir
◄ numb

        Area Code and Telephone Number ►

CERTIFICATION* I, the undersigned, hereby certify that I am the

Check only one ►
{
☐ author
☐ other copyright claimant
☐ owner of exclusive right(s)
☐ authorized agent of _____
}

of the work identified in this application and that the statements made
by me in this application are correct to the best of my knowledge.   Name of author or other copyright claimant, or owner of exclusive right(s) ▲

Typed or printed name and date ▼ If this application gives a date of publication in space 3, do not sign and submit it before that date.

_____   **date ►** _____

👉   Handwritten signature (X) ▼

*17 U.S.C. § 506(e): Any person who knowingly makes a false representation of a material fact in the application for copyright registration provided for by section 409, or in any written statement filed in con
with the application, shall be fined not more than $2,500.

April 1993—100,000

☆U.S. GOVERNMENT PRINTING OFFICE: 1993-342-58°

SHORT FORM SE

For a Serial
UNITED STATES COPYRIGHT OFFICE

REGISTRATION NUMBER

_____

EFFECTIVE DATE OF REGISTRATION
(Assigned by Copyright Office)

Month	Day	Year

APPLICATION RECEIVED
_____

ONE DEPOSIT RECEIVED
_____

TWO DEPOSITS RECEIVED
_____

EXAMINED BY
_____

CORRESPONDENCE ☐

DO NOT WRITE ABOVE THIS LINE.

1   **TITLE OF THIS SERIAL AS IT APPEARS ON THE COPY**

Volume▼   Number▼   Date on Copies▼   ISSN▼

2   **NAME AND ADDRESS OF THE AUTHOR AND COPYRIGHT CLAIMANT IN THIS COLLECTIVE WORK MADE FOR HIRE**

3   **DATE OF PUBLICATION OF THIS PARTICULAR ISSUE**
Month▼   Day▼   Year▼

YEAR IN WHICH CREATION OF THIS ISSUE WAS COMPLETED (IF EARLIER THAN THE YEAR OF PUBLICATION):
Year▼

CERTIFICATION*:   I, the undersigned, hereby certify that I am the copyright claimant or the authorized agent of the copyright claimant of the work identified in this application, that all the conditions specified in the instructions on the back of this form are met, and that the statements made by me in this application are correct to the best of my knowledge.

Handwritten signature (X) _____

Typed or printed name of signer _____

PERSON TO CONTACT FOR CORRESPONDENCE ABOUT THIS CLAIM

Name ▶ _____
Daytime telephone number ▶ _____
Address (if other than given below) ▶ _____

DEPOSIT ACCOUNT

Account number ▶ _____
Name of account ▶ _____

MAIL CERTIFICATE TO

Name▼

Number/Street/Apartment Number▼

City/State/ZIP▼

Certificate will be mailed in window envelope

YOU MUST:
• Complete all necessary spaces
• Sign your application

SEND ALL 3 ELEMENTS IN THE SAME PACKAGE:
1. Application form
2. Nonrefundable $20 filing fee in check or money order payable to *Register of Copyrights*
3. Deposit material

MAIL TO:
Register of Copyrights
Library of Congress
Washington, D.C. 20559

Copyright fees are adjusted at 5-year intervals, based on increases or decreases in the Consumer Price Index. The next adjustment is due in 1995. Contact the Copyright Office in January 1995 for the new fee schedule.

June 1992—50,000

☆U.S. GOVERNMENT PRINTING OFFICE: 1992—312-432/60,001

⊘ Filling Out Short Form SE

BASIC INFORMATION
Read these instructions before completing this form. Make sure all applicable spaces have been filled in before you return this form.

When to Use This Form:
All the following conditions must be met in order to use this form. If any one of the conditions does not apply, you must use Form SE. Incorrect use of this form will result in a delay in your registration.

The claim must be in a collective work.
The work must be essentially an all-new collective work or issue.
The author must be a citizen or domiciliary of the United States.
The work must be a work made for hire.
The author(s) and claimant(s) must be the same person(s) or organization(s).
The work must be first published in the United States.

Deposit to Accompany Application:
An application for registration of a copyright claim in a serial issue first published in the United States must be accompanied by a deposit consisting of two copies (or phonorecords) of the best edition.

Fee:
The filing fee of $20.00 must be sent for each issue to be registered. Do not send cash or currency.

Copyright fees are adjusted at 5-year intervals, based on increases or decreases in the Consumer Price Index. The next adjustment is due in 1995. Contact the Copyright Office in January 1995 for the new fee schedule.

Mailing Requirements:
It is important that you send the application, the deposit copies, and the $20.00 fee together in the same envelope or package. Send to: Register of Copyrights, Library of Congress, Washington, D.C. 20559.

Reproduction for Use of Blind or Physically Handicapped Individuals:
A signature on this form and a check in one of these boxes constitutes a nonexclusive grant of permission to the Library of Congress to reproduce and distribute solely for the blind and physically handicapped under the conditions and limitations prescribed by the regulations of the Copyright Office: (1) copies of the work identified in space 1 of this application in Braille (or similar tactile symbols); or (2) phonorecords embodying a fixation of a reading of that work; or (3) both.

☐ Copies only   ☐ Phonorecords only   ☐ Copies and phonorecords

Collective Work:
The term "collective work" refers to a work, such as a serial issue, in which a number of contributions are assembled into a collective whole. A claim in the "collective work" extends to all copyrightable authorship created by employees of the author, as well as any independent contributions in which the claimant has acquired ownership of the copyright.

Publication:
The statute defines "publication" as "The distributio[n] copies or phonorecords of a work to the public by sale or other transfe[r] ownership, or by rental, lease, or lending;" a work is also "published" if th[e] has been an "offering to distribute copies or phonorecords to a grou[p] persons for purposes of further distribution, public performance, or pu[blic] display."

Creation:
A work is "created" when it is fixed in a copy (or phonorecor[d]) for the first time.

Work Made for Hire:
A "work made for hire" is defined as: ([1]) work prepared by an employee within the scope of his or her employme[nt]; or (2) a work specially ordered or commissioned for certain uses (includ[ing] use as a contribution to a collective work), if the parties expressly agree i[n] written instrument signed by them that the work shall be considered a w[ork] made for hire. The employer is the author of a work made for hire.

The Copyright Notice:
For works first published on or af[ter] March 1, 1989, the law provides that a copyright notice in a specified fo[rm] "may be placed on all publicly distributed copies from which the work [can] be visually perceived." Use of the copyright notice is the responsibility of [the] copyright owner and does not require advance permission from the Co[py]right Office. The required form of the notice for copies generally consists [of] three elements: (1) the symbol "©", or the word "Copyright," or [the] abbreviation "Copr."; (2) the year of first publication; and (3) the name of [the] owner of copyright. For example: "©1992 Jane Cole." The notice is to [be] affixed to the copies "in such manner and location as to give reasonabl[e] notice of the claim of copyright." Works first published prior to March 1, 19[89] **must** carry the notice or risk loss of copyright protection.

For information about notice requirements for works published befo[re] March 1, 1989, or other copyright information, write: Information Sectio[n,] LM-401, Copyright Office, Library of Congress, Washington, D.C. 20559.

PRIVACY ACT ADVISORY STATEMENT Required by the Privacy Act of 1974 (P.L. 93-579)

The authority for requesting this information is title 17 U.S.C., secs. 409 and 410. Furnishing the requested information is voluntary. But if the information is not furnished, it may be necessary to delay or refuse registration and you may not be entitled to certain relief, remedies, and benefits provided in chapters 4 and 5 of title 17, U.S.C.

The principal uses of the requested information are the establishment and maintenance of a public record and the examination of the application for compliance with legal requirements.

Other routine uses include public inspection and copying, preparation of public indexes, preparation of public catalogs of copyright registrations, and preparation of search reports upon request.

NOTE: No other advisory statement will be given in connection with this application. Please keep this statement and refer to it if we communicate with you regarding this application.

SPACE-BY-SPACE INSTRUCTIONS

1 SPACE 1: Title

Every work submitted for copyright registration must be given a title to identify that particular work. Give the complete title of the periodical, including the volume, number, issue date, or other indicia printed on the copies. If possible, give the International Standard Serial Number (ISSN).

2 SPACE 2: Author and Copyright Claimant

Give the fullest form of the author and claimant's name. If there are joint authors and owners, give the names of all the author/owners. (It is assumed that the authors and claimants are the same, that the work is made for hire, and that the claim is in the collective work).

3 SPACE 3: Date of Publication of This Particular Work

Give the exact date on which publication of this issue first took place. The full date, including month, day, and year must be given.

Year in Which Creation of This Issue Was Complete[d]
Give the year in which this serial issue was fixed in a copy or phonorecord fo[r] the first time. If no year is given, it is assumed that the issue was created [in] the same year in which it was published. The date must be the same as or n[ot] later than the publication date.

Certification:
The application cannot be accepted unless it bears th[e] handwritten signature of the copyright claimant or the duly authorized age[nt] of the copyright claimant.

Person to Contact for Correspondence About Thi[s] Claim:
Give the name and telephone number, including area code, of th[e] person to whom any correspondence concerning this claim should be ad[-] dressed. Give the address only if it is different from the address for mailin[g] of the certificate.

Deposit Account:
If the filing fee is to be charged against a Deposi[t] Account in the Copyright Office, give the name and number of the accoun[t] in this space. Otherwise, leave the space blank and forward the $20.00 filin[g] fee with your application and deposit.

Mailing Address of Certificate:
This address must be complete and legible since the certificate will be mailed in a window envelope.

FORM SE/GROUP

UNITED STATES COPYRIGHT OFFICE

REGISTRATION NUMBER

EFFECTIVE DATE OF REGISTRATION
(Assigned by Copyright Office)

Month	Day	Year

APPLICATION RECEIVED

ONE DEPOSIT RECEIVED

EXAMINED BY   CORRESPONDENCE ☐

DO NOT WRITE ABOVE THIS LINE.

1

List in order of publication

No previous registration under identical title

TITLE ▼   ISSN ▼

	Volume ▼	Number ▼	Issue date on copies ▼	Month, day and year of publication ▼
1.				
2.				
3.				
4.				
5.				
6.				
7.				
8.				
9.				
10.				
11.				
12.				
13.				
14.				

2

NAME AND ADDRESS OF THE AUTHOR/COPYRIGHT CLAIMANT IN THESE COLLECTIVE WORKS MADE FOR HIRE

FOR NON-U.S. WORKS: Author's citizenship ▼   Domicile ▼   Nation of publication ▼

CERTIFICATION*:   I, the undersigned, hereby certify that I am the copyright claimant or the authorized agent of the copyright claimant of the works identified in this application, that all the conditions specified in the instructions on the back of this form are met, that I have deposited two complimentary subscription copies with the Library of Congress, and that the statements made by me in this application are correct to the best of my knowledge.

Signature (X) _____   Typed or printed name _____

PERSON TO CONTACT FOR CORRESPONDENCE ABOUT THIS CLAIM

Name ▶ _____
Daytime telephone number ▶ _____
Address (if other than given below) ▶ _____

DEPOSIT ACCOUNT

Account number ▶ _____
Name of account ▶ _____

MAIL CERTIFI-CATE TO

Name ▼

Number/Street/Apartment Number ▼

City/State/ZIP ▼

Certificate will be mailed in window envelope

REPRODUCTION FOR USE OF BLIND OR PHYSICALLY HANDICAPPED INDIVIDUALS

a ☐ Copies and Phonorecords
b ☐ Copies Only
c ☐ Phonorecords Only

MAIL TO:
Register of Copyrights
Library of Congress
Washington, D.C. 20559

17 U.S.C. §506(e): Any person who knowingly makes a false representation of a material fact in the application for copyright registration provided for by section 409, or in any written statement filed in connection with the application, shall be fined not more than $2,500.

April 1991—100,000   ✩ U.S. GOVERNMENT PRINTING OFFICE: 1991–282-170/20,016

Form SE/GROUP

BASIC INFORMATION

Read these instructions before completing this form. Make sure all applicable spaces have been filled in before you return this form.

When to Use This Form: All the following conditions must be met in order to use this form. If any one of the conditions does not apply, you must register the issues separately using Form SE or Short Form SE.

1. You must have given a complimentary subscription for two copies of the serial to the Library of Congress, confirmed by letter to the General Counsel, Copyright Office. Subscription copies must be mailed **separately** to:

   Library of Congress
   Group Periodicals Registration
   Washington, D.C. 20540

2. The claim must be in the collective works.
3. The works must be essentially all new collective works or issues.
4. Each issue must be a work made for hire.
5. The author(s) and claimant(s) must be the same person(s) or organization(s) for all of the issues.
6. Each issue must have been created no more than one year prior to publication.
7. All issues in the group must have been published within the same calendar year.

Which Issues May Be Included in a Group Registration: You may register two or more issues of a serial published at intervals of one week or longer under the same continuing title, provided that the issues were published within a 90-day period during the same calendar year.

Deposit to Accompany Application: Send one copy of each issue included in the group registration with the application and fee.

Fee: A nonrefundable filing fee of $10.00 FOR EACH ISSUE LISTED ON FORM SE/GROUP must be sent with the application or charged to an active deposit account in the Copyright Office. There is a minimum fee of $20.00 for Form SE/Group. Special handling is not available for Form SE/Group.

Mailing Instructions: Send the application, deposit copies, and fee together in the same package to: Register of Copyrights, Library of Congress, Washington, D.C. 20559.

International Standard Serial Number (ISSN): ISSN is an internationally accepted code for the identification of serial publications. If a published serial has not been assigned an ISSN, application forms and additional information may be obtained from National Serials Data Program, Library of Congress, Washington, D.C. 20540. Do not contact the Copyright Office for ISSNs.

Collective Work: The term "collective work" refers to a work , as a serial issue, in which a number of contributions are assembled i collective whole. A claim in the "collective work" extends to all copyright authorship created by employees of the author, as well as any independ contributions in which the claimant has acquired ownership of the c right.

Publication: The statute defines "publication" as "The distributio copies or phonorecords of a work to the public by sale or other transfe ownership, or by rental, lease, or lending;" a work is also "published" if t has been an "offering to distribute copies or phonorecords to a grou persons for purposes of further distribution, public performance, or pu display."

Creation: A work is "created" when it is fixed in a copy (or p orecord) for the first time. For a serial, the year in which the collective w was completed is the creation date.

Work Made for Hire: A "work made for hire" is defined as: work prepared by an employee within the scope of his or her employm or (2) a work specially ordered or commissioned for certain uses (includ use as a contribution to a collective work), if the parties expressly agree written instrument signed by them that the work shall be considered a w made for hire. The employer is the author of a work made for hire.

The Copyright Notice: For works first published on or a March 1, 1989, the law provides that a copyright notice in a specified fe "may be placed on all publicly distributed copies from which the work be visually perceived." Use of the copyright notice is the responsibility of copyright owner and does not require advance permission from the Co right Office. The required form of the notice for copies generally consis three elements: (1) the symbol "©", or the word "Copyright," or abbreviation "Copr."; (2) the year of first publication; and (3) the name of owner of copyright. For example: "©1990 Jane Cole." The notice is to affixed to the copies "in such manner and location as to give reasona notice of the claim of copyright." Works first published prior to Marc 1989, **must** carry the notice or risk loss of copyright protection.

For information about notice requirements for works published be March 1, 1989, or other copyright information, write: Information Secti LM-401, Copyright Office, Library of Congress, Washington, D.C. 2055

SPACE-BY-SPACE INSTRUCTIONS

1 SPACE 1: Title and Date of Publication

Give the complete title of the serial, followed by the International Standard Serial Number (ISSN), if available. List the issues in the order of publication. For each issue, give the volume, number, and issue date appearing on the copies, followed by the complete date of publication, including month, day, and year. If you have not previously registered this **identical title** under Section 408 of the Copyright Act, please indicate by checking the box.

2 SPACE 2: Author and Copyright Claimant

Give the fullest form of the author and claimant's name and mailing address. If there are joint authors and claimants, give the names and addresses of all the author/claimants. If the work is not of U.S. origin, add the citizenship or domicile of the author/claimant, or the nation of publication.

Certification: The application cannot be accepted unless it bears the handwritten signature of the copyright claimant or the duly authorized agent of the copyright claimant.

Person to Contact for Correspondence About Th Claim: Give the name and telephone number, including area code, of person to whom any correspondence concerning this claim should addressed. Give the address only if it is different from the address mailing of the certificate.

Deposit Account: If the filing fee is to be charged against a depo account in the Copyright Office, give the name and number of the accou in this space. Otherwise, leave the space blank and forward the filing with your application and deposit.

Mailing Address of Certificate: This address must be comple and legible since the certificate will be mailed in a window envelope.

Reproduction for Use of Blind or Physicall Handicapped Individuals: A signature on this form and check in one of these boxes constitutes a nonexclusive grant of permissi to the Library of Congress to reproduce and distribute solely for the bli and physically handicapped under the conditions and limitations p scribed by the regulations of the Copyright Office: (1) copies of the wo identified in space 1 of this application in Braille (or similar tactile symbol or (2) phonorecords embodying a fixation of a reading of that work; or both.

FORM G/DN
For Group/Daily Newspapers
UNITED STATES COPYRIGHT OFFICE

REGISTRATION NUMBER

EFFECTIVE DATE OF REGISTRATION
(Assigned by Copyright Office)

Month	Day	Year

APPLICATION RECEIVED

ONE MICROFILM DEPOSIT RECEIVED

EXAMINED BY   CORRESPONDENCE ☐

DO NOT WRITE ABOVE THIS LINE.

1 TITLE OF THIS NEWSPAPER AS IT APPEARS ON THE COPIES ▼   City/State▼

Month and year date on copies ▼   Number of issues in this group ▼   ISSN▼   Edition▼

2 NAME AND ADDRESS OF THE AUTHOR/COPYRIGHT CLAIMANT IN THESE COLLECTIVE WORKS MADE FOR HIRE

3 DATE OF PUBLICATION OF THE FIRST AND LAST ISSUES IN THIS GROUP
Month▼   Day▼   Year▼

(First) _____

(Last) _____

REPRODUCTION FOR USE OF BLIND OR PHYSICALLY HANDICAPPED INDIVIDUALS

a ☐ Copies and Phonorecords

b ☐ Copies Only

c ☐ Phonorecords Only

CERTIFICATION*:   I, the undersigned, hereby certify that I am the copyright claimant or the authorized agent of the copyright claimant of the works identified in this application, that all the conditions specified in the instructions on the back of this form are met, and that the statements made by me in this application are correct to the best of my knowledge.

Handwritten
signature (X) _____

Typed or printed
name of signer _____

PERSON TO CONTACT FOR CORRESPONDENCE ABOUT THIS CLAIM

Name ▶ _____

Daytime telephone number ▶ _____

Address (if other than given below) ▶ _____

DEPOSIT ACCOUNT

Account number ▶ _____

Name of account ▶ _____

MAIL CERTIFICATE TO

Name▼ _____

Number/Street/Apartment Number▼ _____

City/State/ZIP▼ _____

Certificate
will be
mailed in
window
envelope

U.S.C. §506(e): Any person who knowingly makes a false representation of a material fact in the application for copyright registration provided for by section 409, or in any written statement filed in connection with the application, shall be fined not more than $2,500.

☆ U.S. GOVERNMENT PRINTING OFFICE: 1992–312-432/60,005

August 1992—20,000

Form Group/Daily Newspaper

BASIC INFORMATION
Read these instructions before completing this form.
Make sure all applicable spaces have been filled in
before you return this form.

When to Use This Form: All the following conditions must be met in order to use this form. If any one of the conditions does not apply, you must use Form SE. Incorrect use of this form will result in a delay in your registration.
1. The work must be a daily newspaper.
2. The claim must include all issue dates within the calendar month within the same year.
3. The applicant must submit a complete month's issues in microfilm form.
4. Each issue must essentially be an all-new collective work.
5. The work must be a work made for hire.
6. The author(s) and claimant(s) must be the same person(s) or organization(s).
7. The application must be filed within 3 months after the last publication date included in the group.

Deposit to Accompany Application: This application must be accompanied by a deposit of a positive, 35mm silver-halide microfilm that includes all issue dates within a calendar month for the specific title that was published as the last (final) edition.

Fee: The nonrefundable filing fee for registration of a group of newspapers is $40.00. Unless you maintain a Deposit Account in the Copyright Office, the $40.00 fee in the form of a check, money order, or bank draft must accompany your application form and copies. Do not send cash or currency. Make your remittance payable to: **Register of Copyrights**. Remittances must be payable immediately through a U.S. institution in U.S. dollars. Remittances may be in the form of International Money Order only if it is immediately redeemable in U.S. dollars. Special Handling is not available for the group registration of daily newspapers.
NOTE: The Copyright Office has the authority to adjust fees at 5-year intervals, based on changes in the Consumer Price Index. The next adjustment is due in 1995. Please contact the Copyright Office after July 1995 to determine the actual fee schedule.

Mailing Procedures: It is important that you send the application, the deposit, and the $40.00 fee together in the same envelope or package to: Register of Copyrights, Library of Congress, Washington, D.C. 20559.

Reproduction for Use by Blind or Physically Handicapped Individuals: A signature on this form and a check in one of the boxes in space 3 (on verso of page) constitute a nonexclusive grant of permission to the Library of Congress to reproduce and distribute solely for the blind and physically handica under the conditions and limitations prescribed by the regulations c Copyright Office: (1) copies of the work identified in space 1 of this a cation in Braille (or similar tactile symbols); or (2) phonorecords embod a fixation of a reading of that work; or (3) both.

Collective Work: The term "collective work" refers to a work , as a serial issue, in which a number of contributions are assembled i collective whole. A claim in the "collective work" extends to all copyr able authorship created by employees of the author, as well as any inde dent contributions in which the claimant has acquired ownership o copyright.

Publication: The Copyright Law defines "publication" as "the d bution of copies or phonorecords of a work to the public by sale or c transfer of ownership, or by rental, lease, or lending." A wor also "published" if there has been an "offering to distribute copie phonorecords to a group of persons for purposes of further distribu public performance, or public display."

Work Made for Hire: A "work made for hire" is defined as: work prepared by an employee within the scope of his or her employm or (2) a work specially ordered or commissioned for certain uses (inclu use as a contribution to a collective work), if the parties expressly agre a written instrument signed by them that the work shall be consider work made for hire. The employer is the author of a work made for hi

Newspaper: As defined by the Newspaper Section of the Serials Government Publications Division of the Library of Congress, works sified as newspapers are serials mainly designed to be a primary so of written information on current events, either local, national, or in national in scope. Newspapers contain a broad range of news on all jects and activities and are not limited to any specific subject matter. Ne papers are intended either for the general public or for a particular gr

SPACE-BY-SPACE INSTRUCTIONS

1 SPACE 1: Title

Space 1 must identify the work being registered by giving the complete title of the newspaper, the month and year printed on the copies, the number of issues in the group, the city and state, the edition, and, if known, the ISSN number.

2 SPACE 2: Author and Copyright Claimant

Give the fullest form of the author and claimant's name. If there are joint authors and owners, give the names of all the author/owners. (It is assumed that the authors and claimant are the same, that the work is made for hire, and that the claim is in the collective work.)

3 SPACE 3: Date of Publication

Give the exact date on which publication of the first and last issues in this group took place. The full date, including month, day, and year must be given.

Certification: The application cannot be accepted unless it bears handwritten signature of the copyright claimant or the duly authorized ag of the copyright claimant.

Person to Contact for Correspondence
About This Claim: Give the name and telephone number, includ area code, of the person to whom any correspondence concerning this cl should be addressed. Give the address only if it is different from the add for the mailing of the certificate.

Deposit Account: If the filing fee is to be charged against a Dep Account in the Copyright Office, give the name and number of the acco in this space. Otherwise, leave the space blank and forward the $40.00 fi fee with your application and deposit.

Mailing Address of Certificate: This address must be compl and legible because the certificate will be mailed in a window envelope

FORM VA
For a Work of the Visual Arts
UNITED STATES COPYRIGHT OFFICE

REGISTRATION NUMBER

_____

VA   VAU

EFFECTIVE DATE OF REGISTRATION

_____

Month   Day   Year

DO NOT WRITE ABOVE THIS LINE. IF YOU NEED MORE SPACE, USE A SEPARATE CONTINUATION SHEET.

TITLE OF THIS WORK ▼   **NATURE OF THIS WORK ▼** See instructions

PREVIOUS OR ALTERNATIVE TITLES ▼

PUBLICATION AS A CONTRIBUTION If this work was published as a contribution to a periodical, serial, or collection, give information about the collective work in which the contribution appeared.   **Title of Collective Work ▼**

If published in a periodical or serial give: **Volume ▼**   **Number ▼**   **Issue Date ▼**   **On Pages ▼**

2

a

NAME OF AUTHOR ▼   **DATES OF BIRTH AND DEATH**
Year Born ▼   Year Died ▼

Was this contribution to the work a "work made for hire"?
☐ Yes
☐ No

AUTHOR'S NATIONALITY OR DOMICILE
Name of Country
OR { Citizen of ▶ _____
Domiciled in ▶ _____

WAS THIS AUTHOR'S CONTRIBUTION TO THE WORK
Anonymous? ☐ Yes ☐ No
Pseudonymous? ☐ Yes ☐ No

If the answer to either of these questions is "Yes," see detailed instructions.

NATURE OF AUTHORSHIP Check appropriate box(es). **See instructions**
☐ 3-Dimensional sculpture   ☐ Map   ☐ Technical drawing
☐ 2-Dimensional artwork   ☐ Photograph   ☐ Text
☐ Reproduction of work of art   ☐ Jewelry design   ☐ Architectural work
☐ Design on sheetlike material

b

NAME OF AUTHOR ▼   **DATES OF BIRTH AND DEATH**
Year Born ▼   Year Died ▼

Was this contribution to the work a "work made for hire"?
☐ Yes
☐ No

AUTHOR'S NATIONALITY OR DOMICILE
Name of Country
OR { Citizen of ▶ _____
Domiciled in ▶ _____

WAS THIS AUTHOR'S CONTRIBUTION TO THE WORK
Anonymous? ☐ Yes ☐ No
Pseudonymous? ☐ Yes ☐ No

If the answer to either of these questions is "Yes," see detailed instructions.

NATURE OF AUTHORSHIP Check appropriate box(es). **See instructions**
☐ 3-Dimensional sculpture   ☐ Map   ☐ Technical drawing
☐ 2-Dimensional artwork   ☐ Photograph   ☐ Text
☐ Reproduction of work of art   ☐ Jewelry design   ☐ Architectural work
☐ Design on sheetlike material

NOTE

Under the law, the "author" of a "work made for hire" is generally the employer, not the employee (see instructions). For any part of this work that was "made for hire" check "Yes" in the space provided, give the employer (or other person for whom the work was prepared) as "Author" of that part, and leave the space for dates of birth and death blank.

3

a **YEAR IN WHICH CREATION OF THIS WORK WAS COMPLETED** This information must be given in all cases.
◀ Year

b **DATE AND NATION OF FIRST PUBLICATION OF THIS PARTICULAR WORK**
Complete this information ONLY if this work has been published.   Month ▶ _____ Day ▶ _____ Year ▶ _____ ◀ Nat

---

4

COPYRIGHT CLAIMANT(S) Name and address must be given even if the claimant is the same as the author given in space 2. ▼

TRANSFER If the claimant(s) named here in space 4 is (are) different from the author(s) named in space 2, give a brief statement of how the claimant(s) obtained ownership of the copyright. ▼

See instructions before completing this space.

DO NOT WRITE HERE OFFICE USE ONLY

APPLICATION RECEIVED

ONE DEPOSIT RECEIVED

TWO DEPOSITS RECEIVED

FUNDS RECEIVED

MORE ON BACK ▶
• Complete all applicable spaces (numbers 5-9) on the reverse side of this page.
• See detailed instructions.   • Sign the form at line 8.

DO NOT WRITE HE

EXAMINED BY _____

FOR

CHECKED BY _____

☐ CORRESPONDENCE
   Yes

F
COPY
OF
U
OF

DO NOT WRITE ABOVE THIS LINE. IF YOU NEED MORE SPACE, USE A SEPARATE CONTINUATION SHEET.

PREVIOUS REGISTRATION Has registration for this work, or for an earlier version of this work, already been made in the Copyright Office?

☐ Yes ☐ No If your answer is "Yes," why is another registration being sought? (Check appropriate box) ▼

a. ☐ This is the first published edition of a work previously registered in unpublished form.

b. ☐ This is the first application submitted by this author as copyright claimant.

c. ☐ This is a changed version of the work, as shown by space 6 on this application.

If your answer is "Yes," give: **Previous Registration Number** ▼   **Year of Registration** ▼

DERIVATIVE WORK OR COMPILATION Complete both space 6a and 6b for a derivative work; complete only 6b for a compilation.

a. **Preexisting Material** Identify any preexisting work or works that this work is based on or incorporates. ▼

See inst
before c
this spac

b. **Material Added to This Work** Give a brief, general statement of the material that has been added to this work and in which copyright is claimed. ▼

DEPOSIT ACCOUNT If the registration fee is to be charged to a Deposit Account established in the Copyright Office, give name and number of Account.

Name ▼   **Account Number** ▼

CORRESPONDENCE Give name and address to which correspondence about this application should be sent.   Name/Address/Apt/City/State/ZIP ▼

Be su
give y
daytin
◄ numb

Area Code and Telephone Number ▶

CERTIFICATION* I, the undersigned, hereby certify that I am the

check only one ▼

☐ author

☐ other copyright claimant

☐ owner of exclusive right(s)

☐ authorized agent of _____

Name of author or other copyright claimant, or owner of exclusive right(s) ▲

of the work identified in this application and that the statements made
by me in this application are correct to the best of my knowledge.

Typed or printed name and date ▼ If this application gives a date of publication in space 3, do not sign and submit it before that date.

_____ Date▶ _____

👉 **Handwritten signature (X)** ▼

_____

MAIL CERTIFI-CATE TO

Name ▼

Number/Street/Apt ▼

Certificate will be mailed in window envelope

City/State/ZIP ▼

YOU MUST:
• Complete all necessary spaces
• Sign your application in space 8

SEND ALL 3 ELEMENTS IN THE SAME PACKAGE:
1. Application form
2. Nonrefundable $20 filing fee in check or money order payable to *Register of Copyrights*
3. Deposit material

MAIL TO:
Register of Copyrights
Library of Congress
Washington, D.C. 20559-6000

The Copyrig
has the autho
just fees at 5-
vals, based o
in the Consu
Index. The ne
ment is due
Please cor
Copyright O
July 1995 to
the actual fee

July 1993—300,000   ♻ PRINTED ON RECYCLED PAPER   ☆U.S. GOVERNMENT PRINTING OFFICE: 1993-342-58

request for
special handling

SPECIAL HANDLING IS NOT FOR CONVENIENCE ONLY !

NOTE: The special handling of a registration application or other fee service severely disrupts the entire registration process and workflow of the Copyright Office. It is granted only in the most urgent of cases. A request for special handling is subject to the approval of the Chief of the Receiving and Processing Division, who takes into account the workload situation of the office at the time the request is made. A minimum period of five working days is required to process a registration application under special handling procedures.

Why is there an urgent need for special handling?

☐ Litigation ☐ Contractual/Publishing Deadlines

☐ Customs Matter ☐ Other, Specify

If you must have the requested action to go forward with the litigation, please answer the following questions.

a. Is the litigation actual or prospective?

b. Are you (or your client) the plaintiff or defendant in the action? Please specify.

c. What are the names of the parties and what is the name of the court where the action is pending or expected?

ss all
nks are
oleted
r
uest
not be
cessed.

I certify that the statements made above are correct to the best of my knowledge.

(Signature)

(Address)

(Phone)   (Date)

COPYRIGHT
CE USE ONLY

Information Specialist handling matter

remarks

August 1987 - 1,000

NTINUATION SHEET FOR FORM TX

all possible, try to fit the information called for into the spaces
ided on Form TX.

u do not have space enough for all of the information you need
ive on Form TX, use this continuation sheet and submit it with
n TX.

u submit this continuation sheet, clip (do not tape or staple) it to
n TX and fold the two together before submitting them.

T A of this sheet is intended to identify the basic application.
T B is a continuation of Space 2. PART C (on the reverse side of
sheet) is for the continuation of Spaces 1, 4, 6, or 7. The other
:es on Form TX call for specific items of information, and should
need continuation.

REGISTRATION NUMBER
TX   TXU
EFFECTIVE DATE OF REGISTRATION
. . . .
(Month)   (Day)   (Year)
CONTINUATION SHEET RECEIVED
Page _____ of _____ pages

DO NOT WRITE ABOVE THIS LINE. FOR COPYRIGHT OFFICE USE ONLY

A

tification
of
lication

IDENTIFICATION OF CONTINUATION SHEET: This sheet is a continuation of the application for copyright registration on Form TX, submitted fc
the following work:

• TITLE: (Give the title as given under the heading "Title of this Work" in Space 1 of Form TX.)

. . . .

• NAME(S) AND ADDRESS(ES) OF COPYRIGHT CLAIMANT(S): (Give the name and address of at least one copyright claimant as given
in Space 4 of Form TX.)

. . . .

B

inuation
pace 2

NAME OF AUTHOR:

Was this author's contribution to the work a "work made for hire"?   Yes...... No......

DATES OF BIRTH AND DEATH

Born . . . . Died . . . .
(Year)   (Year)

AUTHOR'S NATIONALITY OR DOMICILE:

Citizen of . . . . } or { Domiciled in . . . .
(Name of Country)   (Name of Country)

**WAS THIS AUTHOR'S CONTRIBUTION TO
THE WORK:**

Anonymous?   Yes...... No......
Pseudonymous? Yes...... No......

AUTHOR OF: (Briefly describe nature of this author's contribution)

If the answer to either of these questions i
"Yes," see detailed instructions attached.

NAME OF AUTHOR:

Was this author's contribution to the work a "work made for hire"?   Yes...... No......

DATES OF BIRTH AND DEATH

Born . . . . Died . . . .
(Year)   (Year)

AUTHOR'S NATIONALITY OR DOMICILE:

Citizen of . . . . } or { Domiciled in . . . .
(Name of Country)   (Name of Country)

**WAS THIS AUTHOR'S CONTRIBUTION TO
THE WORK:**

Anonymous?   Yes...... No......
Pseudonymous? Yes...... No......

AUTHOR OF: (Briefly describe nature of this author's contribution)

If the answer to either of these questions
"Yes," see detailed instructions attached.

NAME OF AUTHOR:

Was this author's contribution to the work a "work made for hire"?   Yes...... No......

DATES OF BIRTH AND DEATH

Born . . . . Died . . . .
(Year)   (Year)

AUTHOR'S NATIONALITY OR DOMICILE:

Citizen of . . . . } or { Domiciled in . . . .
(Name of Country)   (Name of Country)

**WAS THIS AUTHOR'S CONTRIBUTION TO
THE WORK:**

Anonymous?   Yes...... No......
Pseudonymous? Yes...... No......

AUTHOR OF: (Briefly describe nature of this author's contribution)

If the answer to either of these questions is
"Yes," see detailed instructions attached.

NAME OF AUTHOR:

Was this author's contribution to the work a "work made for hire"?   Yes...... No......

DATES OF BIRTH AND DEATH

Born . . . . Died . . . .
(Year)   (Year)

AUTHOR'S NATIONALITY OR DOMICILE:

Citizen of . . . . } or { Domiciled in . . . .
(Name of Country)   (Name of Country)

**WAS THIS AUTHOR'S CONTRIBUTION TO
THE WORK:**

Anonymous?   Yes...... No......
Pseudonymous? Yes...... No......

AUTHOR OF: (Briefly describe nature of this author's contribution)

If the answer to either of these questions
"Yes," see detailed instructions attached.

NAME OF AUTHOR:

Was this author's contribution to the work a "work made for hire"?   Yes...... No......

DATES OF BIRTH AND DEATH

Born . . . . Died . . . .
(Year)   (Year)

AUTHOR'S NATIONALITY OR DOMICILE:

Citizen of . . . . } or { Domiciled in . . . .
(Name of Country)   (Name of Country)

**WAS THIS AUTHOR'S CONTRIBUTION TO
THE WORK:**

Anonymous?   Yes...... No......
Pseudonymous? Yes...... No......

AUTHOR OF: (Briefly describe nature of this author's contribution)

If the answer to either of these questions is
"Yes," see detailed instructions attached.

Use the reverse side of this sheet if you need more space for:
* *Further continuation of Space 2*
* *Continuation of Spaces 1, 4, 6, or 7 of Form TX*

NAME OF AUTHOR:	DATES OF BIRTH AND DEATH:	**E**
Was this author's contribution to the work a "work made for hire"? Yes...... No......	Born .... Died .... (Year) (Year)	Contin... of Sp

☐ **AUTHOR'S NATIONALITY OR DOMICILE:**

Citizen of .... } or { Domiciled in ....
(Name of Country) (Name of Country)

WAS THIS AUTHOR'S CONTRIBUTION TO THE WORK:

Anonymous? Yes...... No......
Pseudonymous? Yes...... No......

If the answer to either of these questions is "Yes," see detailed instructions attached.

AUTHOR OF: (Briefly describe nature of this author's contribution)

NAME OF AUTHOR:

Was this author's contribution to the work a "work made for hire"? Yes...... No......

DATES OF BIRTH AND DEATH:

Born .... Died ....
(Year) (Year)

☐ **AUTHOR'S NATIONALITY OR DOMICILE:**

Citizen of .... } or { Domiciled in ....
(Name of Country) (Name of Country)

WAS THIS AUTHOR'S CONTRIBUTION TO THE WORK:

Anonymous? Yes...... No......
Pseudonymous? Yes...... No......

If the answer to either of these questions is "Yes," see detailed instructions attached.

AUTHOR OF: (Briefly describe nature of this author's contribution)

NAME OF AUTHOR:

Was this author's contribution to the work a "work made for hire"? Yes...... No......

DATES OF BIRTH AND DEATH:

Born .... Died ....
(Year) (Year)

☐ **AUTHOR'S NATIONALITY OR DOMICILE:**

Citizen of .... } or { Domiciled in ....
(Name of Country) (Name of Country)

WAS THIS AUTHOR'S CONTRIBUTION TO THE WORK:

Anonymous? Yes...... No......
Pseudonymous? Yes...... No......

If the answer to either of these questions is "Yes," see detailed instructions attached.

AUTHOR OF: (Briefly describe nature of this author's contribution)

NAME OF AUTHOR:

Was this author's contribution to the work a "work made for hire"? Yes...... No......

DATES OF BIRTH AND DEATH:

Born .... Died ....
(Year) (Year)

☐ **AUTHOR'S NATIONALITY OR DOMICILE:**

Citizen of .... } or { Domiciled in ....
(Name of Country) (Name of Country)

WAS THIS AUTHOR'S CONTRIBUTION TO THE WORK:

Anonymous? Yes...... No......
Pseudonymous? Yes...... No......

If the answer to either of these questions is "Yes," see detailed instructions attached.

AUTHOR OF: (Briefly describe nature of this author's contribution)

CONTINUATION OF (Check which): ☐ Space 1 ☐ Space 4 ☐ Space 6 ☐ Space 7

C

Continu...
of oth...
Space

CONTINUATION SHEET
FOR APPLICATION FORMS

This Continuation Sheet is used in conjunction with Forms CA, PA, SE, SR, TX, and VA **only**. Indicate which basic form you are continuing in the space in the upper right-hand corner.

If at all possible, try to fit the information called for into the spaces provided on the basic form.

If you do not have space enough for all the information you need to give on the basic form, use this continuation sheet and submit it with the basic form.

If you submit this continuation sheet, clip (do not tape or staple) it to the basic form and fold the two together before submitting them.

Part A of this sheet is intended to identify the basic application.
Part B is a continuation of Space 2.
Part C (on the reverse side of this sheet) is for the continuation of Spaces 1, 4, or 6. The other spaces on the basic form call for specific items of information and should not need continuation.

NOT WRITE ABOVE THIS LINE. FOR COPYRIGHT OFFICE USE ONLY

FORM ____ /CON
UNITED STATES COPYRIGHT OFFICE

REGISTRATION NUMBER

PA PAU SE SEG SEU SR SRU TX TXU VA VAU

EFFECTIVE DATE OF REGISTRATION

| (Month) | (Day) | (Year) |

CONTINUATION SHEET RECEIVED

Page _____ of _____ pages

A
entification of application

IDENTIFICATION OF CONTINUATION SHEET: This sheet is a continuation of the application for copyright registration on the basic form submitted for the following work:
● TITLE: (Give the title as given under the heading "Title of this Work" in Space 1 of the basic form.)

....●

NAME(S) AND ADDRESS(ES) OF COPYRIGHT CLAIMANT(S) : (Give the name and address of at least one copyright claimant as given in Space 4 of the basic form.)

....

B
ontinuation of Space 2

d

NAME OF AUTHOR ▼

DATES OF BIRTH AND DEATH
Year Born▼   Year Died▼

Was this contribution to the work a "work made for hire"?

□ Yes
□ No

AUTHOR'S NATIONALITY OR DOMICILE
Name of Country

OR { Citizen of ▶ ——————
Domiciled in ▶ ——————

WAS THIS AUTHOR'S CONTRIBUTION TO THE WORK
Anonymous?   □ Yes □ No   If the answer to either of these questions is "Yes" see detailed
Pseudonymous? □ Yes □ No   instructions.

NATURE OF AUTHORSHIP Briefly describe nature of the material created by the author in which copyright is claimed. ▼

---

e

NAME OF AUTHOR ▼

DATES OF BIRTH AND DEATH
Year Born▼   Year Died▼

Was this contribution to the work a "work made for hire"?

□ Yes
□ No

AUTHOR'S NATIONALITY OR DOMICILE
Name of Country

OR { Citizen of ▶ ——————
Domiciled in ▶ ——————

WAS THIS AUTHOR'S CONTRIBUTION TO THE WORK
Anonymous?   □ Yes □ No   If the answer to either of these questions is "Yes" see detailed
Pseudonymous? □ Yes □ No   instructions.

NATURE OF AUTHORSHIP Briefly describe nature of the material created by the author in which copyright is claimed. ▼

---

f

NAME OF AUTHOR ▼

DATES OF BIRTH AND DEATH
Year Born▼   Year Died▼

Was this contribution to the work a "work made for hire"?

□ Yes
□ No

AUTHOR'S NATIONALITY OR DOMICILE
Name of Country

OR { Citizen of ▶ ——————
Domiciled in ▶ ——————

WAS THIS AUTHOR'S CONTRIBUTION TO THE WORK
Anonymous?   □ Yes □ No   If the answer to either of these questions is "Yes" see detailed
Pseudonymous? □ Yes □ No   instructions.

NATURE OF AUTHORSHIP Briefly describe nature of the material created by the author in which copyright is claimed. ▼

Use the reverse side of this sheet if you need more space for continuation of Spaces 1, 4, or 6 of the basic form.

CONTINUATION OF (Check which):　　□ **Space 1**　　□ **Space 4**　　□ **Space 6**

C

Continuati
of other
Spaces

August 1993—100,000　⊕　PRINTED ON RECYCLED PAPER

☆U.S.GOVERNMENT PRINTING OFFICE: 1993-342-582/80,

FORM CA
For Supplementary Registration
UNITED STATES COPYRIGHT OFFICE

REGISTRATION NUMBER

TX	TXU	PA	PAU	VA	VAU	SR	SRU	RE

EFFECTIVE DATE OF SUPPLEMENTARY REGISTRATION

_____ _____ _____
Month Day Year

DO NOT WRITE ABOVE THIS LINE. IF YOU NEED MORE SPACE, USE A SEPARATE CONTINUATION SHEET.

TITLE OF WORK ▼

REGISTRATION NUMBER OF THE BASIC REGISTRATION ▼

YEAR OF BASIC REGISTRATION ▼

NAME(S) OF AUTHOR(S) ▼

NAME(S) OF COPYRIGHT CLAIMANT(S) ▼

LOCATION AND NATURE OF INCORRECT INFORMATION IN BASIC REGISTRATION ▼

Line Number . . . . Line Heading or Description . . . .

INCORRECT INFORMATION AS IT APPEARS IN BASIC REGISTRATION ▼

CORRECTED INFORMATION ▼

EXPLANATION OF CORRECTION ▼

LOCATION AND NATURE OF INFORMATION IN BASIC REGISTRATION TO BE AMPLIFIED ▼

Line Number . . . . Line Heading or Description . . . .

AMPLIFIED INFORMATION ▼

EXPLANATION OF AMPLIFIED INFORMATION ▼

MORE ON BACK ▶ • Complete all applicable spaces (D -G) on the reverse side of this page.
• See detailed instructions. • Sign the form at space F.

DO NOT WRITE HERE

Page 1 of _____ pages

FORM CA RECEIVED

FUNDS RECEIVED DATE

EXAMINED BY

CHECKED BY

CORRESPONDENCE ☐

REFERENCE TO THIS REGISTRATION ADDED TO
BASIC REGISTRATION   ☐ YES   ☐ NO

FORM

FOR
COPYR
OFFI
USE
ONL

DO NOT WRITE ABOVE THIS LINE. IF YOU NEED MORE SPACE, USE A SEPARATE CONTINUATION SHEET.

CONTINUATION OF: (Check which) ☐ PART B OR ☐ PART C

DEPOSIT ACCOUNT: If the registration fee is to be charged to a Deposit Account established in the Copyright Office, give name and number of Account.

Name _____

_____

Account Number _____

CORRESPONDENCE: Give name and address to which correspondence about this application should be sent.

Name _____

Address _____
                                                                    (Apt)
_____
(City)   (State)   (ZIP)
Area Code and Telephone Number ▶ _____

Be sure
give you
daytime
◀ number

CERTIFICATION* I, the undersigned, hereby certify that I am the: (Check one)
☐ author ☐ other copyright claimant ☐ owner of exclusive right(s) ☐ duly authorized agent of_____
                                                                    (Name of author or other copyright claimant, or owner of exclusive right(s) ▲
of the work identified in this application and that the statements made by me in this application are correct to the best of my knowledge.

Typed or printed name ▼   Date ▼

_____   _____

☞   **Handwritten signature (X)** ▼
_____

MAIL CERTIFI-CATE TO

Name ▼

Number/Street/Apt ▼

City/State/ZIP ▼

Certificate will be mailed in window envelope

YOU MUST:
• Complete all necessary spaces
• Sign your application in space F

SEND ALL ELEMENTS IN THE SAME PACKAGE:
1. Application form
2. Nonrefundable $20 filing fee in check or money order payable to
   Register of Copyrights

MAIL TO:
Register of Copyrights
Library of Congress
Washington, D.C. 20559-6000

The Copyright
has the authori
just fees at 5-ye
vals, based on c
in the Consume
Index. The next
ment is due in
Please   contac
Copyright   Offic
July 1995 to de
the actual fee sc

December 1993—25,000   ☆U.S. GOVERNMENT PRINTING OFFICE: 1993-301-241/8

ADJUNCT APPLICATION
or Copyright Registration for a
Group of Contributions to Periodicals

 **FORM GR/CP**

UNITED STATES COPYRIGHT OFFICE

Use this adjunct form only if you are making a single registration for a group of contributions to periodicals, and you are also filing a basic application on Form TX, Form PA, or Form VA. Follow the instructions, attached.

Number each line in Part B consecutively. Use additional Forms GR/CP if you need more space.

Submit this adjunct form with the basic application form. Clip (do not tape or staple) and fold all sheets together before submitting them.

REGISTRATION NUMBER
TX   PA   VA

EFFECTIVE DATE OF REGISTRATION

. . . .
(Month)   (Day)   (Year)

FORM GR/CP RECEIVED

Page _____ of _____ pages

DO NOT WRITE ABOVE THIS LINE. FOR COPYRIGHT OFFICE USE ONLY

A

Identification of Application

IDENTIFICATION OF BASIC APPLICATION:
● This application for copyright registration for a group of contributions to periodicals is submitted as an adjunct to an application filed on: (Check which)

☐ Form TX   ☐ Form PA   ☐ Form VA

IDENTIFICATION OF AUTHOR AND CLAIMANT: (Give the name of the author and the name of the copyright claimant in all of the contributions listed in Part B of this form. The names should be the same as the names given in spaces 2 and 4 of the basic application.)

Name of Author: . . . .

Name of Copyright Claimant: . . . .

B

Registration for Group of Contributions

COPYRIGHT REGISTRATION FOR A GROUP OF CONTRIBUTIONS TO PERIODICALS: (To make a single registration for a group of works by the same individual author, all first published as contributions to periodicals within a 12-month period (see instructions), give full information about each contribution. If more space in needed, use additional Forms GR/CP.)

☐
Title of Contribution: . . . .
Title of Periodical: . . . . Vol. . . . . No. . . . . Issue Date . . . . Pages . . . . . .
Date of First Publication: . . . . Nation of First Publication . . . .
(Month)   (Day)   (Year)   (Country)

☐
Title of Contribution: . . . .
Title of Periodical: . . . . Vol. . . . . No. . . . . Issue Date . . . . Pages . . . . . .
Date of First Publication: . . . . Nation of First Publication . . . .
(Month)   (Day)   (Year)   (Country)

☐
Title of Contribution: . . . .
Title of Periodical: . . . . Vol. . . . . No. . . . . Issue Date . . . . Pages . . . . . .
Date of First Publication: . . . . Nation of First Publication . . . .
(Month)   (Day)   (Year)   (Country)

☐
Title of Contribution: . . . .
Title of Periodical: . . . . Vol. . . . . No. . . . . Issue Date . . . . Pages . . . . . .
Date of First Publication: . . . . Nation of First Publication . . . .
(Month)   (Day)   (Year)   (Country)

☐
Title of Contribution: . . . .
Title of Periodical: . . . . Vol. . . . . No. . . . . Issue Date . . . . Pages . . . . . .
Date of First Publication: . . . . Nation of First Publication . . . .
(Month)   (Day)   (Year)   (Country) ,

☐
Title of Contribution: . . . .
Title of Periodical: . . . . Vol. . . . . No. . . . . Issue Date . . . . Pages . . . . . .
Date of First Publication: . . . . Nation of First Publication . . . .
(Month)   (Day)   (Year)   (Country)

☐
Title of Contribution: . . . .
Title of Periodical: . . . . Vol. . . . . No. . . . . Issue Date . . . . Pages . . . . . .
Date of First Publication: . . . . Nation of First Publication . . . .
(Month)   (Day)   (Year)   (Country)

DO NOT WRITE ABOVE THIS LINE. FOR COPYRIGHT OFFICE USE ONLY

Continued

☐ Title of Contribution: . . . .
Title of Periodical: . . . . Vol. . . . No. . . . . Issue Date . . . . Pages . . . . . .
Date of First Publication: . . . . Nation of First Publication . . . .
                        (Month)   (Day)   (Year)   (Country)

☐ Title of Contribution: . . . .
Title of Periodical: . . . . Vol. . . . No. . . . . Issue Date . . . . Pages . . . . . .
Date of First Publication: . . . . Nation of First Publication . . . .
                        (Month)   (Day)   (Year)   (Country)

☐ Title of Contribution: . . . .
Title of Periodical: . . . . Vol. . . . . No. . . . . Issue Date . . . . Pages . . . . . .
Date of First Publication: . . . . Nation of First Publication . . . .
                        (Month)   (Day)   (Year)   (Country)

☐ Title of Contribution: . . . .
Title of Periodical: . . . . Vol. . . . No. . . . . Issue Date . . . . Pages . . . . . .
Date of First Publication: . . . . Nation of First Publication . . . .
                        (Month)   (Day)   (Year)   (Country)

☐ Title of Contribution: . . . .
Title of Periodical: . . . . Vol. . . . . No. . . . . Issue Date . . . . Pages . . . . . .
Date of First Publication: . . . . Nation of First Publication . . . .
                        (Month)   (Day)   (Year)   (Country)

☐ Title of Contribution: . . . .
Title of Periodical: . . . . Vol. . . . No. . . . . Issue Date . . . . Pages . . . . . .
Date of First Publication: . . . . Nation of First Publication . . . .
                        (Month)   (Day)   (Year)   (Country)

☐ Title of Contribution: . . . .
Title of Periodical: . . . . Vol. . . . No. . . . . Issue Date . . . . Pages . . . . . .
Date of First Publication: . . . . Nation of First Publication . . . .
                        (Month)   (Day)   (Year)   (Country)

☐ Title of Contribution: . . . .
Title of Periodical: . . . . Vol. . . . No. . . . . Issue Date . . . . Pages . . . . . .
Date of First Publication: . . . . Nation of First Publication . . . .
                        (Month)   (Day)   (Year)   (Country)

☐ Title of Contribution: . . . .
Title of Periodical: . . . . Vol. . . . . No. . . . . Issue Date . . . . Pages . . . . . .
Date of First Publication: . . . . Nation of First Publication . . . .
                        (Month)   (Day)   (Year)   (Country)

☐ Title of Contribution: . . . .
Title of Periodical: . . . . Vol. . . . No. . . . . Issue Date . . . . Pages . . . . . .
Date of First Publication: . . . . Nation of First Publication . . . .
                        (Month)   (Day)   (Year)   (Country)

☐ Title of Contribution: . . . .
Title of Periodical: . . . . Vol. . . . No. . . . . Issue Date . . . . Pages . . . . . .
Date of First Publication: . . . . Nation of First Publication . . . .
                        (Month)   (Day)   (Year)   (Country)

☐ Title of Contribution: . . . .
Title of Periodical: . . . . Vol. . . . No. . . . . Issue Date . . . . Pages . . . . . .
Date of First Publication: . . . . Nation of First Publication . . . .
                        (Month)   (Day)   (Year)   (Country)

▲ October 1991—25,000   ☆U.S. GOVERNMENT PRINTING OFFICE: 1991: 312-432/40,00

search request form

Copyright Office
Library of Congress
Washington, D.C. 20559

Reference & Bibliography
Section
(202) 707-6850
8:30 a.m. - 5 p.m. Monday-Friday
(Eastern time)

Type of work:

Book   Music   Motion Picture   Drama   Sound Recording
Photograph/Artwork   Map   Periodical   Contribution   Architectural Work

Search information you require:

Registration   Renewal   Assignment   Address

Specifics of work to be searched:

TITLE:

AUTHOR:

COPYRIGHT CLAIMANT (if known):
(name in © notice)

APPROXIMATE YEAR DATE OF PUBLICATION CREATION:

REGISTRATION NUMBER (if known):

OTHER IDENTIFYING INFORMATION:

If you need more space please attach additional pages

Estimates are based on the Copyright Office fee of $20 an hour or fraction of an hour consumed. The more information you furnish as a basis for the search the better service we can provide.

Names, titles and short phases are not copyrightable.

Please read Circular 22 for more information on copyright searches.

YOUR NAME: DATE:

ADDRESS:

DAYTIME TELEPHONE NO. (   )

Convey results of estimate search by telephone   Fee enclosed?   yes   Amount $
     yes   no   no

DOCUMENT COVER SHEET

For Recordation of Documents
UNITED STATES COPYRIGHT OFFICE

DATE OF RECORDATION
(Assigned by Copyright Office)

Month	Day	Year

Volume _____ Page _____

Volume _____ Page _____

DO NOT WRITE ABOVE THIS LINE.

REMITTANCE _____

the Register of Copyrights:

ase record the accompanying original document or copy thereof.   FUNDS RECEIVED _____

NAME OF THE PARTY OR PARTIES TO THE DOCUMENT, AS THEY APPEAR IN THE DOCUMENT.

Party 1: _____   Party 2: _____
        (assignor, grantor, etc.)   (assignee, grantee, etc.)

_____   _____
              (address)   (address)

DESCRIPTION OF THE DOCUMENT:
- ☐ Transfer of Copyright
- ☐ Security Interest
- ☐ Change of Name of Owner
- ☐ Termination of Transfer(s) [Section 304]
- ☐ Shareware
- ☐ Life, Identity, Death Statement [Section 302]
- ☐ Transfer of Mask Works
- ☐ Other _____

TITLE(S) OF WORK(S), REGISTRATION NUMBER(S), AUTHOR(S), AND OTHER INFORMATION TO IDENTIFY WORK.

Title   Registration Number   Author

Additional sheet(s) attached?
☐ yes
☐ no
If so, how many? _____

☐ Document is complete by its own terms.
☐ Document is not complete. Record "as is."

5 Number of titles in Document: _____

7 Amount of fee enclosed or authorized to be charged to a Deposit Account_____ .

Account number _____
Account name _____

Date of execution and/or effective date of accompanying document _____ .
                    (month)   (day)   (year)

AFFIRMATION:* I hereby affirm to the Copyright Office that the information given on this form is a true and correct representation of the accompanying document. This affirmation will not suffice as a certification of a photocopy signature on the document.

10 **CERTIFICATION:*** Complete this certification if a photocopy of the original signed document is submitted in lieu of a document bearing the actual signature.

I certify under penalty of perjury under the laws of the United States of America that the accompanying document is a true copy of the original document.

_____   _____
             Signature   Signature

                                                Duly Authorized Agent of:

_____   _____
               Date   Date

RDA-
TO:

Name▼

Number/Street/Apartment Number▼

City/State/ZIP▼

ngly and willfully falsifying material facts on this form may result in criminal liability. 18 U.S.C.§1001.

y 1993—50,000   ☆ U.S. GOVERNMENT PRINTING OFFICE: 1993–342-582/60,032

⬛Document Cover Sheet

BASIC INFORMATION

Read these instructions before completing this form. Make sure all applicable spaces have been filled in before you return this form, or the form cannot be used.

When to Use This Form: Use the Document Cover Sheet when you are submitting a document for recordation in the U.S. Copyright Office.

Mailing Requirements: It is important that you send two copies of the Document Cover Sheet, any additional sheets, the document, and the fee together in the same envelope or package. The Copyright Office cannot process them unless they are received together. Send to: *Documents Unit, LM-462, Cataloging Division, Copyright Office, Library of Congress, Washington, D.C. 20559.*

Two copies of this Document Cover Sheet and any additional sheets you include, which must measure 8 1/2 x 11 inches, should accompany **each document**. Cover sheets should be typed or printed. The cover sheet, when completed, should contain all of the information necessary for the Copyright Office to process the document and ensure that the correct data is recorded promptly. The Copyright Office will process the document on the basis of information contained in the cover sheet without verifying its correctness from the document itself. However, to be recordable, a document must satisfy the recordation requirements of the Copyright Act and Copyright Office regulations.

The person(s) submitting a document with a cover sheet are solely responsible for verifying the correctness of the cover sheet and the sufficiency of the document. Recording a document submitted with or without a cover sheet does not constitute a determination by the Copyright Office of the document's validity or the effect of that document. Only a court of law may make such determinations.

This cover sheet and any additonal sheets will be recorded with the document as part of the official recordation.

SPACE-BY-SPACE INSTRUCTIONS

1 SPACE 1: Name of Party or Parties to the Document

Name all of the parties to this document. If additional space is needed, use a white, 8 1/2 x 11 inch sheet of paper to list the parties. The document will be indexed under the names of these parties. For transfers, notices of termination, and other two-party documents, indicate which is assignor, grantor, or party 1 and which is assignee, grantee, or party 2.

2 SPACE 2: Description of Document

Describe the document. This description will be entered in the catalog record of the recordation.

3 SPACE 3: Title(s) of Work(s)

List the titles of all works which are included in the document. Include registration number, names of authors, and other information to identify the work(s) and link them to the original registration. Additional sheets the same size as the cover sheet may be attached, if needed. Indicate that the titles on any addtional sheets are additions to Space 3.

4 SPACE 4: Completeness of Document

All section 205 documents must be complete by their own terms in order to be recordable. Examples of section 205 documents include transfers of copyright ownerships and other documents pertaining to a copyright such as exclusive and non-exclusive licenses, contracts, mortgages, powers of attorney, certificates of change of corporate name or title, wills, and decrees of distribution.

5 SPACE 5: Number of Titles in Document

The number of titles determines the recordation fee. The fee for a document of any length containing one title is $20. Additional titles are $10 for each group of 10 or fewer. The Copyright Office will verify title counts.

6 SPACE 6: Fee

Calculate the fee from the information given in Space 5.
NOTE: The Copyright Office has the authority to adjust fees at 5-intervals, based on changes in the Consumer Price Index. The next adjustment is due in 1996. Please contact the Copyright Office after July 1995 determine the actual fee schedule.

7 SPACE 7: Deposit Account

If a Deposit Account is to be charged, give the Deposit Account number.

8 SPACE 8: Date of Execution

Give the date the accompanying document (not this Cover Sheet) executed and/or became effective.

9 SPACE 9: Affirmation

This space is to be completed by all applicants. The party to the document submitting it for recordation or his/her authorized agent should sign affirmation and authorization contained in this space. This affirmation authorization is not a substitute for the certification required for documents containing a photocopy signature. (See Certification, Space 10.)

10 SPACE 10: Certification

Complete this section only if submitting photocopied documents in of a document bearing the actual signature.

Certification: Any transfer of copyright ownership or other document pertaining to a copyright (section 205) may be recorded in the Copyright Office if the document bears the actual signature of the person or persons executed (signed) the documents. If a photocopy of the original signed document is submitted, it must be accompanied by a sworn or official certification. A sworn certification signed by at least one of the parties to document or their authorized representative (who is identified as such Space 10 will satisfy that requirement.

Copies of documents on file in a Federal, state, or local government office must be accompanied by an official certification.

Index

U

V

W

Y

NOLO PRESS CATALOG

ESTATE PLANNING & PROBATE

Plan Your Estate
Attorneys Denis Clifford & Cora Jordan. Nat'l 3rd ed.

Thoroughly revised and updated, this is the most comprehensive estate planing book available. It covers everything from basic estate planning to sophisticated tax saving stratagies. Includes information on federal estate and gift taxes, estate tax saving trusts, trusts used to control property left to beneficiaries, charitable remainder trusts, durable powers of attorney, living wills, funerals and burials. Good in all states except Lousiana.
$24.95/NEST

Make Your Own Living Trust
Attorney Denis Clifford. Nat'l 1st ed.

Find out how a living trust works, how to create one, and how to determine what kind of trust is right for you. Contains all the forms and instructions you need to prepare a basic living trust to avoid probate, a marital life estate trust (A-B trust) to avoid probate and estate taxes, and a back-up will. Good in all states except Louisiana.
$19.95/LITR

Nolo's Simple Will Book
Attorney Denis Clifford. Nat'l 2nd ed.

It's easy to write a legally valid will using this book. Includes all the instructions and sample forms you need to name a personal guardian for minor children, leave property to minor children or young adults and update a will when necessary. Good in all states except Louisiana.
$17.95/SWIL

The Conservatorship Book
Lisa Goldoftas & Attorney Carolyn Farren. CA 2nd ed.

Provides forms and all instructions necessary to file conservatorship documents, appear in court, be appointed conservator and end a conservatorship.
$29.95/CNSV

How to Probate an Estate
Julia Nissley. CA 8th ed.

Save costly attorneys' fees by handling the probate process yourself. This book shows you step-by-step how to settle an estate. It also explains the simple procedures you can use to transfer assets that don't require probate. Forms included.
$34.95/PAE

audio cassette tapes

5 Ways to Avoid Probate
Attorney Ralph Warner with Joanne Greene. Nat'l 1st ed. 60 minutes

Provides clear, in-depth explanations of the principal probate avoidance techniques: joint tenancy, insurance, living trusts, savings account trusts and pension plans.
$14.95/KWL

Write Your Will
Attorney Ralph Warner with Joanne Greene. Nat'l 1st ed. 60 minutes

If you're getting ready to write your will, this tape is a good place to start. It answers the most frequently asked questions about writing a will and covers all key issues.
$14.95/TWYW

law form kits

Nolo's Law Form Kit: Wills
Attorney Denis Clifford & Lisa Goldoftas. Nat'l 1st ed.

All the forms and instructions you need to create a legally valid will, quickly and easily.
$14.95/KWL

software

Living Trust Maker
Version 2.0

Put your assets into a trust and save your heirs the headache, time and expense of probate with this easy-to-use software. Use it to set up an individual or shared marital trust, transfer property to the trust, and change or revoke the trust at any time. Its manual guides you through the process, and legal help screens and an on-line glossary explain key legal terms and concepts. Good in all states except Louisiana.
WINDOWS $79.95/LTWI2
MACINTOSH $79.95/LTM2

Nolo's Personal RecordKeeper
Version 3.0

Finally, a safe, accessible place for your important records. Over 200 categories and subcategories to organize and store your important financial, legal and personal information, compute your net worth and create inventories for insurance records. Export your net worth and home inventory data to Quicken®.
DOS $49.95/FRI3
MACINTOSH $49.95/FRM3

WillMaker®
Version 5.0

Make your own legal will and living will (health-care directive)—and thoroughly document your final arrangements—with *WillMaker 5*. Its easy-to-use interview format takes you through each document step-by-step. On-line legal help is available throughout the program. Name a guardian for your children, make up to 100 property bequests, direct your healthcare in the event of coma or terminal illness, and let your loved ones know your wishes around your own final arrangements.
WINDOWS $69.95/WIW5
DOS $69.95/WI5
MACINTOSH $69.95/WM5

BUSINESS/WORKPLACE

The Legal Guide for Starting & Running a Small Business
Attorney Fred S. Steingold. Nat'l 1st ed.

An essential resource for every small business owner. Find out how to form a sole proprietorship, partnership or corporation, negotiate a favorable lease, hire and fire employees, write contracts and resolve disputes.
$22.95/RUNS

The Legal Guide to Starting and Running a Small Business on Disk
Version 1.0

The disk version of this best selling book provides instant access to plain-English explanations of the laws that affect your business everyday. Features random access searching, keyword index, hyper-text linking, and "Law in the Real World" examples from businesses just like yours.
WINDOWS $25.95/RUNSWI

Sexual Harassment on the Job: What It Is and How to Stop It
Attorneys William Petrocelli & Barbara Kate Repa. Nat'l 2nd ed.

An invaluable resource for both employees experiencing harassment and employers interested in creating a policy against sexual harassment and a procedure for handling complaints.
$18.95/HARS

Marketing Without Advertising
Michael Phillips & Salli Rasberry. Nat'l 1st ed.

Outlines practical steps for building and expanding a small business without spending a lot of money on advertising.
$14.00/MWAD

Your Rights in the Workplace
Attorney Barbara Kate Repa. Nat'l 2nd ed.

A comprehensive guide to workplace rights—from hiring to firing. Covers wages and overtime, parental leave, unemployment and disability insurance, worker's compensation, job safety, discrimination and illegal firings and layoffs.
$15.95/YRW

How to Write a Business Plan
Mike McKeever. Nat'l 4th ed.

This book will show you how to write the business plan and loan package necessary to finance your business and make it work.
$21.95/SBS

The Partnership Book
Attorneys Denis Clifford & Ralph Warner. Nat'l 4th ed.

Shows you step-by-step how to write a solid partnership agreement that meets your needs. It covers initial contributions to the business, wages, profit-sharing, buy-outs, death or retirement of a partner and disputes.
$24.95/PART

The California Nonprofit Corporation Handbook
Attorney Anthony Mancuso. CA 6th ed.

Shows you step-by-step how to form and operate a nonprofit corporation in California. Includes the latest corporate and tax law changes, and forms for the Articles, Bylaws and Minutes.
$29.95/NON

How to Form Your Own Corporation
Attorney Anthony Mancuso. CA 8th ed.

All the forms, instructions and tax information you need to incorporate a small business yourself and save hundreds of dollars in lawyers' fees.
California $29.95/CCOR
New York $29.95/NYCO
Texas $29.95/TCOR

The California Professional Corporation Handbook
Attorney Anthony Mancuso. CA 5th ed.

Doctors, lawyers, accountants and members of certain other professions must fulfill special requirements when forming a corporation in California. Contains up-to-date tax information plus all the forms and instructions necessary.
$34.95/PROF

The Independent Paralegal's Handbook
Attorney Ralph Warner. Nat'l 3rd ed.

Legal and business guidelines for anyone who wants to go into business as an independent paralegal helping consumers with routine legal tasks.
$29.95 PARA

 books with disk

How to Form a Nonprofit Corporation
Attorney Anthony Mancuso. Nat'l 2nd ed.

Explains the legal formalities involved and provides detailed information on the differences in the law among all 50 states. It also contains forms for the Articles, Bylaws and Minutes you need, along with complete instructions for obtaining federal 501(c)(3) tax exemptions and qualifying for public charity status. Includes incorporation forms on disk.
DOS $39.95/NNP

How to Form Your Own Corporation
Attorney Anthony Mancuso.

Step-by-step guide to forming your own corporation. Provides clear instructions and all the forms you need including Articles, Bylaws, Minutes and Stock Certificates. Includes all incorporation forms on disk.
Florida DOS $39.95/FLCO
New York DOS $39.95/NYCO
Texas DOS $39.95/TCI

Taking Care of Your Corporation, Vol. 1: Director and Shareholder Meetings Made Easy
Attorney Anthony Mancuso. Nat'l 1st ed.

This book takes the drudgery out of the necessary task of holding meetings of the board of directors and shareholders. It shows how to comply with state laws, prepare minutes for annual and special meetings, take corporate action by written consent, hold real or paper meetings and handle corporate formalities using e-mail, computer bulletin boards, fax and telephone and video conferencing. Includes all corporate forms on disk.
DOS $26.95/CORK

How to Form Your Own California Corporation With Corporate Records Binder & Disk
Attorney Anthony Mancuso. CA 1st Ed.

How to Form Your Own California Corporation is also available in a new format. Includes all the forms and instructions you need to form your own corporation, a corporate records binder, stock certificates and all incorporation forms on disk.
$39.95/CACI

How to Form a California Nonprofit Corporation with Corporate Records Binder and Disk
Attorney Anthony Mancuso. CA 1st Ed.

Step-by-step instructions and all the forms you need to form a nonprofit corporation in California. Includes a corporate records binder, index dividers, member certificates and all forms on Macintosh and DOS disks.
$49.95/CNP

Software Development: A Legal Guide
Attorney Stephen Fishman. Nat'l 1st ed.

Clearly explains patent, copyright, trademark and trade secret protection and shows how to draft development contracts and employment agreements. Includes all contracts and agreements on disk.
DOS $44.95/SFT

 software

Nolo's Partnership Maker
Version 1.0

Prepares a legal partnership agreement for doing business in any state. Select and assemble the standard partnership clauses provided or create your own customized agreement. Includes on-line legal help screens, glossary and tutorial, and a manual that takes you through the process step-by-step.
DOS $129.95/PAGI1

California Incorporator
Version 1.0 (good only in CA)

Answer the questions on the screen and this software program will print out the 35-40 pages of documents you need to make your California corporation legal. A 200-page manual explains the incorporation process.
DOS $129.00/INCI

audio cassette tapes

How to Start Your Own Business: Small Business Law
Attorney Ralph Warner with Joanne Greene. Nat'l 1st ed. 60 minutes

This tape covers what every small business owner needs to know about organizing as a sole proprietorship, partnership or corporation, protecting the business name, renting space, hiring employees and paying taxes.
$14.95/TBUS

Getting Started as an Independent Paralegal
Attorney Ralph Warner. Nat'l 2nd ed. Two tapes, approximately 2 hrs.

Practical and legal advice on becoming an independent paralegal from the author of *The Independent Paralegal's Handbook*.
$44.95/GSIP

THE NEIGHBORHOOD

Dog Law
Attorney Mary Randolph. Nat'l 2nd ed.

A practical guide to the laws that affect dog owners and their neighbors. Answers common questions about biting, barking, veterinarians and more.
$12.95/DOG

Neighbor Law:
Fences, Trees, Boundaries & Noise
Attorney Cora Jordan. Nat'l 2nd ed.

Answers common questions about the subjects that most often trigger disputes between neighbors: fences, trees, boundaries and noise. It explains how to find the law and resolve disputes without a nasty lawsuit.
$16.95/NEI

Safe Homes, Safe Neighborhoods:
Stopping Crime Where You Live
Stephanie Mann with M.C. Blakeman. Nat'l 1st ed.

Learn how you and your neighbors can work together to protect yourselves, your families and property from crime. Explains how to form a neighborhood crime prevention group; avoid burglaries, car thefts, muggings and rapes; combat gangs and drug dealing; improve home security and make the neighborhood safer for children.
$14.95/SAFE

GOING TO COURT

Everybody's Guide to Small Claims Court
Attorney Ralph Warner. Nat'l 5th ed. CA 11th ed.

These books will help you decide if you should sue in Small Claims Court, show you how to file and serve papers, tell you what to bring to court and how to collect a judgment.
National $18.95/NSCC
California $18.95/CSCC

Everybody's Guide to Municipal Court
Judge Roderic Duncan. CA 1st ed.

Sue and defend cases for up to $25,000 in California Municipal Court. Gives step-by-step instructions for preparing and filing forms, gathering evidence and appearing in court.
$29.95/MUNI

Represent Yourself in Court
Attorneys Paul Bergman & Sara Berman-Barrett. Nat'l 1st ed.

Handle your own civil court case from start to finish without a lawyer with the most thorough guide to contested court cases ever published for the non-lawyer. Covers all aspects of civil trials.
$29.95/RYC

Collect Your Court Judgment
Gini Graham Scott, Attorney Stephen Elias & Lisa Goldoftas. CA 2nd ed.

Contains step-by-step instructions and all the forms you need to collect a court judgment from the debtor's bank accounts, wages, business receipts, real estate or other assets.
$19.95/JUDG

The Criminal Records Book
Attorney Warren Siegel. CA 3rd ed.

Shows you step-by-step how to seal criminal records, dismiss convictions, destroy marijuana records and reduce felony convictions.
$19.95/CRIM

How to Change Your Name
Attorneys David Loeb & David Brown. CA 6th ed.

All the forms and instructions you need to change your name in California.
$24.95/NAME

Fight Your Ticket
Attorney David Brown. CA 5th ed.

Shows you how to fight an unfair traffic ticket—when you're stopped, at arraignment, at trial and on appeal.
$18.95/FYT

audio cassette tapes

Winning in Small Claims Court
Attorney Ralph Warner with Joanne Greene. Nat'l 1st ed. 60 minutes

Guides you through all the major issues involved in preparing and winning a small claims court case—deciding if there is a good case, assessing whether you can collect if you win, preparing your evidence, and arguing before the judge.
$14.95/TWIN

FAMILY MATTERS

The Living Together Kit
Attorneys Toni Ihara & Ralph Warner. Nat'l 7th ed.

A detailed guide designed to help the increasing number of unmarried couples living together understand the laws that affect them. Sample agreements and instructions are included.
$24.95/LTK

A Legal Guide for Lesbian and Gay Couples
Attorneys Hayden Curry, Denis Clifford & Robin Leonard. Nat'l 8th ed.

This book shows lesbian and gay couples how to write a living-together contract, plan for medical emergencies, understand the practical and legal aspects of having and raising children and plan their estates. Includes forms and sample agreements.
$24.95/LG

Divorce:
A New Yorker's Guide to Doing it Yourself
Bliss Alexandra. New York 1st ed.

Step-by-step instructions and all the forms you need to do your own divorce and save thousands of dollars in legal fees. Shows you how to divide property, arrange custody of the children, set child support and maintenance (alimony), draft a divorce agreement and fill out and file all forms.
$24.95/NYDIV

Nolo's Pocket Guide to Family Law
Attorneys Robin Leonard & Stephen Elias. Nat'l 3rd ed.

Here's help for anyone who has a question or problem involving family law—marriage, divorce, adoption or living together.
$14.95/FLD

Divorce & Money
Violet Woodhouse & Victoria Felton-Collins with M.C. Blakeman. Nat'l 2nd ed.

Explains how to evaluate such major assets as family homes and businesses, investments, pensions, and how to arrive at a division of property that is fair to both sides.
$21.95/DIMO

How to Raise or Lower Child Support in California
Judge Roderic Duncan & Attorney Warren Siegal. CA 2nd ed.

For parents on either side of the support issue. All the forms and instructions necessary to raise or lower an existing child support order.
$17.95/CHLD

The Guardianship Book
Lisa Goldoftas & Attorney David Brown. CA 1st ed.

Provides step-by-step instructions and the forms needed to obtain a legal guardianship of a minor without a lawyer.
$19.95/GB

How to Adopt Your Stepchild in California
Frank Zagone & Attorney Mary Randolph. CA 4th ed.

Provides sample forms and step-by-step instructions for completing a simple uncontested stepparent adoption in California.
$22.95/ADOP

Smart Ways to Save Money During and After Divorce
Victoria F. Collins & Ginita Wall. Nat'l 1st ed.

Here's a book packed with information on how to save money before, during and after divorce. It covers how to keep attorney's fees low, save on taxes, divide assets fairly, understand child support and alimony obligations and put aside money now for expenses later.
$14.95/SAVMO

California Marriage & Divorce Law
Attorneys Ralph Warner, Toni Ihara & Stephen Elias. CA 11th ed.

Explains community property, pre-nuptial contracts, foreign marriages, buying a house, getting a divorce, dividing property, and more. Pre-nuptial contracts included.
$19.95/MARR

Practical Divorce Solutions
Attorney Charles Sherman. Nat'l 1st ed.

Covers the emotional aspects of divorce and provides an overview of the legal and financial considerations.
$14.95/PDS

How to Do Your Own Divorce
Attorney Charles Sherman (Texas ed. by Sherman & Simons). CA 19th ed. & Texas 5th ed.

All the forms and instructions you need to do your own uncontested divorce without a lawyer.
California $21.95/CDIV
Texas $17.95/TDIV

MONEY MATTERS

Stand Up to the IRS
Attorney Fred Daily. Nat'l 2nd ed.
Detailed strategies on surviving an audit, appealing an audit decision, going to Tax Court and dealing with IRS collectors. It also discusses filing delinquent tax returns, tax crimes and concerns of small business people.
$21.95/SIRS

How to File for Bankruptcy
Attorneys Stephen Elias, Albin Renauer & Robin Leonard. Nat'l 4th ed.
Trying to decide whether or not filing for bankruptcy makes sense? This book contains an overview of the process and all the forms plus step-by-step instructions you need to file for Chapter 7 Bankruptcy.
$25.95/HFB

Money Troubles:
Legal Strategies to Cope With Your Debts
Attorney Robin Leonard. Nat'l 2nd ed.
Essential for anyone who has gotten behind on bills. It shows how to obtain a credit file, negotiate with persistent creditors, challenge wage attachments, contend with property repossessions and more.
$16.95/MT

Simple Contracts for Personal Use
Attorney Stephen Elias & Marcia Stewart. Nat'l 2nd ed.
Contains clearly written legal form contracts to buy and sell property, borrow and lend money, store and lend personal property, release others from personal liability, or pay a contractor to do home repairs. Includes agreements to arrange child care and other household help.
$16.95/CONT

law form kits

Nolo's Law Form Kit: Power of Attorney
Attorneys Denis Clifford & Mary Randolph and Lisa Goldoftas. Nat'l 1st ed.
Create a conventional power of attorney to assign someone you trust to take of your finances, business, real estate or children when you are away or unavailable. Provides all the forms with step-by-step instructions.
$14.95/KPA

Nolo's Law Form Kit: Loan Agreements
Attorney Stephen Elias, Marcia Stewart & Lisa Goldoftas. Nat'l 1st ed.
All the forms and instructions necessary to create a legal and effective promissory note. Shows how to decide on an interest rate, set a payment schedule and keep track of payments.
$14.95/KLOAN

Nolo's Law Form Kit:
Buy and Sell Contracts
Attorney Stephen Elias, Marcia Stewart & Lisa Goldoftas. Nat'l 1st ed.
Step-by-step instructions and all the forms necessary for creating bills of sale for cars, boats, computers, electronic equipment, household appliances and other personal property.
$9.95/KCONT

Nolo's Law Form Kit: Personal Bankruptcy
Attorneys Steve Elias, Albin Renauer & Robin Leonard and Lisa Goldoftas. Nat'l 1st ed.
All the forms and instructions you need to file for Chapter 7 bankruptcy.
$14.95/KBNK

Nolo's Law Forms Kit: Rebuild Your Credit
Attorney Robin Leonard. Nat'l 1st ed.
Provides strategies for dealing with debts and rebuilding your credit. Shows you how to negotiate with creditors and collection agencies, clean up your credit file, devise a spending plan and get credit in your name.
$14.95/KCRD

PATENT, COPYRIGHT & TRADEMARK

Trademark: How to Name Your Business & Product
Attorneys Kate McGrath & Stephen Elias, with Trademark Attorney Sarah Shena. Nat'l 1st ed.
Learn how to choose a name or logo that others can't copy, conduct a trademark search, register with the U.S. Patent and Trademark Office and protect and maintain the trademark.
$29.95/TRD

Patent It Yourself
Attorney David Pressman. Nat'l 3rd ed.
From the patent search to the actual application, this book covers everything including the use and licensing of patents, successful marketing and how to deal with infringement. Includes all necessary forms and instructions.
$39.95/PAT

The Inventor's Notebook
Fred Grissom & Attorney David Pressman. Nat'l 1st ed.
Helps you document the process of successful independent inventing by providing forms, instructions, references to relevant areas of patent law, a bibliography of legal and non-legal aids and more.
$19.95/INOT

Copyright Your Software
Attorney Stephen Fishman. Nat'l 1st ed.
What everyone in the software industry needs to know about software copyright protection and infringement. Includes step-by-step instructions and all the forms necessary to register your work with the Copyright Office. Also covers international copyright protection.
$39.95/CYS

The Copyright Handbook
Attorney Stephen Fishman. Nat'l 2nd ed.
Provides forms and step-by-step instructions for protecting all types of written expression under U.S. and international copyright law. Covers copyright infringement, fair use, works for hire and transfers of copyright ownership.
$24.95/COHA

software

Patent It Yourself Software
Version 1.0
Patent It Yourself is also available in software. With separate tracks for novice and expert users, it takes you through the process step-by-step. It shows how to evaluate patentability of your invention, how to prepare and file your patent application and how to generate all the forms you need to protect and exploit your invention.
Windows $229.95/PYW1

HOMEOWNERS

How to Buy a House in California
Attorney Ralph Warner, Ira Serkes & George Devine. CA 3rd ed.
Effective strategies for finding a house, working with a real estate agent, making an offer and negotiating intelligently. Includes information on all types of mortgages as well as private financing options.
$24.95/BHCA

For Sale By Owner
George Devine. CA 2nd ed.
Everything you need to know to sell your own house, from pricing and marketing, to writing a contract and going through escrow. Disclosure and contract forms included.
$24.95/FSBO

Homestead Your House
Attorneys Ralph Warner, Charles Sherman & Toni Ihara. CA 8th ed.
Shows you how to file a Declaration of Homestead and includes complete instructions and tear-out forms.
$9.95/HOME

The Deeds Book
Attorney Mary Randolph. CA 3rd ed.
Shows you how to fill out and file the right kind of deed when transferring property. Outlines the legal requirements of real property transfer.
$16.95/DEED

LANDLORDS & TENANTS

The Landlord's Law Book, Vol. 1: Rights & Responsibilities
Attorneys David Brown & Ralph Warner. CA 4th ed.
Essential for every California landlord. Covers deposits, leases and rental agreements, inspections (tenants' privacy rights), habitability (rent withholding), ending a tenancy, liability and rent control. Forms included.
$32.95/LBRT

The Landlord's Law Book, Vol. 2: Evictions
Attorney David Brown. CA 5th ed.
Shows step-by-step how to go to court and evict a tenant. Contains all the tear-out forms and necessary instructions.
$34.95/LBEV

Nolo's Law Form Kit: Leases & Rental Agreements
Attorney Ralph Warner & Marcia Stewart. CA 1st ed.
With these easy-to-use forms and instructions, California landlords can prepare their own rental application, fixed term lease, month-to-month agreement and notice to pay rent or quit.
$14.95/KLEAS

Tenants' Rights
Attorneys Myron Moskovitz & Ralph Warner. CA 12th ed.
This practical guide to dealing with your landlord explains your rights under federal law, California law and rent control ordinances. Forms included.
$18.95/CTEN

JUST FOR FUN

Nolo's Favorite Lawyer Jokes on Disk
Over 200 jokes and hilariously nasty remarks about lawyers organized by categories (Lawyers as Vultures, Nobody Loves a Lawyer, Lawyers in Love…). 100% guaranteed to produce an evening of chuckles and drive every lawyer you know nuts.
IBM PC $9.95/JODI
MACINTOSH $9.95/JODM

Devil's Advocates: The Unnatural History of Lawyers
by Andrew & Jonathan Roth. Nat'l 1st ed.
A hilarious look at the history of the legal profession.
$12.95/DA

Poetic Justice: The Funniest, Meanest Things Ever Said About Lawyers
Edited by Jonathan & Andrew Roth. Nat'l 1st ed.
A great gift for anyone in the legal profession who has managed to maintain a sense of humor.
$9.95/PJ

29 Reasons Not to Go to Law School
Attorneys Ralph Warner & Toni Ihara. Nat'l 4th ed.
Filled with humor, this book can save you three years, $150,000 and your sanity.
$9.95/29R

OLDER AMERICANS

Social Security, Medicare & Pensions
Attorney Joseph Matthews with Dorothy Matthews Berman. Nat'l 5th ed.
Offers invaluable guidance through the current maze of rights and benefits for those 55 and over, including Medicare, Medicaid and Social Security retirement and disability benefits, and age discrimination protections.
$18.95/SOA

Beat the Nursing Home Trap: A Consumer's Guide to Choosing and Financing Long-term Care
Attorney Joseph Matthews. Nat'l 1st ed.
Guides you in choosing and paying for long-term care, alerting you to practical concerns and explaining laws that may affect your decisions.
$18.95/ELD

REFERENCE

Legal Research: How to Find and Understand the Law
Attorneys Stephen Elias & Susan Levinkind. Nat'l 3rd ed.
A valuable tool on its own or as a companion to just about every other Nolo book. Gives easy-to-use, step-by-step instructions on how to find legal information.
$19.95/LRES

Legal Research Made Easy: A Roadmap Through the Law Library Maze
2-1/2 hr. videotape and 40-page manual.
Nolo Press/Legal Star Communications. Nat'l 1st ed.
Professor Bob Berring explains how to use all the basic legal research tools in your local law library with an easy-to-follow six-step research plan and a sense of humor.
$89.95/LRME

CONSUMER/REFERENCE

Nolo's Pocket Guide to California Law
Attorney Lisa Guerin & Nolo Press Editors. CA 2nd ed.
Get quick clear answers to questions about child support, custody, consumer rights, employee rights, government benefits, divorce, bankruptcy, adoption, wills and much more.
$10.95/CLAW

Nolo's Pocket Guide to California Law on Disk
This handy resource is also available on disk. With this new format you can rapidly search through California law by topic and subtopic, or by using the key-word index. The program tracks and saves searches, and allows you to save text to a file for later use.
Windows $24.95/CLWIN
Macintosh $24.95/CLM

Nolo's Pocket Guide to Consumer Rights
Barbara Kaufman. CA 2nd ed.
Practical advice on hundreds of consumer topics. Shows Californians how and where to complain about everything from accountants, misleading advertisements and lost baggage to vacation scams and dishonored warranties.
$14.95/CAG

Nolo's Law Form Kit: Hiring Child Care & Household Help
Attorney Stephan Elias. Nat'l 1st ed.
All the necessary forms and instructions for fulfilling your legal and tax responsibilities. Includes employment contracts, application forms and required IRS forms.
$14.95/KCHLD

How to Win Your Personal Injury Claim
Attorney Joseph Matthews. Nat'l 1st ed.
Armed with the right information anyone can handle a personal injury claim. This step-by-step guide shows you how to avoid insurance company run-arounds, evaluate what your claim is worth, obtain a full and fair settlement and save for yourself what you would pay a lawyer.
$24.95/PICL

Fed Up with the Legal System: What's Wrong and How to Fix It
Attorneys Ralph Warner & Stephen Elias. Nat'l 2nd ed.
Forty common-sense proposals to make our legal system fairer, faster, cheaper and more accessible.
$9.95/LEG

IMMIGRATION

How to Get a Green Card: Legal Ways to Stay in the U.S.A.
Attorney Loida Nicolas Lewis with Len T. Madlanscay. Nat'l 1st ed.
Written by a former INS attorney, this book clearly explains the steps involved in getting a green card. It covers who can qualify, what documents to present, and how to fill out all the forms and have them processed. Tear-out forms included.
$22.95/GRN

Como Obtener La Tajeta Verde: Maneras Legitimas de Permanacer en los EE.UU.
Attorney Loida Nicolas Lewis with Len T. Madlanscay. Nat'l 1st ed.
The Spanish edition of How to Get a Green Card.
$24.95/VERDE

ORDER FORM

Code	Quantity	Title	Unit Price	Total

Subtotal	
California residents add Sales Tax	
Shipping & Handling ($4 for 1st item; $1 each additional)	
2nd day UPS (additional $5; $8 in Alaska and Hawaii)	
TOTAL	

Name

Address

(UPS to street address, Priority Mail to P.O. boxes)

FOR FASTER SERVICE, USE YOUR CREDIT CARD AND OUR TOLL-FREE NUMBERS

Monday-Friday, 7 a.m. to 6 p.m. Pacific Time
Order Line   1 (800) 992-6656 (in the 510 area code, call 549-1976)
General Information 1 (510) 549-1976
Fax your order   1 (800) 645-0895 (in the 510 area code, call 548-5902)

METHOD OF PAYMENT

☐ Check enclosed   ☐ VISA   ☐ Mastercard   ☐ Discover Card   ☐ American Express

Account #   Expiration Date

Authorizing Signature

Daytime Phone

MAIL YOUR ORDER WITH A CHECK OR MONEY ORDER MADE PAYABLE TO:
NOLO PRESS, 950 PARKER ST., BERKELEY, CA 94710

ALLOW 2-3 WEEKS FOR DELIVERY. PRICES SUBJECT TO CHANGE.

TO ORDER CALL 1-800-992-6656